ONE WEEK LOAN
UNIVERSITY OF GLAMORGAN
TREFOREST LEARNING RESOURCES CENTRE
Pontypridd, CF37 1DL
Telephone: (01443) 482626
Books are to be returned on or before the last date below

RELIGION, IDENTITY AND CHANGE

Religion is of enduring importance in the lives of many people, yet the religious landscape has been dramatically transformed in recent decades. Established churches have been challenged by Eastern faiths, revivals of Christian and Islamic fundamentalism and the eclectic spiritualities of the New Age. Religion has long been regarded by social scientists and psychologists as a key source of identity formation, ranging from personal conversion experiences to collective association with fellow believers.

This book addresses the need for a reassessment of issues relating to identity in the light of current transformations in society as a whole and religion in particular. Drawing together case studies from many different expressions of faith and belief – Hindu, Muslim, Roman Catholic, Anglican, New Age – leading scholars ask how contemporary religions or spiritualities respond to the challenge of forming individual and collective identities in a national context marked by secularisation and postmodern decentring of culture, but asks important questions that are of universal significance for those studying religion: How is personal and collective identity constructed in a world of multiple social and cultural influences? What role can religion play in creating, reinforcing or even transforming such identity?

Published in association with the British Sociological Association Study of Religion group, in the Ashgate *Religion and Theology in Interdisciplinary Perspective Series*.

The editors, Simon Coleman and Peter Collins, teach in the Department of Anthropology, University of Durham, UK.

RELIGION AND THEOLOGY IN INTERDISCIPLINARY PERSPECTIVES SERIES

Series Editors

Professor Douglas Davies, University of Durham, UK
Professor Richard Fenn, Princeton Theological Seminary, New Jersey, USA

Creativity through shared perspectives lies at the heart of Ashgate's new series on *Theology and Religion in Interdisciplinary Perspective*. Central religious and theological topics can be raised to a higher order of expression and clarity when approached through interdisciplinary perspectives; this new series aims to provide a pool of potential theories and worked out examples as a resource for ongoing debate, fostering intellectual curiosity rather than guarding traditional academic boundaries and extending, rather than acting as a simple guide to, an already well-defined field. Major theological issues of contemporary society and thought, as well as some long established ideas, are explored in terms of current research across appropriate disciplines and with an international compass. The books in the series will prove of particular value to students, academics, and others who see the benefit to be derived from bringing together ideas and information that often exist in relative isolation.

Also in the series

Predicting Religion
Edited by Grace Davie, Paul Heelas and Linda Woodhead
ISBN 0 7546 3009 9 (Hbk)
ISBN 0 7546 3010 2 (Pbk)

The Return of the Primitive
A New Sociological Theory of Religion
Richard K. Fenn
ISBN 0 7546 0419 5 (Hbk)
ISBN 0 7546 0420 9 (Pbk)

Christian Language and its Mutations
Essays in Sociological Understanding
David Martin
ISBN 0 7546 0739 9 (Hbk)
ISBN 0 7546 0740 2 (Pbk)

Religion, Identity and Change

Perspectives on Global Transformations

Edited by Simon Coleman and Peter Collins
University of Durham

BSA Sub series of Religion and Theology in
Interdisciplinary Perspectives Series

ASHGATE

Published by
Ashgate Publishing Limited
Gower House
Croft Road
Aldershot
Hants GU11 3HR
England

Ashgate Publishing Company
Suite 420
101 Cherry Street
Burlington, VT 05401-4405
USA

The editors have asserted their moral right under the Copyright, Designs and Patents Act, 1988, to be identified as the editors of this work.

Ashgate Website: http://www.ashgate.com

British Library Cataloguing in Publication Data
Religion, identity and change : British perspectives on global transformations. –
   (BSA sub-series of religion and theology in interdisciplinary perspectives)
   1. Religion and sociology – Great Britain 2. Identity (Psychology) – Great
   Britain 3. Identity (Psychology) – Religious aspects 4. Identification (Religion)
   5. Great Britain – Religion
   I. Coleman, Simon, 1963– II. Collins, Peter III. British Sociological Association
   306.2'0941

Library of Congress Cataloging-in-Publication Data
Religion, identity, and change: perspectives on global transformations / edited by
Simon Coleman and Peter Collins.
   p. cm. – (Religion and theology in interdisciplinary perspectives series)
   ISBN 0-7546-0450-0 (alk. paper)
   1. Religion and sociology – Great Britain. 2. Great Britain–Religion–20th
Century. 3. Identity (Psychology) I. Coleman, Simon. II. Collins, Peter (Peter
Jeffrey) III. Series.

BL60.R323 2003
306.6'0941–dc21

2003048199

ISBN 0 7546 0450 0

Typeset in Times New Roman by LaserScript Ltd, Mitcham, Surrey.

Printed and bound in Great Britain by MPG Books Ltd, Bodmin, Cornwall.

Contents

List of Contributors

Paul Chambers (School of Humanities and Social Sciences, University of Glamorgan)

Simon Coleman (Department of Anthropology, University of Durham)

Peter Collins (Department of Anthropology, University of Durham)

Douglas Davies (Department of Theology, University of Durham)

Kieran Flanagan (Department of Sociology, Bristol University)

David Herbert (Department of Religious Studies, Open University)

Michael P. Hornsby-Smith (Department of Sociology, University of Surrey)

Eleanor Nesbitt (Religions and Education Research Unit, University of Warwick)

Martyn Percy (Lincoln Theological Institute, University of Manchester)

Katy Radford (Currently Policy Researcher, Save the Children, Northern Ireland)

Nancy A. Schaefer (Amsterdam, freelance researcher)

Martin D. Stringer (Department of Theology, Birmingham University)

Steve Sutcliffe (Formerly of Department of Religious Studies, University of Stirling)

Matthew Wood (Richmond, the American International University, London)

Preface

Kieran Flanagan

One of the most surprising shifts in recent sociology has been the centring of issues of identity into its deliberations. Identity has always been an important sociological concept, but until recently it has had a rather dispersed existence in facets of ethnicity, education and roles. It was a term often mentioned but seldom given any theoretical significance. The fallout from debates on postmodernity in the 1990s brought two seemingly unconnected areas of sociology into analytical focus: the self and culture. Identity is the concept that links both. It points to the uncertainties and unsettlements of life in what Bauman has termed 'liquid modernity' (Bauman 2000). In this setting, little is solid, all is malleable and identity can be anything and nothing. Ironically, the endless opportunities of life in 'liquid modernity' have made notions of identity highly problematic.

Identities are increasingly objects of desire and manufacture. This opens out endless avenues of possibility for making an identity, but these opportunities lead to all sorts of knavish tricks. The grammar for arbitrating between distinction and recognition has become untenable, and in the confusion all manners of ambiguity of identity pass for authentic. Some exult in these confusions while others make more. In these confusions, the issue of identity has become a matter of perplexity, if not curiosity, that places the term in the centre of sociological scrutinies.

As a site of affiliation and designation, identity relates to biography, to a sense of recollection, but it also points to forms of identification, how one wishes to be defined. Identity carries a property of distinction, of marking boundaries, but in an era of tolerance some of these become unfixed, leading to more unsettlements. Culture, too, has become dominated by similar frustrations of opportunity but also by denial, for it also faces definitional problems. These conditions of unsettlement have become magnified in the context of globalisation. The processes of embedding and disembedding that Giddens (1991) has used to characterise globalisation have effected a destabilisation of identity and culture.

Increasingly, identity is the term that expresses the need to shape culture into some form of recognisable practice that links to an identifiable way of life. Cultural practice needs a distinctive mark for identification purposes. Identity and culture become matters of importance for those who find the links between each problematic and their bases insecure. The politics of recognition have arisen to reflect the needs of the marginal, those whose identities seem unsecured in a culture where all should rest secured. Identities suffer where others impose definitions that are deemed estranging by the identified. This thwarting of ambitions and a denial of affirmation has generated a response from sociologists to speak for those whose identity is given neither autonomy nor adequate recognition. Thus, lurking in the question of identity is an issue of emancipation and a crucial facet of this demand is the sociologist's role in speaking for the unemancipated, whose identities are in some way indiscernible. In all these questions of identity are ultimate questions about fate, destiny, memory and biography. The question 'who am I?' forms the basis of the self-interrogation of cultures and groups. Personal identity, that which is the responsibility of the actor to craft, is intermingled with collective identities, thus making efforts to reconcile levels of analyses of both highly problematic. In these many shapes and sizes of identities, there is a property of searching, of insecurity and distrust.

Earlier notions of identity, in the 1970s, related to definite questions of its social construction. In this setting, identity had an agenda of certainty, one that related to its conventional sites of exploration in social psychology and education. The issue of identity was one of its transmission in forms of socialisation, so that the formation of the social self in childhood and its movement into adulthood were of critical sociological interest. Quite clearly, in this context the biography of growing up had many problematic dimensions but at least identity was set in relation to a narrowly defined issue of ageing. Now issues of identity arise in almost all areas of sociology, including religion where little sociological attention has been given to the impact of this crucially important term. This collection fills a notable gap in the intellectual marketplace, and in the sociology and anthropology of religion. It marks out a territory that very much needs exploration.

Some reasons for the growing complexity of notions of identity emerged in areas rather removed from the habitual concerns of sociology. These areas were in political sociology, particularly in relation to nationalism. Identity had a political and cultural facet. It related to the responses of the fringes of the state to their apparent disqualification from its cultural consensus. For nationalists, identity was something fractured, peripheral and incomplete. In the 1980s, nationalism in the British Isles was treated as a quest for self-definition and this demand for autonomy pointed to wider issues that were to emerge in other sectors of sociology. Issues of identity are most pertinent when they emerge on the margins of cultural and political consensus.

Identity came into the centre of sociology to signify a property of precariousness, a sense of displacement that gave expression to the insecurities that the term 'postmodernity' was invented to characterise. In this mood of the late 1980s, postmodernity pointed to the conclusion that all facets of life were available for redefinition in the light of a failure of consensus as to what rules of identification were to count. Identity pointed to a paradox: differences were to be treated with indifference, if not tolerance; and similarities were intolerable because they affirmed the monochrome nature of a culture of commodity. As social bonds of commitment and trust unravel, the suspicion and scepticism surrounding the treatment of the construction of identities in traditional realms fades away. This clears the space for a wider issue of how identities are to be constructed in civil society. In the climate of uncertainty regarding the making of identity, those on the margin seek to take advantage of the chaos. Concerns with discrimination and exclusion based on race in the 1960s are amplified in the wider concerns of those who feel culturally disadvantaged, whose dignity is denied and whose claims to recognition are spurned.

The agenda of identity politics seeks to overcome a perceived sense of exclusion and to secure legal redress for those who feel excluded in areas such as gender, sexuality, handicap and of course race and ethnicity. As identities that structure and exclude are marked for uprooting, it is scarcely surprising that some feel they inhabit a rootless culture in which the making of distinctions is in some ways a politically incorrect act of discrimination. The freedoms sought for identity ironically accentuate their destabilisation. Identity is now an accomplishment of the self and the commodification of culture presents a promise that any form can be secured. Therapy, style experts, fashion and the mass media all conspire together to make the social construction of identity unproblematic. Yet it is the expansion of these forms of advice and the fiction of endless opportunities that have rendered the issue of identity unstable both for the self and for adequate sociological scrutiny. In the rootless culture of postmodernity, the finding of a secure identity has become an ambition for many. Such a shift has favourable implications for the concerns of the essays in this collection with how identity and religion are to be linked.

These essays relate to wider shifts in concerns with identity in sociology itself. These bear on three considerations. First is a growing concern with the narrative or story of an actor or culture whose tale needs to be given recognition in sociology. It is difficult to argue that the claims for an authentic voice and for contextualisation granted to those who struggle in identity politics cannot also be recognised for those seeking to make a mark for identity and its social construction in religion. Second, the question of identity is linked to biography, to memory and to the construction of a tradition that gives rise to its position in culture. Third, the question of identity has taken on a property of seeking or journeying. This questing enables sociology to treat religion with a new and greater tolerance, as part of wider issues of culture and ethnicity. These widening concerns of sociology are well reflected in this collection. Rich in ethnography, it is a solid set of case studies in religion and identity that opens out a number of unexpected terrains that are well worth further exploration.

The diversity of fields in the collection points to the present richness of the sociology of religion in the United Kingdom. Increasingly, there is a conscious effort among practitioners to present the concerns of the sociology of religion to the wider interests of the discipline as a whole. This collection takes forward such an ambition most effectively. A pleasing facet of the collection is the mixture of contributions it presents from well-established scholars but also, and most importantly for the future of this important branch of sociology, from younger scholars beginning to make their mark in the field.

The effects of 11 September 2001 are difficult to estimate in relation to the sociology of religion. This event has brought into focus the contrast between the indefinite forms of religious identity that pass in a secularised modernity and those of a decidedly definite form in the context of fundamentalism, most notably in Islam. Sociology of religion is only just coming to terms with the notion that fundamentalism expresses a form of resistance to the indefiniteness of a culture of postmodernity. Identity in relation to religion needs to be treated in a different, more vibrant manner than before and in this regard, this collection is timely.

As anthropologists, the editors have been concerned to give the 'margins' adequate representation. By linking religious identity to ethnicity, they point to a vibrancy on the fringe of mainline religions, but also to the need to reconceive religion in terms of relocations in the context of being British. Space for this relocation arises from the demise of the cultural hegemony of Anglicanism, and to a lesser extent Catholicism, in the United Kingdom. In their diversity, the case studies in this volume supply a critique of notions of secularisation that propagate irresistible processes of disengagement and indifference. The weight of the collection leans towards the notion that religious differences, in terms of a diversity of identities sought, *do* matter and that it makes analytical sense to chronicle these in the context of globalisation. More than anything else, globalisation forces sociologists to look to the local, to the forging of identities against processes of standardisation. For that reason, the chronicling of a diversity of local identities in relation to religion as a series of struggles to search and to find has its own justification. These passages of self-understanding lend a crucial value to the notion of identity as it seeks to bridge the gap between freedom and constraint, ideal and reality, and self-definition and that of the other. These also have crucial implications for the way religion as living force, one that can be situated in a theology, is to be understood. In this regard, the shocking conclusion for sociologists of religion is that the making of a religious identity is intrinsically linked with processes surrounding the social construction of a faith.

In their introduction, the editors draw attention to an important facet of identity and religion, a concern with its self-conscious expression. This is given a diversity of settings, within Christianity but also in relation to the Celtic fringe and some facets of New Age religions. The treatment of religion in terms of time, space, memory and kinship in the essays in the collection marks a shift in sociological understandings that will give rise to further debate. These elements link with identity in ways that indicate how religious affiliations adjust and change according to cultural circumstances that are not entirely in their control. It is these senses of transition and adjustment that are so well chronicled in this collection. In many cases, there is a perplexity about the identities so encountered both for the sociologists and for the respondents themselves.

The quest for an identity linked to religion echoes facets of Weber's notion of elective affinity where affiliations are secured based on choices that bear sociological scrutiny. The self-consciousness located in identity that the editors note relates to a notion of reflexivity. Although the term does not appear often in the collection, many of the contributions complement the importance of the term in recent sociology. Self-awareness and forms of choice underline the social construction of identity. This greatly changes the way the sociology of religion is to proceed. Its understandings can only become less judgemental and more accepting of how identities come to be made within the sphere of religious assumptions. Reflexivity demands a property of introspection and in dealing with the study of religion it is unlikely that sociology can remain immune from the need to inspect its own identity.

Papers selected for a collection that emerges from a conference reflect the market forces of intellectual interests. Some might feel a certain perplexity about the collection in that the fringe rather than the centre forms central concerns of sociological and anthropological characterisation. These concerns seem heirs to the agenda of the sociology of religion in the 1980s, where cults and sects, the fringes of religion, ruled and the theologies of the main religions were of marginal interest. Although issues of Catholicism and Anglicanism appear in the collection, these are treated in terms of decline and uncertainty, assimilation and division. It is as if in some superior and some unexamined way these main forms of Christianity assume that identity is an affliction of the margins. Somehow they feel exempt from considering identity as also being their question. Hopefully, this collection might spur those in these religions to rectify an imbalance and to fill in a startling gap in their own theologies. In the present climate, it is presumptuous to assume that identity is only a question for those outside the theological mainstream.

The well-documented and stimulating essays in this collection should be read carefully as expressions of careful understandings of the problems of identity a variety of religions face within the United Kingdom, where forces of globalisation loom large. Within these large forces, small tales of identities constructed need to be heard and these are well articulated in this collection. Its topics deal with kinship and religion, ethnicity and identity, the self, time and space, clerical identity, the parish church, rich seams of religious life in Islam, spiritualism, Northern Ireland and Wales, and Mormon, Catholic and Anglican cultures. All the essays point to efforts to form identities in hazardous circumstances where manifold dilemmas are faced. A sense of journeying is well conveyed in these essays that supply a rich harvest of sociological accounts. In so creatively opening out the possibilities available in understandings of the link between identity and religion, this collection has performed a valuable service for the study of religion.

Bibliography

Bauman, Z. (2000), *Liquid Modernity*, Cambridge: Polity.
Giddens, A. (1991), *The Consequences of Modernity*, Cambridge: Polity.

CHAPTER 1

Introduction:
Ambiguous Attachments

Religion, Identity and Nation

Simon Coleman and Peter Collins

> All the Patels mix together like one family, but they would normally be Gujarati Patels not Bengali ones. It's very tribal – a bit like the Irish.

The speaker is Shaunaka Rishi Das,[1] a member of the Oxford Centre for Vaishnava and Hindu studies. His depiction of the Patels as akin to a large family evokes images of community often associated with ethnic enclaves and religious collectives. But perhaps the most intriguing part of his statement is the nod towards the tribal Irish. Is Shaunaka revealing the sophisticated, reflexive awareness of self and remote other that is supposedly characteristic of identity in late modernity?[2]

Yes and no. In fact, Shaunaka originally had another name and another identity, as Timothy Kiernan from Wexford. Timothy had wanted to train for the Catholic priesthood before he became a member of Hare Krishna. As a 'Hindu priest', he now spends his time spreading his adopted religion's principles of peace to the citizens of Belfast. He was speaking at the largest festival for young Hindus ever held outside India, an opportunity for some 15 000 people a day to descend on a park in north-west London in the summer of 2001. Not only did the festival bring together members of the 300 000-strong Hindu 'community' from all parts of Great Britain, it also attracted a host of religious and other dignitaries from India itself. Blessings were showered on the proceedings by the Archbishop of Canterbury as well as by Prince Charles, and a recording was made to be broadcast to Hindus in India, the US, South Africa and Australia. Tony Blair, the British Prime Minister, was quoted in the press as saying: 'This event provides British Hindus with an important opportunity to explore their culture and their faith', while the national newspaper the *Guardian* provided its own piece of (rather less sanguine) sociological commentary at the end of a news feature about the festival: 'Although Hindus were not involved in recent riots in Bradford and Oldham, the questions of identity confronting them are similar to those in the Muslim community.'

What are we to make of this event, and what does it tell us about the subjects covered in this book? Note the multilayered levels of identity that the festival encapsulated and even celebrated – certainly religious, but also generational, ethnic, national and global. An expression of a specific faith was also the opportunity to claim more complex, ramifying sets of allegiances, bringing together Gujaratis and Bengalis, Hindus and Christians, British-based and Asian-based leaders. Religious and national identity could be seen as complementary (in Blair's words), but 'Hinduness' was also associated with a transnational community that included both a homeland (India) and an extensive diaspora. Hindu identity could even be conflated with a more generic condition of 'being religious' in contemporary Britain – and thereby given the full approval of an archbishop.

It is a social scientific truism that identity is constructed, at whatever level (individual, cultural, social, national, transnational), through expressions of 'difference' (see especially Nesbitt, Chapter 11, this volume). Though commonplace, this insight is useful because it tells us that identity can never be created in a vacuum – it must always be produced in and through a set of relations with real or imagined others. Identifying the 'in-group' makes little sense from an analytical or lay point of view unless one also identifies the 'out-group(s)', and, similarly, minorities can only be understood in relation to majorities. Personality theorists might present identity in terms of personal distinctiveness and autonomy, as the result of 'the individual's self-construal' (Jacobson 1998:9). However, processes of discrimination and boundary formation do not exist only as internal, psychological states; they are also expressed and constituted in behaviour (Mauss 1996:11). George Mead's symbolic interactionism emphasised how the self emerged through social intercourse with others, with the notion of internalisation describing how society could determine individuality (Aronowitz 1995:114). As Jacobson notes (1998:9–10), sociology and social psychology have therefore tended to focus on how a sense of identity can be formed from a supposed dialectic between individual and society, as membership of social groups shapes the individual perception of self.[3] Ethnic, national and many religious identities help define an 'I' by placing it against a background 'we' (Appiah and Gates 1995:3) as well as a 'they'. In this sense, the allocation of identity in relation to the self is both an inevitable outcome of human interaction and – at times – a more self-consciously adopted stance in relation to others.

As the Hindu festival illustrates, we should not assume that boundaries of identity must be permanent or exclusive. Shaunaka is an intriguing figure here: how does his Catholicism feed into his Hinduism, assuming that it does? Is the latter a reaction against, or does it encompass, the former? Does he identify himself more with Ireland or with India? To what extent does he see a distinction between an ethnic association of self with place of origin, and a chosen commitment to a universalistic religion with a global reach (cf. Jacobson 1998:10)? The chances are that none of these questions can be answered in simple terms. Similarly, the festival itself was a multidimensional combination of pilgrimage and conference: both an *enactment* of various identities and a self-conscious *discussion* of what these identities might consist of. Tony Blair's use of the imagery of 'exploration' captures this sense of an open-endedness in cultural affiliation, of an unfinished project (and one that never *can* be finished).

The *Guardian* headline for the article – 'Young Hindus in Festival Search for Modern Identity' – also invokes the imagery of a quest, but significantly adds the qualifier 'modern' to the notion of religious identity. The paper apparently accepts that it is indeed possible to be modern and religious at the same time, and yet implies that previous Hindu religious formations have been premodern in their attitude. Perhaps the sub-text of the piece, which after all appeared in the most liberal of the mainstream British broadsheets, is actually that to be properly 'modern' in Britain is akin to adopting a kind of pluralism – even postmodernism – in attitude and affiliation. Furthermore, the ambiguity of the event, its celebration not of one identity but of many, seems to have made it a suitable candidate for endorsement by representatives of church, royalty and state. Religious identity, even a previously exotic or foreign one, can implicitly be deemed an acceptable part of the contemporary British public (civil) sphere provided it leavens its more spiritual aspects with other, cross-cutting ties to national and even global citizenship. As the anthropologist Anthony Cohen has pointed out (1986:2–3), it is in the nature of the symbolic to be imprecise. We see here an example of what M.G. Smith (1974) calls cultural pluralism, according to which ethnic identity is explicitly not used as a criterion of national citizenship.[4] The festival supposedly acts to reconcile two ways through which group identity has traditionally been constructed (Boyarin and Boyarin 1995:305): common *genealogy* (in the sense of ethnic or religious continuity) does not fatally undermine a cultural heritage delimited by *geography*.

Nonetheless, a jarring note appears in the *Guardian* article, in the shape of the chilling reference to riots at the end of the piece. The article concludes by reminding the reader of forms of (religious) identity whose practices lead not towards tolerance and ambiguity, but towards violence in the heartlands of the nation. This reminder takes on extra resonance if we remember that the story was published in July 2001, just six weeks or so before the events of 11 September in New York and Washington, DC. If the Hindu festival illustrated the possible affinities between globalisation and multiple, overlapping identities, incidents in the US a few weeks later were to highlight a much more jagged and tragic juxtaposition of the assertion of religious faith on a global stage.

Locating Religion

Religion has long been regarded by social scientists and psychologists as a key source of identity formation and maintenance, ranging from personal conversion experiences to collective association with fellow believers. There are occasions when apparent religious affiliation seems to act largely as a powerful label for a sub-group. Jacobson (1998:120ff.) writes of how many young British Muslim males have little interest in engaging in arduous religious practice, but are nevertheless keen to proclaim their affiliation with pride (see David Herbert, Chapter 10, this volume). The religion's connotations of faith and fervour in the UK resonate with a desire to be assertive in contexts of perceived racism (including for instance the debates surrounding the Rushdie affair): gender, generation and ethnicity are thus encompassed by the term 'Islam'.[5]

However, we should not habitually conflate religion with identity, or assume that the latter acts as a totalising explanation for the former. In other words, we should avoid reductionist, crudely functionalist – and even fetishising – views of religion that account for its revival or persistence purely in terms of the identity it can bestow on its followers. Quite apart from the fact that, on the individual level, there may be many motivations for expressing commitment to a given religious group or ideology, religious practice itself can incorporate elements – belief, ritual, self-surveillance, aesthetics and so on – whose links to identity are evident but only partial.

Religions are likely to vary greatly in the kind of identity they might encompass, not only because of factors 'internal' to the religion, but also as a result of influences pertaining to any given surrounding context. The experience of being a Hindu in Delhi is not the same as being one in Durham. Even the salience of particular aspects of our identity can vary according to the situations we find ourselves in: at one moment our role as practising Jew or Muslim might be stressed, at another our role as parent, and so on. Akeel Bilgrami provides a vivid example of the malleability of identity consciousness in his article 'What is a Muslim?', where he talks (1995:199) of how, despite the fact that he is not a believer in Muslim doctrine, he found himself saying 'I am a Muslim' in a Hindu neighbourhood in India: 'It was clear to me that I was, without strain or artificiality, a Muslim for about *five minutes.* That is how negotiable the concept of identity can be.'[6]

Processes of identity formation are not only malleable, they are also extremely promiscuous in their deployment of cultural resources. Religion, language, skin colour, class, occupation, lifestyle and so on can be used singly or in combination, and identity-related factors may be tightly or loosely integrated with each other (Toulis 1997:83). As Cohen notes (1986:17), a community can make virtually anything grist to the mill of cultural distance (or, one might add, proximity), though such fabrication is often more likely to occur as a partially unpredictable outcome of myriad social interactions than through consciously orchestrated, all-powerful leadership. Identity can also be ascribed to a person or group from without, since processes of labelling are clearly bound up with relations of authority and power.

Previous work has adopted a number of theoretical positions in assessing the formation of identity in general, and here we distinguish between two basic orientations. The 'primordialist' view emphasises the significance of historical continuities in creating attachments to territory and community (cf. Jacobson 1998).[7] Jenkins (1997:44) argues that this model of identity, at least as it is expressed in ethnic terms, has historical roots in Romantic reactions to Enlightenment rationalism (cf. Hobsbawm and Ranger 1983). It is certainly a perspective that is frequently adopted by political cultures as means of self-justification. For instance, Hickman states (1995:7), drawing on Hall (1992):

> It has therefore been a main function of national cultures to represent what is in fact the ethnic mix of modern nationality as the primordial unity of 'one people'. This has been achieved by centralized nation states with their incorporating cultures and national identities, implanting and securing strong cultural institutions, which tend to subsume all differences and diversity into themselves.

If primordialism stresses an internally homogenous justification for, and view of, identity, the situationalist perspective is more concerned with the dynamic formation of boundaries among social groups. The most prominent advocate of this latter view has been the anthropologist Fredrik Barth, for instance in *Ethnic Groups and Boundaries* (1969). In formulating his theory, Barth was himself forming intellectual boundaries in relation to those scholars who still maintained a structural functionalist view of the world as inherently made up of firmly bounded societies or groups (Jenkins 1997:12). He focused on how cultural differentiation was produced and reproduced out of interactions among actors, who were seen as choosing to highlight certain specific elements of culture as emblematic of cultural difference while ignoring others. Barth shifted attention away from the static, corporate group (often labelled as 'the tribe' by anthropologists) and towards strategising individuals; away from alleged historical continuity in the sharing of culture and towards contemporary processes of making distinctions. The cultural resources actors could deploy in building boundaries could be tangible or symbolic, visible or invisible. Boundaries were therefore to be seen as 'legitimated' rather than simply 'legitimate' (Cohen 1994:199–200), and allegiances needed to be regarded as 'created out of cognitive and performative actions directed towards outsiders as well as insiders' (Toulis 1997:170). Jenkins (1997:59) thus points out the homologies between a Goffmanesque view of social selfhood as staged and processual and a Barthian model of ethnicity as transactional.

Barth's approach emphasises a view of identity, and culture in general, that is oriented towards action and the creation of shifting networks in human relations. On the level of the individual, membership of groups can change over time (as we saw above with Shaunaka), even though broader distinctions between such groups can be maintained, albeit with evolving criteria of difference (Wallman 1979:3). He provides a corrective to a 'mosaic' view of human groups, in which social and cultural formations seemingly possess an autonomy that is created for the descriptive convenience of the analyst rather than reflecting 'reality' on the ground.[8] However, Barth has had his critics. Ironically, his theory might be said to have exaggerated consensus within ethnic groups (Jacobson 1998:17) at the same time as emphasising a rather a-sociological individualism (Jenkins 1997:22). Certainly, the depiction of strategising actors needs to be combined with an appreciation of the structural constraints on individuals and groups in their production of boundaries.

Barth suggests that his view of culture as variable and contingent anticipated postmodernist theoretical perspectives (see Jenkins 1997:12), and while this view may seem overstated he undoubtedly contributed to a more sophisticated understanding of the potential instabilities of identity. However, much recent work on ethnic groups has traced processes of migration of groups from single geographical contexts into numerous diasporic spheres, with the result that new questions are being asked of ethnicity and identity. For instance, Gardner (1995:7) writes of how studies of the encapsulation of groups are less salient than they were in the 1970s. Migrants engage in multiple cultural worlds that are dynamically intertwined and are thereby involved in complex processes of self-creation, while contemporary work is at least as interested in differences *within* groups as it is in relations *between* them. Furthermore, as Blair's comments on the Hindu festival indicated, there is now the need to study 'hyphenated' cultures of British-Asians, British-Muslims and so on.

Postmodernist approaches generally identify essentialism (with its obvious resonances with primordialism) as a prime political and epistemological enemy. Appiah and Gates (1995:1) note that 'the calls for a "post-essentialist" preconception of notions of identity have become increasingly common', and the oft-invoked phrase 'the politics of identity' reveals the highly charged character of debates that can move from the pages of textbooks into the social relations of teachers and students themselves. Among the outdated 'essentialisms', Cohen (1994:205) includes the Marxist idea that all social identity could essentially be reduced to class identity. The implication is not that class consciousness does not exist, but that other claims for affiliation – gender, race, age, religion and so on – cannot be reduced to mere epiphenomena in contexts where these different forms of identity appear to be upheld simultaneously, successively or separately.

For Flanagan (2001:241–2), however, the choice inherent in postmodernism is a burden as well as an opportunity. 'Unsettlements and ambitions' emerge (ibid.:253) since the individual supposedly takes on the duty of maximising self-actualisation in relationships supposedly uncluttered by obligation and commitment. In his view, a crisis of identity emerges (ibid.:245): 'Postmodernity signifies the absence of a consensus as to the agenda for an identity, hence the demise of the pilgrim metaphor for travellers of modernity', while people travel without the prospect of relief at arrival. Robin Cohen (1994:205) takes note of some of the same phenomena but puts a more positive spin on things, using not a metaphor of aimless travel (a kind of abnegation of agency) but one of game-playing (a celebration of agency) in 'situational' identity:

> The basic idea here is that an individual constructs and presents any one of a number of possible social identities, depending on the situation. Like a player concealing a deck of cards from the other contestants, the individual pulls out a knave – or a religion, an ethnicity, a lifestyle – as the context deems a particular choice desirable or appropriate.

Cohen does admit that there are some obvious limits to the flexibility of situational identity, since (ibid.:205): 'It is relatively easy to change a religion or one's clothes. It is less easy to change one's accent, manner and language', but the sense of playful ironising that he evokes privileges the experience of middle-class cosmopolitans over those who, for economic and structural reasons, may not have extra clothes or identities to change into. Even the assumption that religion can be changed as easily as putting on a new suit or dress is rather naïve, suggesting that all faiths possess a stereotypical New Age, mix-and-match mentality. However, Cohen does make a further important point, which indicates the complexity in his argument. He notes (ibid.:205) that some forms of identity constructs can emerge – such as the territorially based claims of nationalism – which explicitly seek to overcome postmodern fragmentation. We see how the experience of living in globalising contexts can produce 'fixes' as well as 'flows' of identity (cf. Meyer and Geschiere 1999), and the former just as much as the latter should be seen as products of postmodernity.

An extreme postmodernist perspective that implies a given identity can be adopted or not adopted at will therefore exaggerates the conscious powers of the individual actor. Cohen's indication that some identities are easier to manipulate than others – for instance his implication that clothes are easier to change than accents – implicitly acknowledges the relevance of practice theory and in particular the *habitus* (Bourdieu 1977) in forming the self. In other words, bodily and cognitive dispositions are internalised by the person through engaging in everyday cultural practice. Once identity is seen as complexly embodied within the person, and not merely a removable label or temporary state of empathy, we see how wariness with regard to essentialism needs to be combined with an acceptance of continuities in socially derived and yet 'personal' dispositions. In this regard, Akeel Bilgrami's experience of 'being a Muslim for five minutes', while in a Hindu neighbourhood, is interesting because he may be pointing to a distinction between a consciously articulated lack of belief and a more embodied internalisation of Muslim identity that is disinterred, apparently rediscovered, on certain occasions.

A necessary analytical task in trying to understand the forming of personal and collective identities is consequently to mediate between focusing on history/memory on the one hand, and strategising/conscious agency on the other. The recent work of Hervieu-Léger (2000) on religion as a 'chain of memory' becomes relevant here. As Davie (2000:30) points out, Hervieu-Léger's perspective has Durkheimian roots, propagated through the work of Halbwachs. Concrete or imagined communities, drawing on textual, liturgical and architectural heritages, are seen as key to fostering the memories necessary for religion's projection into the present and future. Hervieu-Léger's perspective emphasises the potential importance of place and history (as in primordialism) but renders these problematic, needing actively to be reproduced, and indeed under threat in contemporary 'amnesiac' societies.[9] Other recent work, in certain respects very different to that of Hervieu-Léger, nevertheless similarly mediates between the limitless cultural play of postmodernism and the necessity to acknowledge the presence of continuities in cultural affilation. The anthropologist Paloma Gay y Blasco's (1999:3, 173–7) depiction of Spanish gypsy identity aims to show how gypsies reproduce their 'singularity' without recourse to territory or even a shared past. Gypsies lack 'permanent' media through which to encode their identity, and in the absence of external media through which to objectify the self, gypsyness is linked to actions or performances rather than essences or substances.

Where do these various debates about identity, briefly summarised above, leave analysts of religion? First, we are cautioning against approaches that suggest a crude analytical hierarchy, according to which religion can be seen as an epiphenomenon of a single other factor, such as the (assumed, post)modern search for identity. Second, we note that intriguing resonances are evident between theoretical approaches to identity and certain religious ideologies. The primordialist emphasis on historical and cultural continuity has some parallels with fundamentalist condemnations of fragmented meanings and floating signifiers. In both cases, the possibility of homogeneity in culture is asserted as part of an oppositional ideology whose character is ironically formed in relation to, and therefore out of, the very plural context it purports to despise. Situationalism is perhaps more akin to a liberal, even New Age, acceptance of contingency and dynamic evolution in human affairs.

The main point to emphasise is that religion is often a comment on, and analysis of, culture – a meta-theory in its own right – as well as being part of culture. The anthropologist Robin Horton (1967) has famously highlighted the importance of an 'awareness of alternatives' in the development of modern cosmologies, suggesting that such knowledge can lead to scepticism but also to the self-conscious formulation and ordering of ideas in relation to other ways of viewing the world. More recently, Giddens and other theorists have interpreted the relativisms of late modernity as leading to reflexivity in the process of clothing oneself in culture.[10] Both perspectives throw light on the British situation, where to say 'I am committed to religion X' is ineluctably (and despite ideologies of multiculturalism) an assertion of the value of X in relation to numerous other possibilities, including the choice to be committed to no faith at all. The adoption of religion becomes – among many other things – the acceptance of commonality as well as difference in relation to numerous others. In this sense religious activity always carries with it a statement of identity, whether the actor intends to make such a statement or not.

Dis-locating Religion

Debates about the impact of postmodernity on identity have prompted us to pose questions about territory in a supposed age of deterritorialisation (Harvey 1989), and about tradition in an era of alleged detraditionalisation (Heelas *et al.* 1996). Given the interests of this book, we are also led into debates concerning secularisation, and indeed many of our contributors frame their arguments in terms of assertions about the decline or efflorescence of religion in Britain and the West generally. One of the intriguing things about these debates is that they reveal concerns that have long been central to sociologists of religion, but are generally much less salient to their anthropological counterparts.[11] In coming to understand why such a difference is evident we may also be able to say something about approaches to identity. First, however, we need to define some of our terms.

When we referred earlier to a crude view of secularisation we basically meant the idea that fewer people 'believe' in God than before. An obvious problem with this view is that belief is a highly problematic area (Ruel 1997), which cannot be assumed to have the same connotations within different religions, while such a focus also fails to explore numerous other possible dimensions of religiosity: ritual, texts, bodily discipline and so on. It is important to realise that advocates of a firm yet much more sophisticated secularisation thesis, such as Bryan Wilson or Steve Bruce, cannot be accused of being unaware of the myriad dimensions of religion; nor indeed are they simply stating that Britain has now become a country where nobody believes in God. Bruce notes (1995:48), for instance, that generally less than a quarter of the population claims to have 'no religion'. In common with Bryan Wilson, his main focus is on the declining influence, the diminishing reach, of religion, although he adds (2002:41): 'I would go further than Wilson and argue that the decline in the social significance of religion, in turn, reduces the number of people interested in religion.'

According to Bruce (whose work we shall concentrate on here), the social importance of religion has been reduced as it has essentially been privatised to the worlds of family and leisure, and rendered a matter of choice rather than inevitability.[12] Thus (as Weber also anticipated) there are enclaves where religion may remain potent – for instance where it can be associated with a threatened ethnic identity – 'but they are only enclaves' (Bruce 1995:125).[13] Belief in the supernatural has not disappeared, but the forms in which it is expressed have often become so diffuse that they have few specific societal consequences (1996:234; 2002:94).

Meanwhile, science has not directly 'disproved' religion *per se*, but naturalistic ways of thinking 'have made the religious approach to life less relevant' (Bruce

1995:133). The material world comes to be seen as 'an amoral series of invariant relationships of cause and effect' (ibid.:133–4). Thus Bruce is not making the intellectualist argument that people have suddenly become 'rational' and come to realise the error of their formerly religious ways; it is more that social and economic conditions have made us (again to adopt Weberian imagery) religiously unmusical. A lack of musicality can be produced and manifested in various ways, and in Britain it seems to have emerged through indifference rather than hostility – indeed, the former can be seen as indicating secular*isation*, while the latter implies an overt ideology of secular*ism*. Other countries, such as France, have experienced more explicit waves of pro- and anti-religious sentiment, often associated with political revolution.

Despite differences among Western liberal democracies, there are some broad features of 'modern' societies as a whole that are seen as relevant to the secularisation paradigm (Bruce 1995:128–35). Many social institutions involving the family, education systems and economic activities are said to have become more specialised and autonomous, and thus not necessarily inherently linked to religion. With technological innovation, occupational change, increased interaction with strangers and a general move from ascribed to achieved identities, societies have become more egalitarian in orientation, and less in thrall to long-standing hierarchies, including those of the church. This kind of argument (also evident in Wilson's work) is rather Durkheimian in its linking of religion to forms of community organisation. Alongside the fragmentation of community comes what Wilson calls 'societalization' (Wilson 1982; Bruce 1995:130), with national, impersonal bureaucracies taking over the functions that were once performed by local organisations.

Bruce's view is therefore as much a 'shrinkage' as it is an out-and-out 'secularisation' hypothesis. Priests give way to secular professionals and the modern world is assumed to run uniformly rather than as the occasional stage for miraculous events, but all sorts of beliefs and small-scale religious organisations can continue to exist. A significant if often ignored part of Bruce's argument is that he intends 'modern' to signify 'possessing certain features' (those summarised above), rather than simply implying 'extant in our time'. In his words: 'The Kalahari bushmen are still about, but no one would cite their culture as relevant to arguments about the effects of modernization' (Bruce 1995:127). Although there is some tension in Bruce's argument here, his usual contention is that what he calls secularisation cannot be seen as universal, or indeed necessarily irreversible (1998, 2002:37). Thus the argument that religion is flourishing in, say, Iran is irrelevant to what he is saying about the contemporary situation in Western industrial societies.

In certain respects, Bruce's presentation of secularisation is affirmed by developments in modern Britain. The title of one of his books refers to the movement from 'Cathedrals to Cults' (1996), expressing a translation of religion from the (visible) centre to the (obscure) margins, and the point that he is making is seemingly illustrated for the editors of this volume when they think about the sacred geography of their own city. At the centre of Durham, and at its highest point, are situated the Norman castle and cathedral. Until the nineteenth century, both were closely associated with the prince-bishops of Durham, figures who held secular and spiritual power in the north-east of England: they had their own parliament, could raise their own taxes and armies and were empowered to set up their own courts. In 1837, however, the castle was handed over to the recently established university, and it is now a college providing accommodation for students. Along with the cathedral, it forms an officially designated World Heritage Site. The contribution of the castle and cathedral to the identity of the city cannot therefore be said to have diminished, but it has been transformed in highly significant ways. Political and ecclesiastical authority have been separated from each other. The former has been ceded to national government and the latter has given ground to a broadly secular institution for the training of professionals. The sacred architecture of the city retains transnational reference points but these are largely to do with world heritage and the commercialisation of place and 'tradition' (Harvey 1989). Heritage does not need to evoke sacred 'memory' so much as a generalised desire to experience a past that is commodified through the demands of tourism, possibly the most lucrative industry in the contemporary world (Coleman and Crang 2002). Durham cathedral is therefore central to the finances of the city, and to the identity of place that is sold to visitors ('Come to Durham, Land of the Prince-Bishops'); yet its significance is less to do with its ritual or legal functions and much more to do with its marketable age and architecture. Its current role can be seen as a metonym for wider shifts in the place of Christianity in a country where Sundays are deployed for leisure rather than liturgy (or where liturgy is seen *as* leisure).

In practice, however, much of the secularisation debate seems to revolve around different interpretations of the same data: is the spiritual glass half full or half empty? For instance, does the fact that most people affirm that they have faith in some kind of divine force exemplify or disprove 'secularisation'? Flanagan (2001:240) notes that:

> The collapse in church figures might suggest an endemic condition of de-spiritualisation. Yet, the spirit of the times points to an endless interest in issues that one thought had long been expelled from culture. As interest in ecclesiastical culture has declined, fixations on its legacy in horror films, and reports of angels and devils have increased.

In other words, people certainly have not stopped thinking about matters relating to religion, but are we to argue that the diffusion of 'ecclesiastical culture' away from the auratic contexts of cathedral and church into the mass-produced, popular context of film indicates the continued salience or the irreversible compromise and fragmentation of faith? It may be significant that Flanagan uses the word 'spiritual' rather than 'religious' here, perhaps indicating a shift towards a more diffuse expression of sacrality.

Identifying the assumptions behind any given interpretation of secularisation is clearly important (cf. Hanson 1997:159). It is after all possible to provide such a broad definition of religion that it can encompass just about everything from brushing one's teeth ('ritual self-purification') to watching football ('producing collective effervescence' – depending perhaps on which team one is watching . . .). Here, we do not want to enter into extended definitional self-justification, other than saying that our contributors focus on activities that are self-identified as religious by actors and generally accepted as such by observers. We are more interested in focusing on two assumptions inherent in the secularisation paradigm as summarised by Bruce, thereby reflecting further on the connections (or otherwise) between religion and identity.

First, Bruce (1995:91–2; 2002:213–14) argues that modern societies are marked by a fairly abrupt division between the public and the private, and that the two spheres have their own values and norms. While the public sphere is supposed to be rationalistic, task-oriented and universalistic, the private sphere of family and friends is more 'permissive' in its orientation to reality.[14] Of course, modern states do differ in the extent to which they permit minorities the right to create their own sub-societies. The US, for example, with its relatively decentralised political and educational structures, provides more *initial* leeway than the UK. In any case, the assertion that a public/private division exists is crucial to the thesis that religion has retreated from the former to lick its wounds in the latter. A differentiation of spheres argument about religion also parallels that made above about the context-based nature of identity: in order to function in a fragmented society, it is deemed necessary to present different identities to others according to different situations. Similarly, in order to function in a secularised society, people are assumed to want to keep their religious convictions away from the office, no matter how exuberantly they might have been dancing in the spirit in church the night before. This kind of contention is also used by Bruce to defend himself against the depiction of major churches regaining a public role through becoming pressure groups in civil society (Casanova 1994; cf. Bruce 2002:20–1), since he argues that religious groups are effective in the public arena only when they represent their case in secular terms.

Whatever the relative merits of Bruce vs. Casanova, our point is slightly different. Notice the implicit hierarchy of importance evident in the use of the blanket-word secularisation to describe this confinement of religious agency to the private sphere. The temptation is presented to invest the macro-politics of government and public affairs with more importance than the micro-politics of the home or other more 'domestic' arenas. This potential tendency also relates to what we said earlier about anthropological versus sociological attitudes towards secularisation. Of course the obvious point has to be made that anthropologists have traditionally studied societies where religion has been less differentiated from other areas of society – kinship, politics, economics and so on; but we also claim that an ethnographic approach is relatively more likely to privilege the everyday and domestic than is a broad focus on surveying the social impact of any given religion or set of religions. Bruce, at least, has tended to do the latter. This is emphatically not to say that one approach is right and the other wrong, but it is to point out that they have different orientations to data.

Bruce's argument does accept the possibility that the contemporary world might house revivals of politicised religious fervour. He quotes examples from Iran or Pakistan (1995:127) to make his case, but implies that these are not 'modern' in the sense that he is using the term, since they occur in contexts that do not predominantly possess the features of modernity that he has identified. The example of the Kalahari Bushmen made a similar point about the context-specific nature of the modern, and the 'enclaved' nature of the non-modern. Bruce tends largely to ignore religions recently brought by immigrants from 'non-modern' to 'modern' contexts, and explains his reasoning not in the main text of his most recent book on the subject, but in a footnote (2002:243). His point is that non-Christians (measured by national surveys) form a small part of the population, and that 'native Britons' do not appear to be joining these religions in great numbers. Thus 'they are so closely associated with ethnic identities that they do not form part of the religious expressions that the former Christians who concern us in these debates could take up'. Furthermore, Bruce argues that there tends to be a regression to the mean for religious impulses, as over time they move towards the secularity of society as a whole. Thus (ibid.:244): 'The evidence suggests that, as immigrants become established and they and their children become upwardly mobile, commitment to their faith is weakened.'

From an anthropological point of view, the 'margins' are often as interesting if not more interesting than the 'mainstream', but Bruce is not referring to inherent levels of interest, rather to relevance to his secularisation paradigm. The use of the term 'native Briton' is more problematic, since it does not deal with the fact that the children of immigrants are born in Britain. If not treated with caution, the term can be taken to imply that there is a stable and easily definable ethnic identity (and indeed 'mainstream') that is 'British'. More broadly, Bruce's argument tends to focus on national contexts without dealing with issues of globalisation. Diasporas are being cemented in Bradford or Manchester that render geographically 'distant' areas of Asia part of the immediate cultural context for many British citizens. There is much truth in the claim that minorities often need to bow to 'the mainstream' in order to make their voice heard (Ardener 1993), but we must also develop an understanding of the contemporary state that takes account of the way cultural processes can bypass formal political borders (alongside an appreciation that the mainstream itself is changeable). As 'national context', Britain will almost certainly continue to house contending visions of the degree to which religion can be divorced from the public sphere, with many such visions being promoted and reinforced through cultural and social impulses originally derived from far beyond the physical boundaries of the nation. To return to Shaunaka for a moment: the festival he attended clearly mediated between diasporic and Indian Hindu communities, asserting both a civil and a transnational identity at one and the same time.

Relocating Religion

Who, then, are 'the British'? Sometimes the term is mistakenly conflated with just one nationality, usually the supposedly 'dominant' English; at other times its reference points go so far as to encompass members of the wider Commonwealth, some of whose inhabitants are said to be 'more British than the British' (Robbins 1993:32).[15]

Even if we accept the point that identity is created in relation to boundaries and the establishment of difference, we do not necessarily get very far. Robin Cohen identifies (1994:7) six 'fuzzy' frontiers against which definitions can be established: the Celtic fringe; the heritage of the Dominions; the Empire and non-white Commonwealth; Atlantic and Anglophone connections; emergent European identities; relationships to aliens. This book focuses on the attitudes and practices of people who spend most of their lives resident in the UK, but of course postwar immigration from the Black and Asian Commonwealth (the Empire 'striking back') has increasingly divorced territory from race and/or colour (ibid.:35). Although British national identity has not had to contend with civil war or military defeat in recent history (unlike some of its European counterparts), its self-confidence has had to face up to the impact of decolonisation (Robbins 1993:32–3) and periods of relative economic marginalisation in the global market.

A simple way of characterising recent religious history might be to say that at the start of the nineteenth century the United Kingdom was a Protestant state (ibid.:87); at the start of the twentieth, it was basically Christian; and at the dawn of the twenty-first, it was decidedly mixed. As the country has become more multicultural, so the historically predominant Christian traditions have inevitably had to adapt to a plurality of faiths (Parsons 1994:8), while ethnic and religious affiliations have entered new combinations, seen for instance in the growth of black Pentecostalism over the past decades (see, for example, Calley 1965; Toulis 1997; Schaefer 2002). In line with Barth's thesis, internal cultural and religious diversification has actually encouraged concerns with boundaries (alongside some blurring of older identities). Thus Scottish and Welsh forms of nationalism have joined that of the Irish on the contemporary political agenda, and actually achieved mainstream approval of limited regional autonomy. In such cases, Europe and the world can be seen as valuable reference points, thus bypassing the rest of Britain. The centre cannot be said to have held in religious terms either. The Church of England, once (at least stereotypically) a bastion of political conservatism, has recently expressed its relative divorce from what is perceived as the status quo through opposition to government policy in military and economic matters.[16]

What kind of religious demographic landscape are we dealing with now? Bruce (1995:30–5, 74–87) gives us some ballpark figures. In 1992 there were around 50 000 churches still left in the UK, although for instance Church of England membership fell from 13.5 per cent of the adult population in 1900 to 3.9 per cent in 1990. Adult Roman Catholic membership in Britain over the same 90 years increased from 5.5 per cent to 9.1 per cent. There are around 300 000 Jews in Britain, probably over 1 million Muslims, and roughly 300 000 Hindus and 300 000 Sikhs. Naturally these figures conceal huge variations in what counts as membership, active or otherwise, and they say little about the extent to which 'believing' can occur without 'belonging' (Davie 1994). For our purposes, the important point is that we cover many of these religious orientations and a few more,[17] and that each has a sizeable community on which to construct identity that can be felt on national and transnational stages.

Religion and Identity: Case Studies

In our opening sections we tried to tease out some of the complex threads that weave together religion and identity in the United Kingdom today. For heuristic purposes we introduced a number of elements and processes that bear directly on this, our central issue: ethnicity, gender, class, secularisation, globalisation. The remainder of this book attempts to develop each of these themes further by exploring them in a series of case studies. We do not underestimate our task. For instance, globalisation is often conceived of as 'a' *process* that can have marked effects on *states* of religious and national identification. However, one problem with such an assumption is the (from a social scientific point of view) naïve idea that forms of religious or national affiliation can ever be seen as static. Another problem is that globalisation is hardly a clearly defined and autonomous social force, even if we can say in general terms that processes of migration, technological developments in the media, improved systems of transport and the breakdown of economic borders have contributed to new questionings of the role of nation-states in the contemporary world. While the boundaries of Britain can be defined relatively clearly in political and territorial terms, its cultural, ethnic, economic and religious boundaries are much more – and increasingly – difficult to determine. In making such a claim, we need to be aware of how, as van der Veer (1995:3) puts it, the discourse of modernity misleadingly emphasises the 'boundedness' of the traditional community and compares it to the supposed individual freedom of movement in modern society. Internal divisions and movements have of course been evident over many years, for instance among the separate countries and regions of the British Isles, or among the more established faiths. Looking outwards, Britain's historical role as a colonial power has meant that it has actually been engaged in extensive international networks of cultural and economic exchange for many centuries. Thus, an institution such as the Church of England, in one sense the quintessential expression of a single nation's identity within the union, has also long been a church whose jurisdiction extends far beyond a small island in northern Europe.

These problems complicate our task but, if anything, make its justification for existence more compelling. We do not intend to provide a formulaic statement of how some abstracted notion of 'identity' relates to an equally abstracted notion of 'religion'. Evident throughout the volume are, however, three basic assertions about religion and identity, as revealed in their manifold forms within contemporary Britain. For the time being, we state these assertions fairly baldly:

1   As Flanagan has remarked (2001:239), issues of religion and identity are increasingly coming into focus in social scientific thinking, despite the fact that a crude reading of secularisation theory might have anticipated the demise of religion as an object of central interest, and an equally crude understanding of postmodernity might have predicted the shattering of sustainable forms of personal or collective identity in a multicultural, plural context such as Britain. Indeed, the assertion of religious identity in a public, and not merely an individual, sense has been important in recent political debates concerning British policies on education, racism, broadcasting, the family, abortion and so on (Parsons 1994:17; cf. Nye 2001).

2   Both religion and identity are of interest because they are important to so many people, but this is not to say that their boundaries of jurisdiction and relevance can be seen as stable. Within both, constantly shifting forms of alliance and fragmentation, homogenisation and heterogenisation, are discernible and need to be mapped out.

3   It is therefore worth studying religion and identity *together* not only because they so clearly interact and at times overlap with each other, but also because both can be seen as key sites of ambiguity and creativity in many parts of the contemporary, globalising world. Transnational processes have the capacity to redefine relevant *contexts* of self-identification for individuals and groups. If localities help to define identities, we should not be surprised if traditional identities are challenged in situations of relative deterritorialisation and consequent reconstruction of the meaning of neighbourhood, locale and so on (Fardon 1995; Appadurai 1996). Bauman (2001) suggests further that, instead of talking about inherited or acquired identities, it would be more in keeping with the realities of the globalising world to speak of 'identification', an always incomplete activity in which we are constantly engaged. The contemporary social world differs somewhat from previous eras in the scale of the meaningful arenas within which many people see themselves and others – in effect, the Schutzian 'life world' has widened (Jenkins 1997:38). More broadly, Robertson (1992:26–7; cf. Coleman 2000) focuses on different kinds of orientation to 'the global circumstance' and highlights four reference points of the global field – selves, national societies, the world system of societies and humankind. As Robertson puts it (1992:27): 'In an increasingly globalized world there is a heightening of civilizational, societal, ethnic, regional and, indeed individual, self-consciousness.' Such self-consciousness is evident in articulations of religiosity as well as of wider forms of identity, and we propose to trace some of these articulations in the chapters of this book.

Some of the chapters were originally delivered at the British Sociological Association, Sociology of Religion Study Group meetings, held on the theme of 'Religion and Identity' in Durham in 1999. In making a selection of papers from the conference, we decided to promote the coherence of our volume by taking papers that focused on the United Kingdom, even though our theoretical aims are far from parochial. We then added other papers to ensure a reasonable geographical and denominational spread of the variety of religions practised in Britain. It may itself be an expression of processes of globalisation that, although we (Coleman and Collins) convened the sociology of religion meeting in Durham, in fact we are both anthropologists who happen to have located our 'tribes' among Western religious groups. In any case, our anthropological instincts prompted us to choose papers that (with some exceptions) had something of an ethnographic flavour, often exploring broader processes through detailed micro-studies.

We hope, therefore, that this book can be read on a number of levels. Each chapter is self-contained and can be consulted individually by the reader searching for information on a specific religious culture. At the same time, the volume as a whole adds up to a contemporary survey of religious activity in Britain at the dawn of the new millennium. In that sense it complements a number of recent and excellent social scientific discussions of British religion (see for instance Aldridge 2000; Bruce 1995; Davie 1994). Of course, even though Britain has a particular religio-political history and genealogy of relationships between church and state (cf. Martin 1978), its movement especially since 1945 away from a Christian religious identity into a much more plural, ethnically complex, context has parallels with, and perhaps lessons for, other Western countries (Parsons 1994:8). On yet another level we hope collectively to make a more general contribution to studies of identity in contexts of globalisation. We cannot claim that all of our authors understand or deal with global processes in the same way or to the same extent; however, all of the chapters of this book deal with how particular religious formations express identities that are forged in relation to audiences that include, but also transcend, the local group or even nation-state.

We could have ordered the chapters in many different ways. In practice, each is self-contained, though common themes occur across the contributions. Chambers, Davies, Hornsby-Smith, Percy, Radford, Stringer and Schaefer present often widely differing varieties of Christianity, while Herbert and Nesbitt examine Asian religions, but one could just as easily say that Schaefer's and Hornsby-Smith's contributions parallel Herbert's and Nesbitt's in focusing on religion and migration. Chambers, Radford and Sutcliffe use specific examples of religious practice to talk about national identities in various parts of what is (stereotypically) called 'the Celtic fringe', but Sutcliffe's work also resonates with that of Wood in discussing the New Age, and so on.

Martyn Percy, in Chapter 2, plunges us ostensibly into the traditional heart of English religion – Steve Bruce's 'mainstream' – by focusing on the current identity of the Anglican parish church. His argument combines both an analysis of the past and present and a proposal for the future, as he documents shifting relationships between *parochia* and *ekklesia*, parish community and church congregation. One of Percy's central questions relates to the issue of context and locality that we raised earlier. He asks: To what extent can a 'parish' church be meaningfully spoken of in mobile, globally conscious communities where many people have lost their sense of belonging to a parochial space? More broadly, he states that public space itself has now become more ambiguous, with numerous possible centres being available for any one community. Percy's response to these issues – and to assertions of secularisation in general – is decidedly upbeat, if considered from the point of view of the church. He argues that church membership and attendance have varied considerably across the centuries. Furthermore, and as others have pointed out (Davie 1994), he notes that almost all forms of collective association have declined steeply in recent decades, so that the Church is hardly alone in dealing with problems of encouraging active membership. Furthermore, there has been an (evolving and extensive) history of relating to the parish church, which has long been a creator and sustainer of identity, without people necessarily attending it regularly. Percy ends by exploring some of the options open to the Church as its identity shifts from the parochial to the local in its purview. In the future, patterns of ministry might no longer be configured solely through geographical space: indeed, the Church might need to create novel spaces for communities and different opportunities for differentiated niche groups.

Michael Hornsby-Smith in Chapter 3 also focuses on mainstream Christianity but in the context of the history of Roman Catholicism in England. He builds on research he has been conducting for many years on the dissolution of the often ethnically reinforced 'fortress church', while also drawing on a distinction made by Philip Hammond (1988) between 'collective-expressive' and 'individual-expressive' views. Apart from looking at postwar social change and post-Conciliar religious change, he reflects on the future for English Catholicism as it enters the twenty-first century. Hornsby-Smith detects a clear movement in Roman Catholicism along a number of dimensions, including sharp increases in marital exogamy, dissent over the reaffirmed teaching on contraception, liturgical changes towards the vernacular, and overall value convergence between Catholics and the rest of the population. Such trends illustrate Steve Bruce's 'reversion to the mean', and indeed a substantial degree of structural and cultural assimilation to English (and English Catholic) norms by second-generation Irish immigrants. In line with a similar point made by Percy about Anglicanism, one of the consequences of such developments is a search for a positive commitment to the faith among some members, rather than a passive acceptance of it. The evolution of English Catholicism, argues Hornsby-Smith, manifests complex connections between class, ethnicity and age and significant changes in these modes of social differentiation. These changes are related to broad cultural and economic shifts related to the mobile nature of belonging, uses of communications technology and the growth in leisure industries. Thus Hornsby-Smith invokes the work of Danièle Hervieu-Léger (see above) in linking his conclusions to the thesis that there has been a fragmentation of collective and individual memory in plural Western societies.

Chapter 4 by Martin Stringer similarly traces the tension between communally based identity and more individual forms. Stringer's chapter also parallels that of Percy in certain respects: both draw on their experiences in the north of England in order to meditate on the condition of the Church of England, both focus on the role of the clergy in relation to the parish, and both are concerned with adapting traditional religious identity to the demands of the present. In other respects, however, they differ widely. Stringer's concern is less with 'the church' in general and more with the relationship between the ministry, gender and sexuality, and specifically with the ordination of women and homosexual priests. He points out that there are conflicts between the self-proclaimed identities of (inner-city) clergy and their role, based on the assumptions of the people to whom they are ministering. Such conflicts lead Stringer to ask whether priesthood, as understood by the Anglican church, is a role, a profession, a job or an identity. Stringer agrees with others that priesthood in the Church of England is no longer seen as a vocation, but rather as a career. He then takes this argument further, by stating that while many ordinary people still assume that the public role and personal identity of priests should be united seamlessly, clergy themselves have been developing individual understandings of identity very much out of tune with such traditional understandings of priesthood. Stringer reminds us that the self-identity of priests is constructed as much through their sexuality as their religious faith and practice and suggests that an appreciation of this fact could positively contribute to the development of the church in the United Kingdom.

Two of our contributions approach the expression, or at least influence, of national identity in other 'Celtic' contexts. Paul Chambers in Chapter 5 traces some important movements in Welsh religion – or perhaps one might say religion in Wales. His tracing of the decline of Welsh Nonconformism over the past century as an organising principle of life is significant, but he also notes that such religious decline is fairly typical of other modern north European societies. Durkheimian influences are evident in his argument that changing social environments have contributed to such changes, including the erosion of a working-class culture that was built around the chapel and neighbourhood. In general, says Chambers, the possibilities for articulating a distinctively Welsh form of religion have declined, as social and geographical mobility have created an increasingly heterogeneous culture. Anglicans and Roman Catholics (historically 'non-Welsh' identities) have surpassed Nonconformism in numerical coverage. Yet, interestingly, it might be that Anglican churches are now recreating at least some forms of identity through helping to preserve the Welsh language and inhabiting the spaces vacated by the declining Free Churches. Chambers, like Percy, is therefore interested in the contemporary meaning of 'the parish', as he illustrates through a focus on Swansea. Meanwhile, says Chambers, evangelicals have been active in Wales but their transnational, fragmented and often exclusivist orientations have divorced them from the concerns of most local populations, creating a situation that is a far cry from the Great Revival of 1904–5. Thus Chambers cogently remarks (see page 76): 'While the link between religion and national identity has now largely disappeared, identity, nevertheless remains a key component of religious affiliations.'

Steve Sutcliffe in Chapter 6 also juxtaposes politics and religion in his analysis of religion in Scotland, but this time in the context of cultural impulses that are seeking a measure of independence from England through a sort of diffuse nationalism that works at many levels – intellectual, artistic, sporting, media-related – and takes in a spectrum of strengths and voices. Sutcliffe's central hypothesis is that the establishment of a measure of political-civic autonomy for Scotland in 1999 will further promote a process of cultural and religious pluralisation within Scotland. He introduces a number of examples, including a brief 'Time for Reflection' slot in the Scottish Parliament that is an arresting example of how 'multifaith' politics can be institutionalised within the legislature itself. In common with Percy, Sutcliffe sees his work as challenging aspects of the secularisation paradigm. He argues that not enough attention has been paid to the growth and impact of diaspora religions and new spiritualities in the country, resulting in a misleading depiction of it as a purely *de-* rather than emergent *post-*Christianised culture. For Sutcliffe, what is striking is the laicisation and domestication of religious discourse and action in the culture at large, so that we should now look for 'vibrant if necessarily unstable' sites of spirituality beyond the boundaries of the large social institutions. In Scotland, it seems, religion is more interestingly characterised by its prolific diversification than by its progressive deinstitutionalisation. Perhaps, given what we have said about Bruce's work above, the difference is in emphasis as much as it is in fundamental argument, but it is significant enough. An irony of Sutcliffe's contribution is that, as Scotland devolves from England, it potentially comes to resemble the British and European experience as a whole in its heterogeneity and democratisation of faiths.

Although other authors in this volume deal at least briefly with issues of time and place none do so in quite the same way as Douglas Davies. His Chapter 7 is unusual in the context of this volume in attempting an exercise in situational analysis. This methodological approach was developed by the anthropologist Max Gluckman and others who were confronted with communities undergoing rapid social change in postwar southern Africa. They focused their attention on social situations, on the coming together of particular people in particular places at particular times.[18] Like Gluckman *et al.*, Davies is interested in structure *and* process, in the particular *and* the universal. After reminding us how powerful and enduring a religious metaphor the journey is, Davies describes how for Mormons such movements facilitate a 'ritual generation of time' (see page 108). He presents us with an example of the physicality of globalisation, of the densely meaningful movement of believers (and beliefs) from one location to another, of wandering and homecoming. As Davies shows, journeys transect both place *and* time. He illustrates his argument ethnographically with reference to commemorative events that the Latter-day Saints call 'Sea Trek' and 'Faith in Every Footstep' during each of which groups of adepts plainly draw on past time as a resource for constructing present identity.

In certain respects, the next two chapters on Christianity provide an alternative strategy to those just discussed regarding the project of creating religious identity in contexts of globalisation. Nancy Schaefer examines recent urban revivals orchestrated in London by the American charismatic Protestant evangelist Morris Cerullo. She argues that the movement of Caribbean migrants to Britain after the Second World War and the subsequent emergence of the black churches have been central to Cerullo's UK constituency. The evangelist, though white himself, appears to have drawn on black 'cultural repertoires' in creating temporary 'free space' (one might even say an enclave) for the mediation and celebration of shared cultural identities among the black audience. Here, as in the case of the Catholics described by Hornsby-Smith, age or generation impacts crucially on religious and ethnic identity. However, if Irish Catholics have moved towards the English mainstream in terms of their broad identity markers, black charismatics have combined the religious and the ethnic, the global and the (English) urban, in recreating rather than merely reviving their sense of distinctiveness in society. It is interesting that Schaefer draws on a metaphor of space in describing this process. Percy, we remember, argued that the English parish church had to discover new spatial contexts of meaning and function in 'locality'; Schaefer's informants deploy 'space' more as a temporary site of liminality, of freedom from a society that they sometimes regard with suspicion. Although somewhat paradoxical, here is a white evangelist who, for primarily historical reasons, successfully provides a 'safe haven' (though a dynamic one) for these black congregations. The diasporic festival that they produce is far less civic in orientation than that attended by Shaunaka, and correspondingly more controversial.

Katy Radford in Chapter 9 also deals with a form of radical and controversial Protestantism, intimately linked to ethnicity, but in her case it is expressed through Orange parades at Drumcree, Northern Ireland. She illustrates our point about the extent to which religious identities interdigitate with other cultural markers when she shows how the members of 'The Shankill Women Support Drumcree Group' express their Protestantism most cogently not through religious worship, but through ostensibly secular loyalist practices such as support for parades. As in Wood's example (see below), these women are prompted to become participants in the events described partly through ties of kinship. And once again, space and place are shown to be relevant here, since the parade is a key means of marking territory in a context where Protestant identity is marked in opposition to that of (geographically adjacent) Roman Catholics. We are dealing here not with a diffusely defined parish, but rather with the exact tracing of a territory through movement that invokes history but at the same time attempts to dominate the present. Although the roots in the past are more evident than they would be at a Cerullo revival, and the conversionary aims much less evident, we see a similar attempt to convert urban space into a form of testimony, a proclamation to the self and others of the correctness of one's beliefs. More broadly, of course, the march is about staking the claim for a Protestant geography of ties with the UK, against the apparently threatening tide of Roman Catholicism (a tide which, according to Hornsby-Smith, is ironically becoming absorbed in the cultural mainstream on the mainland itself). Radford's vivid chapter highlights many further ironies associated with the march. Women participate in and support events associated with witness and protest, but in doing so themselves undergo a process of peripheralisation within their own community. Their assertion of the power of place and history is also largely ignored by global media representations that decontextualise their identities and interpret them through objectified, two-dimensional images. In one sense, the passions expressed on the march illustrate the point made by Bruce and others that religion can appear to take a powerful role even in 'modern' contexts, when it is reinforced by other factors of identification such as ethnicity and gender. Yet Radford also notes that while the Orangemen are attempting to show allegiance and support for a state, the state may itself be progressively distancing itself from Northern Ireland. Furthermore, the quasi-religious rituals alongside mimesis of the military hark back to a once formidable Protestant hegemony in Northern Ireland: Drumcree for many observers symbolises not the power but rather the obsolete nature of Orangeism. The case study therefore presents yet another modulation of the connections between memory and identity, but demonstrates both the changing nature of commemoration and the fact that problematic divisions can be discerned *within* the parading community, and not just created in relation to external forces. As a 'civic' ritual, the parade could hardly be further removed from the self-conscious pluralism (cf. Gilliat-Ray 1999) of the Hindu festival for youth.

David Herbert (Chapter 10) and Eleanor Nesbitt (Chapter 11) shift our attention to two 'migrant' religions whose links with British history and memory are relatively long term and which have in contrasting ways been highly visible and influential in national culture. In discussing Islamic identity and globalisation, Herbert exposes some of the problems and contradictions of bland discourses of 'multiculturalism' and national 'unity in diversity'. He also disputes Western narratives of modernity (see above) that present Islam as the 'other' – a form of the past signifying a time when social life was dominated by religion. One strand of his argument follows Castells (e.g. 1997) in seeing religion as a source of communal identity in contemporary societies, a form of 'project' identity (that is, 'projected holistically towards the transformation of society') that might act as a source of resistance to dominant global systems. More specifically, Herbert argues that controversy over Rushdie's *The Satanic Verses* led, among other things, to the gradual development of a Muslim 'public sphere' in Britain, a series of intersecting social spaces for the representation but also the contestation of Muslim identity and ideology. Complementing some of our points made above, he points to a new development of transnational consciousness resulting not from ties with sending societies, but from areas of the world not strongly represented among British Muslims, such as Bosnia, Palestine and Afghanistan. Furthermore, following Werbner (1996), he talks of how the Muslims' diasporic public sphere might involve an important female collective voice. The pluralisation processes Herbert identifies are of course evident in various forms in all of the religions examined in this book.

A by-product of Herbert's contribution is his deconstruction of the essentialist discourses that seem to surround Western representations of Islam. Nesbitt takes the fluidity and heterogeneity of religious (and ethnic) identities as the fulcrum of her chapter on processes of religious identity formation among young British people from south Asian families. She highlights the crude mismatch between the broad labels of 'Hindu' and 'Sikh' (often deployed in British educational contexts) and the actual self-identification and experience of the young people studied in the Midlands. To some extent the state formally defines 'world faiths' (such as Christianity, Islam, Sikhism and Hinduism) through its construction of locally agreed religious education syllabuses. At school, identities are aligned with these 'world faiths', even when the culture of home challenges such allocation and spans supposed boundaries. But it is also evident from Nesbitt's careful ethnography that one's identity as a child (however formed through religious affiliation) is mutable and certainly changes as one ages – a point clearly made by several other contributors. Indeed, the children interviewed by Nesbitt adopt an almost ludic attitude to these monolithic religious systems. Nesbitt further reflects thoughtfully on methodologies for eliciting information on identity (to the approval of her two anthropological editors, she recommends participant observation, among other things). An example of the complexity of the forms of self-identification that she uncovers is provided in her story of interviewing a young 'Hindu' woman. The latter admitted in her final interview that she was Jain, but explained that she only identified herself in this way when talking with (other) Hindus, as most people in Britain would not actually understand the word 'Jain'.

In the sociology of religion, mention of the 'New Age' has almost become a trope for some of the processes discussed above: pluralisation, individualisation and postmodernism. In the final chapter of the volume, Wood continues the tendency of our authors to complexify categorisations of religious behaviour. Like Nesbitt, Wood adopts an ethnographic approach in his examination of a network of groups in Nottinghamshire which he labels 'nonformative' in the sense that they display a relative absence of formal social structures compared to those which are established in churches, sects and so on. He is at pains to stress, however, that nonformative spirituality does not provide a purely individualised haven for people to escape from their lives and focus on themselves. Rather, it is a means by which people can attempt to interpret and deal with their everyday lives. Indeed, kinship identity, that web of social relations we are all entangled in (though rarely examined so far in work on the New Age), forms an essential part of such spirituality. Thus Wood vigorously argues for a focus on kinship motifs in beliefs and practices, on issues such as the relationship of participants with sexual partners, parents and children. Wood therefore brings kinship, touched on in the majority of the chapters here, to centre stage and argues cogently that it bears a heavy, primarily practical, load in mediating religion and identity.

The reader may draw a number of conclusions from this collection of case studies and we will do no more here than flag up just three that we feel are especially significant. First, we would point to the conspicuous relevance, for these individuals and groups, of religion in forming their sense of identity and belonging. Second is the undoubted subtlety with which various forms of social differentiation – national affiliation, ethnicity, class, generation, kinship, gender, sexual orientation – are combined with religion to construct personal and social identity. Nesbitt (in this volume) quotes Stuart Hall thus: 'Identities are never unified ... never singular but multiply constructed across different, often intersecting and antagonistic, discourses, practices and positions' (1996:4). It is difficult, if not impossible, to separate out a distinctive 'religious identity' in these cases and indeed to try to do so seems to us a pointless act of reductionism. Finally, all these eleven authors indicate clearly the relevance to their particular cases of debates currently central to modern social theory and in particular those relating to larger socio-cultural movements such as globalisation and secularisation. For these reasons alone we believe that, together, these essays constitute a significant contribution to our understanding of the complex development of religious faith and practice in the United Kingdom.

Notes

1 Quoted in the *Guardian*, 27 July 2001, 'Young Hindus in Festival Search for Modern Identity'. The details contained in these paragraphs come from the *Guardian* article.

2 See Giddens (1991).

3 Kipp (1993:9) draws on the work of Marilyn Strathern (1988) to note that unexamined assumptions about the individual and a presumed antinomy between the individual and society underlie Marx as well as Durkheim, with Strathern sceptical that we will find 'society' and 'the individual' wherever we go.

4 Jenkins (1997:26) summarises Smith (1974) as distinguishing between: (a) cultural pluralism, in which although a society is composed of different ethnic groups these are not used as a criterion of citizenship; (b) social pluralism, where ethnicity is important regarding political organisation but does not affect citizenship; (c) structural pluralism, where ethnic identity directly affects citizenship and the incorporation of collectivities into membership of the state.

5 The Rushdie affair provoked anger among large groups of young men who until that time had not appeared especially interested in religion (Jacobson 1998:122).

6 Jacobson (1998:2–3) notes that individuals can at different times orient themselves towards different kinds of minority 'community' – Muslim, Asian, etc. Cross-cutting cleavages among Pakistanis in Waltham Forest include class, birthplace, own and parents' nationality, mother tongue and preferred language.

7 This view thus conflates genealogy and geography in terms of continuity.

8 Jenkins (1997:16) remarks: 'This ontology of the social world emerged from the social anthropological preoccupation – itself a legacy of the long-standing and disproportionate theoretical sway exercised by structural functionalism during the discipline's formative years – with social groups and their systematic interrelationships, and with social order and integration.'

9 Note Flanagan's (2001) shrewd comments in this area. He remarks that Weber's notion of the routinisation of charisma focuses on an issue of the formation of identity which Bourdieu has incorporated in his habitus. This relates to dispositions, to the process of structuring an identity in a field where there is a consensus as to the rules of the game. Whereas New Age presupposes destabilisation, Weber and Bourdieu presuppose a stability of a cultural field upon which an identity is to be constructed: 'The issue of identity in sociology has to be linked to a question of identification. This forms the focal basis of an act of affiliation and self-realisation in transactions that are structured, such as those of ritual or community' (ibid.:24).

10 Flanagan (2001:251) notes that Giddens writes very much without reference to religion in his accounts of personal identity in late modernity. Flanagan goes on to claim: 'But as Jenkins notes, the "ontological insecurity" which Giddens pursues in his worries about the reflexive self as the project of late modernity, is a variation on ideologies of spiritual salvation that sought to recast the self' (ibid.:252). Such ideologies can be traced back to Augustine's *Confessions* but also to Weber's Protestant ethic.

11 See the issue of *Social Anthropology*, **9**(3) (October 2001) edited by Michael Stewart. The emergent anthropological orthodoxy on secularisation is that it has not happened.

12 Bruce can be seen as a clear and prolific defender of the secularisation thesis, not least as it can be applied to the UK.

13 Just as Bruce's imagery tends to divide the public from the private, so he tends to refer to isolated enclaves, cut off from the mainstream (or alternatively to see religion as so diffuse as to render itself socially irrelevant, as in his view of the New Age).

14 There are of course reasons to be sceptical of such a division: some religious movements, such as evangelical Protestantism, sometimes try to annex the rational; nor can we tell the extent to which public policy is determined by religious conviction in the case of Tony Blair, for example.

15 Robbins also notes (1993:33) that in different ways New England, Nova Scotia and New South Wales all testify to the legacy of a kind of Britishness around the world.

16 Most famously with regard to war in the Falklands; at the time of writing, it remains to be seen how the Church of England will respond to government policies on war with Iraq.

17 Though not Judaism.

18 See for example Gluckman, (1940); Mitchell (1956); Van Velsen (1967).

Bibliography   -

Aldridge, A. (2000), *Religion in the Contemporary World: A Sociological Introduction*, Cambridge: Polity.

Appadurai, A. (1996), *Modernity at Large: Cultural Dimensions of Globalization*, Minneapolis: University of Minnesota Press.

Appiah, K.A. and Gates, H.L. (1995), 'Editors' Introduction: Multiplying Identities', in K.A. Appiah and H.L. Gates (eds) *Identities*, Chicago: Chicago University Press, pp. 1–6.

Ardener, S. (ed.) (1993), *Defining Females: The Nature of Women in Society*, Oxford: Berg.

Aronowitz, S. (1995), 'Reflections on Identity', in J. Rajchman (ed.) *The Identity in Question*, New York: Routledge, pp. 111–27.

Barth, F. (1969), *Ethnic Groups and Boundaries*, Boston: Little, Brown.

Bauman, Z. (2001), *Community: Seeking Safety in an Insecure World*, Cambridge: Polity Press.

Bilgrami, A. (1995), 'What is a Muslim? Fundamental Commitment and Cultural Identity', in K.A. Appiah and H.L. Gates (eds) *Identities*, Chicago: Chicago University Press, pp. 198–219.

Bourdieu, P. (1977), *Outline of a Theory of Practice*, Cambridge: Cambridge University Press.

Boyarin, D. and Boyarin, J. (1995), 'Diaspora: Generation and the Ground of Jewish Identity', in K.A. Appiah and H.L. Gates (eds) *Identities*, Chicago: Chicago University Press, pp. 305–37.

Bruce, Steve (1995), *Religion in Modern Britain*, Oxford: Oxford University Press.

Bruce, S. (1996), *Religion in the Modern World: From Cathedrals to Cults*, Oxford: Oxford University Press.

Bruce, S. (1998), 'The Charismatic Movement and the Secularization Thesis', *Religion*, **28**(3), 223–32.

Bruce, S. (2002), *God is Dead: Secularization in the West*, Oxford: Blackwell.

Calley, M. (1965), *God's People: West Indian Pentecostal Sects in England*, London: Oxford University Press.

Casanova, J. (1994), *Public Religions in the Modern World*, Chicago: Chicago University Press.

Castells, M. (1997), *The Information Age: Economy, Society, Culture*, vol. 3 *End of Millennium*, Oxford: Blackwell.

Cohen, A.P. (ed.) (1986), *Symbolising Boundaries: Identity and Diversity in British Cultures*, Manchester: Manchester University Press.

Cohen, R. (1994), *Frontiers of Identity: The British and the Others*, London: Longman.

Coleman, S. (2000), *The Globalisation of Charismatic Christianity: Spreading the Gospel of Prosperity*, Cambridge: Cambridge University Press.

Coleman, S. and Crang, M. (eds) (2002), *Tourism: Between Place and Performance*, Oxford: Berghahn.

Davie, G. (1994), *Religion in Britain since 1945: Believing without Belonging*, Oxford: Blackwell.

Davie, G. (2000), *Religion in Modern Europe: A Memory Mutates*, Oxford: Oxford University Press.

Fardon, R. (1995), *Counterworks: Managing the Diversity of Knowledge*, London: Routledge.

Flanagan, K. (2001), 'Religion and Modern Personal Identity', in Anton van Harskamp and Albert W. Musschenga (eds) *The Many Faces of Individualism* Leuven: Peeters, pp. 239–266.

Gardner, K. (1995), *Global Migrants, Local Lives: Travel and Transformation in Rural Bangladesh*, Oxford: Clarendon Press.

Gay y Blasco, P. (1999), *Gypsies in Madrid: Sex, Gender and the Performance of Identity*, Oxford: Berg.

Giddens, A. (1991), *Modernity and Self-Identity. Self and Society in Late Modern Age*, Cambridge: Polity.

Gilliat-Ray, S. (1999), 'Civil Religion in England: Traditions and Transformations', *Journal of Contemporary Religion*, **14**(2), 233–44.

Gluckman, M. (1940), 'An Analysis of a Social Situation in Modern Zululand', *African Studies*, **14**, 1–30 and 147–74.

Hall, S. (1992), 'The New Ethnicities', in J. Donald and A. Rattansi (eds) *'Race', Culture and Difference*, London: Sage, pp. 252–59.

Hall, S. (1996), 'Introduction: Who Needs "Identity"?', in S. Hall and P. du Gay (eds) *Questions of Cultural Identity*, London: Sage, pp. 1–17.

Hammond, P.E. (1988), 'Religion and the Persistence of Identity', *Journal for the Scientific Study of Religion*, **27**(1), 1–11.

Hanson, S. (1997), 'The Secularisation Thesis: Talking at Cross Purposes', *Journal of Contemporary Religion*, **12**(2), 159–79.

Harvey, D. (1989), *The Condition of Postmodernity: An Enquiry into the Origins of Cultural Change*, Oxford: Blackwell.

Heelas, P., Lash, S. and Morris, P. (eds) (1996), *Detraditionalization: Critical Reflections on Authority and Identity*, Oxford: Blackwell.

Hervieu-Léger, D. (2000), *Religion as a Chain of Memory*, Cambridge: Polity.

Hickman, M.J. (1995), *Religion, Class and Identity: The State, the Catholic Church and the Education of the Irish in Britain*, Aldershot: Avebury.

Hobsbawm, E. and Ranger, T. (eds) (1983), *The Invention of Tradition*, Cambridge: Cambridge University Press.

Horton, R. (1967), 'African Traditional Thought and Western Science', *Africa*, **37**, 50–71.

Jacobson, J. (1998), *Islam in Transition: Religion and Identity among British Pakistani Youth*, London: Routledge.

Jenkins, R. (1997), *Rethinking Ethnicity: Arguments and Explorations*, London: Sage.

Kipp, R.S. (1993), *Dissociated Identities: Ethnicity, Religion and Class in an Indonesian Society*, Ann Arbor: University of Michigan Press.

Martin, D. (1978), *A General Theory of Secularization*, Oxford: Blackwell.

Mauss, A. (1996), 'Identity and Boundary Maintenance. International Prospects for Mormonism at the Dawn of the Twenty-First Century', in D. Davies (ed.) *Mormon Identities in Transition*, London: Cassell, pp. 9–19.

Meyer, B. and Geschiere, P. (eds) (1999), *Globalization and Identity: Dialectics of Flow and Closure*, Oxford: Blackwell.

Mitchell, J.C. (1956), *The Kalela Dance. Aspects of Social Relationships among Urban Africans in Northern Rhodesia*, Rhodes-Livingstone Paper No. 27, Manchester: Manchester University Press.

Nye, M. (2001), *Multiculturalism and Minority Religions in Britain: Krishna Consciousness, Religious Freedom, and the Politics of Location*, Richmond: Curzon.

Parsons, G. (1994), 'Introduction: Deciding How Far You Can Go?', in Gerald Parsons (ed.) *The Growth of Religious Diversity: Britain from 1945*, Vol. II *Issues*, London: Routledge, pp. 5–21.

Robbins, K. (1993), *History, Religion and Identity in Modern Britain*, London: The Hambledon Press.

Robertson, R. (1992), *Globalization: Social Theory and Global Culture*, London: Sage.

Ruel, M. (1997), 'Christians as Believers', in Malcolm Ruel (ed.) *Belief, Ritual and the Securing of Life: Reflexive Essays on a Bantu Religion*, Leiden: E.J. Brill, pp. 36–59.

Schaefer, N. (2002), 'Morris Cerullo's London Revivals as "Glocal" (Neo-) Pentecostal Movement Events', *Culture and Religion*, **3**(1), 105–23.

Smith, M.G. (1974), *Corporations and Society*, London: Duckworth.

Strathern, M. (1988), *The Gender of the Gift: Problems with Women and Problems with Women in Society*, London: University of California Press.

Toulis, N. (1997), *Believing Identity: Pentecostalism and the Mediation of Jamaican Ethnicity and Gender in England*. Oxford: Berg.

Van der Veer, P. (ed.) (1995), *Nation and Migration: The Politics of Space in the South Asian Diaspora*, Philadelphia: University of Pennsylvania Press.

Van Velsen, J. (1967), 'The Extended Case Method and Situational Analysis', in A.L. Epstein (ed.) *The Craft of Social Anthropology*, London: Tavistock Publications, pp. 129–49.

Wallman, S. (ed.) (1979), *Ethnicity at Work*, London: Macmillan.

Werbner, P. (1996), 'Public Spaces, Political Voices: Gender, Feminism and Aspects of British Muslim Participation in the Public Sphere', in W. Shadid and P. van Koningsveld (eds) *Political Participation and Identities of Muslims in Non-Muslim States*, Kok Pharos: Kampen, pp. 53–70.

Wilson, B. (1982), *Religion in Sociological Perspective*, Oxford: Oxford University Press.

CHAPTER 2

Losing Our Space, Finding Our Place?

The Changing Identity of the English Parish Church

Martyn Percy[1]

> Too often we allow ourselves to suppose that
> could we but get back to the beginning we should
> find that all was intelligible and should then be able
> to watch the process whereby simple ideas were
> smothered under subtleties and technicalities. But it
> is not so. Simplicity is the outcome of technical subtlety;
> it is the goal not the starting point. As we go backwards
> the familiar outlines become blurred; the ideas become
> fluid, and instead of the simple we find the indefinite.
>
> (Maitland 1897:9)

The English parish church is part and parcel of the cultural furniture of the nation. To some it is 'more than a place of denominational worship. It is the stage on which the pageant of the community has been played out for a millennium' (Jenkins 1999:3). For others it is the natural focus of the community, 'markers and anchors ... repositories of all embracing meanings pointing beyond the immediate to the ultimate ... [the] only institutions that deal in tears and concern themselves with the breaking points of human existence' (Davie 1994:189). Still for others, the parish church is a place of Christian witness within a defined community. It is the *ekklesia* of the *parochia* (Pounds 2000:37–40); the means of spiritual sustenance, ethical endeavour and social shaping within a given community that becomes 'the social skin of the world ... always laid out in particular ways, *ordered* in such a way as to be suitable for its place' (Hardy 1996:27).

To be sure, these idealist descriptions of the parish church all have their merit. But what does it mean to talk about a parish church today? The question is timely when one considers the various subtle and inimical forces that appear to have eroded the identity of a parish church. Religious pluralism has been a feature of the landscape of English religion since the Reformation; a parish church is no longer the sole focus for the religious rituals of its people or for their spiritual aspirations. Changes in population and church-going habits have also left their mark. Robin Gill has remarked on the Victorian inclination to build greater numbers of churches and of larger sizes, even in areas where substantial depopulation was occurring (Gill 1992). And yet there have been many other periods when the apparent over-provision of church buildings effectively threatened parochial sustainability and viability. For example, Winchester could once claim to be 'the most over-churched city in England' (Pounds 2000:123), with, in the twelfth century, a cathedral, two monasteries and at least 57 churches for a population serving no more than 8000 people; that is one parish church for every 130 people. (Similar figures are cited by

Pounds for Worcester, York, Norwich and other medieval towns and cities.) But what did 8000 people *do* with 57 churches and a cathedral? It would appear that these churches, although mostly proper parish churches insofar as the *parochia* supported the *ekklesia*, were made up of congregations serving relatively small communities. It was economically viable then, but only just. By 1535, the number of parish churches in Winchester had fallen to just 13 – a quarter of the number for the twelfth century.

In this chapter, I will be reflecting on the identity of the English parish church and exploring in what ways the pressures it now faces are particular and specious. In order to do this, it will first be necessary to 'debunk' the myth of secularisation. In a chapter of this length, it is not possible to present an in-depth account of what secularisation theses once attempted to propagate. But it will be enough to know that today, most sociologists of religion no longer accept that modernity necessarily ushers in a less religious era. Steve Bruce (1997) and Bryan Wilson (1966) from a sociological perspective, and Callum Brown (2000) and Owen Chadwick (1975) from a historical perspective, perhaps represent the better-known faces of 'classic' secularisation theories that insist on the inevitable decline of religion as society advances. Meanwhile, Grace Davie (1994), David Martin (1978), Peter Berger (1969) – to name but a few – have identified that religion in the modern world does not suffer as one might immediately suppose; granted, it mutates, is squeezed into new shapes, and patterns of religious affinity and belonging are certainly altering. But it is (arguably) undeniable that the world is *not* a less religious place with the onset of modernity. People continue to possess and express what we scholars of religion variously call 'innate', 'folk' or 'common' spirituality, or 'vernacular religion'. Outside organised mainstream religion, spiritual affinities flourish. I readily acknowledge that my 'sketch' of secularisation (or rather an anti-thesis) is sweeping, but the narrative provides an important foundation for the rest of the discussion.

Second, I wish to comment on the identity of the parish church today by exploring its apparent ambiguities. The idea of a parish church can be said, to some extent, to be a bit of an accident. As Pounds points out, the Saxon age is the first phase in the development of the concept. The *parochia* was a partly secular and partly sacred arrangement. Minster churches – hundreds were dotted around England – devolved spiritual responsibility to smaller *parochia* that were charged with the task of ministering to local communities. Minster churches themselves owed their very existence to royal estates or other dimensions of the feudal system granting rights, privileges and land to the church. A parish was, primarily, a governable and economically viable agrarian or urban community that could not only pay its secular taxes but also afford its spiritual duties. In Saxon England, as today, it cost money to be buried in a churchyard. Even then a system of tithing existed to support the ministry and fabric of the church, and this survived well into the nineteenth century. In short, the viability of a church was deeply connected to the viability of a community; church and parish lived in a relation of intra-dependence. Payment of fees to the church meant that the poor were cared for, sacramental ministry provided, the dead buried honourably, and that the moral welfare of the community was generally catered for – although the secular authorities were mainly responsible for enforcing the law. The church needed a parish; and the parish needed its church. But as I will show, this relationship began to bifurcate even before the Reformation, and so the waning and mutating identity of a parish church has nothing to do with, initially at least, secularisation. So, paradoxically, I argue that while parish churches have lost their pivotal role in public and community life, this process does not necessarily indicate that people are less religious or spiritually inclined.

Third, a conclusion explores the future of the parish church and its identity. With the (undeniable) collapse of parochial identity in the broad delta of contemporary English culture (a process that appears to predate the Reformation), what can a parish church offer to its environment and to its people? To what extent can a space such as a parish church be meaningfully spoken of when many people have lost their conscious sense of belonging to a parochial space? In asking these questions, I realise that there is also an uncertainty about clerical identity to address; however, that will have to wait for another essay – although I will touch on the issue briefly.

The Myth of Secular England: a Brief Sketch

One of the great paradoxes of late modernity is that churches believe in the steady decrease of public faith more than almost any other group. During the last half of the twentieth century, it was popular to believe in a new credo: secularisation. Promoted by a few busy sociologists in league with disenchanted voices in the media, the theory is simple enough. The more advanced or modern society becomes, the less it looks to the spiritual and the religious. *Ergo*, church attendance declines, and the once golden age of Christendom, at least in the West, is coming to its end. The thesis appears to be supported by statistics; fewer people go to church than, say, a hundred years ago, so the long-term prognosis seems to be correct. Correspondingly, the churches suffer from what might be termed a 'collective low-grade (but not clinical) depression', believing themselves to be in the grip of a neuralgic pathology, and increasingly inclined towards panaceas that deal with symptoms, but seldom causes.

As with most things, the truth is not nearly so simple. We now know enough about church-going habits to make a more sober, less bleak judgement about the parish church. It doesn't take a mathematical genius to figure out that church-goers who once went 52 times a year (and on high days and holy days), but now only go 47 times a year (allowing for holidays) cause a 10 per cent drop in attendance. But there are not 10 per cent fewer people attending church; what has changed is the performance of the worshippers. It may be the case that more people come to church less frequently, and that *regular* church-going is in decline, but the appetite for occasional church attendance seems undiminished. Granted, fewer people belong, formally, to a Christian denomination when compared to the inter-war or Victorian periods. But almost all forms of association have declined steeply since those days. As Robert Putnam (2000) perceptively points out, associational disconnection is an endemic feature of modern life, but, ironically, churches are holding up far better than many of their secular voluntary and associational counterparts.

For example, today there are fewer Scouts and Guides; trade union membership has waned; and there are now fewer members of the Conservative Party than there are Methodists. Bodies such as the Freemasons, Round Table, townswomen's guilds and women's institutes have noted steep declines in membership; but the Mother's Union has held out rather well by comparison. Recreationally, there are fewer people in our cinemas and football grounds than 70 years ago – yet no one can say these activities are in decline. Indeed, it is a sobering thought that in so-called secular Britain, there are still more people turning to God each weekend in a church than watching a game of football. During the year 2000 over 35 million people visited an English cathedral. Whether they were tourists, pilgrims, casual inquirers or idle visitors – no one can guess the percentages, or how many visitors who had never prayed before stopped before the statue of the Madonna and Child, and lit a candle for their family – the numbers are highly significant.

Another problem with secularisation is that after sociologists and the media, the body that believes in the thesis most passionately is the churches themselves. Many, if not most, have bought the idea that modernity leads to the gradual and incremental loss of faith. Correspondingly, various interest groups emerge, hoping to make some capital out of the perceived crisis. Liberals propose stripping the faith to its bare essentials in order to make religion more credible. Evangelicals also strip the faith to its essentials, and promote 'the basics' of religion through courses like *Alpha*. But most Christians (and it is never easy to say *who* these people are or what their faith consists of) in the middle ground are bewildered by these approaches to faith and society. For in their day-to-day Christian existence, no matter how intense or how nominal, they do not encounter a 'secular' world at all, but, rather, one in which spirituality, religion and questions of faith remain public and widespread. In short, they do not believe in the modern 'disease' of secularisation, and consequently, they are unpersuaded by those groups that seek to promote their panaceas.

But surely there is some truth in the idea that fewer people are turning to official or mainstream religion? Yes and no. To a large extent, it depends on what periods in history are being compared to the present. For example, the Victorian period saw a revival of religion and religious attendance that lasted for about 40 years. Yet at the beginning of the eighteenth and nineteenth centuries, on the contrary, church attendance was, on the whole, derisory (Percy 2001:55). The medieval and Reformation periods are often characterised as ages of great faith. Certainly, individuals and communities did die for their beliefs. However, the general scale of apathy and antipathy should not be underestimated. The eleventh-century monk, William of Malmesbury, complained that the aristocracy rarely attended Mass, and even the more pious heard it at home, 'but in their bedchambers, lying in the arms of their wives' (Fletcher 1997:476). At least they heard Mass though; according to one scholar, 'substantial sections of thirteenth century society – especially the poor – hardly attended church at all' (Murray 1972:92). Even though a system of fines for non-attendance persisted late into the Middle Ages, the penalties were notoriously difficult to enforce; and anyway, only the head of the household was required to attend church – children, wives, servants and those who were ill were always excused.

Social theorists who attempt to measure and judge 'secularity' against the success or failure of 'official' religion have usually failed to read the plot. There have been very few periods in English history when everyone went to church or

Sunday school, knew right from wrong, and absolutely hung on every word their parish priest uttered. As Keith Thomas notes: 'what is clear is that the hold of organized religion upon the people [of England] was never so complete as to leave no room for rival systems of belief' (Thomas 1971:178). As further evidence, Thomas cites an extract from one of Oliver Heywood's *Diaries*:

> One Nov 4 1681 as I travl'd towards Wakefield about Hardger moor I met with a boy who would needs be talking. I begun to ask him some questions about the principles of religion: he could not tell me how many gods there be, nor persons in the godhead, nor who made the world nor anything about Jesus Christ, nor heaven nor hell, or eternity after this life, nor for what ends he came into the world, nor for what condition he was born in – I ask't him whether he was a sinner; he told me he hop't not; yet this was a witty boy and could talk of any worldly things skillfully enough ... he is 10 years of age, cannot reade and scarce ever goes to churche.
>
> (Thomas 1971:206)

Granted, the Yorkshire region could be argued as a special case. Ever since records for the area began, church-attendance figures have been consistently poor and always below any national average. Yet detailed readings of parochial records from almost any age can illustrate the pragmatic, amateurish nature of 'official' English religion. Here are some extracts from the *Archdiaconal Visitations in 1578* (Bedfordshire Historical Records Society 1990) that make the point no less forcefully:

> *Langford* Our chancell is owte of repayre in tymber & wyndowes, at the parsons defaute. Our churche wyndowes are in decaye by reason of fowle that cometh in at the chancell wyndowes which hathe broken them.

> *Bedford Sancti Petri* [sic] There is no pulpitte in the littel churche. The x commandments are not on the walles. The chancell & churche are not paved in some places.

> *Colmworth* We have had no service on the weeke dayes not from Maye daye last tyll September & no service on Sancte Peters Eve nor Sancte Bartholemewe Eve nor Michaelmas daye at nyghte & they had iiij children christened iiij wayes, & he woold not let the parishe see his licence & one syr Brian Hayward dyd in the like case. Umphrey Austyne churche warden last yere wold not present the lead that was missing oute of the steeple. Item Nicholas Dicons, Thomas Jud, William Quarrell & his wyfe have not receaved this xij monthes. Item the Quenes Iniunctions or the bisshoppes were not made thes iij yeres nor the catechisme taughte.

> *Tylsworth* We have had but one sermone since Michaelmas, which was the Sondaye after New yers daye.

> *Farandiche* The chancell & parsonage are in decaye by the parson's defalt. They have but one sermon this year.

> *Bidham* We doe present that we had no Communion but once this yeare, and that our last churchwardens dyd not make there accompt for the yere.

> *Patnum* [Pavenham] Our chansell is in decaye and redye to faule dwone, at the defaute of Trynitye College in Cambridge.

The picture painted of religion in sixteenth-century Bedfordshire is probably just about enough to raise Bunyan from his grave. The parish churches appear to be in a poor state of repair, with theft of lead and timber being relatively commonplace. Why there are chickens running riot in the church at Langford is anyone's guess, but they were possibly abandoned as part of a tithe payment. It was not uncommon, notes Pounds, for live animals to be left in church (2000:75). Furthermore, the records cited above also suggest that the clergy appear to be mostly absent from their churches, squashing the myth that every parish was (until recently) well served by its own parish priest. In many cases these churches in Bedfordshire have not seen a priest for months or even years. And is it not ironic that the concerns of the laity – here represented by the churchwardens – are similar to the same concerns expressed today by the churchwardens of the twenty-first century? Namely, when will we get our next vicar, bishop? And what is to be done about the state of our church? The agenda for the parish church is as old as the hills: without staffing and proper maintenance, there is fear for the community as a whole.

These observations do raise some interesting questions about the clergy, though. What were they doing about the state of parish churches, and about the apparent vacuum of pastoral and sacramental provision? Not much, it would seem. William Tyndale complained that, in 1530, few priests could recite the Lord's Prayer or translate it into English. When the Bishop of Gloucester tested his clergy in 1551, of 311 priests, 171 could not repeat the Ten Commandments – but this is hardly surprising, as there were few seminaries. Did any of this matter? Hardly. It would seem that the impact of the clergy on their congregations was very slight. As Keith Thomas notes in his magisterial *Religion and the Decline of Magic* (1971), 'members of the population jostled for pews, nudged their neighbours, hawked and spat, knitted, made coarse remarks, told jokes, fell asleep and even let off guns', with other behaviour including 'loathsome farting, striking, and scoffing speeches', which resulted in 'the great offence of the good and the great rejoicing of the bad' (ibid.:61–6, 161–2).

This haphazard, semi-secular, quiet (but occasionally rowdy and irreverent) English Christianity continues well into successive centuries. James Woodforde's *Diary of a Country Parson* (Beresford 1999) provides an invaluable window into the life of the clergy and the state of English Christianity in the eighteenth century. Again, a close reading of the text suggests that whatever secularisation is, it is not obviously a product of the Industrial Revolution. Woodforde clearly thinks it is reasonably good to have 'two rails' (or 30 communicants) at Christmas or Easter, from 360 parishioners. Such figures would be low by today's standards in some rural communities. Woodforde tells us that the only time his church is ever full is when a member of the royal family is ill, or when there is a war on. Generally, the context of his ministry is one where he baptises, marries and buries the people of his parish, but the week-by-week Sunday attendance is not something that would get many ministers into a frenzy of excitement. But Woodforde is not bothered by this – not because he is especially lazy – but because the *totality* of his contact with his parish constitutes his ministry. He is *with* his people in all their trials and tribulations, not just his congregation. He is their man for all seasons; an incarnate presence in the midst of a community that waxes and wanes in its religious affections (Beresford 1999:vii).

More could be said about the apparent indifference of the English towards their parish church, but space does not permit. What needs to be stressed at the end of this short section is that the parish church and the ministry that issued from it were, generally speaking, greatly valued by the parish. However, that valuing did not necessarily translate into frequent and intense church attendance on the part of the masses. Mostly, it seems that the English have tended to *relate* to their parish churches in a variety of ways; in a relationship of affection (sometimes grudging), of vicarious religiosity (having others believe in those things that one can't quite be so certain of – 'say one for me, padre'), and of 'believing without belonging', to borrow the oft-quoted maxim of Grace Davie. Certainly, it can be asserted that statistical surveys continually support the thesis that England is a place where the vast majority of the population continue to affirm their belief in God, but then proceed to do little about it. So church attendance figures remain stubbornly low. Yet this is not a modern malaise, but is rather a typical feature of many Western societies down the ages. Granted, there have been periods of revival when church attendance has peaked. But the basic and innate disposition of the English is typical of Western Europe – one of believing without belonging; of relating to the church, and valuing its presence and beliefs – yet without necessarily sharing them. As the ageless witticism expresses it: 'I cannot consider myself to be a pillar of the church, for I never go. But I am a buttress – insofar as I support it from the outside.'

The Contemporary English Parish Church: an Ambiguous Identity?

With these brief reflections in mind, we now turn to the ambiguity of the parish church in contemporary English culture. What does it stand for? Whom does it serve? In what ways is the parish church the *ekklesia* of the *parochia*? The idea of a 'parish' may seem to be obvious to many: still part of the cultural furniture, and sufficiently resonant to command attention and respect. For many established churches worldwide, the parish is the fundamental unit of organisation, the 'place' where the church is located. It is odd, then, that so little attention has been focused upon identifying what a parish is and means, particularly in relation to theology, ministry and ecclesiology.

As many ministers of religion already know, the shape and content of parish ministry has altered radically over the last century. An increasingly professionalised clergy, coupled to an uneasy mutation in public perceptions of parochial identity, has led to some profound and subtle shifts. While clergy are still all curates – with the 'cure of souls' for the whole parish – it is becoming less and less clear in a mobile, transient, globalised and compressed world what might be meant by terms such as 'community', 'local' and 'place', let alone 'parish'. 'Parish visiting' used to be a standard feature of many parochial ministries, but its tenure as a staple part of the average clergy timetable has been all too brief. While Woodforde and his parsonic predecessors (for example, George Herbert) were often wont to call upon their parishioners for a mixture of social, secular and sacred reasons, it was the Victorians who developed what was a pastoral habit into a systematic discipline – but with mixed results. Wickham's study of religion in industrial cities confirms that, typically, out of one street of hundreds of residents, 'you perhaps see a solitary instance where a whole household of several persons are regular attenders' (Wickham 1957:14). Gerald Parsons's study of Victorian Christianity clearly shows that, in spite of the clergy cultivating a professionalism (including the sporting of 'dog collars' from about 1860, the first time clergy had really begun to dress differently to mark them out in day-to-day wear from other gentlemanly professions), the vast majority of the population remained unmoved, and didn't take 'serious Christianity' that seriously (Parsons 1988:25).

While it is true that rates of church-going were buoyant during the Victorian era, the peaks and troughs of church-attendance figures have nearly always depended as much upon cultural factors (such as the shifting population from agrarian to industrial contexts, or in the case of Billy Graham's evangelistic campaigns of the postwar era the shift from cities to a new suburbia) as upon the intensity of engagement between a church and its parish. Thus, the 'serious Christianity' of the Victorian era engaged in intense parochial ministry for a mixture of reasons: baptism visiting was especially encouraged, but the development of Sunday schools and adult Bible classes, which flourished between 1875 and the late Edwardian period, owed as much to the desire to encourage education and self-improvement as it did to anything else.

So far as one can tell, the impact of all this expended effort was somewhat limited. Parish churches and their ministers throughout the nineteenth century were, in effect, being forced to reinvent their connectedness to the parish. The obligation of tithing was withering, if not altogether defunct, which meant that the parish now had no necessary economic relationship with its church (besides, other denominations had received legal recognition since 1689). Tithing was a mixed blessing for the parish church. In general, it was not resented by most parishes; people understood that this was their due to God, and the church was merely the collector. But many did resent the manner of collection, and the ends for which the moneys were used. Some complained that they were taxed several times over: once for the grass, then for the hay, then for the milk, and then for the cheese – and finally for the cow too. This led to some disgruntled protests, such as pouring a tenth of the milk yield all over the chancel steps. Even as late as the eighteenth century there was a riot in the Cornish fishing village of Madron when the rector attempted to collect the tithe of fish. The fishermen argued that parish boundaries did not extend into the Atlantic Ocean; the clergyman replied that they were landed on the soil of his parish, and he was entitled to his due (Pounds 2000:213).

It was only a question of time before the literal payment in kind of a tenth of all yields was ended; what worked haphazardly for agrarian economies would never translate into the emerging industries of the late eighteenth century. The Tithe Commutation Act duly came into force in 1836. However, it would be another century before tithing was finally phased out, as rents and glebe land persisted well into the twentieth century. Consider, for example, this description of a father's hope for his second son, and a career in the church, during the latter part of the eighteenth century:

> Dr Darwin, a confirmed freethinker, was sensible and shrewd. He had only to look around him, recall the vicarages he had visited, and ponder the country parsons he entertained at home. One did not have to be a believer to see that an aimless son with a

penchant for field sports would fit in nicely. Was the Church not a haven for dullards and dawdlers, the last resort of spendthrifts? What calling but the highest for those whose sense of calling was nil? And in what other profession were the risks of failure so low and the rewards so high? The Anglican Church, fat, complacent, and corrupt, lived luxuriously on its tithes and endowments, as it had for a century. Desirable parishes were routinely auctioned off to the highest bidder. A fine rural 'living' with a commodious rectory, a few acres to rent or farm, and perhaps a tithe barn to hold the local levy worth hundreds of pounds a year could easily be bought as an investment by a gentleman.

(Desmond and Moore 1991:.47)

But fundamentally, parish churches and their ministers were gradually becoming disconnected from the local economy. The 'church rate' that levied a tax on local people for the upkeep of the parish church was abolished by law in 1864, leading to the present anomalous situation, whereby the whole parish has access to the parish church for baptisms, weddings, funerals and other rites, but only the congregation are obliged to pay for the upkeep of the building. In short, the experience of Victorian parochial ministry was one of more intense engagement as the parish and the church underwent rapid bifurcation, with the parish – as a space – ceasing to be defined in ecclesiastical or spiritual terms, and collapsing back into its secular shape, only this time it was ordered by boroughs and civic authorities. Or, to put it another way, the increasing loss of the parish as a recognised 'place' that began in Victorian England – a product of industrialisation, capitalism and early globalisation – led to the parish church becoming a more intense spiritual space, and to the clergy being more obviously differentiated as a professional class, replete with their own separate colleges for training and formation (not something they had existed in previous centuries).

But where do these reflections on spaces and places take us today? In her book *Space, Place and Gender* (1994:146ff.), Doreen Massey, a geographer with interests in cultural theory, feminist theory, philosophy and sociology, makes a number of pertinent and illuminating points in relation to our discussion of the *ekklesia* and the *parochia*. First, places are only defined in relation to or over and against other places. Second, places have many identities – they are not flat or static. Third, place and community do not necessarily correlate. While there may be a longing for such coherence, it is important to grasp that communities are often at odds with their environments. (In distinguishing between 'place' and 'space', I adopt fairly simple definitions based on the etymology of the terms. 'Space' refers to a defined area, whereas 'place' stipulates the value, identity and definition of that space. Or, put more simply, 'place' tends to be a more socially constructed idea than 'space' – but even the idea of 'space' requires some social definition.)

Massey also points out some of the ironies of modernity and locality. Air travel has led to a decline in passenger shipping, which has isolated many remote island communities. Thus, while for some the world is more compressed and globalised, for others it is increasingly lonely and fragmented. Technology also reduces spatial distances – fax, e-mail and video-phone – yet many still travel many miles just to collect water. The city may be alive and well, with everything 'within easy reach'; yet pensioners may still be living in a bed-sit, their presence or absence going undetected for many months. In other words, the mobility of some, while destroying the identity of the 'local' for many, may equally leave many depending even more heavily on their immediate environment and community for support. Once again, we can see here that 'the local' has an ethical dimension to it – the global threatens the local at many levels (for example, the supermarket versus the local corner shop), making it impossible for a prescient pastoral ministry to be limited to the local – because many ethical and social problems will have to be fought on a broader canvas.

Take, for example, my own present locality – Millhouses, a small suburb nestling in the city of Sheffield. The place name comes from a ruined abbey a few miles down the road, which was built in 1178 by a penitent knight who was implicated in the assassination of Thomas à Becket. So Millhouses owes its origins to a Frenchman, who built the abbey on the furthest extent of the arch-episcopal province of Canterbury. Over the centuries, Millhouses moved away from agrarian dependency to water-powered mills making metals and machines. The area prospered. Today the area mostly comprises post-Edwardian housing, whose residents are either retired or youngish middle-aged people who are working in the professions or middle management – the 'posher' parishes lie on its borders. Today, the parish numbers 4000, but with over a third of the area still covered in protected woodland.

Yet that is only one way of describing Millhouses. In terms of education, the infant and junior schools are among the most sought after in the city, which has pushed up the house prices: education by postcode. The parish also falls in the right catchment area for the best secondary schools. Yet in the parish itself, there is a struggling secondary modern school, which draws all its pupils from the poorer parts of the city, including those from the ethnically diverse neighbouring parish. So, every day, there are busloads of children of every ethnic colour and hue coming to school at the bottom of Millhouses Lane, while there are (four-wheeled drive) carloads of children, mostly Caucasian, who leave the top of Millhouses Lane for other schools. In other words, even in a largely unselfconscious parish such as Millhouses, the phenomenon of what David Sibley calls 'geographies of exclusion' have to be faced (Sibley 1995). Millhouses is a place where feelings and images of difference can surface, where borders are ambiguous (for example, educational, class, work-related, residential?), and exclusion and inclusion are no longer confined to physical boundaries.

So for whom is Millhouses local? The answer is 'many more than its 4000 residents' – but they are all experiencing the same shared space very differently. Commercially, the ethnic shops just outside the parish depend on custom from within the parish. But those shops face stiff competition from three large supermarkets, which are fairly 'upmarket'. So for many, whether shop owner or shop worker, Millhouses is a place of work, and perhaps of economic struggle. Then there are the pubs competing for more than local business, and the restaurants that depend more on passing trade than on residents.

Clearly, to minister in such a community would require one's attention being constantly drawn out of the parish, because the identity of the parish can never itself be settled. It is an arbitrary space that is experienced in many different ways by several different types of community. Whatever Millhouses is, it is not static; it is a contested place, an ambivalent locality. The 'cure of souls' for the parish necessarily extends across the simple frontiers of residency.

But let us return to the relationship between the *ekklesia* and the *parochia*. I noted at the beginning of this chapter that their identities had begun to undergo a process of bifurcation that can be dated from the Reformation, and in all probability well before that. For example, even from the early Middle Ages, it became increasingly difficult to order and police growing populations through the auspices of the local church. Courts of law, the rise of civic authorities and guilds, the need for better transport infrastructures and the like meant that many people looked beyond their immediate parochial boundaries for their livelihood. As we observed earlier, in small cities such as Winchester, what passed for 'parochial worship' was essentially congregational in character – a parish church may just have consisted of a few extended families worshipping together, and whatever sacramental ministry they could afford. In turn, this dynamic emerged afresh in the wake of the Reformation, when religious services could easily be said at home, presided over by the head of the house, and gathered around the word, and not sacramental worship. Furthermore, the economic ties that bound parishes to their parish churches were beginning to break down as commerce became increasingly cosmopolitan. The local mattered less and less as people became more mobile. These trends, present long before the Renaissance, never mind the Reformation, were only to increase during the Industrial Revolution. It is possible to identify many points of interaction between the *ekklesia* and the *parochia* where the process of bifurcation began to take root, but two are singled out for discussion here: birth and death.

Minster churches had once monopolised the rite of baptism; it was a sacrament undertaken by patronal churches, and the origin of the phrase 'mother church' partly lies in this sequential control. Under the Saxon minster system, there were chapels and places of worship that were the *parochiae* of the minster, but these places rarely had fonts of their own. The fight to acquire the status of parish church was thus often about local autonomy and prestige, and against the interests of the minster – and perhaps even about finance. Although no fee was levied for the sacrament of baptism, some financial benefit inevitably accrued to the minster through control over who was admitted to the sacred fold (and, by implication, who was excluded, as non-payment of tithes normally led to formal excommunication – although this exclusion could always be overcome upon payment of fines). To be a parish church meant owning a font, and this in turn enabled the local *ekklesia* to be truly a part of the *parochia* in its own right. Parish churches symbolised not only the presence of God in the midst of a community; they also made a powerful economic and social statement: this is a viable, living community that can support itself and support its God. A chapel said something different: we are dependent on another area for our welfare.

To return to Millhouses for a moment. The history of the local churches follows these contours neatly. All Saints Ecclesall is a large church that sits atop a hill that would have once partially overlooked the site of Beauchief Abbey. The original church was built in the thirteenth century for a local dignitary who tired of the journey up and down the hill to hear Mass at the abbey. His solution was to give lands to the abbey for agriculture and milling at the bottom of the valley (Millhouses), and in return he built a chantry chapel next to his manor, and a priest from the abbey came to him each day to say Mass. In the late nineteenth century the Millhouses area acquired its own 'chapel of ease' to accommodate the burgeoning population, and in the twentieth century it became a parish church, symbolising the area's new-found identity.

Yet baptism is only half of the equation that allowed medieval chapels to make the uneasy transition to parish church. The other space that was required was a graveyard. Again, economic factors may have played a part in the development of parish churches. Burials were a source of income for the priest, sexton (who dug the grave) and the church, and also allowed the community to 'own' its place of worship in a very particular way. In other words, the identity of a community could be entirely tied up with the location of the dead, and how the living memorialised them. The right to bury the dead signified that this 'place' was not transitory, but established. Not only was it a viable economic community, it was also a place that had a history and a right to a future.

I make these observations about parish churches in Saxon and medieval times because they were clearly important in maintaining a sense of place and in creating a kind of local identity, which was secular, sacred, religious, civic, communitarian and catholic. Yet many parish churches today struggle to 'connect' with their locations in ways that are similar. In the case of births, baptismal rates have dropped steadily in England since the turn of the twentieth century, the trend accelerating with noticeable speed from the 1960s. The response of the churches, interestingly, to this loss of *extensive* connection, has been to reify baptismal rites into a more *intensive* form of religious experience. Gone are the accommodating cultural customs of bygone eras in which the clergy baptised large numbers of children at times that were mainly convenient to families (like Sunday afternoons). Baptism, as a negotiated point of entry into the life of the church (and who can say where the church begins and ends?), has lost its communitarian and ambiguous feel as a social rite of passage – even the term 'christening' is discouraged – and been replaced by something more definitive. A more demanding series of liturgies requires the parents to say more (the 1662 *Book of Common Prayer* did not expect or demand this), with the baptismal service now more usually being situated within a normal Sunday morning service such as Matins or a Eucharist.

The effect of this is hard to measure, but it would not be unfair to say that the parish church, in its loss of extensive connectedness with its own locality, has attempted to re-engage its disparate community by becoming more intense in its religious expression and by sharpening up its actual identity. Observers may say that this is inevitable: the allegedly invasive forces of modernity such as pluralism and consumerism require commodities in every competitive environment – including the spiritual marketplace – to be clearer about their identity in order to be noticed (or differentiated) in order that they may be purchased. Yet we can also say that such a trend, if it exists, points to the lack of importance we now attach to places as spaces that provide us with our identity. We are where we can go; not where we are.

Similar problems can be seen in relation to death. For most of the twentieth century, new churches that were built did not provide graveyards; gardens of rest for interred remains are a relatively late innovation. Death has moved, sociologically and culturally, from a commonplace event that was central to the life of all small communities and localities, to something that is removed from the mainstream of society, and placed on its margins. Most deaths occur in hospitals, hospices or residential and nursing homes. The vast majority of funerals are conducted in anonymous crematoriums that form no spatial, spiritual or social attachment with the bereaved. The memorialisation of the dead – once the main point and function of a parish church – has been speedily eroded by the contemporary utilitarian forces that have tidied death up (in the name of clinical cleanliness) and swept it into the corners of modern life. Death is not seen; it is not heard; it does not speak (Percy 2001:315–18). Even those graveyards that remain open and accessible are more often than not closed for burial.

Predictably, the responses of the English parish churches have been pragmatic and pastoral. Remembrance Sunday refuses to die, long after its veterans have all been mourned. The festival of All Souls has undergone a renaissance in recent years, as churches have sought to restore the memorialisation of death and the reality of bereavement, as well as speaking of resurrection, into a relationship with the communities they serve. The spaces and places for death may no longer exist in the way they once did, but there is always the compensation of calendrical ritual. And, as many churches discovered after 11 September 2001, or after the death of Diana, Princess of Wales, an open church, in which to light a candle or say a prayer and sign a condolence book, is still the first port of call for many people, and preferred to posting a message on the web.

The Future of the Parish Church and Its Identity

Our reflections so far have suggested that the gradual bifurcation of the *ekklesia* from the *parochia* was a process that began prior to the Reformation, and has been as much about economic realities as it has about anything we might call secularisation. We might also add that the gradual atomisation of public space – a feature of modernity stretching back to the Industrial Revolution – has forced the parish church to reconsider its own sense of place. It is not that long ago that parish churches were the only places within a community that could house debates, discussions and social gatherings. But their monopoly has been broken by the endemic pluralisation of public space: taverns, cinemas, community halls, as well as competing denominations and a host of other arenas. Of course, such places have always been a feature of the English townscape, but there can be no question that public space has now become more ambiguous; there are now many centres for any one community; its focal point is seldom obvious. Arguably, the media – in their most general capacity as purveyors of information, recording and memory – are the new public space. It would appear, then, that parish churches are beginning to lose their point. A parish, as a place, is no longer defined by its capacity to support a church. Modern communities are unsettled and mobile, something recently conceded by the Church of England in its proposals on marriage reform. In future banns will perhaps no longer have to be published (but they may still be said, and so remain as a 'custom'), and there will be greater freedom in choosing venues for matrimony; one need no longer be tied by the constraints of residency.

But it would be premature to sound the death knell for the parish church. True, few couples who apply to be married at their local church (or the one they like the look of, near the reception venue) appear to know which parish they belong to; it is not just the church that is lost in the complex public space of urbanity – the parish has also lost its point and identity for many people. Yet my narration of the parish church in English cultural history clearly suggests that its identity has always been evolving, so there is arguably little cause for alarm. Every generation of churchwardens has had to face an apparently insuperable set of problems ranging from apathy to poverty through to clerical negligence and absence. Indeed, all that we may say here is that the parish church is losing its identity because the concept and feel of parishes has already been lost. The next line of defence, then, is for the recognition of *local* churches, and that is arguably the key mutation of modernity for the parish church: its identity is shifting from the parochial to the local. And of course, the local church – from the Latin word *localis* – is still located and known.

That said, the more pervasive problem identified is this: parish churches are losing their sense of prominence within the public sphere. Public space is more plural and atomised than ever, making it difficult for the church to find its place within contemporary society. If that paradigm is, broadly speaking, the correct context for describing the somewhat troubled identity of the parish church, what can be said about its potential and future? While it is true that Britons are rapidly turning from being religious *assumers* (within the homogenous culture of a 'common' worship and an 'authorised' Bible) to religious *consumers*, and are moving from a culture of religious assumption to religious consumption, in which choice and competition in the spiritual marketplace thrive, there may be little cause for alarm. Perhaps the churches need to panic a little less about the apparently bleak statistics, and their apparent loss of identity, and concentrate a little more on maintaining religion as something that is public, accessible and extensive, while also being distinct, intensive and mysterious. So I have three general comments to make by way of conclusion.

First, even in the most modern societies, there is still demand for religion that is public, performative and pastoral. Furthermore, there are thousands and thousands of private spiritualities and beliefs that flourish in modernity, demonstrating that faith does not wither and die in our culture. Many churches have seen a rise in numbers since 11 September 2001. Religion mutates and lives on; churches, to take advantage of this, must continue to try to be open to the world and extensively engaged with their communities. Very few people choose not to relate at all to the church or to mainstream religion. In any secular age, there is space and demand for religion, faith and spirituality. This is important, for it reminds us that religion provides enchantment within modernity, and that churches are often the only bodies that provide public and open places within a community for tears, grief, remembrance, laughter and celebration.

Second, religion is remarkably resilient in the modern age. Much of our 'vernacular religion' – such as the celebration of Christmas – reveals a nation that still enjoys its carols, nativity plays and other Christian artefacts that long ago moved beyond the control of the church to become part of the cultural furniture. Religion is still in demand, and where it is absent, it is more often than not created, or the gap filled with new forms of spirituality. In the absence of religion, people tend to believe anything rather than nothing, and the task of the church must be to continue to engage empathetically with culture and society, offering shape, colour and articulation to the voices of innate and implicit religion.

Third, the churches can respond to the challenge of an apparently faithless age with a confidence founded on society (yes, society), which refuses to leave religion alone. Often, the best that churches can do is to recover their poise within their social and cultural situations, and continue to offer a ministry and a faith to a public who wish to relate to religion, without necessarily belonging to it. With rare exceptions in history, this is what all clergy have had to work with most of the time: it is both an opportunity and a challenge. So the recipe for a response might look like this: relax; have faith in the resilience of God and the Church; but also respond with tenacity, compassion and wisdom to the many tests of faith that dominate every age. The parish church and the Christian faith have many more supporters than members. We do not live in a secular age, as the sociological prophets of the 1960s once foretold. Our era continues to be a time of questions, exploration, wonder and awe.

I began this chapter by quoting Maitland's words, and it must be obvious by now that the parish church did not begin as something 'simple' that has gradually been complicated over time by its civic, secular and sacred duties. Moreover, even as this chapter has shown, the 'signs' of religion and secularisation point in slightly different ways. The gradual atrophy in the pivotal power of the English parish church since the Industrial Revolution is, in one sense, undeniable. At the same time, a detailed history of parish churches shows that their success and failure, prior to the Industrial Revolution, is not linked to secularisation, and that spirituality and vernacular religion persist, waxing and waning, with or without due regard to the provision of parochial places of worship. That said, since parish churches are no longer linked to the *local* economy and what that space generates in terms of wealth and income, they have to reinvent themselves as places of worship that are less extrinsically linked to their communities. In that sense, it is right and proper to speak of a kind of *institutional* secularisation, provided it is understood that this is not taken to mean that people are less spiritual or religious in late modernity.

So where does this take us? The parish church has always been a complex pottage of competing convictions and interests, brought together in the focus of a building and a ministry, the ownership of which has always been open to interpretation. But the *ekklesia* is, after all, 'the assembly' of aspirations, hopes, memories, celebration and sacramental life, and, where possible, it continues to embody the life of the *parochia*. So what the parish church needs now, arguably, is to continually rediscover its ministry, one that engages with contemporary culture in interrogative, empathetic and critical-friendly ways. And, dare one say it, parish churches perhaps need a little less of the prevailing panacea-mentality that drives so much of the present thinking on mission, and claims to be able to rescue or resuscitate the church from its deathbed. Rumours of its imminent funeral are nearly always greatly exaggerated.

But it does not follow that the meaning, value and ministry of a parish church are immutable. Perhaps now, more than at any other time in history, parish churches need to discover what their identity consists of, and instead of accepting the bifurcation of the *parochia* and the *ekklesia*, look for new patterns of convergence in which the churches begin to engage afresh with their peoples and contexts on many different levels. In short, they may need to accept that the shift from the *parochial* to the *local* might not be entirely deleterious for their identity. In the future, patterns of ministry will no longer be configured solely through geographical space and its constraints. To find its place in the modern world, the church will have to create new spaces for new communities and different opportunities for differentiated niche groups. Such a vision might appear to threaten the very concept of a parish church; but it might also be its saviour. To be a parish church, an *ekklesia* must find its *parochia* and locate itself within it, incarnating the life of God within the given community, in ways that are local and catholic. In the complex and ambiguous spaces of our future, the church will need to find its place in society once again, if it is to continue to offer a religion that is public, performative and pastoral.

Note

1 The reflections in this chapter were originally delivered in my Eric Abbott Memorial Lecture at Westminster Abbey, May 2000, under the title 'A Knowledge of Angles: How Spiritual are the English?', and was subsequently explored in more depth in my *Salt of the Earth: Religious Resilience in a Secular Age*.

Bibliography

Bedfordshire Historical Records Society (1990), *Archdiaconal Visitations in 1578*, Publication no. 69, Bedford.

Beresford, J. (ed.) (1999), *James Woodforde: The Diary of a Country Parson*, Norwich: Canterbury Press.

Berger, P. (1969), *A Rumour of Angels*, Garden City, NY: Doubleday.

Brown, C. (2000), *The Death of Christian Britain*, London: Routledge.

Bruce, S. (1997), *Religion in Modern Britain*, Oxford: Oxford University Press.

Chadwick, O. (1975), *The Secularization of the European Mind in the Nineteenth Century*, Cambridge: Cambridge University Press.

Davie, G. (1994), *Religion in Britain since 1945: Believing without Belonging*, Oxford: Blackwell.

Desmond, A. and Moore, J. (1991), *Darwin*, Harmondsworth: Penguin.

Fletcher, A. (1997), *The Barbarian Conversion*, New York: Holt.

Gill, R. (1992), *The Myth of the Empty Church*, London: SCM Press.

Hardy, D. (1996), *God's Ways with the World*, Edinburgh. T. & T. Clark.

Jenkins, S. (1999), *England's One Thousand Best Churches*, London: Allen Lane.

Maitland, F. (1897), *Domesday Book and Beyond*, Cambridge: Cambridge University Press.

Martin, D. (1978), *A General Theory of Secularization*, Oxford: Blackwell.

Massey, D. (1994), *Space, Place and Gender*, Cambridge: Polity.

Murray, A. (1972), 'Piety and Impiety', *Studies in Church History*, **8**, 110–22.

Parsons, G. (1988), *Religion in Victorian Britain*, vol. 4, Manchester: Manchester University Press.

Percy, M. (2001), *Salt of the Earth: Religious Resilience in a Secular Age*, Sheffield: Sheffield Academic Press.

Pounds, N. (2000), *A History of the English Parish*, Cambridge: Cambridge University Press.

Putnam, R. (2000), *Bowling Alone*, London: Simon & Schuster.

Sibley, D. (1995), *Geographies of Exclusion*, London: Routledge.

Thomas, K. (1971), *Religion and the Decline of Magic*, London: Weidenfeld & Nicolson.

Wickham, E. (1957), *Church and People in an Industrial City*, London: Lutterworth Press.

Wilson, B. (1966), *Religion in Secular Society: A Sociological Comment*, London: Watts & Co.

CHAPTER 3

The Changing Identity of Catholics in England

Michael P. Hornsby-Smith

Anthony Giddens defines *self-identity* very simply as 'the self as reflexively understood by the individual in terms of his or her biography' (1991:244). For Berger and his colleagues, identity meant 'the actual experience of self in a particular social situation ... the manner in which individuals define themselves. As such, identity is part and parcel of a specific structure of consciousness' (1974:73). These will serve for our present purposes. What I have in mind is the response which people in England who acknowledge themselves to be Roman Catholic make to the question: 'What do you mean when you say you are a Roman Catholic?' I aim to explore to what extent an individual Catholic identity has replaced a more ascribed, communally based, religio-ethnic identity.

Phillip Hammond has provided a useful framework for the analysis of the changing nature of the English Catholic identity over the past half-century. Following Hans Mol (1978), he distinguished two kinds of identity: one which is involuntarily held, such as is the case of a religio-ethnic immigrant minority, which is nourished in primary, face-to-face groups and community interaction; another which is transient and dependent on the nature of social encounters and where a great deal of social interaction takes place outside primary groups. Thus Hammond distinguishes two views of the church in contemporary society:

> On the one hand, there is ... the 'collective-expressive' view, in which involvement is largely involuntary because it emerges out of overlapping primary group ties not easily avoided. On the other hand, there is the 'individual-expressive' view, in which involvement is largely voluntary and independent of other social ties ... the social conditions eroding the first view are the same conditions that permit, perhaps even encourage, the second view.
>
> (1988:5)

Following Luckmann's contrast between church-related and invisible religion (1970), Hammond suggests that people can be located on a grid in terms of their involvement in overlapping primary groups and in secondary groups. This leads him to distinguish two main types of religious identity. First, church-affiliated people who place a high stress on primary group involvement and on 'localism' (Roof 1978) and a low stress on secondary group involvement are said to have a 'collective-expressive' involvement in the church and the first type of 'involuntary, immutable' religious identity. Second, those with a low local involvement but high secondary group ties are said to have an 'individual-expressive' involvement in the church and a 'transient, changeable' religious identity (Hammond 1988:6).

Hammond's theory, which was constructed largely with the American immigrant churches in mind, nevertheless seems likely to be useful in the case of English Catholics since, as I have noted elsewhere (1987:24–6), between two-fifths and one-half of all Catholics in England and Wales in 1971 were either first- or second-generation immigrants, half of them Irish. I have also argued previously (ibid.:208–14) that the defensive walls of the 'fortress church', which up to the 1950s substantially preserved a distinctive Catholic sub-culture (see also Coman 1977), have largely been dissolved in the solvent of postwar social change and post-Conciliar religious change. It is the main aim of this chapter to illustrate the effects of these changes for the identity of English Catholics in the light of Hammond's theory and to speculate about the implications for English Catholicism as it enters the twenty-first century.

Catholic Identity in the Fortress Church

Up to the 1950s the Roman Catholic Church in England (and Wales) displayed a sect-like exclusiveness and defensiveness against what it perceived to be a hostile society. This was the time of the 'fortress church', feverishly reinforcing its defences: separate Catholic schools, parish clubs and organisations, a strongly enforced stress on marital endogamy, and a distinctive sub-culture. It was the time of 'closed' Catholicism, as John Whyte (1981) has called it, a time when the church defined itself *against* the world. Peter Coman summarised the position well:

> In an important sense the Catholics in mid-twentieth century England, preponderantly of Irish ancestry and origin, were members of a subsociety and constituted a subculture by virtue of their specific norms and values in sexual, marital and familial morality, their allegiance to Rome, the importance attached to the Mass, their belief in life after death and their numerous distinguishing symbols such as Friday abstinence ... educational segregation and marital endogamy in combination with an array of ... Catholic associations ... [which] were designed to protect the Catholic subculture.
>
> (1977:4–5)

Coman noted that 'virulent anti-papal prejudice in England provoked its own antithesis in the special loyalty to Rome among English Roman Catholics' (ibid.:12) and argues that:

> Common allegiance to Rome bound together the diverse English and Irish elements which made up the Roman Catholic Church in England. The precise, disciplined, distinctive and intransigent standpoint of Rome on many controversial issues in a mid-twentieth century helped to give this community the character of a minority subculture, sharply distinguished from the other Christian denominations and from the increasingly secular wider society.
>
> (ibid.:14)

Coman went on to suggest that in adhering to norms and values (relating, for example, to artificial contraception and divorce) 'not shared by the wider culture of which they were members', increasingly they felt themselves to be 'different' from their compatriots and to have their own distinct identity. Their separateness was fostered by such peculiarly Roman Catholic practices as the retention of Latin as the liturgical language and abstinence from the eating of meat on Fridays in memory of the Crucifixion on Good Friday.

(ibid.:16)

Mary Douglas (1973:62) has pointed out that Friday abstinence gained significance as a symbol of allegiance simply by its 'lack of meaning for other cultures'. 'No empty symbol, it means allegiance to a humble home in Ireland and to a glorious tradition in Rome' (ibid.:59–60). The migrant worker in a hostile or unfriendly England would have lived in the context of 'cultural defence' (Wallis and Bruce 1992:17–18) and hence perhaps be even more likely to adhere to such identifying practices than Catholics in Ireland, at least in the early stages of adapting to a new society and before the onset of any processes of assimilation.

The whole point of Coman's book is to show that the great hostility of Catholics in England to the proposals for the construction of a welfare state in the early postwar years reflected their fierce determination to defend their own distinctive sub-culture and religious and social value system from what was perceived to be the dangerous arrogation of power by the state. This was particularly expressed in the bitter battles to defend the right to control over their own schools and to proper levels of state funding for them.

Interviewed in the mid-1970s, George Woodcock, former General Secretary of the Trades Union Congress (TUC), expressed the traditional view about his Catholic identity when he said: 'I couldn't leave the Catholic Church just as I couldn't leave my family.' Steven Fielding gives a flavour of the Whit walks in Manchester which were a massive demonstration of religio-ethnic identity. He suggests that:

> The Catholic Church used religious processions and ceremonial to reinforce adherents' sense of belonging to a separate culture. They complemented, in ritual form, the Church's more mundane attempts to raise structural fences around Catholics ... The walk gave Catholics a chance to publicly assert their individual and collective self-importance in the midst of a society where it was usually denigrated.
>
> (Fielding 1993:72, 75–6)

Mary Chamberlain conveys the flavour of convent education in the early 1960s:

> We were fed on a diet of masochism, self-sacrifice and devotion. It was an intense emotional experience, undiluted Catholicism. The sense of exclusivity, uniqueness and destiny was here multiplied. We were a beleaguered island. It reflected all the religious xenophobia of English Catholicism with a primitivism which would have done credit to the early mystics.
>
> (Chamberlain 1989:32)

Anthony Archer, in his analysis of working-class Catholicism in Newcastle, observed that 'religion was an inheritance that was largely taken for granted' (1986:112). In this sense it was largely true that 'once a Catholic, always a Catholic' and this form of identity can be seen to persist, for example in the case of hospital patients or on the deathbed. All of these examples are consistent with Hammond's 'collective-expressive' type of involvement in the church where being a Catholic was an involuntary and immovable part of one's intrinsic identity, like one's gender or ethnicity, an indication of ancestry and membership of an identifiably distinct religio-ethnic community, something unchangeably ascribed.

It is likely that the majority of Catholics in England have an Irish ancestry over several generations. The identity of Irish Catholics, therefore, provides a particularly critical test of the thesis that there has been a shift from a 'communal-expressive' to an 'individual-expressive' form of identity over the past half-century.

In the first decade after the Second World War there was a massive influx of Irish migrants to Britain. Cardinal Griffin, in a pastoral letter in 1955, acknowledged the huge contribution which they had made to the church in Britain and went on to urge their full integration into the Catholic community (Hickey 1960:55–7). What evidence there was from studies around this time in Birmingham (YCW 1951), Cardiff (Hickey 1967), Liverpool (Ward 1965) and London (Jackson 1963), suggested that, in the main, processes of assimilation were not far advanced. One study reported that in the case of the new Irish immigrants in Birmingham there was

> an unfortunate tendency to preserve the Irish in an Irish atmosphere. There has been in the past, a tendency to evade the problem of absorbing the immigrants into the parish and parish life because of the difficulties involved. Very few of the stabilised societies have been able to recruit the Irish into their ranks and most parish societies in Birmingham are either Irish or English, seldom a mixture of both.
>
> (YCW 1951; quoted in Hickey 1960:28)

All these examples clearly express a 'culturally expressive', religio-ethnic form of Catholic identity. How, if at all, has this identity changed over the past half-century? As Mary Chamberlain observed of her convent schooldays in the early 1960s: 'Try as they might, the nuns could not finally control what went on in our lives beyond the School' (1989:33). Indeed, the social world was changing rapidly and the challenges of the Second Vatican Council were about to raise questions which had hitherto been suppressed.

Catholic Identity at the End of the Twentieth Century

Studies of English Catholicism over the past quarter of a century have, however, demonstrated convincingly that there have been major transformations as a result of postwar social changes, especially the impact of the 1944 Education Act, and post-Vatican II religious changes, including the encouragement of new ecumenical approaches. I have argued previously (1987:208–14) that the effect of these changes was substantially to dissolve the boundary walls which previously had defended the distinctive sub-culture. The evidence for this is overwhelming: the sharp increase in marital exogamy; the dissent over the reaffirmed teaching on contraception; liturgical changes, such as the use of the vernacular, and the encouragement of lay

ministries, including the greater participation of women; the easing of disciplinary
rules, such as those involving religiously mixed marriages, and the rules concerning
fasting and abstinence; the evidence for substantial value convergence between
Catholics and the rest of the population; the growth of friendlier contacts with the
members of other churches; declining hostility towards Catholics and their
acceptance as largely domesticated and respectable members of British society; and
so on.

Mary Douglas regretted the modernising processes in the church and
complained that 'Friday no longer rings the great cosmic symbols of expiation
and atonement; it is not symbolic at all, but a practical day for the organization of
charity. *Now the English Catholics are like everyone else*' (1973:67; emphasis
added). Coman summed up the transformations well:

> The gradual assimilation through education and mixed marriage, the dissent over
> traditional teaching in birth regulation, the questioning of the limits of papal authority,
> the gradual substitution of English for Latin in the liturgy, the tentative movements
> towards ecumenism, the softening of traditional disapproval of mixed marriages and
> the abolition of Friday abstinence all pointed to the weakening and erosion of the
> traditional homogeneous Roman Catholic subculture.
>
> (1977:105)

Other unanticipated consequences of the liturgical and related changes were
pointed out by Anthony Archer who, with some justification, suggested that
whereas the church up to the 1950s had been an important source of identity for
working-class Catholics, the post-Vatican II church had increasingly become a
vehicle for the achievement of the aspirations of articulate middle-class enthusiasts
who are in open competition with older forms of clerical domination. Archer
regarded the liturgical changes which were so enthusiastically welcomed by
middle-class reformers as new forms of elitism. The very language of the new Mass
was classist in origin. Archer, therefore, interpreted the changes as new forms of
class oppression, and it is hardly surprising that with the dissolution of a distinctive
Catholic identity, 'working-class indifference coincided ... with the relinquishment
of an Irish identity, and their subsequent failure to find anything of particular
interest to them in the Catholic Church' (1986:141–5, 234–6).

By the 1970s it was becoming increasingly clear that English Catholicism was
emerging slowly but surely from its fortress, somewhat apprehensively engaging in
a higher level of social contact with non-Catholics and the 'outside' world, with a
consequential decline in its defensive mentality. By the time the pope came to
Britain in 1982, a nun could say gleefully, 'Now we can come out from under the
bushes'!

Various researches in the 1970s and 1980s pointed to this conclusion. The
national survey of English Catholics in 1978 showed that Catholics were
experiencing as much or more upward social mobility as the population generally
(Hornsby-Smith 1987:77) and were moving out of the inner-city ghetto-like
parishes and into new suburban parishes and estates where contacts with non-
Catholics were more likely. From the 1970s this was reflected in a noticeably higher
rate of marital exogamy with over one-third of Catholics married between 1970 and
1977 in canonically invalid marriages and two-thirds in religiously mixed marriages

(ibid.:92–4). Various measures of communal involvement also demonstrated major differences between prewar generations and those coming to adulthood in the postwar years (ibid.:183). Surveys of electors in four parishes in the mid-1970s also demonstrated that on a wide range of social, political and moral questions, Catholic attitudes had converged closely to those of the population generally (ibid.:109, 165). All these changes 'necessarily entailed radical changes in the nature of Catholic identity' (ibid.:214).

Evidence from a large number of interviews carried out with a wide range of Catholics in the 1970s showed how much Catholics in England (and Wales) had changed. By this time there was clearly a pluralism of Catholic beliefs and practices which pointed to a distinct 'hierarchy of truths' in the minds of most Catholics. It seemed likely that up to the 1950s Catholics differentiated relatively little between creedal beliefs, non-creedal beliefs such as papal infallibility, teachings on moral issues (whether dealing with personal sexuality such as contraception, or socio-political issues such as the nuclear defence strategy or racism or development issues), and disciplinary rules (such as the Mass attendance obligation, the prohibition of inter-communion or frequency of confession). In a strongly rule-bound and guilt-ridden church, where notions of mortal sin and eternal damnation were strongly emphasised, it seems that Catholics were just as likely to feel coerced to conform on matters of abstinence from eating meat on Fridays as they were to avoid contraception or to believe in the Trinity (Hornsby-Smith 1991:215). In David Lodge's memorable phrase (1980), there was a 'loss of the fear of hell' from the 1960s with a consequent emergence of a much more differentiated and discriminating form of Catholicism.

The qualitative interview data reviewed in a range of studies in the 1970s and 1980s pointed to a pluralism of both beliefs and legitimations of religious authority and of the nature and meaning of religious belonging, what it meant to be a Roman Catholic in England in the last quarter of the twentieth century. The data point to the conclusion that with the dissolution of the distinctive Catholic sub-culture, there was an associated shift in the nature of Catholic belonging to the church. No longer was being a Catholic a part of one's intrinsic identity, an indication of ancestry and membership of an identifiably distinct religio-ethnic community, something normally ascribed. In the last quarter of the twentieth century Catholics were increasingly required to make a positive choice and affirm the calling to participate fully in the work of the whole 'People of God'. From being a given aspect of their cultural identity which they accepted passively, Catholics were invited to see their Catholic faith as having meaning, and requiring from them a positive commitment to the task of mission in the world. Whereas previously 'cradle' Catholics regarded themselves as Catholics unless they positively 'opted out', there is a sense in which in the post-Vatican II church, Catholics were being asked to 'opt in', rather as converts had always had to. It seems, therefore, that the basis of meaningful belonging for the English Catholic had been transformed from one of religio-ethnic identity to one of voluntary religious commitment (Hornsby-Smith 1991:9).

Of course, the above contrast has been presented in ideal-typical terms. The empirical reality varies from parish to parish, depending, for example, on how strict the parish priest is in allowing access to the sacraments (for example, baptism) to those whose attachment to the local parish community is only nominal. The reality inevitably lies somewhere in between the two types. There seems little doubt, though, that there has been a significant shift away from the 'communal-expressive' form of identity, even if the element of choice sits alongside remnants of older forms of belonging, including the habitual and nominal, and the instrumental (for example, in order to get one's child into a favoured Catholic school). The 'individual-expressive' view of the church, then, appears to prevail in the contemporary society, where 'English Catholics are like everyone else' and where continuing commitment is much more likely to be voluntarily chosen but changeable, and where the church (or parish) is regarded as but one of several more or less salient institutions in the life of the individual Catholic (ibid.:20).

Irish Catholics

The most stringent test of Hammond's thesis would be provided by a strong religio-ethnic immigrant community of which the huge Irish Catholic community would be the archetypal case. Analysis of the social backgrounds of both first- and second-generation Irish immigrants using samples from the annual General Household Survey of households in Great Britain for 1979 and 1980 (Hornsby-Smith and Dale 1988) showed that the social origins of the Irish were decidedly more working class than those of the 'English' control group. What has happened to the identity of these Irish immigrants over the past few decades?

The extent to which Irish Catholic immigrants lost their Irish identity over two or more generations is a matter of debate. In their study of Sparkbrook in the mid-1960s, Rex and Moore seem to regard the processes of assimilation as largely inevitable over time even if there are variations in the extent to which individual migrants follow that route. Most of the Irish they interviewed had arrived in the 1950s and 1960s. 'The majority ... seem to retain their Irishness. Perhaps losing their Irishness, succeeding, and moving out of Sparkbrook all come at the same point in a process of urbanization, anglicization, and assimilation' (1969:85).

A number of researchers have argued that over a period of time, which may be two or more generations, and given favourable conditions, such as an absence of religious hostility, national grievances or barriers to upward social mobility, and the relative invisibility of the immigrant group, a process of assimilation gradually but steadily takes place. Such appeared to be the view of Rex and Moore in Sparkbrook and of John Hickey (1967) in his historical study of Irish Catholics in Cardiff.

In the early 1970s, Liam (W.) Ryan (1973) and his assistants interviewed a total of 1432 people in three areas in Greater London who had emigrated from the Irish Republic since the Second World War and had been in Britain for at least a year. He reported that one-third had achieved economic and residential 'accommodation', one-third 'structural integration', and one-third were 'well on the way toward identi-ficational and cultural assimilation with their adopted country' (Ryan 1973:231–2).

In the late-1970s a nationally representative sample of 1023 adult Catholics included around 134 first-generation married Irish immigrants (28 per cent of whom had married a non-Catholic) and 114 second-generation (50 per cent of whom had married a non-Catholic) (Hornsby-Smith and Lee 1979:200). These numbers were sufficiently large to allow comparisons with other British-born Catholics and to test the extent to which there was evidence for a process of assimilation to the norms of other Catholics by the second generation. On five of the six scales of religious outcomes – adult religious practice, doctrinal orthodoxy, church involvement, private prayer and sexual orthodoxy – the average scores show clearly a convergence to the norms of the 'other British born' by the second generation in the case of those who had married a non-Catholic spouse. In the case of those who had married a Roman Catholic spouse there was evidence of slower convergence in the case of doctrinal orthodoxy; on the other four scales the second-generation Irish scored higher than either the first-generation Irish or British samples.

Further analyses provided further evidence in support of the assimilation hypothesis. The social mobility experiences of second-generation Irish Catholics were identical with those Catholics born in England (Hornsby-Smith 1987:75) and there was also evidence for convergence in the case of marriage patterns (ibid.:124–5). Analyses of religious outcomes provided similar results (ibid.:124–31). In sum, it was concluded that by the second generation there had been a general convergence in the religious beliefs, attitudes and practices of Irish Catholics towards the norms for English Catholics. In other words, the evidence pointed to a substantial measure of religious assimilation by the second generation. However, the assimilation of Irish Catholics was not a simple process but was mediated in particular by the patterns of social and religious endogamy or exogamy. While social mobility and assimilation were accelerated by national intermarriage, religious convergence and assimilation to the norms of English Catholicism were accelerated by religious intermarriage. Since the rates of exogamy have been increasing rapidly in recent decades, the ease and speed of assimilation of Irish Catholics seem likely to increase (ibid.:130–2).

Confirmation and elaboration of these findings were provided by data from the 1979 and 1980 General Household Surveys for Great Britain for those aged 16–49. Hornsby-Smith and Dale (1988) compared a total of 330 first- and 536 second-generation immigrants from the Irish Republic and 146 first- and 197 second-generation immigrants from Northern Ireland with a control sample of 1200 'English', currently living in England, who had been born in Great Britain and both of whose parents had also been born in Great Britain. The analyses showed that 'both men and women from the Republic of Ireland have, by the second generation, achieved levels of educational qualifications and occupational statuses and rates of upward social mobility that exceed those of the English control sample' (ibid.:541). Assimilation, seen as a process in which both cultural and structural differences between the immigrant group and the indigenous population are progressively reduced over an extended period of time, seemed clearly to be taking place for those immigrants from the Irish Republic from where the bulk of Irish Catholic immigrants come.

This view of general Irish assimilation has been strongly contested by Mary Hickman (1995, 1999). Hickman's interests are primarily historical and ideological. She is concerned to demonstrate that there was a convergence of interests between the Roman Catholic Church in England and the British state in their strategies of coping with the huge influxes of Irish migrants in the nineteenth century but also in the 1950s and 1960s. On the one hand, the Catholic hierarchy was concerned to demonstrate the loyalty and respectability of Catholics to the British state following Catholic emancipation in 1829 after three centuries of persecution, and also to safeguard the faith of its adherents. On the other hand, the Protestant British state was concerned to incorporate the Irish into British society but also to diffuse incipient socio-political unrest and divide the working class by segregating the Irish immigrants from the indigenous working class. The emergence of a separate Catholic school system in the nineteenth century served these purposes well. Hickman argues that the invisibility of the Irish was socially constructed by processes of incorporation, differentiation and denationalisation. Considered analytically, the argument is a valuable exercise in historical sociology and of the processes involved.

Where her argument is misleading is in its interpretation of the results of structured interviews with around 100 teenagers in four schools in London and Liverpool around the late 1980s. All the London sample were second-generation Irish with both parents born in Ireland. The Liverpool sample consisted mostly of third-, fourth- and fifth-generation Irish who had been subjected to incorporation for a number of generations (Hickman 1999). In a survey of their identities, Hickman reports that:

> Amongst the London pupils 81 per cent named either 'Irish' or 'of Irish descent' as their primary identity, thus privileging their parents' national origins over the national identity of the country in which they were born. In Liverpool, in contrast, only 12.5 per cent chose an Irish identity as primary. On the other hand 65 per cent of the Liverpool sample perceived themselves to be Liverpudlians before all else; thus privileging a regional identity over the national identity of the country in which they were born. Only 18 per cent of the pupils of Irish descent selected 'British/English' as their primary identity.
>
> (Hickman 1995:244–5; see also 1999)

Such findings are not inconsistent with an assimilation thesis. She correctly argues that:

> The survival of Irish identity is more likely if the individual of Irish descent is of working-class origin, lives in an Irish area, visits Ireland regularly and participates in Irish social and cultural activities. In these circumstances someone of Irish descent who is third or fourth generation Irish would select an Irish identity to describe himself or herself.
>
> (Hickman 1995:246)

This is undoubtedly the case. One might also add as further conditions that they experience no upward social or outward geographical mobility and that they practise strict marital endogamy. Such conditions describe the classic case of 'cultural defence', traditionally employed by immigrants in the early years after migration to a hostile environment. Hickman seems unaware that her research design was faulty in that it did not offer a valid test of the retention of Irish identity but only investigated the most favourable possible circumstances. Intermarriage was zero in London and probably very low in the stable and static area of Liverpool. But national average statistics indicate that over one-quarter of first-generation Irish Catholics marry a non-Catholic while the proportion rises to one-half of second-generation Irish. In other words, her sample was heavily skewed in favour of retention of Irish identity.

One cannot help feeling that much of Hickman's disagreement with the assimilationists is partly semantic, partly ideological, and partly an exercise in political correctness in an increasingly transparent multicultural Britain. Hickman appears to see the term assimilation as threatening, implying the dissolution of all Irish characteristics in the English 'melting pot'. She prefers to use the concept of 'incorporation' which differs from assimilation 'in that it assumes state and institutional intervention in the regulation of the experience and identity of significant labour migrant groups' (1995:13) and because it points to a strategy used *against* the Irish. All the same, the end result appears to be, to a greater or lesser extent, cultural and structural assimilation and it is this that is reflected in changing identities.

The conclusion must remain, on the basis of the wide range of empirical evidence, including that of Hickman, which we have reviewed, that in the last quarter of the twentieth century and in general, there has been a very substantial degree of both structural and cultural assimilation to English (and English Catholic) norms by second-generation Irish immigrants. The evidence is consistent with a shift of Catholic identity from the 'collective-expressive' to the 'individual-expressive'.

Generational Differences

Evidence for the shift of identity is most apparent when considering generational differences. One of the most striking findings from the 1978 national survey of English Catholics was that 'Catholics are more likely to be critical of the institutional Church or of its authorities or of its official teachings or regulations the younger they are' (Hornsby-Smith and Lee 1979:130–1). There were numerous examples of quite radical differences between the generations in the qualitative interviews reported in *Roman Catholic Beliefs in England* (Hornsby-Smith 1991). The testimony of many 'core' Catholics speaking about their children's generation was that they would have to 'find new but authentic bases of loyalty for themselves. They would not feel obliged to accept meekly, as an earlier generation once had, a religious teaching which did not seem to make sense of their deepest everyday experiences' (ibid.:83–4).

Using cross-sectional data at one point in time, as in the national survey, it is not possible to distinguish between age, generation and cohort effects. Nevertheless, findings from the European Values Surveys in the Irish Republic for 1981 and 1990 (Hornsby-Smith and Whelan 1994) show strikingly that a large number of measures of religiosity remained remarkably constant within a cohort over the nine-year period. There was relatively little evidence of ageing effects but clear indications of 'a significant cultural shift among those cohorts born since the 1950s' (ibid.:42). If this comparison has any validity, then there are good grounds for believing that though there might be some life-cycle effects (for example, to do with the sacraments of initiation for their children), the lower levels of belief, practice and commitment among young English Catholics will be carried with them throughout their lives. Among these new cultural styles is the substantial loss of the sense of membership of an embattled religio-ethnic community and the greater salience of an 'individual-expressive' form of identity.

Differences between prewar and postwar generations on matters of religious authority and loyalty were already apparent to Kokosalakis (1971) in his study of a Liverpool parish in the late 1960s. In the mid-1970s, a Catholic Marriage Advisory Council counsellor in her sixties summed up the position well:

> The younger generation do not see life as being lived on 'nos' only ... and are not prepared to take it, whereas my generation would have done ... I remember in my youth resenting a lot of this 'Thou shalt not' stuff but doing it because that was the rule ... The younger people have decided that they are not going to sit through this mumbo-jumbo.
>
> (Hornsby-Smith 1991:158–9)

Other evidence pointed clearly to the rejection of older forms of traditional clerical authority and its replacement by new forms of legitimation based on consultation and shared decision-making (ibid.:198). Taken with the loss of the fear of hell (Lodge 1980), many Catholics dissented from the official teaching of the church on contraception without any sense of guilt, fear or shame and 'made up their own minds' on most matters on which they had relevant everyday experiences and in the light of their own circumstances. This was

> overwhelmingly the case with the youngest cohorts. Arguably this would not have been the case a generation ago, or up to the 1950s. The threat of religious sanctions which previously intimidated many Catholics into a more or less resentful compliance no longer had the power to convince or persuade. The research evidence was that most Catholics will, in the last analysis, make up their own minds on moral issues pragmatically and commonsensically.
>
> (Hornsby-Smith 1991:207–8)

John Fulton, on the basis of in-depth interviews with 'core' and 'super-core' Catholics in the 18–30 age group in England, reports that for them 'obedience is no longer a virtue ... It has been replaced by personal moral discernment and following one's conscience.' This 'differentiates them from their parents' generation of Catholics' (Fulton 1999:169). He concludes that 'a subtle but significant change in Catholic identity has occurred over the past thirty years' (ibid.:180). These very committed young Catholics remain in the church even though they disagree with its leadership (ibid.; see also Fulton *et al.* 2000).

Mary Eaton (1999), in an interesting study of three generations of Catholic women, has also pointed to the evidence of a generational shift. She interviewed a number of professional women who belonged to the same student cohort educated at a Catholic college of education in the late 1960s. Whereas their mothers had either married a Catholic or their father had converted on marriage and had been closely involved with parochial organisations, only a small minority of this cohort had married a Catholic man, and although nearly all continued to attend Mass weekly, unlike their mothers they did not join parish-based organisations such as the Union of Catholic Mothers or the Catholic Women's League, though many were involved as catechists, eucharistic ministers and so on. Most of these women, now in their fifties, were critical of failures of religious education and saddened that most of their own children, now teenagers or young adults, were no longer practising.

In order to understand the generational shifts which have been noted, it is useful to place them in the context of postwar social changes. Sylvie Collins has provided a useful overview and has suggested that over the past half-century

> Spirituality amongst young people has moved from a modern spirituality located in a stable Christian tradition (in Wuthnow's terms a 'spirituality of dwelling', 1998); through to a late modern spirituality mainly located in the search for the inner or higher self (Wuthnow's 'spirituality of seeking'); through to a postmodern spirituality that reflects more of an aesthetic/ethical understanding, that is to say, a dislocated spirituality which focuses on experience *per se* rather than a specific object, and primarily the experience of intimacy (a spirituality of intimacy). Running alongside these forms of spirituality … there has been an increasingly salient ethic of consumption which can provide an alternative non-spiritual, materialistic basis around which young people may organize their lives, but which has increasingly become heavily implicated in spirituality itself.
>
> (Collins 2000:223)

In sum, the evidence we have briefly reviewed points clearly to a massive cultural shift in the nature of belonging, understanding of religious authority, and moral decision-making of the younger generations of Catholics. Such a paradigm shift, which parallels the shift from a manufacturing-based form of modernity to an economic system based heavily on information and communication technology and in which consumption and leisure industries assume ever greater salience, has had inevitable consequences for the nature of Catholic identity.

Prospects for the New Millennium

We set out to explore the change in the identity of English Catholics in the postwar and post-Vatican II years and test the utility of Hammond's (1988) analysis for religio-ethnic minorities. The evidence we have reviewed about social and religious changes in English Catholicism over the past half-century appears wholly consistent with Hammond's suggestion of a shift of identity from the 'communal-expressive' to the 'individual-expressive' and the decline of an involuntary, ascriptive and automatic form of communal identity. A consideration of the case of Catholics of Irish descent provided a particularly demanding test of the hypothesis, but again the evidence from the 1978 national survey pointed unambiguously to the steady 'assimilation' of Irish Catholics to the norms of 'English' Catholics by the second generation, especially for that substantial proportion who married out of the Irish community. The alternative claim by Mary Hickman (1995) that a strong Irish identity is retained was argued to apply only in special circumstances of 'cultural defence' where there was strong community support and no marital exogamy or mobility out of the community. Strong evidence in support of Hammond's hypothesis was also found in the case of the analysis of generational differences.

It would seem that this shift of Catholic identity both reflects and is a consequence of the pervasive cultural shift in Western societies generally. This is associated not only with the break-up of the old colonial empires in the postwar period but also and more recently with major technological advances, economic developments and processes of globalisation. This major cultural shift has been variously characterised as one from modernity to postmodernity (Bauman 1998) or late modernity (Giddens 1991), and (in my view misleadingly) from materialism to post-materialism (Inglehart 1990). Others have pointed to a growing cultural and religious pluralism and the emergence of the imperative of individual autonomy and choice in *The Individualizing Society* (Ester *et al*. 1993).

With their emergence from the 'fortress church', it was sociologically inevitable that English Catholics would be affected by these powerful societal forces, like everyone else. Given their previous defensiveness in the face of hostility and discrimination and their substantial conformity to community constraints in a situation of 'cultural defence', it was only to be expected that, with the decline of hostility, their experiences of social and geographical mobility and achievement of a measure of social respectability in a more ecumenical climate in English society in the last quarter of the twentieth century, English Catholics would enthusiastically embrace the cultural shifts and give them expression in the way they live their lives. Indeed the evidence points strongly to there having been a paradigmatic shift in the nature of Catholic belief, practice, sense of belonging and responses to ecclesiastical authority around the 1960s and 1970s.

Danièle Hervieu-Léger (1997) proposes that there has been a fragmentation of collective and individual memory and an individualisation of belief in the current phase of cultural pluralism which threatens the sense of continuity and identity of the believer in a 'line of believers'. In modern societies characterised by change and mobility, 'social identities are less and less inherited from one generation to another; they are built out from the diversity of the social and personal experiences in which individuals are involved' and can be reconstructed by reconfiguring and combining the communitarian, cultural, ethical and emotional dimensions of the 'line of believers' (Hervieu-Léger 1997:131). John Fulton concludes that today: 'historical and institutionalized religion ... becomes one of a set of options for the restoration of moral consciousness to the public and private sphere, to the workings of social institutions and to self-identity' (Fulton:122).

In other words, the answer to our initial question 'What do you mean when you say you are a Roman Catholic?' at the turn of the millennium is much more ambiguous and varied and individually selected than it was 50 years ago when it was still largely involuntary and communally based in the distinctive Catholic subculture.

Acknowledgements

I am grateful to Sylvie Collins for helpful comments on an earlier draft of this chapter. The research base for this chapter relates primarily to England. Similar trends are likely in Wales and Scotland, though after a time lag.

Bibliography

Archer, A. (1986), *The Two Catholic Churches: A Study in Oppression*, London: SCM Press.

Bauman, Z. (1998), 'Postmodern Religion?', in P. Heelas (ed.) *Religion, Modernity and Postmodernity*, Oxford: Blackwell, pp. 55–78.

Berger, P.L., Berger, B. and Kellner, H. (1974), *The Homeless Mind: Modernization and Consciousness*, Harmondsworth: Penguin.

Chamberlain, M. (1989), 'Growing Up Catholic', in R. Samuel (ed.) *Patriotism: The Making and Unmaking of British National Identity*, Vol. II *Minorities and Outsiders*, London: Routledge, pp. 18–36.

Collins, S. (2000), 'Spirituality and Youth', in M. Percy (ed.) *Calling Time: Religion and Change at the Turn of the Millennium*, Sheffield: Sheffield Academic Press, pp. 221–37.

Coman, P. (1977), *Catholics and the Welfare State*, London: Longman.

Douglas, M. (1973), *Natural Symbols*, Harmondsworth: Penguin.

Eaton, M. (1999), 'What Became of the Children of Mary?', in M.P. Hornsby-Smith (ed.) *Catholics in England 1950–2000*, London: Cassell, pp. 219–241.

Ester, P., Halman, L. and de Moor, R. (eds) (1993), *The Individualizing Society: Value Change in Europe and North America*, Tilberg: Tilberg University Press.

Fielding, S. (1993), *Class and Ethnicity*, Buckingham: Open University Press.

Fulton, J. (1997), 'Modernity and Religious Change in Western Roman Catholicism: Two Contrasting Paradigms', *Social Compass*, **44**(1), 115–29.

Fulton, J. (1999), 'Young Adult Core Catholics', in M.P. Hornsby-Smith (ed.) *Catholics in England 1950–2000*, London: Cassell, pp. 161–81.

Fulton, J., Abela, A.M., Borowik, I., Dowling, T., Marler, P.L. and Tomasi, L. (2000), *Young Catholics at the New Millennium: The Religion and Morality of Young Adults in Western Countries*, Dublin: University of Dublin Press.

Giddens, A. (1991), *Modernity and Self-Identity*, Cambridge: Polity.

Hammond, P.E. (1988), 'Religion and the Persistence of Identity', *Journal for the Scientific Study of Religion*, **27**(1), 1–11.

Hervieu-Léger, D. (1997), 'La Transmission Religieuse en Modernité: Eléments pour la Construction d'un Objet de Recherche', *Social Compass*, **44**(1), 131–43.

Hickey, J.V. (1960), *The Irish Rural Immigrant and British Urban Society*, London: Newman Demographic Survey.

Hickey, J. (1967), *Urban Catholics: Urban Catholicism in England and Wales from 1829 to the Present Day*, London: Geoffrey Chapman.

Hickman, M.J. (1995), *Religion, Class and Identity*, Aldershot: Avebury.

Hickman, M.J. (1999), 'The Religio-Ethnic Identities of Teenagers of Irish Descent', in M.P. Hornsby-Smith (ed.) *Catholics in England 1950–2000*, London: Cassell, pp. 182–98.

Hornsby-Smith, M.P. (1987), *Roman Catholics in England: Studies in Social Structure Since the Second World War*, Cambridge: Cambridge University Press.

Hornsby-Smith, M.P. (1991), *Roman Catholic Beliefs in England: Customary Catholicism and Transformations of Religious Authority*, Cambridge: Cambridge University Press.

Hornsby-Smith, M.P. (ed.) (1999), *Catholics in England 1950–2000: Historical and Sociological Perspectives*, London: Cassell.

Hornsby-Smith, M.P. and Dale, A. (1988), 'The Assimilation of Irish Immigrants in England', *British Journal of Sociology*, **39**(4), 519–44.

Hornsby-Smith, M.P. and Lee, R.M. (1979), *Roman Catholic Opinion: A Study of Roman Catholics in England and Wales in the 1970s*, Guildford: University of Surrey.

Hornsby-Smith, M.P. and Whelan, C.T. (1994), 'Religious and Moral Values', in C.T. Whelan (ed.) *Values and Social Change in Ireland*, Dublin: Gill & Macmillan, pp. 9–44.

Inglehart, R. (1990), *Culture Shift in Advanced Industrial Society*, Princeton, NJ: Princeton University Press.

Jackson, J.A. (1963), *The Irish in Britain*, London: Routledge & Kegan Paul.

Kokosalakis, N. (1971), 'Aspects of Conflict Between the Structure of Authority and the Beliefs of the Laity in the Roman Catholic Church', in M. Hill (ed.) *A Sociological Yearbook of Religion in Britain*, Vol. 4, London: SCM Press, pp. 21–35.

Lodge, D. (1980), *How Far Can You Go?*, London: Secker & Warburg.

Luckmann, T. (1970), *The Invisible Religion*, London: Collier-Macmillan.

Mol, H. (1978), *Identity and Religion*, Beverly Hills, Calif. Sage.

Rex, J. and Moore, R. (1969), *Race, Community and Conflict: A Study of Sparkbrook*, London: Oxford University Press/Institute of Race Relations.

Roof, W.C. (1978), *Commitment and Community*, New York: Elsevier.

Ryan, W. (1973), *Assimilation of Irish Immigrants in Britain*, unpublished Ph.D. thesis, St Louis University.

Wallis, R. and Bruce, S. (1992), 'Secularization: The Orthodox Model', in S. Bruce (ed.) *Religion and Modernization: Sociologists and Historians Debate the Secularization Thesis*, Oxford: Clarendon Press, pp. 8–30.

Ward, C. (1965), *Priests and People: A Study in the Sociology of Religion*, Liverpool: Liverpool University Press.

Whyte, J.H. (1981), *Catholics in Western Democracies*, Dublin: Gill & Macmillan.

Wuthnow, R. (1998), *After Heaven: Spirituality in America Since the 1950s*, London: University of California Press.

Young Christian Workers (YCW) (1951), *Report on the Irish in Birmingham*, London: YCW.

CHAPTER 4

Identity and the Anglican Priesthood

Debates on the Ordination of Women and Homosexuals in Sociological Perspective

Martin D. Stringer

In the last quarter of the twentieth century contributions from feminist and gay theorists have become central to the academic debate on identity. Likewise the concept of 'identity' has been central to the writing and theories of feminism and gay studies. Not all those writing within these disciplines are going to agree on what they mean by 'identity' or on the role it might play within their theories. Some of the writing is dense, convoluted and highly complex. Underlying much of this writing, however, is the fundamental assumption that identity is a function of the self; it is something that needs to be claimed by the individual over and against the social. In both feminist and gay writings the given identity of society, whether seen in patriarchal or homophobic structures, or seen in terms of stereotypes and media representations, is understood to be intrinsically negative and detrimental to the individual. It is the role of feminist or gay theory to oppose these societal identities (the identities for the most part given by middle-class straight men) and to claim identities that have been created by women or gays for themselves. Exactly on what basis these new reclaimed identities are to be constructed is, of course, open to debate.

In the case of feminist or gay theologies, then, the same fundamental concern for questions of self-claimed identity, over and against the identities imposed by the church or by straight male theologians, is also apparent. Where this has come most to the fore I would argue has been in the various debates and disputes over the priesthood in Anglicanism since about 1980. To say that there has been a 'crisis of ministry' in all the mainline churches since the mid-1970s is probably to state the obvious. The nature of this crisis, however, has many different elements. At one level there has been a decline in numbers. The number of people coming forward for professional ministry within the churches in Britain has been falling faster than the number of church-going Christians (Bruce 1995:34). At the same time there was an ongoing discussion throughout most of the twentieth century about the possibility of women taking on professional ministry within the churches. By the end of the century, apart from the Catholics and a few smaller denominations, there were women ministers and priests in all the mainline churches in Britain. We have not, however, reached the end of this debate. Women are still not allowed to take on the role of bishop in the Anglican churches and many local congregations of all denominations are still reluctant to call, or have imposed upon them, a woman minister. In the last ten to fifteen years of the twentieth century this debate also widened to include gays and lesbians. Should practising homosexuals be ordained (or their current ordination recognised or rescinded)? Underlying all these discussions, I would argue, and central to the sense of crisis in the ministry, is the concept of 'identity'.

Some traditionalists within the Church of England look back to the days when the parish priest was a significant person within the community. The vicar or parson was somebody to be respected and somebody who, alongside the local squire, the doctor and perhaps the headmaster of the local school, could be expected to represent and maintain the social order of society. Such a situation may never have occurred in quite the way it is envisaged, and many people would tell us that if it had then it was clearly part of an oppressive structure in which the Anglican clergy were complicit. This does not stop those looking for security and 'identity' in the priesthood to look back with some sense of nostalgia to such a perception. What is more, this essentially rural model of the ideal times is only one of a number of different versions of the myth of Anglican priesthood and not all of them are so clearly oppressive or so easy to dismiss as romantic fantasy.[1] These images of what the Church of England parson is supposed to be are deeply rooted in society, even, and I might suggest especially, in those parts of society that have had least to do with the church, such as our inner urban areas. It could also be argued that such images are central to the debates over the ordination of women and homosexuals. Finally, and going back to my opening statements, such images represent societal identities which are given to, and expected of, the clergy and their 'role' in society.[2] In the late twentieth century, with the rise of feminist and gay theories, and the implicit rejection of such societal identities, the clergy themselves (even the straight white males) were reluctant to have such roles imposed upon them. This, I would argue, is at the heart of the crisis that the church is currently facing

In this chapter I want to explore three specific contexts in which I have been very closely involved. I want to look at the changing role of Anglican clergy in the inner city and the conflict between the self-proclaimed identity of the clergy involved and the assumptions of the people they were ministering to. In doing this I want to explore the relationship between self-given identities and societal identities or roles, and the nature of the conflict that has grown up between them. In the second section I want to translate this debate into the context of the discussions surrounding the ordination of women in the late 1980s and early 1990s. Again I want to look at these discussions specifically through the lens of identity and see how far this helps to understand some of the underlying currents of the debate. Finally, I want to look briefly at contemporary debates over the ordination of practising homosexuals. While I will argue that disputes over identity are still central to this discussion, I think that it is important to see how these disputes differ from those involved in the discussions over the ordination of women. I will conclude with a broader discussion about the nature of identity and role as they affect our sociological, and by implication, our theological understanding of the Anglican priesthood.

Priesthood and Identity in the Inner City

Between 1987 and 1993 I worked on a Church Urban Fund-supported project in an inner urban area of Manchester (Stringer 1993). I was employed by the Anglican deanery in the area to help the 13 congregations in their work with young families. Much of my job involved working directly with the congregations, raising their confidence, training certain members for particular tasks, helping them in raising money for further projects and so on. Some of my time was also spent in working with and listening to the people of the area, especially the young mothers and their immediate families. One of the issues that kept being raised within this work was the role of the clergy, both within the congregation and within the community. *Faith in the City* and similar reports commissioned by the Church of England had already highlighted that there was something of a crisis among the clergy in the inner city, a crisis that was more acute than that of the church as a whole (ACCUPA 1985). As with the wider church this was, in part, a crisis of recruitment. Congregations in our part of Manchester were small (15 to 20 on average). Clergy houses were a constant target for vandalism. The local schools were not considered adequate for children of the clergy, and the general environment, both social and physical, was not thought to be suitable for clergy with young families. Finally, the job itself was stressful and most of the clergy suffered illnesses directly relating to the stress of their situation.

The sense of crisis, however, was not all based on the fact that many Church of England clergy simply did not want to work within the inner city. Throughout my time in Manchester all the posts were filled and it was never too difficult to replace clergy who left. There was also a sense of crisis, I would suggest, in what the clergy in this area were expected to do. As I have already indicated, the congregations were low in terms of numbers. These congregations were also elderly, consisting largely of people who used to live in the area before the housing had been demolished and new flats built. The congregations were scarred: they were worn down by vandalism and abuse; they dreaded baptism Sundays when their worship would be swamped by local people; and they felt as though their churches and all they had worked for were dying and disappearing. There was a clear sense of a siege mentality among the congregations I worked with. It was them against the world. The clergy, however, were very seldom prepared to go along with this kind of attitude. They always tried to look beyond the congregation at the people of the area, at their many and complex needs, and at the sheer lack of resources they, the congregations or anybody else appeared to have to meet those needs. All the clergy were committed to working in socially deprived neighbourhoods and all of them were frustrated by the lack of resources of any kind that were available to them to do anything.

What frustrated the clergy most, however, was the attitude of the people, both within the congregations and within the neighbourhood. These clergy, all but one male and all well educated and well motivated, wanted to encourage their congregations and the local people to do things for themselves, to improve their lives, to protest against injustice and to work for the good of their community. What they met, however, was what one of the clergy described to me as 'militant apathy'. Local people had seen many projects and schemes come and go, whether sponsored by the church, by the local authority or by charities. They had built up their hopes as the project arrived only to see them dashed as the project left three years later. They had learnt not to get excited about the big plans and schemes dreamed up by outsiders. Rather they simply got everything they could from each project with the minimum of commitment and investment on their own part, and then moved on to the next one. The clergy never had access to the level of resources or political initiatives needed to change this cycle of cynicism and exploitation.

What is more, the clergy themselves came and went with a high level of regularity and they came to be seen like all other outsiders within the community, there to be tapped for what they could give but not to be trusted or supported. As far as the clergy themselves were concerned, they had one big advantage: they actually lived within the neighbourhood, unlike all the other professionals trying to deal with the situation. This, however, only made them vulnerable and even more isolated within the community. The clergy also had one big disadvantage: the historical assumptions about the church, and about clergy, that were held by practically all the people of the neighbourhood, and by many in the congregations.

One thing became clear to me within a short time of beginning to work in this area. When the local people realised that I was not ordained, they would begin to talk to me openly and often at some length about the church and particularly about the clergy. Many of the people in the area were ex-Catholic, as this particular area of Manchester had traditionally been the focus for the Irish community. Much of what the people wished to tell me, therefore, related to their experiences and understandings of the Catholic Church. Most of what they told me was highly critical and very negative. They felt betrayed, let down and even abused by the church. There were no specific stories of physical or other direct abuse by the clergy. However, as representatives of the church the priests came in for a great deal of criticism. This was associated with another very common discourse that I heard on many occasions from different people in the area. Christians, it was assumed, were supposed to be good, loving, generous and tolerant. Most people who went to church, particularly the neighbours of those I talked to, were none of these things, or at least they were not in the eyes of their neighbours. Most people who went to church, therefore, were condemned as 'hypocrites'. If this was true of neighbours then this was especially true of clergy, especially in the light of many popular stories of meanness, drunkenness, anger and haughtiness on the part of the priests who were remembered.

Alongside this general denigration of the clergy, which was directed at priests and ministers of all denominations, as most people were not all that clear about the differences, there was a further discourse about what these people expected of their clergy today. When churches were encouraged to develop lay teams of pastoral visitors to work within the community, the local people often complained that the 'church' as such took no notice of them because the priest never came to visit. Visiting was perhaps the most obvious context in which the expectations of the clergy were voiced by ordinary people but there were also other expectations about what clergy were supposed to do for them when they were in difficulty and what they could expect of clergy in numerous different situations. On the whole it appeared that contemporary clergy did not live up to any of these expectations; they did not live up to the 'societal identity' of the distant, slightly aloof source of regular sympathy and charity that the people had come to associate with the 'role'. This was a view that was also commonly held by members of the congregation, particularly the older members who had once lived within the area, and was certainly not held by the clergy themselves.

What we see here can be presented as a traditional distinction between the self-identity of the individual and the stereotype or societal identity as held by the community. If this is the case, then the obvious direction of the argument, if we follow the theorists within feminist and gay studies, would be that the clergy should assert their own self-identity and challenge the accepted stereotypes of the society around them. A number of the clergy were very keen to do this. They saw part of their role as challenging and, they hoped, overturning the stereotypes of priesthood held by the local people and giving those who lived around the church a different view of both the clergy themselves and the church that they represented. It is not entirely clear, however, that this is really the kind of response that was needed. Is it possible to equate the expectations of community about the 'role' of a particular profession with the notion of 'stereotype' as used of significant groups within society such as women and gay men? Is priesthood, as understood by the Anglican church, a 'role' or even a 'profession'? Is it something that the person performing the role simply takes on with the job? Or is it an identity? These are the kinds of questions that the situation I met within the inner city left me thinking about. I now wish to turn to the two debates that have dominated Anglican thinking about ordination since the mid-1970s. I want to see whether some of these questions of identity and role can help to make any sense of these disputes, or whether these disputes can help to make sense of our understanding of 'role' or 'identity' in relation to the Anglican priesthood.

The Debate over Women Priests

The debate over the ordination of women in the Church of England came to a head while I was working with the Anglican deanery in Manchester. As the vote in Synod approached I was elected as Chair of the Diocesan Church Union, the principal group opposed to the motion from within the Catholic wing of the church. This position meant that I was in the thick of the debate itself, so far as the Manchester Diocese was concerned, and I had a good opportunity to observe the effect of the debate on clergy and lay members of the church. My own position was always somewhat ambiguous. I did not believe that the General Synod had the right, as an elected body, to make the necessary decisions through a purely democratic process. It was on the basis of the authority of the Synod, therefore, rather than the merits or otherwise of whether women should or should not be ordained that I argued against the legislation. Most others involved, however, on both sides of the debate were far more concerned with the substantive issues, and what this said about the nature of the priesthood and the church, rather than the process by which the decision was to be made.

From the main Catholic opposition the arguments against the ordination of women were twofold. First there were those who objected on the basis of tradition. Jesus, they argued, had never appointed women as disciples and the church had always rejected women as priests. Therefore it was impossible to change this now. Second, there was the opposition that was based on ontology. These opponents argued that a priest celebrates the Eucharist in the person of Christ and that women, as women, could never undertake that role. Those who argued in favour of the ordination of women on the other hand tended to focus on three principal arguments, two that followed or mirrored the arguments of the opponents and one other. First, they argued that society has changed and that the church should continue to keep up to date with cultural changes. This meant that while it was understandable for Jesus not to appoint women as disciples within the culture of first-century Palestine, he did give women a very high profile in his ministry and, in the contemporary culture, he would undoubtedly have appointed women to the priesthood. Second, there was an argument which mirrored the ontological argument of the opposition. All of humanity, it was suggested, is saved through Jesus, not just men. The clergy represent that saved humanity and must therefore include women as well as men to be fully inclusive. The third argument was based on the fact that many women actually felt called to be priests and believed that this call came from God. How, it was argued, could God call individuals to something that was fundamentally wrong? These are obviously simplifications of what were at the time developed as very sophisticated arguments (Chapman 1989; Watts 1993). What is also clear is that there were other subsidiary arguments being used on both sides of the debate.

It is not, however, the details of the arguments that particularly concern me in this chapter. I am more interested in the way in which these issues were understood on the ground, among ordinary people, people who may have been faced either with the possibility of a woman as priest in their own church, or with the experience of women's ministry in their own parish. What became very clear both before and after the vote in Synod was that the experience of having a woman as either a deacon or a priest within a church made a significant difference to ordinary people's opinions and understandings about the role of women in ministry. This may seem to be obvious and common sense. However, I think that the point is important because of the kind of questions and discussions that most ordinary people, both inside the church and within the neighbourhood, had about the place of women's ministry when discussed in the abstract.

If we go back to the discussion of Anglican clergy in inner-city areas we can see that people generally held very clear views of what they expected of the clergy. It was these expectations, I would suggest, matched by their own personal experience, which tended to colour people's views about the ordination of women. These expectations and experiences could be divided into two areas. The first involved their pastoral experience of the clergy, the second their liturgical experience. I will look at each of these in turn before coming back to the main issues of identity.

I have already said that many people in the inner city felt that the church was not interested in them if the clergy themselves did not come to visit. The main experience of the church, therefore, as far as most of these people were concerned, was at a pastoral level. This did involve the clergy in visiting the people in their own homes, but it also extended to the experience that people had of the clergy when they went to the church or the vicarage to see the clergy in their own environment. In many inner-city areas, because the clergy were the only professionals who lived within the neighbourhood, people would turn to them for many different reasons, from trivial matters such as small loans to major family crises. This meant that people had considerable experience, either at first hand, or from neighbours, about the pastoral expertise of the particular clergy in their area.

What was very obvious is that for those people, and they were usually women, who had the option of turning to a woman minister for pastoral care, the account of the experience was positive. The women of these neighbourhoods, and I would guess of many other areas, felt very positively towards women in the role of pastoral carers. There are, of course, a number of stereotypes working in this situation. People are generally used to women in the role of carers, including professionals such as teachers, nurses, social workers and so on. There is also considerable evidence that people generally, and women in particular, prefer to turn to women in these roles as opposed to men. It would not be surprising therefore that a population that set a high store on the pastoral role of the clergy felt that women in that role were preferable to, or at least just as good as, men.

The other context in which the general population met with women as clergy was that of worship and liturgy. Here the situation was somewhat different to that of the pastoral context. Many of the theological disputes about the rightness or otherwise of women's ordination involved the potential role of the woman as a representative either of Christ or of the congregation in the context of worship. It was in this arena, therefore, rather than that of the pastoral role of the clergy, that the real controversy occurred. Of course there are theological arguments between the different factions of the church about the ontological nature of the priesthood and the priest's particular function in worship, especially in connection with the Eucharist. It is arguable, however, that most ordinary members of the congregation, and certainly many of those outside the church, did not really understand the subtlety of these arguments. The question, I would suggest, was much more straightforward and involved, once again, the expectations of people about the societal identity of the priest.

At one level there are issues that could be encapsulated by the term 'tradition'. People simply do not expect to see women dressed up in the vestments of the clergy and at first they find it somewhat odd when they do. This, however, is a short-term perception and soon passes. The more significant issue, I would suggest, concerns understandings of power and authority. Ordinary members of the congregation, and particularly people from outside the church, see the priest as a figure of authority. What is more, this authority is seen particularly within the context of worship. The priest is the one who leads worship. For example, it is usually the clergy who preach and this can be seen as an authoritative role. However, people are more than used to women teachers and I am not sure that it is the preaching role that is the real issue. It is, I would argue, the fact that the clergy are seen to control what is going on during worship that presents them as figures of authority. They announce the hymns, they tell people when to stand up and sit down, they act, in some ways, like the conductor of an orchestra, guiding who is doing what and what is happening next. It is this simple, presidential, role that is seen by many people as authoritative and in many cases a little unnerving. People today are not really used to being told what to do in quite such an authoritative way.

In talking to people about their expectations concerning women ministers it is this presidential role, within the context of worship, that appears to cause most difficulties, both for men and for women. Once again, as with the pastoral roles of clergy, this response is a function of stereotype and prejudice. Women are still not seen in our society as naturally fulfilling such an authoritative role and people would claim to feel much more comfortable with men in that role than with women. It is interesting in this context, therefore, that women are actually preferred in the case of funerals and marriages. Here we might expect the same problems as with worship generally. However, this exception can in some ways be seen to prove the rule. The celebrant's role in both marriages and funerals has become increasingly less authoritative and far more facilitative, putting the grieving family or the couple being married to the fore. It is arguable that it is precisely because people do not want an authoritative controlling hand in liturgies of marriage and funerals that women are thought to be particularly appropriate. Such a facilitative response to ordinary worship, however, is much more difficult to achieve, and is something that people feel far less comfortable with.

What I have talked about, up to this point, in relation to the debate about women's ministry is the question of 'role', or rather the expectations held by ordinary people, what I have called the 'societal identity'. This clearly needs to be matched against the women's own understanding of their individual identity, and this would bring in the third argument in favour of women's ministry, the sense of being called which has been common to so many women. Before doing this, however, I wish to turn to the debate over homosexual clergy, as the questions of 'societal identity' here are somewhat different, where the questions of individual identity, I would suggest, may be very similar.

The Debate about Homosexual Clergy

The question of the ordination of openly gay or lesbian clergy was not a major issue in the Anglican church at the time that I was working in Manchester. However, as a partially open gay man myself, working for the Anglican church, I was obviously aware of a number of sides of the debate and knew a relatively large number of gay clergy within the Manchester diocese. The gay clergy I knew came from all strands of Anglicanism, Catholic, liberal and, to a far lesser extent, evangelical. They were also present on both sides of the debate about the ordination of women. A small number of these clergy had regular partners and so, to use the church's own terminology, were 'practising' homosexuals. It was only after the decision to ordain women had been passed through Synod, however, that the questions surrounding the ordination of gay and lesbian clergy became a real issue. Since 1992, however, the issue has, on a number of occasions, come close to breaking up the church in a way that the ordination of women debate never really did.

If we go back to the analysis I was offering about the way in which the expectations concerning the role of clergy in the Church of England affected popular views on the ordination of women, we can find a similar set of positions in relation to homosexual clergy. Like those churches that had had experience of the ministry of women, those who had had gay clergy (whether the clergy were known to be gay or not) often commented positively on the pastoral care of these clergy. As with the case of women's ministry, this obviously reflects some kind of stereotyping, with the homosexual man being presented as more 'sensitive', less 'masculine' and more 'feminine' than the average straight male. This perception, however, is clearly important and the fact that ordinary parishioners raised the issue, even when they were not aware that their own priest was gay, must indicate that there is, in this case, some kind of truth behind the stereotype. What is also true, however, is that the other 'role' which caused problems for potential women ordinands, the authority implied in the liturgical role, was not an issue for gay men. Gay men appeared to share in the common assumptions of male authority and, however 'camp' the individual concerned, the question of presidential authority in worship was never an issue. In fact the ability of many of the more 'camp' clergy to 'perform' well within the context of worship actually meant that such priests were often spoken of very highly in this context as well as in relation to pastoral care (Stringer 2000). It appears, therefore, that the gay clergyman actually has a double advantage in terms of the public perception of their role or societal identity from the point of view of the congregation. They are seen to be good pastorally, being sensitive and open, and they are seen to be right liturgically. It is not, however, at the level of the public perception of the 'role' that the debate over homosexual clergy has focused.

If I go back to the issues I was raising in relation to clergy in the inner city, the public expectations of the clergy were only one of the two ways in which people judged the appropriateness of particular priests. The other issue related to the widespread assumption of hypocrisy on the part of all people who attended church. It was within this discourse, I would suggest, that the questions concerning the ordination of 'practising homosexuals' occurred. It may seem an obvious point to make. However, it is clear that it is not what the priest is doing in the pastoral or liturgical context that matters in the debate about homosexual clergy; it is what that priest may be doing when he is not being a priest that really matters. It is what happens in the bedroom that causes the problems. Of course, in the case of straight men or women the question of what the clergy do in the bedroom is of no real interest at all, although the more misogynist arguments against women's ordination that focused on the question of pregnant clergy may arguably be related to this issue. For gay clergy, however, as for the possibility of lesbian clergy, sexual activity matters. This is in part because 'gay' and 'lesbian' societal identities are constructed around sexual preferences. However, it also has something to do with the way in which Christianity in general has come to confine sexuality to specific genital acts. The fact that the Church of England, and a number of other non-Catholic churches in this country, have made a clear distinction between 'practising' and non-practising homosexuals within the debate about ordination only serves to reinforce this point. It is the homosexual act that is considered 'sinful' and it is the priest who engages in this act who, in some ways, is understood as compromising the 'goodness' or 'sinlessness' expected of the clergy, and is seen as 'hypocritical'.

Given this analysis, we can also see that there are other more significant differences between the debates over the ordination of women and the ordination of homosexuals, which have more to do with the kind of discussions on identity with which I opened this chapter. A woman is, in most circumstances, openly and obviously a woman. As a person she will be caught up in and treated according to people's perceptions of what it is to be a woman, whether she wishes to or not. She has no choice. If she then decides to explore, for herself, what it means to claim particular identities as a woman this does not, to any great extent, affect the way in which the general mass of the population responds to her. As a priest in the Church of England has traditionally been seen as male, then it is also the case that to claim the role, or identity, of priest, as a woman, means that she, and those who come into contact with her, have to make sense of what it means to be a 'woman priest' whether they really want to or not. The case of the gay man is not at all the same. It is perfectly possible for a gay man to hide his homosexuality from those around him. Most people who meet him on a casual basis (unless he is in a situation where being gay is expected) would automatically respond to him without reference to his 'gayness'. Such a man can, therefore, claim the role of 'priest', so long as he does not publicly announce that he may be gay, without anybody having to worry about anything. It is only if this man chooses to claim the identity of a 'gay priest', and makes a public statement to that effect, that the issues begin to be raised. The debate in relation to gay clergy, therefore, is not so much whether the church should ordain practising homosexuals as whether those homosexuals (practising or not) who have already been ordained should 'come out'.

What is most interesting in this context is the kind of situation that was far more common before the debates about the ordination of women and homosexuals became a serious issue. In a number of parishes the parish priest was gay, and was generally assumed to be gay by members of the congregation. In many cases he may have played out a particular gay stereotype, acting in a camp fashion or affecting a very effeminate manner. In other cases a partner would be living permanently within the vicarage or rectory. The clergy in question, however, would never have dreamt of announcing publicly that they were gay and most of the parishioners, even if pushed, would have denied that their priest was 'of that persuasion'. Even the 'nice young man' living at the vicarage could be explained on the basis of the generosity or pastoral sensitivity of the clergyman, rather than recognised as his 'boyfriend'. Within the whole of this situation a certain level of denial or deceit was central and all involved were, for their different reasons, willing to be involved in that denial. The debates that have happened within the church, however, have meant that such situations are much more difficult to sustain and subsequently far rarer. For psychological and ethical reasons this is probably no bad thing, but it does, I would suggest, make the question of 'identity' in relation to gay and lesbian clergy a much more difficult issue than that of straight women clergy.

Conclusion

As a conclusion to this chapter I want to focus on the particularly Anglican aspects of some of these debates. In doing this I would hope to draw together some of the main themes and ideas that have been running through the chapter. One thing that became very clear during the debates on the ordination of women was that there was no one theology of the priesthood that could be claimed by all Anglicans. The evangelicals, the Catholics and the liberals all developed different kinds of theology, all claiming to draw on 'traditional' Anglican sources. Despite this diversity of theological thinking, however, I would want to argue that, at least at the sociological level, there was in fact a common understanding of priesthood within the Church of England. This common view, I would argue, was based on the merger, for individual clergy, of the understanding of 'role' and 'identity', or the equivalence of the societal identity and the individual identity.

We are often told that the priesthood in the Church of England has become increasingly professionalised since about 1970. It is no longer seen as a vocation, but rather as a career. I would agree with this, but I would also want to go further. From the end of the sixteenth century up to the middle years of the last century I would suggest that Anglican clergy not only saw themselves in the role of the 'priest' but actually understood their identity in terms of that role. It was the particular status, the social standing, the tasks associated with the role that defined who these men were. This was true whether the priest in question understood the priesthood in evangelical, liberal or Catholic terms. The particular theology did not really matter. This association of role and identity defined the gentlemen clergy of the eighteenth century, it drove the slum priests of the nineteenth century, it was the bedrock of the Christian socialists and of those involved in the struggle for education or social reform. It was present in the self-understanding of the chaplains in the First and Second World Wars. These men were 'priests' in terms both of 'role' and of 'identity'. It is this dual feature of the Anglican clergy that has led to many of the expectations of the clergy that I have discussed in this chapter. Most ordinary people, however, both inside and outside the church, still assume that the role and identity of those individuals defined as 'priests' should be one, and that the whole of their lives will be devoted to their task. This, as I have suggested, is where many of the problems lie.

I began by commenting on the way in which feminist and gay or lesbian authors have developed understandings of identity that are focused primarily on the individual, and on the particular attributes and experiences of the individual, rather than on the roles or stereotypes that have been put on them by society. This, I have suggested, has also been present in recent discussions and understandings of priesthood in the Anglican church, particularly in the disputes over women priests and homosexual clergy. This individual understanding of identity, however, is entirely out of tune with the traditional understanding of priesthood in the Anglican church and is, I would say, 'therefore' at odds with the expectations of the public and the bulk of the congregations of the church. As clergy have continued to claim their 'identity' in an individual sense, in association with, but in no sense defined by, their role as priests, then the traditional understanding of the priesthood in the Church of England has begun to collapse. Of course the church cannot go back. It is society as a whole that has moved on, and the church has to recognise this change. However, I would want to argue that by recognising this change it can perhaps find new and exciting ways out of the current crisis, which would never be possible if it continues to stick with the older understanding of the priest as both a role and an identity.

Notes

1 The image of the ritualist slum priest or the evangelical campaigner on prison reform are only really variations on this same myth. There are undoubtedly many others within the recent history of the Church of England.

2 Throughout this chapter I use the terms 'societal identity' and 'role' almost interchangeably. I do not, however, intend both to mean the same thing. The 'role' is the accepted norm or stereotype associated with a particular occupation or position in society. 'Societal identity' refers to the identity that is given to performers of that role by those who come into contact with them, the society in which they practise.

Bibliography

ACCUPA (1985), *Faith in the City: A Call for Action by Church and Nation*, London: Church House Publishing.

Bruce, S. (1995), *Religion in Modern Britain*, Oxford: Oxford University Press.

Chapman, J. (1989), *The Last Bastion: Women Priests – the Case For and Against*, London: Methuen.

Stringer, M.D. (1993), *Final Report of the Ardwick Deanery Young Families Project*, Ardwick Deanery Young Families Project.

Stringer, M.D. (2000), 'Of Gin and Lace: Sexuality, Liturgy and Identity among Anglo-Catholics in the Mid-Twentieth Century', *Theology and Sexuality*, **13**, 35–54.

Watts, M. (ed.) (1993), *Through a Glass Darkly: A Crisis Considered*, Leominster: Gracewing.

CHAPTER 5

Religion, Identity and Change in Contemporary Wales

Paul Chambers

Religion and Contemporary Societies

One of the most striking aspects of social change in northern European societies over the past century has been the radical transformation of the religious sphere. This has been most apparent in that area of public life defined as 'civil society' (Thomas 2000) and its most visible expression has been in the rapid decline of visible public participation in organised religion. Individual religious belief itself remains a widespread phenomenon, measurable through such indices as the European Values Survey (Davie 1994, 2000) and the continued relevance of institutional religion to the vitality of the public sphere should not be under-estimated (Casanova 1994; Fukuyama 1995). Nevertheless, as Steve Bruce (1995) notes, organised religion in northern European societies progressively lost both power and influence throughout the twentieth century and this loss of social significance is most visible in the decline of both denominational membership and attendances at places of worship. This chapter will seek to focus primarily on the relationship between religious adherence, institutional forms of belonging and group identity formation as they relate to Wales and the Welsh people.

Wales itself has historically had a close relationship with religion and for a 100-year period (1850–1950) Welsh social and cultural identity was closely tied to Protestant Nonconformity (Williams 1985). The translation of the Bible into Welsh in 1588 both rescued the language, fixing it in its literary form, and decisively shaped the way in which Welsh culture developed. Increasingly Protestant Nonconformity and the chapel became a central organising principle in Welsh social and cultural life and by the latter part of the nineteenth century, to all intents and purposes, most Welsh people lived their lives within the orbit of the chapel. The Welsh chapel was the concrete expression of solidaristic communities that lived, worked and worshipped in tightly circumscribed locales. It was the voice that encapsulated the social, political and economic life of the community, the totalising expression of habitus, both derived from and informing community life. Of course, there were alternative religious identities, both Anglican and Roman Catholic (approximately 20 per cent of worshippers), and a significant proportion (possibly as much as 50 per cent) of the population did not darken the doors of the churches and chapels (Jenkins 1992). Nevertheless, the social and cultural influence of Nonconformism was such that it might be termed pervasive (Williams 1985) and even triumphant, as radicalism, Nonconformity and cultural nationalism became defining features of modern Welshness (Jenkins 1992). Religion in Wales can now no longer be said to constitute a key source of identity formation or maintenance for any but a minority of the population. This is well illustrated by the rate of decline in church and chapel attendances in Wales, which for the past 50 years has been running at twice that of comparable religious institutions in England. The percentage of the general population who attend church or chapel is now slightly lower than in England and recent national surveys (Christian Research Association 1995; Bible Society 1997) paint a bleak picture of wholesale chapel closures, where areas of decline within institutional forms of belonging far outstrip areas of growth.

The 1995 Welsh Churches Survey (Bible Society 1997) makes interesting reading. Wales still retains a higher density of places of religious worship per head of population than England or Scotland. However, the majority of church and chapel buildings are situated in the less densely populated rural counties and their congregations are both rapidly ageing and decreasing in size. The average age of Welsh congregations is 45 years or over and the average size of congregations is 25 or fewer, with the most frequently reported congregational size being 10. The use of the Welsh language in worship remains widespread and indeed more so than among the general population. Whereas roughly 20 per cent of the Welsh population use Welsh in some form, among the churches, in liturgical terms, 35 per cent are monoglot Welsh and 10 per cent bilingual. In terms of theological orientation, the Welsh churches remain deeply conservative. Evangelicalism has a lower profile than in England or Scotland, although it does constitute a significant force within the Welsh religious economy. Mention should also be made of the Roman Catholic Church, concentrated in the industrial areas of south Wales and now the second largest denomination in Wales, which retains a strong link with Irish ethnic identity. Another major force is Anglicanism, which is now the dominant grouping numerically, having supplanted the declining traditional Free Churches as the majority expression of Welsh religious identity. Largely conspicuous by their absence outside the two Welsh cities is any significant presence of non-Christian religious institutions. The generally conservative nature of Welsh religion is in part a reflection of an ageing church population who are resistant to change. Indeed, it is this resistance to change that is cited by the authors of the Bible Society survey as the main barrier to effective maintenance and mission strategies and the primary source of the growing gap in cultural relevancy between the churches and the general population.

While Wales offers a striking example of religious decline at the institutional level, it is also fairly typical in this respect of other modern north European societies. Social scientific explanations of secularisation have tended to view modernity itself as a corrosive agent, eroding both the social significance of religion within the public sphere and patterns of belief and practice in the private sphere. However, a consensus is now emerging which suggests that this is only true as far as the populations of northern Europe are concerned (Davie 2000:1, 24–33). Elsewhere in the world, religion remains a significant force, both in its influence on national cultures and on international events (see, for example, Lawrence 1989; Fukuyama 1995; Esposito and Watson 2000). It is no longer enough to equate modernity with religious decline, as the experience of some modern industrialised societies, for example the US and Japan, where modernity and a vibrant religious culture coexist with little apparent tension, suggests otherwise. Indeed, the emergence of a postmodern and globalised world has created the conditions for a complex system of cultural flows, resulting in both the resurgence of traditional forms of religion and the increasing global mixing of religious cultures (Robertson 1992; Featherstone 1995). Attempts to clarify this picture, both at national and international levels, through the use of macro-societal concepts such as secularisation have not been entirely successful and there is a growing recognition among many social scientists that secularisation is a multidimensional concept that operates on many diverse levels (see, for example, Dobbelaire 1981; Sharpe 1983; Beckford 1989; Casanova 1994). The secularisation debate itself appears to have descended into little more than the discovery of ever more analytic concepts with which to engage in increasingly speculative (and abstract) accounts of the transformation of religion in modern societies and it is perhaps time to return to a more anthropological approach to religion.

Religion does not exist in a vacuum. It is embedded in societies and, by implication, it finds its life in local communities (Durkheim 1995). From a Durkheimian perspective, religion is 'an eminently social thing' (Fields 1995:xvii) and is therefore both grounded in the experience of community and, more importantly, situated within the life of communities. True, life in these communities has become progressively more complex and atomised under modernity, and in conditions of postmodernity traditional organisations (exemplified by institutiona-lised religion) are likely to struggle to retain social significance at the local level (Harris and Startup 1999). The aggregate effects of this are to be seen in the apparent decline of religion at the 'national' level. It follows that the health of religion generally is highly dependent on events and processes working themselves out at the local level. Local religious organisations are not abstract entities. They are composed of groups of real people operating in real communities, and the fate of local congregations is highly dependent on the nature of the relationships that individuals within these religious organisations have with families, friends and acquaintances and their particular local social, cultural and economic environments. Crucial to the reproductive health of local religious communities is the presence of social networks linking individual congregations to populations and capable of providing a source of fresh recruitment through strategies of autogenous or allogenous growth. This holds true both for the establishment of religious groups in local communities and for their subsequent maintenance, processes which are highly dependent on the nature of local social environments.

In Wales, it was the progressive erosion of a homogenous traditional working-class culture, built around the chapel and neighbourhood, that led to the parallel decline of religion. On a national level, structural changes – the collapse of the Liberal–Nonconformist political consensus and the emergence of socialism as a competing ideology; the progressive erosion of traditional industries; the secularisation of cultural life; the contraction of the Welsh language; and the spread of social and geographical mobility – have all contributed to the general decline in social significance of religion in Wales and the numerical decline of many individual congregations. At the local level, religious life was traditionally informed by the close proximity of kin in a limited locality, a high degree of social, occupational and economic homogeneity and close ties of mutual co-operation between kin and neighbours (Rosser and Harris 1965:126–38). Subsequent pervasive social and geographical mobility has progressively undermined the foundations which informed religious life, dispersing those families that were the lifeblood of the chapels and radically altering the nature of those local social environments which informed religious life. In place of cultural and social homogeneity, there is now heterogeneity, and this has proved fatal to the continuity of a distinctively Welsh form of religion based on both the experience of community and collective and individual identifications with particular places of worship.

Religion and Social Identity

While it is possible to characterise the historical cultural and social domination of Protestant Nonconformity in Wales as a form of civil religion (and a powerful source of social and 'national' identity), it was nevertheless always a very fragmented phenomenon, the product of those perennial schismatic tendencies that distinguish the practice of Welsh religion (Harris 1990; Chambers 1997). Welsh Nonconformity has persisted in dividing and sub-dividing itself denominationally and linguistically, resulting in a proliferation of factions, small denominations and independent congregations and an emphasis on identifying itself with the local congregation rather than with national denominational structures (Harris 1990; Davie 1994:94–5). This has made religious practice in Wales particularly susceptible to social-environmental change at the level of community (Chambers 1999), exemplified by the progressive collapse of those denominations associated with a particular form of cultural identity, the Welsh language. While the profile of the Welsh language has been maintained through the state educational system, at the local level many of those Welsh-speaking communities which sustained these chapels are disappearing and their chapels are disappearing with them. At the national level, while the profile of nationalism has been raised by the upturn in the fortunes of the nationalist political party Plaid Cymru, the historic link between the Nonconformist denominations and nationalism has been progressively eroded to a point where religion no longer constitutes a base for national identity and solidarity. Conversely, as the base of Nonconformism has been eroded within the religious sphere, it has been the Anglicans and Roman Catholics (historically associated with 'non-Welsh' identities) who have become the numerically superior groupings within Wales's religious economy. Despite these changes in the religious and social landscape of Wales, there remains a living memory of a distinctive Welsh (and working-class) culture grounded in collective community structures which reflected a solidarity of attitudes and values (Chambers 1999:128–60). Churches and chapels were central to the notion of local social identity and were located at the heart of those local social networks which were the lifeblood of individual communities. It follows that social and geographical mobility has been of particular significance in that it has radically changed the social constitution of communities, transforming the nature of local social identities and eroding the local social networks that linked chapels and churches to their surrounding communities.

In general, any simple equation between social identity, church and community is now increasingly problematic. D.-C. Martin (1995) suggests that within the open systems of group interaction characteristic of modern Western societies, individual identity formation is based on an open-ended synthesis of many overlapping strands of identity. Stuart Hall (1992) sees personal identity as reconceived in the form of multiple identities. The 'decentred subject' is increasingly defined in terms of personal narratives deriving from multiple reference points, reflecting a move from societies characterised by monocultural identities to something rather more 'postmodern'. This transformed landscape is reflected within the religious sphere in Wales. On the one hand, individuals and groups within civil society, while no longer actively involved in church-going, nevertheless retain to some extent their memories of familial involvement and identification with specific churches and chapels, allowing them to retain some level of nominal allegiance to religious institutions. On the other hand, the progressive atomisation of local populations has undercut the basic premise of sociality which informed and underpinned Welsh religious life. Local religious institutions are becoming increasingly divorced from their surrounding local populations as the networks that linked them with these populations unravel. If there remains any correspondence with these populations, it is within the vestigial social networks that the elderly inhabit and this is reflected in the average age composition of those 89 per cent of Welsh congregations in which older people are over-represented (Bible Society 1997:8–10).

This progressive erosion of traditional forms of community and the fragmentation of social life have created something of a national crisis of identity throughout Wales. Certainly, the 'old' Wales of chapel, coal and choirs is now in the process of being relegated to the glossy brochures and tourist attractions of the heritage industry, while the 'new' Wales, reflected in films such as *Twin Town* and *House of America*, is a project still in the making (Smith 1999:20–8). Contemporary debates about Welsh social identity increasingly emphasise the diversity and plurality of Welsh experiences (Thompson 1999) and it is within this transformed social, economic and cultural landscape that religious institutions must find a new identity, reflecting the fact that religion merely constitutes just one (minority) aspect of social life in Wales. If Nonconformist religion once constituted a 'symbolic mirror' of a monocultural Welsh society then this mirror now appears shattered, reflecting the increasing diversity of Welsh social and religious identities. While the future of Welsh religion remains open, on present trends it is likely that those traditional Free Church denominational structures, which formerly operated as both cultural carriers and a source of collective social identity, will continue to contract to the point where they will eventually disappear. As the remaining religious institutions increasingly operate in a pluralistic climate based on competing social and religious identities, the crucial question for Wales is whether organised religion will continue to retain some distinctive 'national' characteristics or whether it will increasingly come to resemble the generalised patterns of religious belief and practice that have been associated with modern societies elsewhere in Europe.

The Decline of Mainstream Religion?

The idea that the future of religion in modern societies lies in the proliferation of sects and cults and the diminution of traditional churches and denominations has been highly influential among social scientists (see, for example, Wilson 1966;

Bruce 1995; Stark and Bainbridge 1985). Among religious professionals, an equally influential (and related) idea is that evangelicalism represents the one religious ideology capable of successfully reaching a population that is increasingly detached from the churches (Carr *et al.* 1992).

Both these speculations about the future of religion draw heavily on the proposition that there will increasingly be a move from inclusive religious ideologies to exclusive religious ideologies and from religious organisations that have soft boundaries to religious organisations with hard boundaries. This can be seen to have both negative and positive outcomes for the health of religion. On the one hand, the end result is religious institutions almost entirely divorced from their surrounding populations, with religion becoming merely a marginalised practice restricted to a marginalised people. On the other hand, the ideologies that typically underpin sectarian groupings represent both an effective means of dealing with the cognitive dissonances produced by the tension between religion and the forces of secularisation and a powerful (and attractive) source of identity in a postmodern landscape in which individuals typically experience multiple social roles and many overlapping strands of social identity. Persuasive as these arguments are, there is little contemporary evidence to support either proposition.

While not disputing the fact that in general terms religion in northern Europe has become disengaged from the lives of ordinary people, this disengagement is only partial. In an exhaustive analysis of religion in modern/postmodern societies, Jose Casanova (1994) suggests that religion is undergoing a process of 'deprivatisation' whereby it re-enters the public sphere of civil society with renewed vitality. Casanova sees the future of religion in modern societies not in world-rejecting sectarian movements but in terms of mainstream traditional religious groupings who have come to terms with modernity. This revitalised religious sphere is essentially the province of national or liberal churches and not sectarian groupings and it draws strongly on pre-existing identifications of populations with their traditional religious structures. Grace Davie (2000) also suggests that memory and social identity are still powerful factors that need to be taken into account in any analysis of the modern European religious landscape. The proliferation of sectarian religious groups with hard boundaries (epitomised for Davie by the rise of evangelicalism) is only one element of a transformed religious landscape. She finds little evidence to support the contention that the historic churches have become an irrelevancy, suggesting rather that in a transformed European landscape there remains both considerable demand for civil religion and a continued social identification with the historic churches, which act as powerful reservoirs of collective memories. While there is no doubt that Wales has undergone a radical transformation within the religious sphere and that the most visible part of this process has been the marked numerical decline of the membership of the historic Welsh Nonconformist churches, Protestant religion in Wales still retains signs of life and any rumours of its imminent demise are premature.

This vacuum left by the collapse of traditional Welsh Nonconformist denominations has been filled to some extent by both Anglicans and evangelicals. Roman Catholicism, although now the second largest denomination in Wales, remains a free-standing entity that is overwhelmingly dependent on autogenous growth for its continued health. The level of converts received into the Roman

Catholic Church is so low as to be negligible. The Anglican Church in Wales now accounts for 30 per cent of all Christian congregations in Wales and 28 per cent of the church-going population, and represents the largest denomination in Wales (Bible Society 1997:12). This suggests that there is still a latent demand for an inclusively oriented, loosely bounded religion with historical antecedents. Assessing the state of evangelicalism in Wales is rather more problematic, given that it is not a church but a movement and as such individual evangelicals can be expected to be found within the mainstream denominations. In a recent survey, 29 per cent of all congregations in Wales defined themselves as 'evangelical', with another 6 per cent defining themselves as neo-Pentecostal (Bible Society 1997:26). The survey does not indicate where these congregations are placed in terms of denominational affiliation, although it is likely that among mainstream denominations, many Baptist congregations would define themselves as evangelicals (ibid.:26). What we can say with rather more certainty is that sectarian groupings, evangelical and Pentecostal denominations, 'new churches' and non-aligned evangelical churches account for only 9 per cent of congregations and 12.8 per cent of church-goers in Wales (Bible Society 1997:12–13). Statistical evidence would also appear to support the contention that the most striking growth levels are to be found among evangelical congregations (Christian Research Association 1995:25–8, 237–77). However, a number of factors need to be considered in any analysis of contemporary statistics relating to church growth and decline. First, many of those evangelical groupings demonstrating the most impressive growth rates are operating from a relatively small base, which means that the numbers of those added are relatively small when compared to those added to larger historic churches (Davie 1994:62–3). It follows that there is little impact on the general population in terms of visibility. Second, it is not clear from statistics of this type why people are joining and where these recruits come from (Bible Society 1997:53). If, as Steve Bruce (1995:69) suggests, autogenous growth and transfers in and out of different evangelical groupings are a significant factor in the growth of evangelical congregations, then it follows that these churches are again failing to make an impact on the general unchurched population. Third, statistics suggest that those evangelical groupings gaining new recruits at the fastest rate are also losing new recruits at the fastest rate (Christian Research Association 1995:26–7). This suggests either that questions should be raised about the efficacy of evangelical 'conversion experiences' or, more likely, that what these figures are highlighting is the presence of a high level of transfers in and out of competing evangelical churches.

When all these factors are taken into account, it becomes clearer that the 'myth' of evangelical success in recruiting from the general population is not all that it first appears to be. Furthermore, recruitment figures for the Anglican churches in both England and Wales remain the highest overall. This fact is usually either ignored by evangelicals or explained away as the product of the fact that the Anglicans start from a base of more congregations and can therefore be expected to gain more recruits. The authors of the 1997 Bible Society Survey fail to establish any strong argument for the privileging of evangelicalism in terms of mission. Among evangelical congregations in Wales, the percentage rate of growth within charismatic congregations is 7 per cent, but this growth is actually derived from a relatively low base in both individual and congregational terms. Furthermore, these congregations are mainly to be found in urban areas, while the geography of Wales is primarily rural or semi-rural. The same authors suggest that Anglicanism is able to attract new recruits in significant numbers because it appeals to those individuals who value historical tradition and religious orthodoxy. This is seen primarily as a consolidation of Anglicanism and not as a trend which is meaningful in terms of mission to the general population.

This conclusion is puzzling, because as the authors themselves recognise, orientations towards religious belief and practice in Wales remain resolutely conservative and resistant to change. Wales is a small country located on the periphery of Europe, with an ambiguous relationship to nationalism and national identity, and with a religious tradition that has historically functioned as a key carrier of cultural and social identity. While the link between religion and national identity has now largely disappeared, identity nevertheless remains a key component of religious affiliations. Danièle Hervieu-Léger suggests that a key element in the formation of religious identities is the process whereby individuals or groups are incorporated into belief communities. This process depends on a shared stock of references to the past and a remembered experience which can be handed on to future generations (Hervieu-Léger 1994:125). D.-C. Martin (1995:12–13) outlines three key elements in the formation of identity narratives: relationships to the past, relationships to social space and relationships to culture. It is axiomatic that all these elements are mediated and sustained through the interaction of people, whether individually or collectively, and that these interactions will exhibit patterns or regularities over time. Therefore we might add a fourth element, the presence of social networks, linking individuals to groups and establishing the conditions for both individual and group orientations to the past, social space and culture.

Religious growth within the Anglican sphere may well be, as the authors of *Challenge to Change* (Bible Society 1997) assert, a phenomenon associated with traditionalism. Certainly, it involves a particular (conservative) orientation towards the past, social space and culture (Harris and Startup 1999). However, the same conditions apply to evangelicalism, which has its own traditions and its own distinctive orientations to the past, social space and culture (Bebbington 1993). It is clear that both Anglicanism and evangelicalism constitute identity narratives but it is not so clear how these relate to the general population, or why one identity narrative, evangelicalism, should be privileged over another identity narrative, Anglicanism, in terms of reaching beyond the spiritual community in which they originate. The Church in Wales is uniquely placed to tap into the process of religious identity formation. As a historic church that operates on the principle of apostolic succession, it has a clear and unambiguous relationship with the past. True, in Wales, this past has historically been associated with English political and economic dominance, but disestablishment in 1920 opened up the possibility of a distinctively 'Welsh' form of Anglicanism. Indeed, it could be argued that both historically and in the present, too much is made of the 'English' character of Anglicanism in Wales, particularly in rural areas (Harris and Startup 1999:7–12). Certainly, in the present, the Church in Wales is doing more than any other denomination (or even all the Welsh denominations taken together) to preserve the Welsh language (ibid.:37–9, 191–3). As a territorial organisation it increasingly both inhabits the spaces vacated by the declining Free Churches and also provides a symbolic space for those occasional participants who are typically defined as 'nominal Christians'. Lacking the hard boundaries associated with more conversionist groupings, Anglican churches increasingly constitute focuses for those individuals and families who retain a residual religious identity, but who would not define themselves as particularly 'religious'. The 'occasional offices' (baptisms, weddings and funerals) that Anglican churches provide form a crucial point of intersection between Anglican parish churches and their surrounding (non-aligned) populations. Within this context, Bernice Martin's comments on the incarnational and vicarious nature of Anglican ministry demonstrate clearly the appeal of a loosely bounded religious organisation operating among a population she characterised as 'the sleeping partner in a compact with the church' (Carr *et al.* 1992:102). As a cultural institution that is inclusive in orientation, the Church in Wales has been able to adapt to cultural change in a way that more exclusive evangelical churches have not. This is exemplified in formal innovations such as the ordination of women, the loosening of the restrictions on the remarriage of divorced persons in church, and informal, localised accommodations with shifts in moral values and lifestyle among the general population. This 'accommodation' is exemplified by an increasing willingness to include those individuals who, on the grounds of lifestyle, have been traditionally excluded by religious institutions with harder boundaries.

Conversely, evangelicalism in Wales has become increasingly divorced culturally and socially from the general population. Evangelicals generally retain an ambiguous relationship with the past and this is exemplified in their ambiguity towards 'tradition' (rather than Biblicism) as a basis of action and their assertion that evangelicalism is essentially unchanging in form and content (Bebbington 1993). In Wales evangelicalism, which owes so much to the 'age of revivals', has had to contend with a marked loss of social significance for the last century. Evangelicalism in Wales can be said to have been the dominant religious force from the period of the 'Great Awakening' of 1735 to the last 'Great Revival' of 1904–5. This last Revival represented a watershed for evangelicalism in Wales and the twentieth century was characterised by the progressive decline of the pervasive influence of evangelicalism upon Welsh society in terms of morals and values, and numerical decline among evangelical groupings. In terms of social space, evangelicalism has witnessed a retreat from the community into the laager of the congregation. If the idea of 'community' represents anything now, it is in terms of the traditional evangelical opposition between the 'church' and the 'world', and this is translated into a strong identification with the wider 'community' of evangelicals, over and above any identification with the specific communities within which evangelical communities are located. The ambiguities which characterise evangelicalism in Wales are further exemplified by the relationship of evangelical congregations to culture. The progressive fragmentation of evangelicalism in Wales is highlighted by the confused nature of the debate among these churches as to what constitutes cultural relevance. The principal axes around which this debate revolves are language and age. In terms of language, Welsh-speaking evangelical congregations have been loath to relinquish this aspect of their cultural identity, even in the face of a general decline in the day-to-day use of the language in many parts of Wales. In an interesting example of the increasingly transnational character of evangelicalism, Welsh-speaking Southern Baptist missionaries from the US are now active among congregations of the Baptist Union of Wales, although their impact on the churches and chapels appears to be restricted to those (predominantly rural) areas of Wales where the Welsh language is still in daily use. This 'impact' is as yet difficult to assess in terms of the undermining or complementing of local and national identity, although this may change as transnational links become stronger. Conversely, within urban areas of Wales, evangelicalism (in common with secular institutions) has become progressively anglicised, breaking the chain linking collective memories and religious identities among the general population. It has also become more fragmented, with evangelical attitudes to cultural change (expressed either as 'cultural relevancy' or 'compromise') becoming increasingly polarised between conservative evangelicals in one camp and neo-Pentecostals and their fellow travellers in another camp. This polarisation strongly correlates with age (Chambers 1999:107–10), with congregations dominated by older evangelicals demonstrating a resistance to compromise or change. These congregations are suspicious of any discourse that seeks to supplant a strong Biblicism in favour of a religious worldview that accommodates a recognition of cultural factors. For these individuals and groups, it is axiomatic that the message of the Bible remains unchanging and there is no necessity for them to adapt the message to changing cultural conditions. For the newer groupings, the issue of cultural relevancy is the key to solving the problem of the under-representation of younger people within Welsh congregations. While no less Biblicist and no less sure of their evangelical identity, these groups recognise the need to distinguish belief from practice and reorganise their church structures and liturgies in line with the cultural characteristics of their surrounding populations (Chambers 1999:295–300). This particular cultural orientation is reflected in the age and gender profiles of the 'new churches' which most approximate those of the general population. Conversely, both traditional evangelical congregations and non-evangelical congregations tend to have few young people, fewer men and older congregations. In terms of class, all religious institutions are becoming more middle class (Bible Society 1997).

In practice, neither evangelical orientation has led to any significant breakthrough in reaching a general population who appear either ignorant of, or indifferent to, the claims of evangelicalism. Conservative congregations remain locked within a particular form of religious identity that conforms to the practice of 50 years ago while the 'new churches' appear to grow largely through transfers from conservative congregations of younger, disaffected, evangelicals. None of this suggests that the claims made on behalf of evangelicalism, that it (over and above other church types) constitutes the primary vehicle to 're-evangelise society', stand up to sustained examination.

Religion, Identity and Change: an Illustration

Grace Davie (1994:18–27) suggests that we cannot view religious institutions as free-standing entities. They are institutions that operate within society and are subject to external pressures which inevitably shape (but do not entirely determine) the life of these institutions. It is to the localised experience of religious institutions that we now turn in order to illustrate the more general processes described above. The following material is drawn from a detailed three-year (1994–7) study by the author of the state of the Christian religion in the city of Swansea. Drawing from data that include a survey of 217 Christian congregations, interviews with 28 religious professionals and 4 detailed case studies of congregations, this section seeks to illustrate those local socio-ecological processes which have effected change in the areas of religion and identity at the 'national' level.

Swansea is a city that encompasses two social worlds. One world is that of the original traditional solidaristic working-class communities that defined Swansea as an industrial town. The other world is that of the suburban communities that spread out to the west in postwar years, the product of a process of social and geographical mobility which drew families and individuals from working-class communities in the east to the atomised middle-class communities of the western suburbs (Rosser and Harris 1965). This movement has had significant implications both in terms of its corrosive effects on the social and cultural homogeneity that defined Swansea in the past and in terms of a radical transformation of the religious ecology that also defined Swansea in the past. For this religious ecology, the present is now defined by an east–west divide: in the long-established communities of the east, all churches and chapels are struggling to survive in the face of a progressive diminution of their local social significance; conversely, in the western suburbs, religious institutions are rather more buoyant and a healthy religious economy is operating, albeit one that is rather different in nature from traditional expressions of Welsh church life.

It is unsurprising that the effects of social and geographical mobility should have impacted on a religious culture that was highly dependent for its life on a surrounding homogenous social, cultural and economic environment. This is particularly so in the case of Free Church populations, who were the first to take advantage of postwar educational opportunities and the first to vacate their traditional localities in favour of the western suburbs. Others followed, and the social and cultural composition of the communities they left changed accordingly. The pervasive social networks that linked family and neighbours and churches and local populations atrophied and the collective social and cultural characteristics of these communities were transformed accordingly. This has left churches and chapels to struggle with the effects of a radically transformed landscape and a loss of those traditional functions that they fulfilled so effectively in an earlier phase of their collective history. Evangelical congregations (despite their reputation for effective evangelisation) are struggling with rapidly declining numbers in the same way as their sister churches within the Free Church sector and seem no more immune to these socio-environmental changes. Conversely, Anglican churches remain in a relatively healthy position and in some cases individual congregations even reported modest numerical growth. A significant factor in Anglican churches' continued ability to operate effectively in these localities was the continued presence of local social networks linking congregations to their surrounding populations. Unlike their Free Church and evangelical counterparts in working-class areas, Anglican families demonstrated much less social and geographical mobility and their continued presence in these communities provides a continuing focus for religious life. Indeed, from the evidence that Swansea furnishes, an inclusive parish-based system can be seen to be a particularly effective means of retaining a religious presence for two reasons. In its 'denominational' mode it operates for its members and their families, while in its *ekklesia* aspect, it reaches beyond the boundaries of congregation and family to meet the continuing religious needs of the surrounding population. These needs may encompass the occasional offices, individual counselling, or merely the continued presence of an institution that represents a focus for vicarious memory and identity, whereby a minority retains the tradition for a majority.

The picture of religious life in the western suburbs of Swansea is somewhat different. In localities with highly atomised populations there is an absence of the type of local social networks that traditionally linked congregations with their surrounding populations. Religious institutions are far more anglicised and middle class, and demonstrate little continuity with traditional modes of Welsh religiosity which were located firmly within familial allegiances to particular church or chapel congregations. Generally, churches and chapels in the suburbs have proved more resistant to decline and this trend is most apparent within some evangelical congregations who have achieved significant growth rates. However, closer examination of recruitment trends within these growing churches showed that numerical growth was also overwhelmingly the result of transfers from other evangelical congregations, reflecting the fragmented nature of Welsh evangelicalism generally and also the trend towards a decreasing familial identification with particular churches or chapels. What was surprising in Swansea was the ease and frequency with which individuals and their families transferred their allegiances from different evangelical congregations, and this rootlessness represents an important shift in the nature of Welsh religiosity, which has traditionally been grounded in a strong social identification with the 'family' chapel or church. It was also apparent that the presence of social networks was an important factor in facilitating recruitment, but that the nature of these networks linking churches to populations was very different from in the past. In the absence of strong local networks, evangelical congregations seeking sources of new recruits have by necessity been driven towards those networks linking the wider community of Swansea evangelicals together, resulting in a high level of transfer growth but little or no recruitment from local unchurched communities. This competition has led to a significant disparity between membership (declining) and attendance (growing), reflecting the fact that a considerable proportion of evangelicals are now circulating through the various churches without stopping in any particular one for any great length of time. It is also worth noting that those evangelical churches experiencing marked growth are overwhelmingly of a world-accommodating nature and do not require their adherents to conform to those strict standards of behaviour that characterise world-rejecting groups. While this shift has not resulted in any significant recruitment among non-evangelicals it has proved attractive to evangelicals seeking a less sectarian mode of religious expression.

It is within the non-evangelical Free Church sector that decline is most marked. While Free Church congregations in the suburbs are in a better position relative to sister congregations in traditional working-class localities, all the indications are that they are beginning to experience the onset of those processes that will inevitably result in their eventual terminal decline. Located in areas with atomised populations and lacking effective links with their local communities or with a wider religious economy, these congregations, among which older people are over-represented, are insular in character and appear to lack the will or the resources for effective recruitment. It is this sector of the Welsh religious economy that most approximates traditional notions of Welsh religious and social identity and it is the change in fortunes among these churches and chapels which most poignantly exemplifies the radical transformations going on in Welsh religion at the national level.

Religion, Identity and Change

Historically, the Welsh people have had a close relationship with religion and a strong national identification with Protestant Nonconformity, which dominated Welsh society through a network of local chapels situated in the heart of homogenous communities. This collective identification with Nonconformity was essentially an identification of local communities with local churches and chapels. In the twentieth century, increasing social and geographical mobility led to the progressive erosion of a communitarian homogenous working-class culture and the undermining of the pattern of local social identification with local religious institutions. Consequently, traditional 'Welsh' expressions of religion are declining; nevertheless, the pattern of religion in Wales remains distinct from that of other modern societies. There is little evidence in Wales of a significant shift towards identification with sectarian forms of religion and this is reflected in the lower national profile of evangelical congregations relative to their counterparts elsewhere in Britain and northern Europe. The most striking transformation in Wales has been the way in which some religious groups traditionally perceived as on the margins of the religious economy, notably Anglicans and anglicised evangelicals, have increasingly filled the spaces vacated by traditional Welsh Nonconformity.

These changes have created the conditions for new forms of social and cultural identification with religion to emerge. Anglicanism constitutes one focus for identification, both as a national institution and, more crucially, as a parish-based presence within local communities. Nationally, the raised profile of Anglicanism has much to do with its ability (through its ubiquitous territorial organisation) to present itself as a 'major Welsh institution'. Locally, this network of highly visible places of worship with which people can identify themselves, combined with a centrally funded, parish-based ministry, ensures a continued local religious presence, improving the potential for increasing active membership, either through bringing inactive members into a more active role or through attracting new converts. Evangelicalism also constitutes a focus for identity, with evangelicals strongly identifying with the community of fellow evangelicals, but decreasingly identifying with local congregations and local communities and increasingly prone to regularly change their congregational allegiances. This represents a significant shift from the traditional sociality of Welsh religion and historic patterns of familial identification with individual places of worship. It also suggests that a movement that has historically been associated with the periodic religious revivals in Welsh society is progressively losing its 'Welsh' cultural character and identity.

Roman Catholicism, despite now being the second largest Welsh denomination, remains marginal in its impact on the non-Roman Catholic population. Essentially a pillarised institution, it remains the focus for a particular type of religio-ethnic identity that is to be found in those towns and cities of south and west Wales marked by historical Irish in-migration. Much the same can be said for non-Christian religious institutions catering for recent migrant groups although these are few in number and generally restricted to Wales's two cities.

The transformation of the religious sphere in Wales furnishes a particularly striking example of the type of decentring of culture associated with postmodernity and raises questions about the crucial role of local expressions of culture and sociability in identity formation. From the evidence presented, it is clear that the type of 'national' identification of populations with a particular form of religious belief and practice is only 'national' in the sense that it is the aggregate of countless local experiences. In the past, Wales was a society characterised by homogenous communities, demonstrating a high level of similarities with each other in their individual social, cultural and economic conditions. Within this particular social and cultural landscape a pattern of localised identification with localised religious institutions emerged that could with some confidence be described as 'national'. As heterogeneity has replaced homogeneity and communities have become increasingly internally fragmented and differentiated from each other, religion as the symbolic mirror of Welsh society has also been shattered. What remains is a fragmented sense of national identity and an uncertainty about what it is to be 'Welsh'. Elsewhere in Europe and globally, revitalised forms of civil religion have attached themselves to or have been co-opted by various types of nationalism. Unusually, for a country inhabited by a historically 'religion-shaped' people, nationalism in Wales has progressively broken its links with the religious sphere in favour of a pragmatic secular inclusivism which seeks to unite the disparate and multiple social and cultural identities which are emerging in Wales. Nevertheless, even if the close relationship between religion and national identity has been irrevocably broken, religious belief and practice, ranging from individual experiences to collective associations, still remains a key source of identity formation and maintenance for a significant minority of the Welsh population.

Bibliography

Bebbington, D.W. (1993), *Evangelicalism in Modern Britain*, 2nd edn, London: Routledge.

Beckford, J.A. (1989), *Religion and Advanced Industrial Society*, London: Routledge.

Bible Society (1997), *Challenge to Change: Results of the 1997 Welsh Churches Survey*, Swindon: Bible Society.

Bruce, S. (1995), *Religion in Modern Britain*, Oxford: Oxford University Press.

Carr, W. *et al.* (1992), *Say One for Me; The Church of England in the Next Decade*, London: SPCK.

Casanova, J. (1994), *Public Religions in the Modern World*, Chicago: Chicago University Press.

Chambers, P. (1997), ' "On or off the Bus": Identity, Belonging and Schism. A Case Study of a Neo-Pentecostal Housechurch', in S. Hunt, M. Hamilton and T. Walter (eds) *Charismatic Christianity: Sociological Perspectives*, Basingstoke: Macmillan, pp. 140–59.

Chambers, P. (1999), *Factors in Church Growth and Decline*, unpublished Ph.D. thesis, University of Wales.

Christian Research Association (1995), *UK Christian Handbook*, 1996/97 edn, London: Christian Research.

Davie, G. (1994), *Religion in Britain since 1945: Believing Without Belonging*, Oxford: Blackwell.

Davie, G. (2000), *Religion in Modern Europe: A Memory Mutates*, Oxford: Oxford University Press.

Dobbelaire, K. (1981), 'Secularization: A Multi-dimensional Concept', *Current Sociology*, **29**(2), 1–204.

Durkheim, E. (1995), *The Elementary Forms of Religious Life*, trans. K.E. Fields, New York: Free Press.

Esposito, J.L. and Watson, M. (eds) (2000), *Religion and Global Order*, Cardiff: University of Wales.

Featherstone, M. (1995), *Undoing Culture: Globalisation, Postmodernism and Identity*, London: Sage.

Fields, K.E. (1995), 'Translator's Introduction: Religion as an Eminently Social Thing', in E. Durkheim, *The Elementary Forms of Religious Life*, New York: Free Press, pp. xvii–lxxiii.

Fukuyama, F. (1995), *Trust: The Social Virtues and the Creation of Prosperity*, Harmondsworth: Penguin.

Hall, S. (1992), 'The Question of Cultural Identity', in S. Hall, D. Held and T. McGrew (eds) *Modernism and Its Futures*, Cambridge: Polity, pp. 273–326.

Harris, C. (1990), 'Religion', in R. Jenkins and A. Edwards (eds) *One Step Forward? South and West Wales Towards the Year 2000*, Llandysul: Gomer, pp. 49–59.

Harris, C. and Startup, R. (1999), *The Church in Wales: The Sociology of a Traditional Organization*, Cardiff: University of Wales Press.

Hervieu-Léger, D. (1994), 'Religion, Memory and Catholic Identity: Young People in France and the New Evangelisation of Europe', trans. R. Greaves, in J. Fulton and P. Gee (eds) *Religion in Contemporary Europe*, Lampeter: Edward Mellen, pp. 125–38.

Jenkins, P. (1992), *A History of Modern Wales*, London: Longman.

Lawrence, B. (1989), *Defenders of God: The Fundamentalist Revolt Against the Modern Age*, New York: Harper Row.

Martin, D.-C. (1995), 'The Choices of Identity', *Social Identities*, **1**(1), 5–20.

Robertson, R. (1992), *Globalization*, London: Sage.

Rosser, C. and Harris, C. (1965), *The Family and Social Change: A Study of Family and Kinship in a South Wales Town*, London: Routledge & Kegan Paul.

Sharpe, E. (1983), *Understanding Religion*, London: Duckworth.

Smith, D. (1999), *Wales: A Question for History*, Bridgend: Seren.

Stark, R. and Bainbridge, W.S. (1985), *The Future of Religion: Secularization, Revival and Cult Formation*, Berkeley: University of California Press.

Thomas, S. (2000), 'Religious Resurgence, Postmodernism and World Politics', in J.L. Esposito and M. Watson (eds), *Religion and Global Order*, Cardiff: University of Wales Press, pp. 38–65.

Thompson, A. (1999), 'Nation, Identity and Social Theory', in R. Fevre and A. Thompson (eds) *Nation, Identity and Social Theory: Perspectives from Wales*, Cardiff: University of Wales Press, pp. 233–49.

Williams, G.A. (1985), *When Was Wales?*, Harmondsworth: Penguin.

Wilson, B. (1966), *Religion in a Secular Society; A Sociological Comment*, London: Watts & Co.

CHAPTER 6

Unfinished Business – Devolving Scotland/Devolving Religion

Steve Sutcliffe

A multiplicity of groups within (and outwith) Scotland hold different views of the place, its canons, and its culture. So we have Catholic Scotland, which means not only those constituent individuals and areas of Scotland which might be identified as Catholic, but also the views of Scotland which the Catholic community holds, and which are likely, in some ways at least, to differ from those of Islamic Scotland or Protestant Scotland. So we have Gaelic Scotland, whose vision is constructed through and by the Gaelic language, we have Scots Scotland, Urdu-speaking Scotland, English-speaking Scotland. And there are Scotlands beyond our national boundaries, yet which construct their own Scotlands that in turn influence our state: the Scotlands of Japanese corporate investment, of the descendants of those cleared from the Highlands, the Scotlands of Australia and New Zealand. It is Scotlands which make Scotland for us.

(Crawford 1994:56)

For the late UK Labour Party leader John Smith (1938–94), the achievement of political devolution, or 'home rule', in Scotland was 'unfinished business' left over from the rancorous failure of the 1979 referendum, and this phrase of his entered folk vocabulary in the run-up to the new referendum on devolution in 1997. The complex political backdrop to the ensuing mobilisation of a yes/yes vote on, first, establishing a Scottish Parliament and, second, allotting it tax-raising powers, need not concern us here.[1] But the negotiation of religious, ethnic and civic identities in Scotland under its restored Parliament of 1999 cannot be divorced from a diffuse cultural nationalism that at all levels – intellectual, artistic, sport, media – and across a spectrum of strengths and voices, kept John Smith's 'unfinished business' on the road, from Edward Heath's 'Declaration of Perth' in 1968 to the Scotland Act 1998, to cite just the latest stages in a veteran campaign for some measure of 'home rule' within (or without) the UK.[2]

Indeed, is devolution the end? Or is it merely a staging-post to a final settlement, whether this be a federalist British state or an independent Scotland – and the 'break-up of Britain' (Nairn 1977)? Does devolution represent the settled will of 'the Scottish people'? And who exactly are 'they'? What constituencies have been written out of this collective subject which are, at a grassroots level, already staking out claims to a 'Scotland' of their own? In other words, to return to Robert Crawford's invocation of Bakhtinian heteroglossia: just how many 'Scotlands' are there? These are some of the questions that this chapter seeks to address through disaggregating culture and religion in contemporary Scotland and mapping out some new lines of inquiry into their cross-fertilisation in a devolved civic 'space'.

This 'space' in turn mediates the somewhat polarising global–local flow model posited by globalisation theory through drawing upon rich seams of cultural nationalism which, according to Harvie (1998:277) among others, functioned as a 'surrogate politics of Scottish institutions' in a 'polity without an omnicompetent legislature' from the union of English and Scottish parliaments in 1707 up to the devolved settlement of 1999. Most obviously these cultural resisters have taken the form of Scotland's distinctive ecclesiastical, educational and legal establishments but the popular culture of 'Scotland the brand' (McCrone *et al.* 1995) – from tartanry and 'kailyard' literature to the 'heritage' sites of Culloden and Bannockburn – has played a diffuse and underestimated role. From this perspective, the recovery of a partial legislature in 1999 might have been expected to trigger vigorous reassertions of national identity. And yet the sentence with which one prominent contemporary historian opens her post-devolution popular history – '"Scotland" exists – obviously' (Watson 2001:11) – is oddly diffident, the author's rhetorical insistence tempered by her simultaneous repudiation of an unambiguous, meta-narrated Scotland. Indeed, this sentence comes in a preface entitled 'The Trouble with "Scotland"', which evokes a poststructuralist identity constructed from 'an ever-increasing list of contested component parts' (ibid.) rather than a triumphalist assertion of a singular nationalism.[3] Nevertheless the simple fact of the continued assertion of a politically and culturally discrete Scottish identity – 'Scotland Is Different, OK?' (Dickson 1989) – in the face of the dedifferentiating economies of globalisation requires note in a volume about the British experience as a whole. In this context, in sharp contrast to the contemporary anxieties attending attempts to mobilise cultural identity within England, elite and popular cultures in Scotland manifest a range of acts of national self-identification, from the literary-cultural 'Scots renaissance' centred on Hugh MacDiarmid's modernist poem 'A Drunk Man Looks at the Thistle' (1926) to the wide adoption of the *Daily Record*'s car stickers in the mid-1990s which proclaimed 'I'm a real Scot from Falkirk' (or wherever).

These various questions can be reduced to this simple hypothesis: at the same time as institutionalising a viable political identity to mediate (at least in theory) the excesses of global–local culture flows, the establishment of a measure of political-civic autonomy for Scotland in 1999 will serve to exacerbate a process of ongoing cultural pluralisation *within* Scotland, including diversifying and deregulating the roles of those cultural institutions – not least the Church of Scotland within the realm of 'religion' – which previously functioned as definers and guardians of 'Scottishness' in the absence of a legislature before 1999. To test this hypothesis I will move progressively from macro-scale questions of the contemporary representation of collective identity to a micro-scale example of popular 'post-Presbyterian' practice. Hence I begin with institutionalised practices of cultural pluralism within Scottish politics, move on to a panorama of contemporary religious diversity, and conclude with a brief ethnography of firewalking as an example of a 'secular' or 'lay' spiritual practice which takes us beyond the historic 'Presbyterian paradigm' altogether – and perhaps gives a hint of more to come.

Devolving Culture

> The structures of coherence and hegemony devised by the English-speaking communities in Britain and North America, against which Scottish culture has in the past measured itself, are now fiercely questioned from within.
>
> (Editorial, *Scotlands*, **1**, 1994, n.p.)[4]

Devolution is an uncertain process in the sense that 'internally' it brings risk and insecurity to some social groups just as it increases others' cultural capital and social power, and 'externally' it introduces political liminality within a now-asymmetrical 'United' Kingdom in the comparative context of the Welsh and Northern Irish Assemblies and the persistent, if eroded, hegemony of Westminster. In this sense devolution does not resolve John Smith's 'unfinished business' but actually institutionalises it. On the one hand, the Scottish National Party's (SNP) commitment to a referendum on full independence, its consistent polling as second-place party north of the border throughout the 1990s, and a persistent current of nationalist sympathies within the Labour Party in Scotland mean that the devolved Parliament of 1999 may quite plausibly be interpreted not as the final word but as a new stake in a longer-term process of political negotiation on the future of Scotland and the modernisation of the UK as a whole. On the other hand, both the temporary home of the new Scottish Parliament (in late 2003 a new Parliament building is still under construction, at escalating cost) and the election, in November 2001, of the Parliament's third First Minister in two years[5] underscore an enduring uncertainty about the cohesion and direction of what Glaswegian comedian Billy Connolly has publicly mocked as 'a wee pretendy parliament'.[6] These political uncertainties apart, the Parliament's temporary location is symbolically significant, for it occupies the Church of Scotland's Assembly Hall beside New College, Edinburgh, the location of the church's annual general assembly which is the highest ecclesiastical forum of the Presbyterian church in Scotland. Furthermore, to access the chamber MSPs (Members of the Scottish Parliament) must pass a giant statue of John Knox in full preaching flow within the New College courtyard. Thus far, when the church assembly meets annually in May, the Parliament gives way, moving in 2000 to Glasgow, in 2001 to an Edinburgh conference venue, and in 2002 to Aberdeen. In addition to the absence of political 'closure', then, a complex intercourse between (new) civic power and (old) ecclesiastical platform has formalised – at least for the time being – a quasi-state settlement between 'established' church and civic government. Of course, it also raises the question of the place and function within civic society of 'other' identities in Scotland today, particularly the multiplicity of self-consciously 'religious' or 'spiritual' constituencies now seasoning the cultural landscape.

Engagement with the perennial issue of potentially divergent cultural-ethnic and civic identities which arises in this scenario is further complicated by the nationalist debate on securing and articulating Scottish identity within or without the UK. In SNP circles and elsewhere there has been some discussion of the parameters of an inclusive civic nationalism. Two small public bodies are interesting if restricted indices in this regard. 'New Scots' is a coalition made up of about 50 per cent English migrants with smaller proportions of Chinese and south Asians; its first convener was French and its current spokeswoman is a Londoner. It propagates Scottish independence and encourages international settlement in Scotland. New Scots emerged at the end of 1994 within the general orbit of the SNP, partly in direct opposition to the anti-English racism of a small but high-profile group called 'Settler Watch', which briefly in the early to mid-1990s publicly monitored house purchases by English incomers – so-called 'white settlers' – in rural Scotland, and partly to refute Unionist political slurs on the narrow, implicitly 'ethnic' – and hence racist – nature of Scottish nationalism. At its peak, around 1997–8, New Scots had a membership of around 500, but currently it lives largely through a core of activists.[7] In contrast, 'Asian Scots' reflects interests of South Asian groups in Scotland and has been active as an SNP member organisation since the 1990s. There are federated groups in the bigger cities – notably Glasgow, Edinburgh and Aberdeen – and membership is around 500 and growing. Different religious affiliations are represented among Asian Scots but Muslims predominate.[8]

In addition to these small but pioneering groups, a brief 'Time for Reflection' slot in the Scottish Parliament is an arresting if restricted example of the institutionalisation of a 'multifaith' politics of representation within the legislature itself. Each Wednesday afternoon as a preface to the parliamentary session, the chamber is addressed by a representative of a particular religious tradition or charity. Flicking more or less at random through records for 2000–1, we find Norman Shanks, leader of the ecumenical Iona Community (19 January 2000), Ian Baillie from the Royal National Mission to Deep Sea Fishermen (26 April 2000), S.L. Gajree, president of the Hindu Mandir (17 May 2000), Joseph Devine, Roman Catholic Bishop of Motherwell (25 October 2000) and Gelongma Lhamo, a nun from the Karma Kagyu Order, Samye Ling (21 March 2001): their addresses respectively included a Celtic blessing, a fisherman's folk prayer, an exposition from the *Upanisad*, the Lord's Prayer, and a *bodhisattva* vow. This institutionalisation of heteroglossia within Parliament has at least symbolic power, bolstered by ecumenist impulses among senior figures such as the long-standing patronage of the Samye Ling Tibetan Buddhist Centre in Dumfriesshire by the Parliament's inaugural Presiding Officer, former Liberal Party leader Sir David Steel (1938–). But the extent to which 'Time for Reflection' transcends tokenism to exert actual policy pressure remains an open question. Certainly when I attended the session in November 2001 the Presiding Officer's introduction of the speaker to the chamber was dignified but perfunctory, and the female Baptist lay member who on this occasion was addressing MSPs on the needs of asylum seekers in Glasgow was received by a chamber less than 20 per cent full (and which noticeably swelled by around half as much again once the 'real' business of the afternoon began). Nevertheless the careful management of policy presentation in contemporary politics – in the current vernacular, its 'spin-doctoring' – means that even 'gesture politics' are part of the spectrum of cultural representations and must be incorporated into analysis, no more so than in the avowedly 'new' Scotland.[9]

Restricted though these institutionalised examples of cultural pluralism may be, they are tangible evidence that, just as political sovereignty has been considerably devolved in Scotland, so have religious and cultural identities. The aforementioned examples are drawn from the Scottish Parliament and Scottish party politics, but there are also signs of an emergent cultural pluralism diffused across the community. Evidence of this is as yet small, both because the actual scale of change has not yet impacted quantitatively upon the graphs beloved of positivistically inclined social scientists and also because those who have heretofore concerned themselves specifically with religion in Scotland have largely been ecclesiastical historians and sociologists preoccupied with Catholic–Protestant sectarianism. The result is a marginalisation of the growth and impact of diaspora religions and new spiritualities which has the effect of confining the story of religion in Scotland to a chapter in the history of an implacable 'secularisation process' in western Europe rather than making it a case study in an emergent *post-* rather than *de-*Christianised culture that the fluid yet compact cultural geography of contemporary Scotland more interestingly represents. If we take this latter tack, we can engage in a pluralist debate on religious identity in Scotland without, crucially, losing historical awareness. Indeed, a genealogy of cultural – specifically, religious – plurality within modern Scotland actually gives us back an adequate history of our time and place. I propose the 'post-Christianisation' of Scotland in these terms, then, as a thoroughly historical trope for application at a panoramic level of cultural analysis. It periodises contemporary practice by locating diversity within the cultural conditions moulded by a particular social history, which in this case is one of a diffusive popular Christian culture which remained ascendant into the 1960s (Brown 2001). These diffuse Christian values must now, however, compete both with 'other' religious traditions and a more nebulous yet pervasive discourse of 'spirituality' in the culture at large. The latter owes as much to a 'New Age' idiom and popular values of 'personal development', health and well-being (Sutcliffe 2003) as it does to more traditional notions of Christian piety, self-sacrifice and intellectual struggle, and has been aptly termed 'humanistic expressivism' (Heelas 2000) or the 'turn to life' (Woodhead 2001). By analogy, the correlate to 'post-Christian' (in the wider culture) must be 'post-Presbyterian' (within Scotland's specifically Christian cultures). While these terms do indeed denote a rapidly hybridising culture in Scotland at the turn of the twenty-first century that is a long way in time and conception from the 'godly commonwealth' of John Knox, it is also a far cry from the historical and sociological extinction of discursive Christian culture and institutional participation respectively envisaged in Callum Brown's *The Death of Christian Britain* (2001) and Steve Bruce's *God Is Dead* (2002).

In short, I want to argue that a process of identity pluralisation has been shadowing the debate on, and delivery of, political devolution from Westminster to Holyrood. The process entails not so much the *de-*Christianisation as the *post-*Christianisation – that is to say the post-Presbyterianisation – of Scotland and our attention should shift correspondingly from theorisations of secularisation as a 'de-religioning' factor in the modern world to a revisionist theory of secularisation as the laicisation and domestication of religious discourse and action in the culture at large: literally, in 'profane' culture (Latin *pro*/before or outwith, *fanum*/temple). This relocates rather than erases religion: we look now for vibrant – if necessarily unstable – sites beyond the boundaries of those large social institutions (the churches) which have historically been treated as the hegemonic signifiers of 'religion'. In fact the more interesting story of 'secularisation' is less the social contraction of corporate religious structures than the appropriation of religion from the 'professionals' (literally, 'the religious' in the specialist sense of a professional class: priests, ministers, monks/nuns) by 'amateurs' (literally, lovers and enthusiasts, with connotations of 'untutored' or 'unofficial' hermeneutics and even a 'recreational' approach to practice). Accordingly our attention must refocus on the multiple popular religious discourses at work in the culture at large which have yet fully and securely to embed themselves in primary institutions and which may consequently lurk on the periphery of our gaze, mystified as this is by received wisdoms both theological and sociological as to the 'true' location and bounds of our subject. Innovation and risk are now the order of the day: just as the Scottish Parliament occupies a liminal space between outright independence and federalism within a UK state, so no one group commands sufficient support across the Scottish population to define a national religious identity. The religious identity of Scotland at the symbolic level, like the materialist polity, is unresolved, unfinished, and this situation is likely to dominate the immediate future: neither entirely 'lost' nor fully 'secured' by any one camp or coalition.[10]

Post-Presbyterian Trends

> The religiosity, the non-secularity, of [Scotland] is still detectable in its cultural air as the smell of the Atlantic and the North Sea can be sniffed in its winds ... Let me try to get over the point by repeating the story of the Scots scientist who was 'ranting and raving' against the 'Bishops in Presbytery' proposals. 'Why are *you* so worked up?' asked his friend. 'I thought you were an atheist?' 'So I am', replied the scientist, 'but I'm a *Presbyterian* atheist.'
>
> (Highet 1972:268)

In his analysis of Protestant responses to an increasingly vigorous and acculturating Catholicism in twentieth-century Scotland, Stewart Brown (2000:275–9) treats the election of the Irish Catholic scholar, James Mackey, to the Thomas Chalmers Chair of Divinity at New College, Edinburgh, in 1979 as a defining moment in the dethroning of Presbyterian ascendancy in the religious landscape of modern Scotland. Brown argues that this appointment to a professorial chair formerly occupied by the fiercely Reformed theologian Thomas Torrance, and indeed newly renamed after *the* radical figure (Thomas Chalmers) in the 1843 Disruption in the Protestant Church, symbolised the institutional legitimation in Scotland's Presbyterian redoubt of what was already ongoing in contemporary lay culture: namely, the emergence of a 'post-Presbyterian' Scotland, a Scotland 'beyond John Knox', to cite the phrase of the Church of Scotland's own parliamentary liaison officer (Blount 1999). That is, not a *non*-Presbyterian culture but one 'after' Presbyterian hegemony yet infused to a greater or lesser extent with Presbyterian values: in short, a civil culture in which presbyteries are but one forum within a spectrum of ecclesiastical structures and presbyters (elders) but one role model among a corresponding spectrum of laicised religious functionaries.

But the political symbolism of Mackey's appointment also needs to be located in an ongoing 'haemorrhage' of faith which, so Brown (2001) argues, has characterised Scottish Christianity since the early to mid-1960s. Based on an analysis of institutional measures, Brown (ibid.:188) finds that Sunday school enrolments had dropped to just 19 per cent of Scottish children by the early 1970s while only 17 per cent of baptised members of the Church of Scotland were being recruited into full adult membership by the mid-1990s. Working from opinion polls, Field (2001:169) has corroborated this 'haemorrhage thesis', finding that, while 87 per cent of one poll (n = 911, adults 18+) knew of American evangelist Billy Graham's 1991 Scottish tour, only 40 per cent held a favourable opinion of him, and just 8 per cent said they intended to hear him (in sharp contrast to Graham's 1955 Scottish crusade, when the total attendance figures at his meetings amounted to more than one-fifth of the entire Scottish population (Brown 2001:173). In another poll conducted in 2000 (n = 1027, adults 18+), a mere 1 per cent of Scottish adults cited Jesus Christ as the most inspirational influence in their lives (Field 2001:169). In other words, the secular agnosticism of dechurched and unchurched alike in Scotland would seem now to be little different from the rest of the UK and western Europe, and indeed on the basis of evidence from these countries Field (ibid.:168) finds that Scotland 'only manages to hover around the mean on most measures of belief and practice' and 'falls well and consistently below Catholic countries such as Ireland, Portugal and Spain'.

Cultural identity in terms of a corporate religious tradition now needs to be understood to be as much in decline in 'Presbyterian' Scotland as it is in 'C of E' England or 'Methodist' Wales, *pace* the 'Presbyterian atheist' joke recounted by Highet in the early 1970s (above). Historically observers have detected a political function of the Church of Scotland – particularly in its annual assemblies – in maintaining a sense of national unity in the absence of a legislature, a function that is read as cultural hegemony, parochial responsibility or radical social conscience, depending on emic convictions. But contemporary cultural change also makes plain that corporate religion is increasingly unable or unwilling to function in this role and that, at the point of delivery of increased political autonomy, the Church of Scotland is freed to relinquish its symbolic (and congregational) capital as guarantor of Scottish identity. In sociological terms this means it is becoming less of a 'national' church and more of a 'British' denomination. However, although at the conclusion of his narrative Stewart Brown is keen to stress not the collapse of Knox's 'Commonwealth of Faith' but the triumph, at least in intellectual and middlebrow cultures, of ecumenical Christianity in a 'pluralist' society (Brown 2000:281), the panorama of contemporary pluralist culture I attempt here must question the validity of positing a recognisably *Christian* discourse *at all* in broad swathes of the culture at large. Rather, the Christian communities, like other religions, must organise themselves as distinctive pockets, networks and resource nodes within a broader cultural pluralism. Certainly the argument advanced as recently as the early 1970s (Highet 1972) that Scotland, like Northern Ireland but in sharp contrast to England, was an exception to the trend of institutionally eroding and culturally pluralising processes characteristic of the modern world is no longer tenable. The available data show admittedly slightly higher, but still proportionately declining, indices of church affiliation across the Scottish population (Brierley and MacDonald 1995:112, 246). In turn this trend fits the thesis of 'cultural convergence' between Scotland and the rest of mainland Britain. According to this thesis – which is made in both strong and weak forms (Smout 1992) as well as denied categorically (Highet 1972; Dickson 1989) – despite the historical distinctiveness of Scottish institutions of law, education and ecclesiastical governance, despite the long tradition of a 'surrogate politics' enacted in and by elite artistic and intellectual cultures (Harvie 1998:277) and notwithstanding even the return of a legislature in 1999, the populistic and dedifferentiating Anglo-American cultural flows of the 'global' marketplace are eroding indigenous Scottish cultures. In these circumstances Highet's (1972:267) defiant claim at the beginning of the 1970s that 'Scotland's cultural atmosphere is still that of a religious – specifically of a largely Presbyterian – society' looks increasingly tendentious.

Nevertheless this thesis of (Anglo-American) cultural convergence must be nuanced by reference to pockets of 'post-Presbyterian' ethnological resistance. Scotland retains vigorous indigenous oral and material cultures and has speakers of both Gaelic and English as well as several Scots dialect forms.[11] Diverse traditions of folk music flourish, focusing on distinctively Scottish instruments and genres such as accordion, bagpipes, clarsach, fiddle, ballads (Scots 'muckle sangs') and 'mouth music' (Gaelic *port-a-beul*) (Duesenberry 2000), and fuelled by a significant – and ongoing – revival since the 1950s of indigenous music-making (Munro 1996). This had recently been renewed by the successes of the *feisean* ('festival') movement in local communities in the Highlands and Islands and, since 1988, of Edinburgh's Adult Learning Project Scots Music Group in traditional music teaching and learning. These and other 'traditional' forms cumulatively supply an ethnological platform of resistance to a perceived 'McDonaldization' of Scotland (Ritzer 1993) – a 'McScotland', if you like. Muslim communities in contemporary Scotland supply functionally similar if substantively quite different cultural and ethnological resistance to the popular market and resistance from these and other minority ethnic communities to the erosion of traditional cultural identities and values – including the possibility of joint mobilisation on selected moral issues with other such minorities – is likely to grow rather than diminish as the Parliament beds in.

A Conspectus of Contemporary Religious Plurality

> The spiritual commons has never been more diverse or capacious, more open to new fusions of faith and belief.
>
> (Editorial, *Sunday Herald* (Glasgow), 20 February 2000, p. 6)

As early as 1975 the directory *Alternative Scotland* was reporting 'a great upsurge of non-Christian religion' and 'an increasing number of groups interested in borrowing from any religion or none for the purpose of developing the potential of the individual' (Wright and Worsley 1975:114). By the early 1990s Drane (1993:57) reported that 'most unchurched people in Scotland today are more likely to construct their worldview from aspects of the New Age outlook than from elements of mainstream Christianity'. Yet the extensive historiography on 'religion'[12] in modern and contemporary Scotland has been overwhelmingly preoccupied with Christian denominations,[13] Christian innovations[14] and Christian sectarianism.[15] There has been remarkably little comparative analysis pertaining to wider religious and cultural plurality in Scotland. The Christian landscape has been dominated by two big issues, namely the effect on congregational culture of the so-called 'secularisation process', and a constructed Catholic/Protestant antisyzygy.

One consequence is that the extent of diversity even within Christianity has often failed to register. For example, Whaling (1999:18–21) points out to salutary effect that there are Presbyterian, Roman Catholic, Episcopal, Orthodox, Baptist, Methodist and Pentecostal expressions of Christian identity in Scotland and that these can in turn be differentiated according to internal ethnic-cultural tradition: Orthodox Christianity, for example, sub-divides into Greek, Bulgarian, Russian, Ukrainian, Syrian, Ancient, British, Celtic and Coptic branches in Scotland alone. With respect to occlusion of internal differentiation, 'Christianity' turns out to be as mischievous a collective subject as 'Scotland' itself.

If Christian diversity has been mimimised, still less has there been sustained engagement with 'other' religions in Scotland or with the various multicultural, postcolonial, and globalisation debates as these impact upon Scotland – and this despite a large Scottish stake in British colonialism and a considerable international diaspora of Scots.[16] For example, Muslims have been living in Scotland for at least 130 years, although one would scarcely credit this from the extant secondary sources; Joseph Salter, a Christian missionary, recorded in his *Missionary to Asiatics in England* [sic] (1873) that he had met Muslims in Aberdeen, Glasgow and Edinburgh as well as in other towns and cities in England (Wardak 2000:22). By the early 1880s there were small 'colonies' of Indians in Glasgow and Edinburgh, swelled by students at the prestigious Edinburgh medical school (ibid.:24). Following Indian independence in 1947, the population increased to around 4000 by 1960, 16 000 by 1970 and around 31 000 at the time of the 1991 census, of whom 21 000 were Pakistani Muslims largely based in three urban regions: Strathclyde (that is, greater Glasgow), Lothian (Edinburgh and environs) and Tayside (Dundee) (Maan 1992:162, 168; Wardak 2000:28, tables 2 and 3). At the time of writing the results of the 2001 census are being formulated, and these numbers will almost certainly have risen substantially. And yet this community is under-represented in primary Scottish institutions: it was unable to register a single 'Asian Scot' MSP in the elections to the new Parliament in 1999, and its one existing Muslim representative in the UK Parliament at Westminster, Mohammad Sarwar, MP (Labour, Glasgow Govan), was subject to some racist media and political treatment during the closely fought campaigns that gained him both his constituency nomination and his seat in the late 1990s.[17]

Similarly, Sikhs – of whom there are 1000 living in Edinburgh (Nye 1995:36ff.) – and the Chinese community – with over 10 000 members at the 1991 census (Wardak 2000:28) – are almost completely invisible in the scholarship on religion and culture in Scotland. Buddhism has also been ignored by scholars, despite its strong appeal to indigenous converts, as is attested by the presence of the Glasgow Buddhist Centre (run by the Friends of the Western Buddhist Order) in Sauchiehall Street, the heart of Glasgow, since 1973, and long-established Theravadan and Zen groups in Edinburgh. Most prominently, Tibetan Buddhists have been developing the Samye Ling centre in Dumfriesshire since 1967, where one of the largest Buddhist temples in Europe was unveiled in 1988. In 1993 Samye Ling was visited by the present Dalai Lama, Tenzin Gyatso (b. 1935), who also viewed its sister site, Holy Island, off Arran in the Firth of Clyde, where Buddhist retreat facilities and an inter-faith centre have been in the process of planning and construction since 1992.

Indeed, the Holy Island project is an interesting example of the recuperation of an established tradition by a migrant practice: in this case, the 'Buddhification' of a

Christian site, since Holy Island has a cave by tradition associated with a seventh-century Christian hermit saint, Molaise. Samye Ling has made reference to Molaise and his cave in the course of propagating a delicate discourse on inter-faith dialogue in the context of a new, gently hegemonic Buddhist narrative. More diffuse examples of the recuperation of 'tradition' concern the 'neo-paganisation' of ancient monuments such as the large stone formation at Callanish on the island of Lewis and the Kilmartin stone circles in Argyllshire, and the creation in the 1990s of a popular Beltane Fire Festival on Calton Hill at the east end of Edinburgh's famous Princes Street. Such activity is a sign of the increasingly confident public profile of this most theatrically 'deviant' of religious identities: the Pagan Federation has recently claimed up to 10 000 practising pagans in Scotland.[18]

But such a claim only exemplifies the contemporary confidence and vitality of 'heteroprax' popular religiosity in Scotland. At a corporate level alone, Whaling (1999:22–3) lists a 'delicious chaos' of nearly 40 new religions active in Scotland in recent decades. This field, too, has been virtually ignored despite the Scottish origins of several important 'alternative' currents.[19] These include the Camphill Village movement for the care of disabled adults, linked to Rudolf Steiner's Anthroposophical movement, which began life outside Aberdeen in the 1930s; the prominent British career of the Spiritualist medium Helen Duncan (1898–1956), born in Callander near Stirling, which was instrumental in the rescinding of the Witchcraft Act (1736) in 1951 (thus legalising Gerald Gardner's new cult of Wicca); and the internationally renowned 'New Age' colony at Findhorn, established in 1962. Epitomising the dissemination of a pragmatic, populist Anglo-American culture against the grain of Presbyterian rectitude, a thriving grassroots culture of alternative and holistic healing grew up in the 1980s and 1990s, from Highland networks (Forsyth 1995) to centres, fairs and workshops scattered across central Scotland, including one of the longest-running holistic health ventures in the UK, the Westbank Centre in rural Fife (established 1959). There is also a renewed interest in folklore as a recreational and educational resource which can be mapped in a wide range of outlets including museums, tourist attractions and the popular arts. Among museums we can mention two projects from the 1990s: the St Mungo Museum of Religious Life and Art in Glasgow, established in 1993, and the Carfin Pilgrimage Centre in Lanarkshire, a small Catholic exhibition on pilgrimage in a variety of religious cultures, set up in 1996. These are, to my knowledge, unique UK curatorial projects, but they have received minimal academic attention.[20] The Breadalbane Folklore Centre at Killin should also be mentioned: it has the added interest of holding a collection of healing stones associated by tradition with a seventh-century Christian saint, Fillan, which are occasionally handled in healing rituals by visitors and some locals. Tourist attractions include 'Highland Mysteryworld' at Glencoe, where visitors are enjoined to 'discover the myths, learn the legends and sense the superstitions in a magical world of the Ancient Highlands' (leaflet). Arts projects include a large music event, 'The Seer Festival', in the Black Isle in September 2001, celebrating Coinneach Odhar, better known as the Brahan Seer, who was a prominent exponent of 'second sight' visions and premonitions (Gaelic *an da shealladh*, literally 'two sights').[21] Finally such subjects as the 'monster' of Loch Ness (Holiday 1968), the ghostly 'big grey man' of Ben MacDhui (Gray 1994), UFO activity in central belt 'hot spots' (Halliday 1998) and the esoteric Templar mysteries of Rosslyn chapel (Wallace-Murphy and Hopkins 2000) all attract a loyal following among *cognoscenti* as well as supplying spiritual exotica for UK popular culture magazines like *Bizarre* and *Fortean Times: The Journal of Strange Phenomena*.

'Mind, Body and Spirit': Culture in Scotland

> There are many younger generations in Scotland who are already involved in a diffuse search for some kind of spiritual identity. Whether it's bookstore shelves groaning with volumes devoted to 'mind, body and spirit', or lifestyle sections of newspapers proposing all manner of therapies and self-actualisations, the popular appetite for some element of the non-material in the midst of our materialist lives is undeniable.
>
> (Editorial, *Sunday Herald*, 20 February 2000, p. 6)

This brisk editorial could be replicated in a variety of other sources, not least in a report by the Church of Scotland's Board of Social Responsibility (1993:44) which described in the early 1990s 'the active promotion of New Age ideas and practices in Scotland', citing 'well organised and business-like communities' supplying 'courses and literature dealing with astrology, alchemy, the occult, tarot, aromatherapy, I Ching, reflexology, the paranormal and reincarnation'. These diffusive kinds of secular spirituality – secular in the important sense of being laicised and domesticated rather than 'irreligious' practices – can no longer be ascribed solely to 'deviant' sub-cultures and enclaves or confined to a sequestered 'private' sphere. In line with established practice elsewhere (Puttick 2000), many Scottish businesses from small entrepreneurs to major companies are now exploring the benefits for morale (and, of course, productivity) of techniques to enhance 'spiritual well-being'. For example, to mark the third birthday of the bank First Direct, staff at its Hamilton headquarters were offered 'reflexology, Indian head massage, yoga, facials and positive imaging seminars'.[22] Elsewhere, spirituality has an established business profile, from the Edinburgh 'New Age' bookshop 'Body and Soul' (established 1988) to small businesses like 'Celtic Trails Scotland' which offers residential courses 'exploring Scotland's spiritual landscape'.

The following brief ethnography of firewalking does not purport to encapsulate a 'new Scottish religiosity' but it does illustrate the kinds of post-Presbyterian vernacular motifs, values and practices now at work in the majority ethnic culture. This kind of 'alternative spirituality' (Sutcliffe and Bowman 2000) has come to the fore in Scotland as elsewhere in the UK especially since the 1960s, marked by pragmatic and egalitarian Anglo-American values. It can be theorised as a 'grafting' of religion from primary to secondary institutions – particularly to biographies (Sutcliffe 2000b) and small groups (Heelas and Woodhead 2001) – which bolsters the popular appeal and accessibility of religion as a 'cultural resource' (Beckford 1989:170) while suggesting uncertain medium- to long-term structural impact. The functional porosity of boundaries demarcating firewalking (say) from cognate spiritualities has generated a populist discourse fusing motifs and tropes of 'spirituality' and 'healing' which finds peripatetic institutional representation – at 'Celticised' Christian sites (such as Iona), the Samye Ling Tibetan Buddhist Centre, the Findhorn Community and Edinburgh's Salisbury Centre (established 1973), to name a few. These and other organisations have in turn become new resources for the customisation and propagation of lay or secular spiritual hybrids, of which firewalking is as good an example as any.[23]

Firewalking in Fife

> To walk unharmed over incandescent coals is to take a step into a different and somehow magical world where all things become possible, where we begin to see clearly that all limits are self-imposed and ultimately illusory.
>
> (Shango 1996:12)

The ritual of the firewalk enjoyed considerable popularity in Anglo-American culture in the 1990s. In its contemporary popular cultural format – that is, largely isolated from an indigenous context and packaged as a 'workshop' – firewalking dramatises a blend of positive thinking, emotional well-being and spiritual self-empowerment. Early in 1996 I received a poster headed 'Firewalking: A Sacred Ritual of Personal Empowerment' from the Westbank Natural Health Centre in rural Fife. It contained the following invitation:

> Firewalking is an ancient practice intended to empower and heal. Walking barefoot over hot coals burning at over 1200 degrees Fahrenheit seems impossible, yet over half a million Americans and many in the UK have done it. How many other things in your life seem impossible?

I telephoned Westbank for further information. 'How long does the firewalk last?' I ask. 'Well, once we're into sacred time it's difficult to say,' says the firewalk tutor, Hazel. 'Wait until you're standing in front of the coals before you decide whether or not to walk,' she says, 'but I promise you, the workshop will impact on the whole of your life.'

Snow was lying as I drove to the firewalk on a grey winter Sunday. The Westbank Centre – a family home and cluster of outbuildings with a worn and rambling appearance – stands behind the village of Strathmiglo. About 30 people had gathered in a large rectangular room, with french windows leading out onto a small garden. Chairs stood in rows facing a flipchart. Apart from two boys, all looked over 30, with a scattering of older people. Women were slightly in the majority, and with two exceptions we belonged to the ('white') majority ethnic group in Scotland.

Hazel, our firewalk instructor, appeared. An American woman in her late thirties, she had long, straight hair, and wore a full skirt with bands of primary colour, a turquoise blouse and a 'devil's eye' pendant. She flipped over the top page on her chart. This read:

1 Whoever shows up are exactly the right people
2 Whenever it begins is always the right time
3 Whatever we co-create here together is the only thing that can possibly happen
4 When it's over it's over.

Firewalking, Hazel announced, was about breaking down limiting 'cages' of belief. 'Let's break the ice a bit', she said, sizing us up. 'Do you know this one?' She began to sing: 'If you're happy and you know it, clap your hands.' 'Come on!' she called out. Soon we were all singing, clapping and stamping feet. 'Okay,' Hazel said, 'that's good, we're getting some energy moving.' Now she spoke of her teacher, Tolly Burkan, the 'father of the firewalking movement' in the US (Danforth 1989). Burkan, she said, stressed the significance of intentionality: that the true basis of healing and growth lies in *how* we do what we do, not necessarily in *what* is done. 'Fire burns, *or* fire heals,' Hazel said. The difference lay in our intention or faith: 'Flesh cannot firewalk, but Spirit can, moving *through* the flesh.'

She showed us slides of her visits to native firewalkers in Hawaii and Sri Lanka. Originally the preserve of 'mystics and shamans', she said, firewalking was opening up to everyone 'through the shift in consciousness I think we're all aware of'. But first we needed to face our fears – including public speaking. 'So I want you to tell us all why you're here tonight!' she announced. Dutifully we stood up around the room to introduce ourselves. Brief confessions quickly became the norm: 'I've *always* wanted to walk on fire,' said one. 'I want to walk on fire because I'm scared of being myself,' said another. 'I've done it three times already, but I'm already trembling at the thought of walking again.' 'I got lost coming here tonight, and I think that says something about my life.' After each introduction, the rest of us applauded vigorously.

Now it was time to build the fire. Silently we filed out to the small garden where turf had been removed to form a shallow rectangular trench about 1.5 by 3 metres. Hazel began to shake a rattle to consecrate the space, making slow, swooping movements around the trench. We built up a square stack of logs in the middle and then formed a circle round the trench, holding hands in the twilight, some of us skipping up and down against the cold. Then Hazel's helper doused the stack with vegetable oil and she lit it. She moved gracefully around our circle, blessing each person's 'aura' and giving us herbs – a twist of sweet grass 'for sweetness', a pinch of sage 'for purification'. Flames took hold of the stack; smoke billowed out and up. Hazel blessed the fire and thanked the earthworms for giving up their lives for our spiritual development.

We went back inside to wait for the fire to burn down. The mood was now restrained and expectant. Hazel unveiled this acronym on her flipchart:

F alse
E vidence
A ppearing
R eal

'That's what it is', she said, and told the tale of the man who, primed with warnings against poisonous snakes, mistook a coil of rope for a cobra. So, if we *think* the fire will burn us, it will – but its heat is 'false evidence' that can't fool an 'awakened spirit'. A moral fable followed about life's purpose. Three men are hitting rocks with a sledgehammer (Hazel acted this out with relish). The first is in a chaingang: he cries, 'I'm breakin' rocks in the hot sun!' The second is a breadwinner: he cries, 'I'm workin' to feed my family!' But the third says quietly: 'I'm breaking rocks to build a cathedral to the glory of God.' My neighbour caught my eye and nodded approvingly.

But how will we know it's right for us to walk the fire, Hazel asked. The secret was that our 'Higher Self' or 'inner voice' would know. We needed to get 'in touch' with this source of spiritual wisdom by listening quietly and trusting our guidance. The catch was that this voice lives only in the present moment and is infallible only then. A minute too early or late will not work: conditions will have changed. The inner voice had to be heeded *now*.

As we digested this Hazel called us to our feet again. 'It's time to dance!' she said. 'Find a partner!' We formed a circle again, and she taught us a simple dance in a folk style. We had to sing the following words as we danced and we were to look each other directly but softly in the eye as we did so:

> Maybe this is the healing, that we share this feeling
> and find a compassionate love,
> flowing from my heart to yours, flowing from my heart to yours.

As we sang the first line, we faced our partner and spread our arms out and down to bless each other's aura. To the second line, we crossed hands on our chests, still facing each other. To the third, we placed one hand on our partner's chest, just over the 'heart centre' or 'chakra', and then moved on to a new partner. It required considerable concentration to execute these moves and I found it a little unnerving to look directly into so many strangers' eyes. When we finished, Hazel asked us to stand quietly for a few minutes in order to experience the 'energy' now present in the room.

Suddenly her helper entered the room: 'The fire is ready!' he announced dramatically. 'Let's go!' called Hazel. 'Remember, bliss is on the other side of that fire!' Outside, the village street lights glowed down the short rise. The stack of logs had burnt down into a heap of glowing charcoal. We stood in a circle and held hands while Hazel raked it out over the bed of the trench. Then a few logs were scattered along one side: these gradually flamed up. We took off our shoes and stood barefoot. Hazel shouted: 'The Fire is now open!' and began a chant, with no explanation of the words. We took it up, clapping hands and stamping feet. After a hiatus, the first person – a man – came to the top of the trench, paused, then briskly crossed the coals to a great cry of excitement. The way was opened up. A trickle followed, soon becoming a busy procession: people would move to the head of the jostling circle and cross the trench to whoops, applause, continual chanting and clapping. Some walked quickly or half-ran, and were caught by helping hands on the other side; others walked more slowly or lightly; a few danced across or stepped deliberately as if to test the heat. I went across twice, in four or five longish steps. The bed of charcoal felt crunchy underfoot, like warm cornflakes. My feet were already cold from the ground, so it was difficult to gauge the heat, but I didn't linger.

Finally Hazel cried, 'Last call!' A camera flashed several times, freezing phantom figures on the coals. She motioned us to stop chanting, and said solemnly: 'I invite anyone who chooses to walk the fire in silence. Say your intention before walking, and we will say it back to you.' A few did so, calling out words like 'love', 'healing', and 'transformation'. We stood in silence, watching the coals glow. An hour had passed: it was becoming very cold. On the way in we washed each other's feet in bowls of warm water. Inside people sat with cups of tea and biscuits. The final ritual was to compose a letter to ourselves that Westbank would post on in a year's time as a delayed fruit of the event. 'Write what you like,' said Hazel, 'but remind yourselves of what you did here tonight. Feel your own power!'

To Be Continued

> One day one of my children was asked, 'What are you?' He replied, 'I really don't know. My mother is French, my father is Scottish and we are Jewish.'
> (Testimony in St Mungo Museum of Religious Life and Art, cited in Sutcliffe 1994)

In simple terms, my argument in this chapter has been that the historical diversity of religion in modern Scotland has been severely underplayed, and that the recent popularisation in lay, secular culture of previously counter-cultural values and practices – sampled in the firewalk – must be theorised against a recovered history of at least moderate religious plurality and innovation. The deregulation and proliferation of religious practice in Scotland has been further encouraged in the second half of the twentieth century, and since the 1960s in particular, by the severe decline in traditional religious adherence and the qualitative dilution of Presbyterian discourse comprehensively mapped by Brown (1997, 2001) and Field (2001). I began to uncover this process of pluralisation at the beginning of the chapter by examining the 'big picture' of cultural identity and representation within contemporary Scottish politics. In particular we saw how certain empirically restricted but ideologically potent practices pertaining to cultural-religious identity formation had become institutionalised in and on the fringes of the post-1999 Parliament in the shape of the regular 'Time for Reflection' slot and in pressure groups like New Scots and Asian Scots. I then provided a panoramic snapshot of religious plurality in modern Scotland before ending with a grassroots case study in popular post-Presbyterian practice. The account of firewalking that you have just read demonstrated some important characteristics of contemporary majority ethnic religion. Chief among these are Anglo-American popular values: the firewalking 'workshop' is an American innovation, the chief trainers and practitioners are American, and the informing methodology clearly draws upon pragmatic, egalitarian and idealistic, even utopian, principles that are well represented in American praxis both popular (the 'New Thought' movement and exponents of 'positive thinking') and academic (James's pragmatism and Dewey's instrument-alism). But the firewalk itself is also an example of a broader appropriation and reconstruction of 'indigenous' ritual (Johnson 1995) in Scotland 'after' Presbyterianism, which includes aspects of counter-cultural pagan practice (at neolithic sites) as well as the articulation of a popular 'Celtic' identity spanning the Atlantic seabord. We should also note the relocation of practice firmly beyond traditional ecclesiastical boundaries, 'sacrality' becoming in the process a fluid, unstable property assigned to objects, acts and values in the demotic arena of everyday life.

Throughout the chapter I have stressed the function of the national-cultural discursive space of Scotland – in the singular or in the plural, with or without inverted commas – as a collective act of mediation between the reductive polarities of locality and globality, or 'glocalization' in Robertson's (1995) apt but ugly phrase. That is, in Scotland at least, there is no royal road from the global to the local: the tenacity of distinctive Scottish identities from 1707 to 1999, the ability among the population at large to put multiple cultural identities to work (Scottish/ British, Muslim/Scottish/British), and now a devolved Parliament – the most powerful legislative mechanism in the UK after Westminster – function to qualify and regulate at least partially the global flows of international capital and Anglo-American culture in what was once quaintly named 'north Britain'.

In any case, my ethnographic snapshot of firewalking shows that, statistical 'haemorrhage of faith' notwithstanding (Brown 2001; Field 2001), the ritual practice of 'religion' in Scotland manifestly continues, under different rubrics, in unexpected places and in 'other' communities. When we start systematically to look elsewhere for 'religion' rather than in the familiar haunts of churches, mosques and 'new religious movements', we find modest but vigorous cultures of discourse and practice stretching from varieties of Islam to Celtic Christian traditions to Mind Body Spirit groups, rich in subjectivities and firmly wedded to qualitative rather than quantitative theories of practice. In this, Scotland is surely a microcosm of the British and European experience as a whole: there are few neat patterns to be discerned, mainly a heterogeneous, contestatory, self-regulating field of human practice. New cultural institutions of spiritual biography, dyadic confession and group encounter – as my ethnography in part demonstrates – are now significant strategies in the majority ethnic culture whereby religion is in the process of (re)construction. These strategies are in turn highly 'secularised' in the sense of representing a laicised practice rooted in an amateurist ethos of self-education, emotional expressivity and moral improvement. Secularised rituals such as firewalking represent the mutation of previously counter-cultural practices into popular hybrids of 'alternative' spirituality (York 2000) and 'personal development' (Puttick 2000). The example here is firewalking, but I might just as easily have chosen 'Celtic' shamanism or pagan pilgrimage, or approached the issue via the diffusion of a humanistic and psychologistic discourse in popular media and culture (Heelas 2000). Accusations of soteriological frippery or social irrelevance on the part of firewalkers and other 'seekers' (Beck 2000; Sutcliffe 2000b) frequenting the contemporary 'spiritual marketplace' (Roof 1999) – such as Wilson's (1976:97) famous dismissal of the 'highly privatized preference that reduces religion to the significance of pushpin, poetry or popcorn' – miss the opportunity to isolate and theorise a new social-psychological functionality in religion. By this I mean that previously latent or implicit functions of religious practice in constructing biographies and collective cultural identities are replacing claims to historical uniqueness and truth centre stage in public discourse on 'religion'. In my ethnography such functional praxis is primarily bound up with legitimating a post-Presbyterian culture of secularised piety and emotional expressivity on the part of the dominant ethnic group in Scotland, but it may also take the form of political representation, particularly among minority ethnic groups, such as the calls for public respect and protection made by Muslim leaders in Scotland following the bombing of the World Trade Center in New York in September 2001 and a corresponding rise in expressions of 'Islamophobia' in Scotland (which included the firebombing of a mosque in Edinburgh in October 2001). Rarer instances of counter-cultural political representation include McIntosh (1998), composed at the self-styled 'Pollok Free State' encampment against the M77 motorway development outside Glasgow in the mid-1990s: his text splices biblical, pagan and literary sources in an eclectic poetic fusion that is presented less as authored composition than a collective narration of eco-protest (ibid.:202). In all these cases the more or less explicit social-psychological functionality of 'religion' bolsters Beckford's seminal argument on its utilisation as a cultural resource in modern societies (Beckford 1989:170–1). The full implication of this argument, of course, is that 'culture' rather than 'religion' is now in the driving seat: religious practices of all kinds are effectively recast as a sub-category of cultural politics. And on the preliminary evidence of multicultural practice in and on the fringes of the devolved Parliament, the 'return of Scotland' – in Nairn's (2000) pungent rhetoric – will only exacerbate this process north of the border.

A final, reflexive, consideration is this. The compact demography of Scotland means that theory can less easily be divorced from practice in public life; or cannot, at least, risk *being seen to be so*. Whichever genealogy of religion, culture or ethnicity we trace in Scotland, we end up in a small but multivocal territory that is as much an empirical locality as a postmodernised 'imagined community' (Anderson 1991), one that cannot but mediate, at least partially, local–global culture flows. So whether we who are politically enfranchised interpret post-devolution Scotland as a 'diverse assembly'[24] or, more cynically, as a 'wee pretendy Parliament' (Billy Connolly) drives home the reflexive implications of this unfinished business.

Acknowledgements

I am very grateful to Callum Brown, Malory Nye and the present editors for their critical comments on an earlier draft of this chapter.

Notes

1 The Campaign for a Scottish Assembly's (1988) *A Claim of Right for Scotland* is a seminal document formulated by an exclusively Labour/Liberal Democrat campaigning group following the withdrawal of the SNP, Conservatives and Scottish Green Party. Mitchell (1996) is a valuable historical survey of twentieth-century 'home rule' projects. See Lynch (2001) on the workings of the new devolved parliament.

2 The selected sources in Paterson (1998) document the devolution debate since the late 1960s. For good examples of the historiography of cultural and political nationalism in Scotland, see Marr (1992), Finlay (1998), Nairn (2000), McCrone (2001[1992]) and – in a comparative context – Lynch (1996) and Keating (1996).

3 Watson's book followed her role as presenter of a similarly tentatively entitled BBC television series, *In Search of Scotland*, in 2000.

4 Five volumes of the literary theory/cultural studies journal *Scotlands* were published between 1994 and 1998 by Edinburgh University Press.

5 Jack McConnell succeeded Henry McLeish, who resigned after a year in office following financial irregularities at his constituency office in Fife. McLeish himself had been unexpectedly promoted to the post following the sudden death of the inaugural First Minister, Donald Dewar.

6 Connolly's aside to the media has been widely reproduced – see the *Guardian*, 'Special Report: Devolution in Scotland' (5 September 2000; accessed at www.guardian.co.uk/Scotland/Story/): 'If there is any feeling at all for the parliament on the streets, it is the one neatly summarised by Billy Connolly who calls it "a wee pretendy parliament".'

7 Information on 'New Scots' from Dot Jessiman, telephone conversation, November 2001.

8 Information on 'Asian Scots' from Glasgow representative Bashir Ahmad, telephone conversation, November 2001. I am grateful to Mhairi Hunter of the SNP for providing these contacts.

9 Verbatim copies of the addresses are available in the official reports of parliamentary business published by the Stationery Office, Edinburgh. I am currently researching the history of 'Time for Reflection', including analysis of content, performance and audience reception.

10 There are pragmatic polity implications involved in failing to come to terms with the pluralising profile of contemporary Scotland where – in contrast to England and Wales – the population has been declining slowly but surely since the 1971 census (Kenefick 1998:98). At current rates it is projected to drop below 5 million by 2025. Although a falling birth rate is the largest contributory factor, at least one political commentator has recently questioned the absence of policy to attract skilled asylum seekers and other economic migrants to settle in Scotland (A. Young, 'A Vibrant Economy Needs its People too', *Sunday Herald*, 18 November 2001, p. 3, and 'Scottish Population Predicted to Fall Below 5 million', *The Herald*, 16 November 2001, p. 13).

11 See the 13-volume series 'Scottish Life and Society: A Compendium of Scottish Ethnology' in preparation under the auspices of the European Ethnological Research Centre, Edinburgh (Storrier and Kemp 2000).

12 There is a considerable literature on operationalising the polyvalent category 'religion' in a cross-cultural context. It is part of the argument of this chapter that we cannot get to grips with contemporary cultural debates in Scotland (as elsewhere) without, first, revisiting the conceptual confusions and political tensions attendant upon the coexistence of different folk and academic models of 'religion', and, second, understanding the dynamic function played by these unresolved *and necessarily unresolvable* ambiguities and disjunctions in bolstering religion's cultural capital – that is, its potency as a 'cultural resource' (Beckford 1989:170–1). For incisive examples of scholarship on the politics of defining religion, see McCutcheon (1997), Smith (1998) and Fitzgerald (2000).

13 See for example Highet (1960), Brierley and MacDonald (1995), Bissett (1989), Maver (1996), Walker (1996), Brown (1998) and Brown (2000). The classic monograph on the history of religion in Scotland is Brown (second, revised edition, 1997[1987]), but this unfortunately – and, given the opportunity for a second edition, puzzlingly – contains only a few passing references to non-Christian religion(s).

14 See, for example, Monteith (1997, 2000) on the ecumenical Iona Community and Meek (2000) on different aspects of the revival/creation of 'Celtic' Christianity.

15 From a wide literature see Bruce (1985), Gallagher (1987), Bradley (1995), Boyle and Lynch (1998) and the recent attack on anti-Catholicism by Macmillan (2000).

16 As with religious practice, a diffuse ethnic-cultural heterogeneity pulses beneath the surface of traditional representations of 'Scotland', making Crawford's invocation of Bahktinian heteroglossia appropriate beyond mere literary theory. On the history of south Asian settlement in Scotland, see Dunlop and Miles (1990) and Maan (1992). Edensor and Kelly (1989) and Kay (1996) sample oral history across a variety of ethnic backgrounds. 'Multicultural' debates surface in Wishart and St. Clair (1984) on Edinburgh cultural politics, Miles and Dunlop (1987) on racism in Scotland, Nye (1993, 1995) on Hindus in Edinburgh, Whaling (1999:32–5) on the inter-faith movement, Ziarski-Kernberg (2000) on the history and demography of the postwar Polish community, Audrey (2000) on comparative social policy issues concerning Irish, Jewish, Italian and Pakistani communities in Glasgow and Wardak's (2000) study of constructions of social control and deviance by Edinburgh

Pakistanis. A more occluded 'multicultural' issue concerns the ambiguous relationship of 'native' Scots at several levels of discourse with their 'auld enemy', England. This can be mapped both in the elite debate about the anglicisation of Scotland's 'democratic intellect' (Davie 1986;Walker 1994) and in populist tensions between 'native' Scots and English 'incomers' in some plebeian and rural cultures (see Jedrej and Nuttall 1996 for a rare treatment). Given the rise in postwar English migration into Scotland – from 4.5 per cent of the total population in the 1951 census to 7 per cent in 1991 (Kenefick 1998:115) and 8 per cent in the 2001 census results – this is one elided 'minority ethnic' history in urgent need of recovery.

17 There is now a Centre for the Study of Islam and Muslims in Scotland within the Al-Maktoum Institute for Arabic and Islamic Studies at the University of Abertay in Dundee.

18 There is a joint Scotland–Ireland branch of the UK-wide Pagan Federation (established 1971) currently based in Fife. The flagship UK pagan magazine *Pagan Dawn* (no.139, Beltane 2001) lists regular Scottish 'moots' (open gatherings, usually in public houses) in Aberdeen, Ayr, Edinburgh, Galashiels, Glasgow, Perth, Prestwick, St Andrews, Stirling and Stranraer. A Pagan Federation spokesman claimed a total of between 4000 and 10 000 full members and Scottish-based subscribers to the Pagan Federation's London-produced magazine *Pagan Dawn* ('Enjoying a Spell of Growth', *The Herald* 12 July 1999, p. 15). The split figure reflects the fact that one can subscribe to *Pagan Dawn* without becoming a full member, although full members also receive it. These figures look highly inflated compared to the total UK subscriptions to *Pagan Dawn* which in 1997 were running at around 4 000 in total (Pengelly *et al.* 1997:50).

19 But see Wright and Worsley (1975) and Fleming and Loose (1992) on 'alternative' and 'holistic' Scotland respectively, and Sutcliffe (1995, 2000a, 2003) on Findhorn, holistic healing networks and other 'New Age' centres and sites.

20 On the St Mungo museum (Glasgow Museums 1993) – which Paine (1998:xvi) says is one of only six comparable projects worldwide – see Sutcliffe (1994), Lovelace *et al.* (1995) and Michel (1999). I am grateful to Dr Malcolm Brown for drawing my attention to the last item.

21 Leaflets in my collection; on second sight, see Cohn (1999).

22 'The Reflexology Way to Keep that Workplace Stress at Bay', *Sunday Herald*, 13 May 2001, business section, p. 26.

23 An expanded version of the following ethnography can be found in Sutcliffe (2003:188–194). Pseudonyms are used throughout except for the venue. I am grateful to Routledge for permission to reproduce material from the passage in question.

24 The phrase is from Robert Crawford's poem 'A Scottish Assembly' borrowed for the title of Paterson (1998).

Bibliography

Anderson, B. (1991), *Imagined Communities: Reflections on the Origin and Spread of Nationalism*, New York: Verso.

Beck, U. (2000), 'Living Your Own Life in a Runaway World: Individualisation, Globalisation and Politics', in W. Hutton and A. Giddens (eds) *On the Edge: Living With Global Capitalism*, London: Jonathan Cape, pp. 164–74.

Beckford, J. (1989), *Religion in Advanced Industrial Society*, London: Unwin Hyman.

Bissett, P. (1989), 'Kirk and Society in Modern Scotland', in P. Badham (ed.) *Religion, State and Society in Modern Britain*, New York and Lampeter: Edwin Mellen, pp. 51–66.

Blount, G. (1999), 'Beyond John Knox: Churches and the Scottish Parliament', in *Soundings II: Proceedings of a Day Conference for the Methodist Church in Scotland*, Edinburgh: Heriot-Watt University, pp. 7–9.

Boyle, R. and Lynch, P. (eds) (1998), *Out of the Ghetto? The Catholic Community in Modern Scotland*, Edinburgh: John Donald.

Bradley, J. (1995), *Ethnic and Religious Identity in Modern Scotland*: *Culture, Politics and Football*, Aldershot: Ashgate.

Brierley, P. and MacDonald, F. (1995), *Prospects for Scotland 2000: Trends and Tables from the 1994 Scottish Church Census*, Edinburgh and London: National Bible Society of Scotland/Christian Research.

Brown, C. (1997 [1987]), *Religion and Society in Scotland since 1707*, Edinburgh: Edinburgh University Press.

Brown, C. (1998), 'Religion', in A. Cooke *et al.* (eds) *Modern Scottish History 1707 to the Present*, Vol. 2 *The Modernization of Scotland, 1850 to the Present*, East Linton: Tuckwell Press/Open University in Scotland/University of Dundee, pp. 142–60.

Brown, C. (2001), *The Death of Christian Britain: Understanding Secularization 1800–2000*, London: Routledge.

Brown, S. (2000), 'Presbyterians and Catholics in Twentieth-Century Scotland', in S. Brown and G. Newlands (eds) *Scottish Christianity in the Modern World*, Edinburgh: T. & T. Clark, pp. 255–81.

Bruce, S. (1985), *No Pope of Rome: Anti-Catholicism in Modern Scotland*, Edinburgh: Mainstream.

Bruce, S. (2002), *God Is Dead*, Oxford: Blackwell.

Campaign for a Scottish Assembly (1988), *A Claim of Right for Scotland*, Edinburgh (Report of the Constitutional Steering Committee).

Church of Scotland Board of Social Responsibility (1993), 'Young People and the Media', section 7.5 in the *Report of the Church of Scotland Board of Social Responsibility*, Edinburgh: Church of Scotland, pp. 28–73.

Cohn, S. (1999), 'A Historical Review of Second Sight: the Collectors, their Accounts and Ideas', *Scottish Studies*, **33**, 146–85.

Crawford, R. (1994), 'Bakhtin and Scotlands', *Scotlands*, **1**, 55–65.

Danforth, L. (1989), *Firewalking and Religious Healing: The Amercian Firewalking Movement and the Anastenaria of Greece*, Princeton, NJ: Princeton University Press.

Davie, G. (1986), *The Crisis of the Democratic Intellect*, Edinburgh: Polygon.

Devine, T. (2000), *Scotland's Shame? Bigotry and Sectarianism in Modern Scotland*, Edinburgh and London: Mainstream.

Dickson, A. (1989), 'Scotland Is Different, OK?', in D. McCrone *et al.* (eds) *The Making of Scotland: Nation, Culture and Social Change*, Edinburgh: Edinburgh University Press, pp. 53–69.

Drane, J. (1993), 'Coming to Terms with the New Age Movement', Appendix C in Church of Scotland Board of Social Responsibility, *Report of the Church of Scotland Board of Social Responsibility*, Edinburgh: Church of Scotland pp. 54–7.

Duesenberry, P. (2000), 'Scotland II: Traditional Music', *New Grove Dictionary of Music and Musicians*, London: Macmillan.

Dunlop, A. and Miles, R. (1990), 'Recovering the History of Asian Migration to Scotland', *Immigrants and Minorities*, **9**(2), 145–67.

Edensor, T. and Kelly, M. (1989), *Moving Worlds*, Edinburgh: Polygon.

Field, C. (2001), '"The Haemorrhage of Faith?" Opinion Polls as Sources for Religious Practices, Beliefs and Attitudes in Scotland since the 1970s', *Journal of Contemporary Religions* **16**(2), 157–76.

Finlay, R. (1998), 'National Identity', in A. Cooke *et al.* (eds), *Modern Scottish History 1707 to the Present*, Vol 2 *The Modernization of Scotland, 1850 to the Present*, East Linton: Tuckwell Press/ Open University in Scotland/University of Dundee, pp. 25–46.

Fitzgerald, T. (2000), *The Ideology of Religious Studies*, New York and London: Oxford University Press.

Fleming, B. and Loose, G. (eds) (1992), *The Holistic Handbook for Scotland*, Glasgow: Green Crane Press.

Forsyth, L. (1995), *Directory of Holistic Health Care in the Highlands and Islands of Scotland 1995–1996*, Achnasheen: Watershed Publication.

Gallagher, T. (1987), *Glasgow, the Uneasy Peace: Religious Tension in Modern Scotland*, Manchester: Manchester University Press.

Glasgow Museums (1993), *The St Mungo Museum of Religious Life and Art*, Edinburgh: Chambers.

Gray, A. (1994[1970]), *The Big Grey Man of Ben MacDhui*, Edinburgh: Birlinn.

Halliday, R. (1998), *UFO Scotland*, Edinburgh: B & W Publishing.

Harvie, C. (1998), 'Culture and Identity', in A. Cooke *et al.* (eds) *Modern Scottish History 1707 to the Present*, Vol. 2 *The Modernization of Scotland, 1850 to the Present*, East Linton: Tuckwell Press/ Open University in Scotland/University of Dundee, pp. 277–98.

Hassan, G. (ed.) (1999), *A Guide to the Scottish Parliament: The Shape of Things to Come*, Edinburgh: The Stationery Office.

Heelas, P. (2000), 'Expressive Spirituality and Humanistic Expressivism: Sources of Significance Beyond Church and Chapel', in S. Sutcliffe and M. Bowman (eds) *Beyond New Age: Exploring Alternative Spirituality*, Edinburgh: Edinburgh University Press, pp. 237–54.

Heelas, P. and Woodhead, L. (2001), 'Homeless Minds Today?', in L. Woodhead, P. Heelas and D. Martin (eds) *Peter Berger and the Study of Religion*, London: Routledge, pp. 43–72.

Highet, J. (1960), *The Scottish Churches: A Review of their State 400 Years after the Reformation*, London: Skeffington.

Highet, J. (1972), 'Great Britain: Scotland', in H. Mol (ed.) *Western Religion: A Country by Country Sociological Enquiry*, The Hague: Mouton, pp. 249–69.

Holiday, F. (1968), *The Great Orm of Loch Ness: A Practical Inquiry into the Nature and Habits of Water-Monsters*, London: Faber.

Jedrej, C. and Nuttall, M. (1996), *White Settler: The Impact of Rural Repopulation in Scotland*, Luxembourg: Harwood Academic Publishers.

Johnson, P. (1995), 'Shamanism from Ecuador to Chicago: A Case Study of New Age Ritual Appropriation', *Religion*, **25**(2), 163–78.

Kay, B. (ed.) (1996), *The Complete Odyssey: Voices from Scotland's Recent Past*, Edinburgh: Polygon (single-volume reissue of two vols published in 1980 and 1982).

Keating, M. (1996), *Nations against the State: The New Politics of Nationalism in Quebec, Catalonia and Scotland*, London: Macmillan.

Kenefick, B. (1998), 'Demography', in A. Cooke *et al.* (eds) *Modern Scottish History 1707 to the Present*, Vol. 2 *The Modernization of Scotland, 1850 to the Present*, East Linton: Tuckwell Press/ Open University in Scotland/University of Dundee, pp. 95–118.

Lovelace, A. *et al.* (1995), 'St Mungo's Museum of Religious Life and Art: A New Development in Glasgow', *Journal of Museum Ethnography*, **7**, 63–78.

Lynch, P. (1996), *Minority Nationalism and European Integration*, Cardiff: University of Wales Press.

Lynch, P. (2001), *Scottish Government and Politics: An Introduction*, Edinburgh: Edinburgh University Press.

Maan, B. (1992), *The New Scots: The Story of Asians in Scotland*, Edinburgh: John Donald.

McCrone, D. (2001[1992]), *Understanding Scotland: The Sociology of a Nation*, London: Routledge; rev. edn.

McCrone, D., Morris, A. and Kelly, R. (1995), *Scotland the Brand: The Making of Scottish Heritage*, Edinburgh: Edinburgh University Press.

McCutcheon, R. (1997), *Manufacturing Religion: The Discourse on* Sui Generis *Religion and the Politics of Nostalgia*, New York: Oxford University Press.

McIntosh, A. (1998), 'The Gal-Gael Peoples of Scotland', in J. Pearson, R. Roberts and G. Samuel (eds) *Nature Religion Today: Paganism in the Modern World*, Edinburgh: Edinburgh University Press, pp. 180–202.

Macmillan, J. (2000), 'Scotland's Shame', in T. Devine (ed.), *Scotland's Shame? Bigotry and Sectarianism in Modern Scotland*, Edinburgh and London: Mainstream, pp. 13–24.

Marr, A. (1992), *The Battle for Scotland*, Harmondsworth: Penguin.

Marwick, A. (1998), *The Sixties: Cultural Revolution in Britain, France, Italy and the United States c.1958–1974*, Oxford: Oxford University Press.

Maver, I. (1996), 'The Catholic Community', in T. Devine and R. Finlay (eds) *Scotland in the Twentieth Century*, Edinburgh: Mainstream, pp. 269–84.

Meek, D. (2000), *The Quest for Celtic Christianity*, Edinburgh: The Handsel Press.

Michel, P. (1999), *La Religion au Musée: Croire dans l'Europe Contemporaine*, Paris: L'Harmattan.

Miles, R. and Dunlop, A. (1987), 'Racism in Britain: The Scottish Dimension', in P. Jackson (ed.) *Race and Racism: Essays in Social Geography*, London. Unwin.

Mitchell, J. (1996), *Strategies for Self Government: The Campaigns for a Scottish Parliament*, Edinburgh: Polygon.

Monteith, W.G. (1997), *Paths to Wholeness: An Investigation in Terms of Discourse Analysis of 'Divine Healing' in the Iona Community and Associated Activities on Iona*, unpublished Ph.D. thesis, University of Edinburgh.

Monteith, W.G. (2000), 'Iona and Healing: A Discourse Analysis', in S. Sutcliffe and M. Bowman (eds) *Beyond New Age: Exploring Alternative Spirituality*, Edinburgh: Edinburgh University Press, pp. 105–17.

Munro, A. (1996[1984]), *The Democratic Muse: Folk Music Revival in Scotland*, Aberdeen: Scottish Cultural Press.

Nairn, T. (1977), *The Break-Up of Britain*, London: Verso.

Nairn, T. (2000), *After Britain: New Labour and the Return of Scotland*, London: Granta.

Nye, M. (1993), 'Temple Congregations and Communities: Hindu Constructions in Edinburgh', *New Community*, **19**(2), 201–15.

Nye, M. (1995), *A Place for Our Gods: The Construction of an Edinburgh Hindu Temple Community*, Richmond: Curzon.

Paine, C. (1998), 'Preface', in C. Paine (ed.) *Godly Things: Museums, Objects and Religion*, London: Leicester University Press, pp. xiii–xvii.

Paterson, L. (1998), *A Diverse Assembly: The Debate on a Scottish Parliament*, Edinburgh: Edinburgh University Press.

Pengelly, J., Hall, R. and Dowse, J. (eds) (1997), *We Emerge: The History of the Pagan Federation*, London: Pagan Federation.

Puttick, E. (2000), 'Personal Development: The Spiritualisation and Secularisation of the Human Potential Movement', in S. Sutcliffe and M. Bowman (eds) *Beyond New Age: Exploring Alternative Spirituality*, Edinburgh: Edinburgh University Press, pp. 201–19.

Ritzer, G. (1993), *The McDonaldization of Society*, Newbury Park, Calif.: Pine Forge Press.

Robertson, R. (1995), 'Glocalization: Time–Space and Homogeneity–Heterogeneity', in M. Featherstone, *et al.* (eds) *Global Modernities*, London: Sage, pp. 25–44.

Roof, W.C. (1999), *Spiritual Supermarket: Baby Boomers and the Remaking of American Religion*, Princeton, NJ: Princeton University Press.

Shango, J. (1996), 'The Firewalk: A Tool for Healing and Growth', *Caduceus*, **33**, 11–12.

Smith, J. (1998), 'Religion, Religions, Religious', in M. Taylor (ed.) *Critical Terms for Religious Studies*, Chicago: Chicago University Press, pp. 269–84.

Smout, T. (1992), 'Patterns of Culture', in A. Dickson and J. Treble (eds) *People and Society in Scotland*, Vol. III *1914–1990*, Edinburgh: John Donald, pp. 261–81.

Storrier, S. and Kemp, H. (2000), *The European Ethnological Research Centre Handbook and Guide for Contributors*, Edinburgh: European Ethnological Research Centre/National Museums of Scotland.

Sutcliffe, S. (1994), 'Worlds that Meet but Don't Collide' [review of the St Mungo Museum of Religious Life and Art], *The Herald* (Glasgow), 21 May 1994, 'Weekender' section, p. 24.

Sutcliffe, S. (1995), 'Some Notes on a Sociology of New Age and Related Countercultural Religiosity in Scotland', *Journal of Contemporary Religion*, **10**(2), 181–4.

Sutcliffe, S. (2000a), 'A Colony of Seekers: Findhorn in the 1990s', *Journal of Contemporary Religion*, **15**(2), 215–31.

Sutcliffe, S. (2000b), 'Wandering Stars: Seekers and Gurus in the Modern World', in S. Sutcliffe and

M. Bowman (eds) *Beyond New Age: Exploring Alternative Spirituality*, Edinburgh: Edinburgh University Press, pp. 17–36.

Sutcliffe, S. (2003), *Children of the New Age*, London: Routledge.

Sutcliffe, S. and Bowman, M. (eds) (2000), *Beyond New Age: Exploring Alternative Spirituality*, Edinburgh: Edinburgh University Press.

Taylor, B. (1999), *The Scottish Parliament*, Edinburgh: Polygon.

Walker, A. (1994), *The Revival of the Democratic Intellect: Scotland's University Traditions and the Crisis in Modern Thought*, Edinburgh: Polygon.

Walker, G. (1996), 'Varieties of Scottish Protestant Identity', in T. Devine and R. Finlay (eds) *Scotland in the Twentieth Century*, Edinburgh: Mainstream, pp. 250–68.

Wallace-Murphy, T. and Hopkins, M. (2000), *Rosslyn: Guardian of the Secrets of the Holy Grail*, Shaftesbury: Element.

Wardak, A. (2000), *Social Control and Deviance: A South Asian Community in Scotland*, Aldershot: Ashgate.

Watson, F. (2001), *Scotland: A History 8000 B.C.–A.D. 2000*, Stroud: Tempus.

Whaling, F. (1999), 'Religious Diversity in Scotland', in *Soundings II: Proceedings of a Day Conference for the Methodist Church in Scotland*, Edinburgh: Heriot-Watt University, pp. 10–45.

Wilson, B. (1976), *Contemporary Manifestations of Religion*, Oxford: Oxford University Press.

Wishart, P. and St. Clair, R. (1984), *Multicultural Edinburgh: A Short Background to Some of Our City's Ethnic Communities*, Edinburgh: Multi Educational Centre.

Woodhead, L. (2001), 'The Turn to Life in Contemporary Religion and Spirituality', in U. King (ed.) *Spirituality and Society in the New Millennium*, Brighton and Portland: Sussex University Press.

Wright, B. and Worsley, C. (eds) (1975), *Alternative Scotland*, Edinburgh: EUSPB/Wildwood House.

York, M. (2000), 'Alternative Spirituality in Europe: Amsterdam, Aups and Bath', in S. Sutcliffe and M. Bowman (eds) *Beyond New Age: Exploring Alternative Spirituality*, Edinburgh: Edinburgh University Press, pp. 118–34.

Ziarski-Kernberg, T. (2000), *The Polish Community in Scotland*, Hove: Caldra House.

CHAPTER 7

Time, Place and Mormon
Sense of Self

Douglas Davies

This chapter shows how aspects of identity in contemporary Mormonism may be given additional depth against the cultural background of motifs of wandering and homecoming present in ancient Near Eastern and Mediterranean mythology and developed within Christian liturgy and elements of contemporary British civic ritualism. The comparative sociological method underlying these discussions comes to focus on the issue of what might be called the ritual generation of time, or of a sense of the significance of time within the dynamic development of the identity both of groups and of their constituent members.

Time and place frame and foster human identity just as the cultural enhancement of religious creativity forges destiny from mere duration. While animals may never be safe in the spaces they defend, humans too are ever alert to their political-religious boundaries and the need to police them. Part of this unease over locality interweaves with the desire for utopia, that good place where alertness of defence may give way to reflective enjoyment. Christianity is but one religious tradition ensuring a transcendence that eliminates change, replete with its numerous forms of spiritual geography, anticipated experience and motivating drive of desire for 'that sublime abode' encountered in hymnody. Similarly, and conversely, theoreticians of postmodernity are often preoccupied with critical self-reflection upon the absence of somewhere to call home (Bauman 1995:47ff.). Their rooting of self within consciousness has been so thorough an implementation of Cartesian philosophical doubt, with consciousness divorced from its embodied base, that locales have been evacuated of their capacity to foster identity, let alone to confer that heightened sense of self so characteristic of salvation. Eliade's magisterial configuration of the history of religions as a frame for the Western individual in the second half of the twentieth century, echoing Nietzsche's reflection upon the 'eternal return' and the 'death of God', did much to depict the banality of time and the longing to flee the sense of history's weight that alienated minds could no longer bear (Eliade 1969:47ff.). Subsequent trends in critical social theory, with their reflexive engagement in significant absences of time, space and belonging, took this direction still further (Gell 1992; Augé 1992/1995). Against that broad background this chapter moves from a consideration of ancient and classical mythical-historical motifs of wandering and homecoming into a general Christian appropriation of time and place as intersecting axes of salvation before, finally, exemplifying this framing of identity in contexts of contemporary Mormonism.

Making Time

The theoretical issue driving this discussion, which might best be described as the 'ritual generation of time', seeks to account for ways in which ritual events may generate a distinctive sense of time. This notion is used to show how events take their respective cultures in distinct directions and make available quite diverse life options, including different ideas of salvation. Some time ago, Edmund Leach, while self-consciously expressing a Durkheimian perspective on the distinction between the sacred and the profane and implicitly enunciating Durkheim's sense of the social origin of the categories of thought, argued that 'we create time by creative intervals in social life' (1961:135; original emphasis). Leach had in mind those repeated events that are exemplified in the Christian Eucharist or, perhaps, the King's College Festival of Carols in which he was involved as Provost of King's. Though discussing elements of repetitive rites and their place in the ritual maintenance of time, this chapter also furnishes examples of a different kind of activity in which a unique event 'repeats' an earlier and soteriologically significant event. Here 'repeat' is a problematic word and really indicates a commemorative celebration of a past event, as will become clear. But, just as such a commemoration could not occur without the original event so are many cultural activities influenced by pre-existing motifs and values. It is with that in mind that we begin by comparing elements of classical Greek and Hebrew mythical-historical aspects of movement and salvation as a background for considering specific features of Western Christianity in its Anglican liturgical and Mormon commemorational modes.

Wandering and Homecoming: Nomads and Postmodern Life

The idiom of life as a journey marks major traditional Greek, Jewish and Christian cultural sources while, in the adapted forms both of wandering and homecoming and of listless vagrancy, it has provided sociologists such as Schutz (1964:106–19) and Bauman (2000) with motifs for their own form of social and existential analysis. In many respects the history of Western intellectualism is a history of 'being' interpreted through movement. Destiny is depicted as spatial with humanity taking time to attain the goal of reaching a city within a promised land. Key existential verbs such as 'to find' oneself depict the nature of land, of an environment of life, within which identity may be discovered. Just as Anne Salmond once demonstrated the power inherent in images of land, field and territory as models of knowledge, so we might see the means by which such land is traversed as an image of human self-reflection (1982:65–88). This is, perhaps, an inevitable model of self-awareness, given the very fact of the human species and its proclivity to movement in the evolutionary process of exploration and expansion. Yet, while to move is natural, to describe that movement is essentially an act of culture that has long been an essential image for the meaningfulness of human life itself. Without mentioning the pervasive journey motif within shamanistic traditions, something reflected in contemporary accounts of near-death experience, there are three obvious sources of the journey of life in Middle Eastern and Western cultural thought, Babylonian, Greek and Hebrew.

Three Mythical Journeys

The Babylonian epic of *Gilgamesh*, dating from something like 2000 BCE, tells of Gilgamesh, the young ruler, who sets out to find the remedy for death, having been grief stricken after the death of his bosom friend Enkidu. Amidst the oldest of world literature we discover a quest for immortality that is nearly successful, but not quite. For Gilgamesh has, ultimately, to return home to his city of Uruk and accept that his immortality will consist in whatever memory will accrue to him from the very walls of the city that he has built (George 1999). His destiny lies in an identity rooted in a city: immortality is civic.

Exemplifying the Greek tradition, Homer's *Odyssey* describes an adventure-filled journey from home to strange and dangerous lands, a descent to Hades, and a final return to restored love and relationships with kin and servants alike. Like *Gilgamesh* it is a story of journeys within a journey. Odysseus' homecoming, first in disguise and then disclosed, led to the slaughter of his enemies. At the very threshold of his home – the very *limen* as the Romans would call it, and later as Van Gennep (1960) and Turner (1969) would invoke in theory – he vanquished them. In this ancient myth the journey is the frame for destiny and for the depth of relationships made, strained, tested and restored in the identity of the hero. His destiny is ultimately domestic.

From the Hebrew mythical tradition movement begins the very moment Adam and Eve are thrust out of Eden to go wandering. The symbolic evil of the tower of Babel results from the human desire to stop wandering and to build a city. Its destruction ensures ongoing movement: there will be no settlement apart from divinely instigated covenant. Later Egyptian captivity and Exodus, then Babylonian captivity and ultimate restoration of Jerusalem move the tale from myth into history and, through the subsequent diaspora and establishment of the state of Israel, into contemporary politics and religion. Destiny lies in the covenanted land of promise.

Christian Theological Journeys

This movement motif passed into Christian perspectives where 'Jerusalem the Golden', as one pilgrim hymn describes heaven, became a supernatural goal of the self that had traversed life depicted as a vale of tears. Within the New Testament not only do the disciples live a partially mobile life with their wandering rabbi but a central episode of the life of Christ, one who is said to have nowhere to lay his head, concerns his crucial journey to Jerusalem: a theme I have explored in association with the existential theme of betrayal (Davies 2000a). The newborn sect following from Jesus' destiny-laden arrival in Jerusalem is soon dispersed but only to mushroom around the Mediterranean world. Its literary outcome, the New Testament, then becomes a ready source book for journeying motifs, not least once the early church fathers interleave it with Greek mythology (Rahner 1963).

Christian self-identity as a group *en route*, both spiritually and politically, extended from the Mediterranean into the whole world as European Christianities set about colonisation through their imperial and colonialist expansion. Some of Christianity's subsequent holy places became, in their turn, sites for holy journeys, triggering the mass popular movements of the crusades and pilgrimages in the medieval period. Yet, wherever the map of the world was painted pink the members of the British Empire, the world's largest of all time, also explicitly spoke of themselves, in their regular common prayer to God, as those who had 'erred and strayed from Thy ways, like lost sheep'. India and Africa, North America and Australia may have been reached by purposeful journey, but the conqueror confessed to lostness. That biblical image of the hapless lost sheep was complemented by the tragic moral tale of the prodigal son whose journey into the far country and into riotous living led to penury and to words universalised by the *Book of Common Prayer*: 'I will arise and go unto my father'. This image of the prodigal son was taken up by Karl Barth, a key twentieth-century Protestant theologian. Jesus is the prodigal son: the one whose incarnation is, as he puts it, the way of the 'Son of God' into the far country and whose resurrection and ascension become 'the homecoming of the Son of Man' (Barth 1956: IV, 59). This dramatic image was developed in the Church of England's *Alternative Service Book* (1980) and retained in its *Common Worship* book (2000) as a prayer: 'Father of All we give you thanks and praise that when we were far off you met us in your son and brought us home, dying and living he declared your love, gave us grace and opened the gate of glory.'

While such Christian self-reflection indicates the power of soteriological movement underlying religious identity, it has also come to attract wider meaning in less Christian and even in more secular contexts in relation to life understood as a 'journey'. It has, for example, become significant in literature on death, grief and bereavement so that the explicitly religious journey that led Bunyan to write *Pilgrim's Progress* is now echoed by many a religious and secular commentator alike as they speak of life as a journey with its trials, whether or not they see any postmodern destination awaiting the traveller. One potentially interesting feature of this shared discourse lies precisely in its availability as an open-ended concept capable of use by traditionally religious and existentially 'spiritual' people alike. In other words 'journey language' is spiritual language and spiritual language is part of the language of civil religion in America and of a generalised religiosity in Britain.

One interesting example lies in Charles E. Winquist's theological phenomenology, *Homecoming*, subtitled *Interpretation, Transformation and Individuation*, published as long ago as 1978. Winquist's homecoming is about coming home to the self, homecoming as self-understanding (1978:108, 50). Integral to this homecoming of self-understanding is the power inherent not only in language but in language deployed as story-telling. The very notion of life as a journey involves an awareness of the potential inherent in talking in this way for, he reminds us, language possesses an ontological as well as a descriptive purpose (ibid.:3). Winquist highlights the development of what came to be called narrative theology or the theology of story that complemented the growth of popular religious interest in pilgrimage within some Christian theology of the later twentieth century. Crucial to such story-telling are the social contexts in which it occurs, not least religious groups as arenas of narrative rehearsal.

Sociological Journeying

It is beyond the scope of this chapter to reflect on the power of journeys in other major religious traditions, whether in the post-mortem journey of the soul across the judgemental bridge of destiny as portrayed in Zoroastrianism, or the journeys of the Buddha, Muhammad or Guru Nanak, or even the great March of Chairman Mao. In contemporary innovations more otherworldly journeys, whether of shamanic ascents or mystic descents, could also be documented at some length. Instead, I consider the motif of wandering and homecoming in two sociologists: Alfred Schutz and Zygmunt Bauman. One of the clearest analyses of homecoming in the classic literature of sociology is Schutz's paper entitled 'The Homecomer' (1945). In some ways it presages the film *Born on the Fourth of July* and concerns the returning war veteran but it also raises issues of phenomenological sociology of person, time, place and experience. The soldier at war experiences anomie towards the enemy but on returning home encounters anomie within his own society, a switch that is problematic. The homecomer's society need to know about the world in which he has lived if his homecoming is to be potentially successful. The very symbolic character of the notion of 'home' is emotionally evocative and yet hard to describe (Brodersen, 1971:108). Home means life in primary groups, the term Charles Cooney used to describe face-to-face relationships (ibid.:109). The man who has left home replaces vivid experiences with memories. The situation of the separated person is, to a certain degree, that of those in bereavement for whom 'parting is to die a little'. It involves a different system of relevance. In the disruption of personal relationships involved in going away there is an 'irreversibility of inner time' (ibid.:115). This is important, argues Schutz, as a reminder that 'the analysis of any concrete sociological problem, if only driven far enough, necessarily leads to certain basic philosophical questions which social scientists cannot dodge by using unclarified terms such as "environment", or "cultural pattern" (ibid.:115). The homecomer is not the same as the man who left; indeed Schutz wants us to know that some 40 per cent of discharged veterans in the US did not want to return to their old jobs or even to their old communities.

Death and Homecoming

The difference between Schutz and Bauman is profound. Schutz's task of accounting for homecoming in relation to the concrete issue of military veterans is unlike Bauman's contrast between modernity and postmodernity in the form of the pilgrim and the nomad, whether that nomad was a vagabond, a *flâneur* or leisurely stroller, a tourist or player. Schutz's task is directly descriptive: it holds a firmness of touch grounded in a philosophical sense of the worthiness of the venture. Bauman (2000) also describes, but in a style that combines an intense cultural criticism with a desire for morality grounded in individual choice. Bauman's is a moral crusade achieved through a description of the movement of selves. The final chapter of *Liquid Modernity*, for example, is entitled 'Afterthought: On Writing; On Writing Sociology' (2000:202ff.), and is replete with passing references to Malabou and Derrida's *Contre-allée* in which they invite readers 'to think in travel', or to 'think travel'. He even hints that Derrida's intellectual 'home on the cross-roads' was grounded in texts because his native Algerian French intruded into his preferred professorial French of the Sorbonne. What interests me is the goal of this game-playing, in particular Bauman's description of sociology as possessing the practical problem of 'enlightenment aimed at human understanding' (2000:211). Here there is a similarity in that Schutz also saw his sociology of homecoming as possessing a degree of application to everyday life. If there is a difference between them it lies in the intensity with which they see sociology as possessing a moral mission: Bauman emphasises the nature of human freedom and the capacity to be free in choosing ways of life in relation to 'sociological enlightenment' (2000:212). Here it is the sociological public, the reading community and, perhaps, the conference community, that is the arena within which language can serve, in Winquist's sense, an ontological purpose, though the degree to which this can be achieved must be doubted.

Revitalising Remembrance

One example of the journey motif standing as a ready cultural symbol available for further development was furnished by events surrounding Remembrance Day in November 2000, a year in which 'millennial' idioms fired many erstwhile secular projects. These particular Remembrance events involved a decision to focus on young people with a special ceremony at London's Millennium Dome and another at the Cenotaph on the Saturday, the day before Remembrance Sunday. This involved two young people carrying a 'millennial flame' from the dome to the Royal Albert Hall on the Saturday night. One of the carriers, a teenage boy, also recited a vow including the words, 'we hold high the millennial flame, a light to guide us forward into the future'. This innovatory rite took the motif of a journey, one to be taken by young people, and added to it the notion of guidance, though exactly what the guiding power of a millennial flame might be was unsure, at least in interpretative terms. In fact this is an extremely interesting rite if pressed for propositional meaning as a form of decodable language. It would have to be assumed that light is, in and of its natural function, something that guides, and because flame produces light, it makes broad sense to use the image. But what of a millennial flame? What does the notion of millennium add to the function of light? What does the qualifier bring to the model? Here our opening comments on time and place as frames for human identity relate directly to the cultural enhancement of ritual creativity. Even so we bear in mind how ritual often achieves its goal when functioning not as a decodable language but as a behavioural act in and of itself. The significant point is that the annual Remembrance Sunday set of ritual events at the Royal Albert Hall celebration of the military, of the Royal British Legion, the notion of service, the monarchy, the place of the Anglican and other churches in relation to all these things, and also of the Sunday morning Cenotaph event, had added to them the notion of youth remembering the past and looking to the future.

Such a rite mobilises cultural symbols to revitalise the values and sentiments of groups, much as Chapple and Coon argued in their now rather overlooked notion of rites of intensification (1942:507ff.). A form of cultural energy is generated by the event and is used to reaffirm pre-existing beliefs, sometimes through the mediation of a new rite. For this to happen such rites must contain some ideological content bearing a degree of self-evident meaning. It might be argued that the Christian cultural background of Britain already makes such a value addition in the notions of Christ as the light of the world or, analogically, that the millennium is a Christian measure of time and that a light that is a millennial light will, inevitably, participate in the Christian multivocality of light that embraces a sense of divine guidance. Not many, perhaps, will be sufficiently familiar with Christianity to perceive this connection. But the values and sentiments involved in this case are also problematic because Remembrance Day events speak directly only to the military and other personnel who have experienced war and, in contemporary Britain, this does not include most people in their mid-fifties and certainly not entire generations of teenagers and very young adults.

Revitalising Time in Mormonism

The Latter-day Saint (LDS) cases, to which we now turn, take the form of specific cultural re-enactments celebrating historical events, and relate to a much narrower constituency than that of British remembrance rites. As a background to 'Faith in Every Footstep' and 'Sea Trek', as these events are called, it is important to recall that Mormonism originated in the 1830s as one example of an Adventist and millenarian Protestant group whose distinctive feature, generated through the revelations of the prophetic figure Joseph Smith Jr, was that the Latter-days would witness Christ's second advent in the US and not in Jerusalem (Underwood 1993). From the six men present at the church's inauguration in 1830 Mormonism had grown to approximately 11 million members by the year 2000, with some 176 000 in Great Britain and with approximately 34 000 members serving a two-year mission in different parts of the world (Almanac 2000:585–6). As what would, subsequently, turn out to be the quintessential American religion, Mormonism would take time in hand, frame it in eternity, valorise it in history through the concrete expression of architectural space of temples and produce a religious movement that, in the early years of the twenty-first century, would firmly diverge from general notions of postmodernity. While Mormonism's engagement with time reflects many aspects of wider Western and Christian notions of time discussed earlier, it activates these values and sentiments in distinctive ways and thereby generates Mormon 'time' for today.

This ritual generation of time in Mormonism involves a complex process of interrelated activities grounded in the well-known temple rituals and their associated genealogical pursuits through which individuals are both taught about and inducted into the 'plan of salvation' beginning in the 'pre-existence', continuing throughout earthly life and passing into the ever expanding realms of post-mortem worlds. The rituals of endowment and of baptism for the dead constantly refuel beliefs in this scheme of the relationship between 'time' and 'eternity' within the LDS reckoning of duration while also locating Mormon identity within historically defined soteriological terms, as I have shown elsewhere (2000b:73ff. and 1989:168ff. respectively). Here I draw attention to a different kind of behavioural activity that, while sporadic and almost incidental, yet serves quite powerfully to 'generate time'. Two examples are found in what came to be called 'Faith in Every Footstep' and 'Sea Trek', each a 150th anniversary. The first, in 1997, was a re-enactment of the 1847 migratory shift of Mormons from Nauvoo, Illinois, into the Great Salt Lake Basin and the second, in 2001, portrayed the migration of many Scandinavians and Britons to the US in the 1850s. As an intellectual background to these very specific events it is worth rehearsing several elements of mythical and doctrinal thought that gave valency to Christian thought at large which, in turn, invested the earliest Mormon migrations with significance and provided values and sentiments that are, today, considered worthy of reproduction.

'Faith in Every Footstep' and 'Sea Trek' engage with values and ideas that resonate across a broad Mormon constituency. Both concern the migrants who joined the church, especially in the 1840s and 1850s, and who are regarded as Mormon Pioneers: individuals who committed themselves to a journey, whether the transcontinental 1300-mile trek from Nauvoo, Illinois, through to the Salt Lake Basin of Utah, or the intercontinental voyage and trek from Europe. At the heart of this movement lay a bundle of religious and social hopes of a better life and of a different kind of salvation than was offered in the established churches of the day. In Mormon terms these migrants demonstrated obedience to the message of the prophet and his call to an American Zion. Numerically, those involved probably numbered some 80 000 or so while those in recent re-enactments were far fewer, involving several hundred people but with the church's publicity and public relations organisation many thousands were informed of the events.

'Faith in Every Footstep' involved people, often family groups or church groups, literally walking, with handcarts, part of the way taken by their literal forebears. So, too, with the 'Sea Trek' venture. Here Mormonism provided a pragmatic base for engagement with that genealogical research for which Mormonism is best known and which normally manifests itself in temple rites or family gatherings. History takes on a different significance when descendants seek some form of practical experience echoing that of their ancestors. In LDS cultural terms, with its high priority of a deep sense of controlled emotion, this afforded many participants a deepening of their 'testimony' of the truthfulness of Mormonism as a religious scheme.

The 'Sea Trek' episode, for example, involved mostly American Latter-day Saints flying to Europe and taking their berths on tall sailing ships, on which they were expected to perform physical tasks and not merely be passengers, something that came as a shock to some individuals, including older people unfamiliar with manual work. More than that, some experienced the wretchedness of seasickness. These negative experiences enhanced their positive appreciation of their ancestors' commitment and pain of separation from the old country. This was much in evidence, for example, at Liverpool where a ceremony at the dockside unveiled a permanent statue of a Victorian family awaiting departure from Liverpool for the States. Numerous LDS at the event spoke of their sense of awareness of what their ancestors must have gone through as they made this break from one world to another. The very fact that Mormonism has flourished and that descendants should now be able to engage in such an event of their own enhanced the significance of the past, validating its truthfulness within the testimony of the living. The presence of Liverpool's Lord Mayor and others, including officials of Liverpool's museums who accepted the permanent sculpture for the quayside, along with the Anglican Rector of Liverpool asked to say grace at a celebration dinner of VIPs present, all validated the historical past.

This particular day's festivities concluded with a concert and fireworks. The concert, held at Liverpool's Anglican cathedral, took the form of a popular oratorio entitled 'Saints on the Seas', described as 'A Musical Journey of Faith' (Sadleir 2001). Written and composed by Cori Connors with Kurt Bestor and Mark Robinette, all American, it was performed with the Royal Liverpool Philharmonic Orchestra and Choir. An overture led into three 'Actes' along with an Epilogue. The orchestral, vocal soloists and choral elements were interspersed with readings of texts derived from the personal journals of nineteenth-century emigrants and projected onto large screens set up in the form of sailing ship sails. Each text and song reflected both the human experience involved in early church membership and some aspect of LDS doctrine. 'One Heart, One Mind' documented the baptism and healing of an early Swedish convert and 'The Call' reflected the Prophet's call for all converts to come to Zion in America. 'Farewell My Native Land' echoes the 'grief' of leaving the homeland for the New World. A folksy conversation between the ship's blacksmith and a five-year-old emigrant, Josiah Baker, whose father has already died prior to his emigration with his mother, answers the lad's question of how the ship knows where to go. A song, 'True North', both focuses on the guidance of the North Star and reminds Josiah's mother of the 'home she has left and the pull of her heart toward Zion' (Sadleir 2001:7). Acte 2 begins with 'How Hard Can It Be', telling of the Mormons' organisation of practical details and problems. Reflecting the LDS doctrine of the pre-existence, part of the song runs, 'We come to earth with problems at birth, We get 'em, we face 'em. We solve 'em'. From the communal to the personal, 'I Come to You' is one young Norwegian emigrant's song as she journeys to Utah following her husband who has already settled there. The Mormon ideal of husband and wife bound by Zion is romantically reinforced, only to be questioned in the following song, 'If You Were Mine Completely', in which Jean, the boy Josiah's mother, now laments her boy's sudden death and burial at sea. Bereft of husband and son she still travels hopefully, acknowledging the fact that Josiah had come from the eternal home of God and would now proceed back into the divine care. In these songs of love and devotion the pathos of human suffering entwines with faith and divine purpose and easily transcends the century and a half separating migrating Saints from their descendants now retracing the journey by sea and from the many thousands who would hear this work not only in Liverpool but also at performances in Hull, Portsmouth, Copenhagen, Gothenburg, Oslo and, finally, New York. Acte 3 shifted the mood to the activities of sailors in 'Haul Away Joe' and in a 'Storm at Sea' that nearly overcomes the ship. Nevertheless, 'True North Reprise' announces that the North Star has pierced the sky as the storm abates. After the chaos of the storm the Saints, in chorus, bid final 'Farewell My Native Land', leading into the most famous of all LDS hymns 'Come Come Ye Saints' which marks the transition from the 'Sea Trek' to the land trek lying before them. The 'Epilogue', entitled 'Good Winds', is marked in the concert programme with the note that 'In 1911 The First Presidency of the Church sent a message urging overseas Latter-day Saints not to emigrate but to build Zion, a people of one heart and one mind, on their native soil' (Sadleir 2001:11). This final element is, itself, an interesting interpretation of the major transition in Mormonism from an active Adventist and millenarian group to an established sect that certainly became a distinctive denomination and is believed by some to be on the path to becoming a new religion.

This 'Sea Trek' venture was not, however, an official activity of the Church of Jesus Christ of Latter-day Saints but of individual church members Bill and DeAnn Sadleir of Utah who established the Sea Trek Foundation, initially as a personal venture, having been prompted by 'Faith in Every Footstep'. They are LDS, as are most others involved in the venture. At the Liverpool event there was even a pop music group from Utah playing in a very professional way on the riverside. The major emphasis of the concert, as of the bronze statuary of a migrating family group, was upon the Mormon cultural dimension of individuals and families migrating in accord with their religious belief. Interestingly, also at the Liverpool function, an LDS who is a US Senator for Oregon spoke and acknowledged his own European ancestry. The presence of such a person 'in his own right' and not as a church functionary emphasised the broad cultural nature of Mormonism and not its narrower institutional format.

In both the formal reception of the quayside bronze and the following concert some of today's Saints engaged in one distinctive form of the ritual generation of time by talking about concrete episodes from Mormon history, making the past come alive in the present. The past is not allowed to be forgotten. The LDS preoccupation with ancestors includes the diaries, journals and whatever other information can be gleaned about them. These are employed in the construction of rich familiar tapestries of knowledge within which many Saints come to embed themselves and their living relatives. This preoccupation with history serves the goal of salvation, making the concept of 'salvation history' – a broad theological notion of the nineteenth century – quite distinctive in the case of Mormonism. In many traditional forms of Christianity history is treated as 'tradition', whose 'direction' is from the past to the present and where the duty of the faithful is to receive and treasure what comes to them. While this may involve a sense of having to interpret the tradition afresh in each new generation the weight of significance lies with the past but, even so, it is in the ritual action of today that the weighty tradition is made significant and allowed to flourish. So to speak of the ritual 'generation of time' is to emphasise the power of the present and of distinctive forms of contemporary behaviour in reasserting the significance of the past to the present. Religious values, attitudes and sentiments are given a new and personal significance as they influence people's motivations and worldview. For those immediately involved in these endeavours on land and sea the fact of embodied learning exerts powerful influences. While historical events can be learned from written histories and may generate a sense of empathy with the hardships of the past, the acquisition of experience through handcart pulling or seasickness and the tactile encounter with heavy seas confers a different quality of knowledge and a different sense of participation in the lives of far-distant relatives. These very distinctive treks are also, however, examples of a phenomenon very well established in Mormonism through the missionary programme in which young adults leave home and work hard as missionaries and, in so doing, enter into a sphere of communal experience shared by thousands of Mormons both past and present. There is a sense in which the ongoing and ever increasing missionary scheme furnishes its own ritual for the generation of religious sentiments associated with this outreach movement of Mormonism, one that is nearly as old as the Church itself. The missionary programme is, in its own way, a form of ritual affirmation of the past generations of men and women who helped maintain church life. Although bearing some family resemblance to pilgrimage, it would stretch the meaning of that overworked category too far to identify either ordinary missionary activity or the treks with it even though aspects of group integration, of shared community and of numerous individual life commitments could easily be discerned within these events (cf. Eade and Sallnow 1991:3ff.).

Conclusion

Theoretically speaking, 'history' needs careful description as far as most Latter-day Saints are concerned, given its ideological and existential potency. A great deal of Mormon historical 'fact' is derived from documentary material related to genealogical and family history research and contributes to the dynamic, emotion-laden sentiments providing the matrix of personal and group religiosity and, with it, of identity. Here, the ritual generation of time ensures a sense of involvement with the past that is, theologically and philosophically, deemed to be foundational as the arena within which God restored truth to the world through Joseph Smith in a specific time and place. Viewed in concrete specificity, the past serves the commitments of today's believers as they reach back to validate the past and take from it the means of vocalising today's historical convictions. The fact that critical historical methods employed by some Mormon scholars can cause great difficulty as far as the 'mythical' or folk history of Mormonism is concerned lies beyond the scope of this chapter. From what we have seen, the image of wandering and homecoming, already invested with long-term cultural significance, presented Mormons with an opportunity of seeing themselves as a peculiar people, in the world but not of it.

Bibliography

Almanac (2000) *Deseret News, 2001–2002 Church Almanac*, Salt Lake City: Deseret News.
Augé, M. (1992/1995), *Non-places: Introduction to an Anthropology of Supermodernity*, trans. J. Howe, London: Verso.
Barth, K. (1956), *Church Dogmatics*, vol. IV *The Doctrine of Reconciliation*, ed. G.W. Bromiley and T.F. Torrence, Edinburgh: T. & T. Clark.
Bauman, Z. (1995), *Life in Fragments*, Oxford: Blackwell.
Bauman, Z. (2000), *Liquid Modernity*, Cambridge: Polity Press.
Brodersen, A. (ed.) (1971), *Collected Papers of Alfred Schutz*, Vol. 3, The Hague: Martinus Nijhoff.
Chapple, E.D. and Coon, C.S. (1942), *Principles of Anthropology*, New York: Henry Holt.
Davies, D.J. (1989), 'Mormon History, Identity and Faith Community', in E. Tonkin, M. McDonald and M. Chapman (eds) *History and Ethnicity*, London: Routledge.
Davies, D.J. (2000a), *Private Passions*, Norfolk: Canterbury Press.

Davies, D.J. (2000b), *The Mormon Culture of Salvation*, Aldershot: Ashgate.

Eade, J. and Sallnow, M.J. (eds) (1991), *Contesting the Sacred: The Anthropology of Christian Pilgrimage*,. London: Routledge.

Eliade, M. (1969), *The Quest, History and Meaning in Religion*, Chicago: University of Chicago Press.

Gell, A. (1992), *The Anthropology of Time*, Oxford: Berg.

Gennep, A. van (1960), *The Rites of Passage*, trans. M.K. Vizedom and G. Caffee, London: Routledge & Kegan Paul.

George, A. (1999), *The Epic of Gilgamesh*, New York: Barnes & Noble.

Leach, E. (1961), *Rethinking Anthropology*, London: The Athlone Press.

Rahner, H. (1963), *Greek Myths and Christian Mystery*, trans. B. Battershaw, London: Burns & Oates.

Sadleir, W.K. (2001), *Saints on the Seas, a Musical Journey of Faith*, The Sea Trek Foundation.

Salmond, A. (1982), 'Theoretical Landscapes', in D. Parkin (ed.) *Semantic Anthropology*, London: Academic Press, pp. 65–88.

Schutz, A. (1945) 'The Homecomer', *American Journal of Sociology*, **50**(4), 363–76.

Turner, V. (1969), *The Ritual Process*, London: Routledge and Kegan Paul.

Underwood, G. (1993), *The Millenarian World of Early Mormonism*, Urbana and Chicago: University of Illinois Press.

Winquist, C.E. (1978*), Homecoming: Interpretation, Transformation and Individuation*, Ann Arbor, Mich.: American Academy of Religion, Scholars Press.

CHAPTER 8

American-led Urban Revivals as Ethnic Identity Arenas in Britain

Nancy A. Schaefer

The globalisation of the Pentecostal-charismatic movement has received much scholarly attention, especially regarding Latin America, Africa and Asia, while the European scene, including the UK, has received less notice, with some notable exceptions (see Coleman 2000; Hunt *et al*. 1997; Percy 1996; Martin 2002: chap. 2). Attempting to help redress the oversight, this chapter examines a controversial US-based, white-led organisation that in Britain is backed primarily by black[1] Pentecostalists. During the 1990s, the American healing revivalist Morris Cerullo attracted public attention and criticism concerning his Mission to London (MTL) revivals.[2] The issue of 'race',[3] though largely unstated, was an integral sub-text, originating from the fact that Cerullo's core of support derived mainly from the British 'black churches'.[4] Elsewhere I have looked at the controversy in detail (see Schaefer 2002, 2000); here I will identify these churches, focusing on the older, more prevalent African-Caribbean churches, and offer reasons for their support of Cerullo and MTL.

The key to unlocking the riddle of Cerullo's UK constituency can be found in the movement of Caribbean migrants to Britain after the Second World War, and the subsequent emergence of the black churches. These two trends coincided with the rise of Cerullo's career as a healing evangelist and his activities in the Caribbean (among other places). In Britain, the black churches arose to meet the collective and individual needs of African-Caribbean (and more recent African) immigrants[5] (Beckford 1998; Kalilombe 1997; Edwards 1997, 1993). Hence, a central focus of this chapter is the roles black churches play in the life worlds of believers.

I will attempt to show that Cerullo's meetings, utilising black cultural repertoires, were specifically designed to appeal to black Pentecostalists in Britain. Drawing partly on fieldwork undertaken between 1992 and 1996,[6] I will further elaborate my thesis that Cerullo's MTL meetings, among other things, temporarily created 'free space' (e.g. collective liminality)[7] for the mediation and celebration of their shared cultural identities among the predominantly black audience. But before we consider that dynamic, we must first look briefly at the history of Caribbean migration to Britain and the formation of the black churches.

Historical Context: the African-Caribbean Immigrant Experience

Although blacks have lived in Britain since Roman times (Fryer 1984), the mass migration of people from the Caribbean (and the Indian sub-continent) began after the Second World War. The pool of migrants from the old Empire provided a ready labour supply for urban areas such as London which were losing inhabitants (Holmes 1997:15). Following the pattern of chain migration (Kershen 1997:5), the first postwar Caribbean migrants arrived in 1948 when 492 Jamaicans aboard the *Empire Windrush* landed at Tilbury. Like their African and Asian counterparts, many planned a temporary stay, expecting to return home shortly after amassing a small fortune (ibid.:78; Kalilombe 1997:309). The wave lasted until the 1960s, when new legislation (1962) restricted immigration to dependants of UK residents and those with essential job skills. Subsequent acts (1968, 1971) imposed further limitations, effectively curtailing primary immigration from Commonwealth countries (Mason 1995:28–9).

About 60 per cent of Caribbeans came from Jamaica, more than all the other islands combined (Nanton 1997:112). And despite the racial diversity of Jamaica, most were of African extraction (Hiro 1991:viii). Many migrants had previously identified with Britain, and confidently expected a warm welcome to the 'Motherland'. Instead they experienced culture shock resulting from the discrepancy between their expectations and the realities of immigrant life that for many included poverty, poor housing, and racism (Kalilombe 1997; Edwards 1993; Howard 1987). Anthropologist Malcolm Calley observed at the time that African-Caribbeans were often ill, not only because they were unused to the weather, but also because they were 'less well nourished and well housed than English people', living in over-crowded and uncomfortable accommodation (Calley 1965:44).

By the 1960s, the issue of 'race' became politicised and public policy was 'confused' (Marwick 1987:169). Parliamentarians on both sides of the aisle wanted to keep 'race' from becoming a national political issue, but were divided over methods. Yet the issue did not go away; instead it became 'a new source of open social conflict', one which some commentators predicted would even replace class as the most far-reaching, intractable cleavage in contemporary British society (ibid.:166–7, 225). 'Race' became shorthand for 'black' and translated into 'problem'[8] in political rhetoric and public discourse (Mason 1995; Gilroy 1991; Fryer 1984). Rooted partly in the problems associated with postwar housing shortages, white hostility was also fuelled by fascist groups, especially in London (Holmes 1997:19). In 1966 the National Front was created and Enoch Powell's infamous 'Rivers of Blood' speech two years later captured the mood of at least a segment of the population (Marwick 1987:169). During the disturbances of the 1970s, blacks became associated with criminality and their communities came to be viewed as 'pathological' (Gilroy 1991). In 1979, Prime Minister Margaret Thatcher talked about Britons feeling 'swamped' by the newcomers (Ismond 2000:127). Over the next decade, these attitudes hardened, with further rioting linked by government officials to issues of law and order rather than to underlying problems of urban deprivation, unemployment and racism (Benyon and Solomos 1991:22–43).

The situation for many blacks nowadays has not significantly improved, according to indices of social deprivation (see McGuigan 1996:135–53). A new government study – described as 'the most comprehensive and up to date portrait of racial disadvantage' – predicts that the gap between whites and ethnic minorities will worsen over the next 20 years unless the government intervenes (Wintour 2001). Today, one-third of all African-Caribbean households are located in the poorest 10 per cent of English wards, with 13 per cent living in 'unfit' (private sector) housing. African-Caribbean graduates are twice as likely as white graduates to be unemployed, and despite the fact that black children possess 'equal, if not higher, ability than white children on entrance to school ... [African-Caribbean] boys make the least progress through school' (ibid.).

Blacks are also heavily concentrated in urban areas, with over half of all Caribbeans – by 1991, estimated at 490 000 for the West Indian/Guyanese-origin population – living in London (Nanton 1997:110–13). Immigration scholar Anne Kershen writes of the capital city, 'xenophobia, anti-alienism and racism ... have all featured in the London experience and sadly continue to play their part today' (1997:7). Remarkably, the issue of their citizenship lingers in public discourse (Ismond 2000; McGuigan 1996), despite the fact that by 1990, 57 per cent of the African-Caribbean population were born in Britain (Nanton 1997:110–11). Yet, 'racist assumptions that being British is a matter of being white' persist in the popular mind (Jacobson 1997:248).

Stunned by the crude 'black–white' polarity that whites used to classify them as 'outsiders' (and inferior), Caribbeans came to formulate a new 'black' identity which had not existed before (Gilroy 1991; James 1989; Hiro 1991). As Winston James summarises, 'the English ... helped Afro-Caribbean people in Britain to *feel* "West Indian" and *feel* "black"' (James 1989:237; original emphasis), in effect, creating a pan-Caribbean identity.

It would be mistaken, however, to suppose that only one 'black identity' represents all African-Caribbeans, since the process of identity formation is much more complex and, in any event, does not remain constant (McGuigan 1996:135). Thus, it is more accurate here to speak about 'black identities' (Hall 1995; Gilroy 1991; James 1989).

One secular expression of a Caribbean identity was cultivated in the social clubs created by West Indians where they could meet and dance to records from the Islands (Hiro 1991:35; Gilroy 1991). It has also been suggested that the Notting Hill Carnival functions as a celebration of a pan-Caribbean identity (Cohen 1993). While it may indeed represent a secular expression of black community, I want to suggest that a religious idiom of this collective identity can be found in the black Pentecostal churches (Beckford 1998; Edwards 1997; Kalilombe 1997), and was evident at Cerullo's Mission to London meetings as well.

There are, of course, alternative expressions such as Rastafarianism, which is both religious and political. While Rasta culture was significant in raising black awareness during the 1970s and early 1980s, its appeal is limited primarily to younger men. Other black movements include Black Power of the 1970s, and the Nation of Islam ('Black Muslims'), although the latter number only between 500 to 2000 adherents in Britain today (Branigan 2001).

Furthermore, not all black Christians are Pentecostalist, but most are (Brierley 2000; Beckford 1998; Kalilombe 1997). There are also differences among black Pentecostalists (see below) and between Caribbean and African congregations (Hunt and Lightly 2001; Beckford 1998; Kalilombe 1997). Nevertheless, experts agree that these churches have become the most significant black institution in Britain for the postwar settler community (Beckford 1998; Toulis 1997; Kalilombe 1997; Edwards 1993).

The Black Churches in Britain

The black churches are notable for several reasons. First, a higher proportion of the black population attend church, with estimates as high as 20 per cent (Kalilombe 1997:314), compared to less than 10 per cent for the general public (Brierley 2000; Bruce 2001). Moreover, black Christians are heavily concentrated in inner London, where three out of every eight church-goers are black (Brierley 2000:139).[9] So higher church attendance rates distinguish black believers from the general public, who may 'believe without belonging' (Davie 1994). Second, black churches attract more young people and male attenders than the mainstream churches, which draw disproportionate numbers of older women (Bruce 1996:112). Third, the black churches are more successful in retaining their members, including children, at a time when the historical mainline denominations are losing members (Brierley 2000; Bruce 2001). And finally, these churches are known for their expressive cultural styles (see below).

Among African-Caribbean Christians, the majority are Jamaican or of Jamaican parentage, and while some have joined the mainstream churches, the majority are members of Pentecostal churches (Brierley 2000:136; Kalilombe 1997:314). This is unsurprising, since Pentecostalism in Jamaica 'is a religion for every man regardless of race or class, and it offers both respectable status and popular enthusiasm' (Wedenoja 1980:37).

Beliefs and Practices

Black Pentecostalists in Britain share the basic tenets of Pentecostalism, summarised by black church leader Joel Edwards,[10] as 'a literalist approach to Scripture, the baptism of the Holy Spirit, tongues and spiritual gifts, healing, spontaneity in worship, inspirational preaching and confrontation with evil spiritual powers' (1997:47). There are differences, however, between black Pentecostalists; some are Trinitarians, for example, like the New Testament Church of God congregations, others are 'Pentecostal Oneness' or 'Jesus Only' such as Oneness Apostolic adherents (Beckford 1998; MacRobert 1989). Nevertheless, some commentators argue that it is possible to talk about 'Black Christianity' in Britain (Kalilombe 1997).

At the heart of the Pentecostal experience is personal holiness. Expected to live sanctified lives, 'saints' socialise and worship together as a community, using ecstatic forms that are described as joyful, life affirming and generally 'uplifting' (Edwards 1993, 1997; Beckford 1998). For this reason, Edwards calls the black church a 'celebration community' (Edwards 1993:105).

Like all Pentecostals, the black churches highlight spiritual gifts, but their accent on healing stands out (Beckford 1998:30; Howard 1987:15). The other practice that distinguishes them from their white counterparts is ritual foot-washing (see Toulis 1997:145, 151–4). On the whole, however, the theological beliefs of black Pentecostalists differ little from their white brethren; the real distinction resides in their emphasis on music and performance styles (MacRobert 1989).

It is difficult to overstate the significance of music and performance styles for black culture in general, as these serve as important markers for boundary maintenance. Part of the expressive repertoire of British black popular culture, these distinctive forms, it is suggested by Stuart Hall, emerged from communal experiences of oppression and resistance, difference or otherness (Hall 1992:27). Consequently, 'style' is not merely a façade or overlay, but is itself important. As Robert Beckford notes, 'Black popular culture is deeply attached to music, in contrast to mainstream culture's logocentric commitment to the written word' (1998:136).

In Britain, these ecstatic styles 'are fixed and essentialised in the mainstream [white] psyche as "loud", "crude", and far too "emotional"' (ibid.:35). Indeed, a common misconception among outsiders is that worshippers are 'whipped up into a frenzy' but, as Lincoln and Mamiya point out, 'a deciphering of the "frenzy" is particularly important' in order to understand the black sacred cosmos (1990:5). They explain the typical worship service in terms of a cathartic outpouring of emotion, 'that eclipses the harshness of reality for a season and leaves both the preacher and the congregation drained in a moment of spiritual ecstasy' (ibid.:6).

The ultimate aim is not merely catharsis, however, but *transcendence*. The climax is the worshipper's experience of God, and all group rituals, including prayers, singing, preaching and testimonies, are aimed towards this end (Beckford 1998; MacRobert 1989; Calley 1965). Writing about the British scene, Beckford suggests that:

> Within Black Pentecostal Church cultures, divine activity, the work of the Holy Spirit, is understood to be ever-present in the life and worship of the church. Consequently, cultural activities – such as singing, praying and other acts of devotion – are said to be inspired or anointed ... [these] cultural forms within the Black church are also understood to have a transcendent quality reflecting an other-worldly presence and power.
>
> (1998:17)

Music is essential to the service and performance styles include syncopated rhythms, melisma[11] singing, call and response, and motor movements such as swaying, hand-clapping and 'dancing in the Spirit', which are striking by the level of emotional intensity. While black churches employ different musical traditions in their services, gospel music remains popular (Beckford 1998). One reason is undoubtedly the *power* of gospel music; its pounding dance rhythms aid in the attainment of euphoric states that help to create a transcendent atmosphere in which everyday reality is suspended (Pratt 1990:63). For many blacks, gospel music likewise expresses a feeling of community, experienced in what Pratt calls 'the spiritual moment' – that is, 'a new, free space in a world of trouble' (ibid.:66). The music also symbolises cultural resistance which has multiple meanings, both spiritual and political (ibid.; also Beckford 1998:55, 190).

When thinking about the UK context, it is important to recognise that '*Black Britain defines itself crucially as part of a diaspora*' (Gilroy 1991:154; emphasis added), inspired by black populations from elsewhere, especially the US and the Caribbean. The fact that many African-Caribbeans in the UK have chosen the black churches as a medium to express their cultural identities is not wholly unexpected, given the long historical precedent of black churches derived from black diaspora culture in the Caribbean, among other places. In fact, David Martin describes Jamaica – the country of origin of most British Caribbeans – as 'a country of the

African diaspora' (1990:114–15). Moreover, Jamaican culture dovetails neatly with Pentecostalism, as one Jamaican bishop explained to anthropologist Diane Austin-Broos: 'Jamaicans ... accepted Pentecostalism because they already lived in a spirit-filled world. They were Africans. They were emotional. They liked rhythm in their worship and they knew what it was to be spirit-filled' (Austin-Broos 2001:149). From this perspective, the British black churches are an integral part of the current black diaspora, evident in black preaching and black gospel music (Beckford 1998:139).

The Multiple Roles of Black Churches in African-Caribbean Life

The black churches undoubtedly came into being to meet the specific needs of Caribbean-origin Christians in Britain. During the 1950s and 1960s, black believers experienced the stresses and strains resulting from their status as 'ethnic minority' immigrant groups and turned to the 'sacred canopy' of existing churches. Many devotees found them inhospitable, however, detecting little that they could relate to (Edwards 1993:103; Kalilombe 1997:310). As Iain MacRobert points out: 'Most white congregations ... lacked characteristics which Black Christians considered concomitants of authentic faith and spirituality: demonstrable love, life and spiritual power; a high degree of visible Christian commitment; a strong sense of community and full opportunities to participate at every level' (1989:127). Even so, some did remain in the mainline churches,[12] while others dropped out altogether. Still others formed their own churches, with names such as Bethel, Beulah and Shiloh designating their status as places of refuge (Beckford 1998:137). Some of the new congregations had links with denominations 'back home'; others were created *ex nihilo* (Austin-Broos 2001:142; Kalilombe 1997:313–14; Toulis 1997:119).

While the black Pentecostal churches serve as 'pneumatic communities' that interact with the supernatural, they also operate a vital network of support, especially during emergencies or misfortune (MacRobert 1989:129). For this reason, Beckford calls the black church a 'brilliant social-welfare institution' (1998:13). Other observers agree, adding that cultural as well as spiritual and social needs are fulfilled by the black churches (Edwards 1993:104–5; also Kalilombe 1997:306).

Moreover, some insist that emotional and psychological benefits accrue to black church-goers, who may thereby derive a sense of belonging, personal dignity and raised self-esteem (MacRobert 1989:128; Howard 1987:12). Church membership offers congregants opportunities for participation and service, the chance to develop leadership skills, and the possibility of class mobility too (MacRobert 1989:129; Beckford 1998:28–9).[13] To the list of possible benefits, Beckford adds mental health as well (1998:26–7). Based on his own experiences as a second-generation African-Caribbean growing up in England, he credits the 'love, fellowship and nurture' of his church with his educational achievements, and argues that '*the church promotes a system of thought and action which ensures the spiritual and psychological well-being of African-Caribbean British people*' (ibid.:41; emphasis added). He states unequivocally that '*worshipping in the Black Church has kept me sane as a Black man in Britain*' (ibid.).

Beyond the needs of their own congregants, the black churches also seek to serve the wider society and indeed the wider world (Kalilombe 1997:307, 323; Edwards

1993:117; Howard 1987:12). Pentecostalism's emphasis on foreign missions encourages a global orientation among believers, and support for international ministries like Cerullo's. Some UK black churches have links with congregations and organisations elsewhere, including the US, Africa and the Caribbean (Hackett 1995; Gifford 1998).

Today the black churches are grappling with challenges on a number of fronts. One of the most serious is an 'identity crisis' reflected, for example, in the battle over labels (e.g. 'black churches', 'black-led churches', 'black Christianity'). As the boundaries of black identities come under growing pressure, and the contours are increasingly contested (Ismond 2000; Nanton 1997), British blacks struggle 'to maintain an identity which is true to its African-Caribbean heritage without becoming a cultural irrelevance to other sections of the community' (Edwards 1993:115).

The question of identity is closely intertwined with the ongoing problem of racism (Edwards 1997). The black churches have adopted an openness towards whites (see Toulis 1997:168) and an explicitly anti-racial stance, but at the same time, they seek to meet the particular needs of their own black members. Like their US counterparts, British black churches help to mediate tensions between congregants and the wider world, between the universalism of the Christian message and the particularism of their racial history (Lincoln and Mamiya 1990:12–13). While the latest English Church Attendance Survey (ECAS) indicates an increase of non-white members in the mainline churches (Brierley 2000:133–41), insiders note that blacks are still under-represented in leadership positions (Aldred 1999:87; Beckford 1998:44; Edwards 1993:116). Moreover, the apparent optimism of some observers notwithstanding (see Brierley 2000:134), attempts on the part of black churches to attract many white members have often fallen short (Hunt and Lightly 2001; Aldred 1999:87).

Another issue facing black churches concerns their appeal among children. Although more successful than mainline churches in retaining their offspring, some church leaders warn that 'a growing number of young blacks are becoming disenchanted with the black churches which meant so much to their elders' (Kalilombe 1997:309–10). Despite such misgivings, the ECAS shows that these churches are still going strong (Brierley 2000).

To summarise so far, the black UK churches enable Caribbean Pentecostalists to worship God in ways that they find culturally relevant and personally satisfying. As institutions, these churches provide 'free social space' (see Martin 1990:278–80), where individuals can find solace and dignity, sustained by a caring community of like-minded believers. As black theologian James Beckford explains, 'The worshipping tradition ensures that the Black Church is one of the only safe spaces where Black identities are celebrated and perpetuated. For many, the church is a place of affirmation and empowerment' (1998:26).[14] Therefore, Britain's black churches may perhaps be best understood as local adaptations of complex interplays between local and national contexts and external influences from the Caribbean and the US.[15] While striving to meet the needs of black members, congregations likewise reach out to their communities and to the wider world, as part of their missionary mandate. Moreover, these churches implicitly (if not explicitly) facilitate the means to construct and affirm a positive ethnic, as well as religious, identity. Cerullo's Mission to London conventions offer a similar forum – albeit temporarily – for these constituencies, as I will attempt to demonstrate next.

Morris Cerullo, World Evangelism (MCWE) and the Black Churches in Britain

At its peak, MTL drew about 500 sponsors and crowds of between 10 000 and 15 000.[16] The black churches stood out in terms of official sponsorship and participation, confirmed by many observers, including me, at these meetings (1992–6) (Schaefer 1999b; Pain and Manning 1993). According to *The Church of England Newspaper*, no other evangelist had ever attracted black audiences of that size in Britain (20 August 1993, p. 6). In fact, MCWE conceded that over half of its sponsoring congregations were independent and black-led (*MCWE* 1994:6, 7; *MTL Official Programme* 1993; *Victory* [n.d.]).[17]

The two largest black Pentecostal denominations in Britain are the New Testament Church of God and the Church of God of Prophecy, with 7220 and 4785 members respectively (Brierley 1998/9:9.12). About a quarter of all African-Caribbean church-goers are concentrated in these two denominations alone (Kalilombe 1997:314). Importantly for our case, both of these churches lent vital support to MTL in terms of sponsoring congregations and organising board members. Another major backer was Kensington Temple (KT), with 10 000 worshippers and 130 satellite churches (Brierley 2000:31). Although technically a white-led Elim Pentecostal church, it acts as an independent entity, known for the exuberant black worship styles preferred by its large African-Caribbean congregation (Walker 1997:24; Scotland 1995:13). Consequently, KT can be classified as a black church.

African congregations were also involved, represented by churches such as Kingsway International – led by Matthew Ashimolowo (originally from Nigeria) – and the Redeemed Christian Church of God, the largest West African church in Britain (*MTL Official Programme* 1995:8; Hunt and Lightly 2001:105). Added to these were scores of smaller denominations and independent congregations, with names such as Shiloh Pentecostal Church (Oneness), Glory Bible Church and Mustard Seed Church, to name only a few.

Importantly, the two largest *non*-Pentecostal black churches – the African Methodist Episcopal Church and the African Methodist Episcopal Zion Church – also appeared on sponsorship rolls (MacRobert 1989; *MTL Official Programmes* 1992–6). Admittedly meagre in terms of official sponsorship numbers, their presence nevertheless lends credence to my contention that Cerullo's revival meetings also functioned (albeit latently) as a forum for black identity articulations and celebration. Further corroborating evidence may be found in Greg Smith's assertion that there were MTL attenders among the African-Caribbean members of the (white-led) Baptist church in London he studied, although the church did not formally sponsor the event.[18]

While black support was considerable, it was not exclusive; whites and Asians together made up as much as 40 per cent of MTL audiences (Pain and Manning 1993:56; *MCWE* 1994:6, 7), a figure that roughly corresponds with my own estimates. Although the general absence of 'traditional' white-led denominations was noted at the time, other Elim congregations besides Kensington Temple backed the meetings, which were also endorsed by a few British white church leaders: namely Elim Superintendent Wynne Lewis (now retired); Anglican vicar John Starr; and Gerald Coates, head of the ('new church') Pioneer (*MTL Official Programmes* 1992–6; Pain and Manning 1993:40, 56). But in the end – despite his efforts to do so – Cerullo won less support from white Britons. Indeed, with few exceptions, charismatics and evangelicals tended to remain aloof, while some even criticised Cerullo publicly.

Discussion

When seeking to discern the reasons why some black churches backed Cerullo's London revivals, a variety of factors are relevant for our discussion. Much of Cerullo's success among his UK constituents is undoubtedly due, in various degrees, to the message, revivalistic style and cultural forms evident at his London meetings. But there were additional factors that ought to be taken into account, such as the timing of Cerullo's professional career, which coincided with the migration of Caribbeans to Britain. Equally important, in my view, was the absence of black revivalists of the same stripe.

One decisive factor is certainly Cerullo's message, involving power, success and healing, meaning physical, emotional and financial 'health' (Schaefer 2000). His emphasis on personal empowerment is illustrated in MCWE's slogan, 'There is a Power so Strong it makes the Rulers of this world Tremble', appearing on MTL programmes and posters, and repeated by Cerullo from the platform. Since this notion of divine power is limitless and supreme, knowledgeable practitioners ('Spirit-filled' Christians) are exhorted to access God's power in much the same way as they can tap into his unlimited provision of prosperity. As one MTL worshipper happily exclaimed, 'We're plugged in!'[19]

A major corollary of Cerullo's conception of power is spiritual warfare. MCWE supporters, if they heed 'God's prophet', are assured '100% VICTORY, OVER 100% OF THE ENEMY, 100% OF THE TIME!' (*VML* 1996:24; original emphasis). Indeed, Cerullo's success-oriented, 'can-do' attitude – according to one informed black pastor – appeals to aspiring working-class blacks who identify with Cerullo's 'poor' origins and believe his success demonstrates that he was 'called by God'.[20] Apparently Cerullo's teaching also resonates among some middle-class blacks, who use prosperity doctrines 'to justify their status and augment the conservative behavioural outlook of the Church' (Beckford 1998:29).

In terms of cultural forms and revivalistic style, Cerullo draws upon black cultural repertoires, evident in his preaching and use of gospel music. Cerullo's preaching is characterised by interaction ('call and response') between himself and his audience, who inject shouts of 'Praise God' and 'Thank you Jesus' at various junctures during the sermon. After he warms up, Cerullo customarily 'shouts the sermon'. Given his Orthodox Jewish upbringing in New Jersey, it may seem surprising that Cerullo borrows from the Southern US 'black' style of chanted sermons (Rosenberg 1970), but this may be explained in terms of his target audience. In this case, however, Cerullo appears to lack the musical ability to chant

– he ordinarily sings off-key – so instead, he turns to his African-American song leader, Archie Dennis, to break into song at the appropriate times.

Black gospel music is another prominent feature of MTL (Pain and Manning 1993). Although other types of music are played, such as pop and country and western, gospel music predominates, characterised by rhythmic 'black' performance styles manifested in melisma singing, call and response, and motor movements (such as clapping, swaying and dancing). Also notable is the participatory nature of the performance; when the 300-strong black gospel choir is on stage, everyone sings along. Unlike the European tradition that makes a dichotomy between the performers and the audience, African styles – from which gospel derives – do not make this distinction (Curtis 1987). At MTL, the music is buoyant and rousing,[21] helping to stimulate the levels of emotional intensity necessary for the healing ritual, the most important signifying practice for many of Cerullo's followers at these meetings.

During the healing ritual, participants are instructed to place their hands over the area of their bodies needing healing, while Cerullo commands the evil spirits (believed responsible for illness) to depart. Invoking the Holy Spirit, described as 'liquid fire', Cerullo calls out ailments that are purportedly being miraculously cured. Then, after some time, several devotees clamber to the platform in order to give their miracle testimonies and demonstrate their healing. At every MTL, people claimed that they had been healed, confirmed by public testimonials given on the spot, which are then recorded for TV playback and cassette tapes, as well as recitation in ministry literature.

Hence, Cerullo's ideology is refracted through the prism of ritual practices, both collective and individual, characterised by ecstatic worship styles that emphasise the immediacy of the divine encounter, manifested in supernatural healing, glossolalia and emotionalism. His focus on healing and message of empowerment and prosperity correspond to those found in many black churches,[22] and his revival style (for example, preaching and gospel music) conforms to black styles. The evidence suggests that Cerullo draws upon black cultural repertoires as part of his niche marketing strategy. As one knowledgeable black pastor (an MTL supporter who had first heard of Cerullo as a boy in the Caribbean) opined, many black churches share Cerullo's theology, including the belief that God is active and present in daily life, and can be invoked in time of need. Cerullo proclaims healing and deliverance, like the UK black churches, and the atmosphere of his meetings is 'of the Spirit moving'.[23] More than one pastor told me that Cerullo also shares their missionary 'vision' (to 'save' London and Britain for Christ).[24]

Interestingly, MCWE openly admitted that it concentrated its efforts on 'ethnic minorities, immigrants and the less educated working classes' in Britain, and that its MTL meetings – based on experience in Africa and the Caribbean – were 'structured in a way that is attractive to them' (*MTL Official Programme* 1993:9). MCWE also suggested that its UK activities 'compliment[ed]' (*sic*) other British churches that were 'reaching out to the more educated middle classes' (ibid.).

It may seem surprising that black Pentecostalists backed a white revivalist, especially if we suppose (as we do) that for many attenders, MTL served as ethnic identity arenas. However, black church leader Joel Edwards, in calling for increased black leadership, explains: 'On the whole, it is easy for black people to be led by white people. It has happened within the colonies and Commonwealth countries for many centuries and is natural to a minority experience ... [It is a] psychological pattern of many centuries' (Edwards 1993:117). Paul Gifford (1998), in his study of Pentecostalism in Africa, makes a similar point.

Still, we might very well wonder why African-Caribbean Pentecostalists would choose to support this particular US-based ministry. The association with American organisations, in itself, is not unusual. Some UK black churches have affiliations with churches in the US; for example, the denominational headquarters of the New Testament Church of God and the Church of God of Prophecy are located in the States (Trotman 1992:24; Beckford 1998:33–4). Among his followers, Cerullo is regarded as an 'anointed man of God', a view confirmed by the 'signs and wonders' accompanying his ministry, and expressed by many of my contacts. When pressed to explain the support of the British black churches for his London meetings, one black church leader responded, 'black working-class Christians show up at MTL due to the immediacy of the encounter; to hear the Gospel story of hope, power, and a God who intervenes on their behalf'.[25]

But from an external perspective, there are other crucial factors that should be taken into account. Part of the first generation of post-Second World War healing revivalists in the US, Cerullo was promoted by Gordon Lindsay's influential organisation, The Voice of Healing (TVH), where he came into contact with prominent Pentecostal leaders such as Demos Shakarian, David du Plesis, Oral Roberts, Kenneth Hagin, A.A. Allen and Lester Sumrall, among others. In fact, TVH and Shakarian's Full Gospel Business Men's Fellowship International apparently financed Cerullo's first trip to Jamaica in 1955 (*TVH* 1955). Afterwards, Cerullo continued to visit the Caribbean and built up a loyal following there.[26]

Meanwhile, Cerullo's trips to the Caribbean and Africa in the 1950s and 1960s coincided with the movement of migrants from the Commonwealth to Britain. In his book about the 1993 MTL, writer Timothy Pain remarked, 'it's only natural that the people who've been helped by him back in their home countries, should invite him to preach when they migrate to Britain' (Pain and Manning 1993:13). He continues: 'London's Black-led churches believe that Morris Cerullo is a man who communicates the Gospel in a way which is right for their culture. In fact, they think that he reaches their ethnic group better than anyone else' (ibid.:12–13). Even so, another critical piece to the puzzle of Cerullo's black constituency certainly has to do with the lack of viable alternatives. When Cerullo first began holding his revivals in Britain in the 1960s, they were the only large-scale event of this kind around. As one black pastor explained, one of the main 'selling points' of MTL was that it was a 'unifying event' for London's churches that (for a while at least) was held on an annual basis. Futhermore, many black Pentecostalists identified with Cerullo's missionary goals, pledging to support MCWE as evidence of their devotion – 'the extra mile of personal sacrifice'.[27]

That is not to say that black church backing for Cerullo was unqualified; in fact, after Cerullo became embroiled in a public controversy, some black believers reconsidered their support. MCWE's contentious ad campaigns accentuated pre-existing tensions between British evangelicals and Pentecostalists, and Cerullo was unable to provide satisfactory evidence of miracle healing to appease his critics (see Schaefer 2002, 2000). By 1996, Cerullo had lost control of MTL[28] and was pressured to resign from an important UK evangelical organisation. Given his advancing age of 72 years (as of October 2003), coupled with his inveterate disputes with British critics, it seems unlikely that Cerullo will be able to make a strong comeback in the UK.

Moreover, the local religious scene is changing. With a new generation of black Pentecostal preachers growing in stature and popularity, we can expect church leaders such as Matthew Ashimolowo or Ayo Oristejafor to lead such events in future. Indeed, the 1997 MTL was supposed to be directed by a joint black/white partnership led by Matthew Ashimolowo (Kingsway International) and Colin Dye (Kensington Temple). However, the alliance apparently broke down and Ashimolowo backed out, leaving Colin Dye in charge.[29]

Concluding Remarks

In this chapter, we have explored the various reasons why Cerullo found support for his Mission to London meetings among UK black churches. Crucially for our case, Pentecostalism continues to provide a vital forum for the construction and expression of black cultural identities among African-Caribbean and (more recent) African migrant groups. The evidence suggests that many believers see themselves not only as part of a worldwide community of Christians (Toulis 1997), but also as part of a black diaspora (Beckford 1998; Kalilombe 1997; Edwards 1993). It is intriguing that an American evangelist has managed to capitalise on this niche in the UK religious marketplace, with some success. Cerullo's UK meetings utilise black cultural styles borrowed from black diaspora culture, and the emphasis on miracle healing, power, and prosperity conforms to that found in many Pentecostalist churches. Ultimately, these meetings provided African-Caribbean participants an arena for the expression of ethnic identities. Indeed, Paul Gifford, writing about Cerullo's UK meetings, characterised them as distinctly 'counter-cultural' and noted their dependency on the immigrant churches (1998:328, fn 49).

However, in advancing this interpretation, the reader should keep the following caveats in mind. Not all attenders were black, although the majority were, as we have already seen. For many devotees, these gatherings constitute moments of 'effervescence', when the mundane routine of everyday life is temporarily suspended. From their perspective of faith, believers describe these experiences as the 'movement of the Holy Spirit', 'miracle healing power' or 'Pentecostal power'.

At the same time, there were other activities, such as daytime lectures, concerts and an exhibition hall where 'celebrity' speakers and performing artists sometimes signed autographs and marketed their products. The atmosphere was festive; vendors sold Caribbean cuisine, some attenders 'dressed up' for the occasion, while others spent their summer break at the week-long meeting (Pain and Manning 1993:26). Although the atmosphere was relaxed and friendly, it was also expectant and charged with excitement. In effect, these conventions operated on many different levels, with people attending for all sorts of reasons, as my own contacts bore out (also Gifford 1998:234). Some came for spiritual refreshment, for a 'closer walk with the Lord'; others hoped for miracle cures for specific medical conditions or flagging businesses, or to heal broken relationships with loved ones. Still others came to meet new people, to enjoy themselves generally, or to win temporary respite from tedious chores or awkward spouses – or any combination of the above.[30]

Also problematic are superficial generalisations about identity formation, a process which is complex, multifaceted and shifting. In our case, the best evidence suggests that there are generational differences between Britain's black Pentecostalists in terms of their own self-identities. In her study of first-generation African-Caribbean Pentecostal women, Nicole Toulis suggests that many see themselves 'not as Blacks in a White society, but as "Christians" in an imperfect society and world' (1997:274). While Toulis's conclusion is undoubtedly true for some believers, Robert Beckford argues that many second- and third-generation black Pentecostalists in Britain are increasingly 'aware of the global struggle for a full Black humanity' (Beckford 1998:1–2). To this end, Beckford has sought to create a framework for black liberation theology based on the notion of a 'Dread Jesus' (ibid.). His clarion call to young black Pentecostalists may portend an interesting future development for the ongoing discussion about African-Caribbean identity in Britain.

Notes

1 The terms 'black' or African-Caribbean are used here to designate people in the UK of Caribbean origin, in line with common usage (Toulis 1997:xi).

2 The controversy centred on Cerullo's faith healing claims, when an evangelical physician – during a live TV broadcast – challenged him to 'prove' them. The BBC devoted two episodes in its religion documentary series *Heart of the Matter* to investigating Cerullo and MTL, and, in turn, helped to fuel a panic about the American revivalist and his UK meetings (see Schaefer 2002, 2000).

3 While 'race' is a discredited biological concept, it remains meaningful as a social category linked to ethnicity (Newman 2000:115–16).

4 The term 'black church' has replaced the former reference of 'Negro Church' utilised until the 1960s in the US (Lincoln and Mamiya 1990:1). Here the term will be applied to churches that are 'black' controlled, or 'black led', with predominantly black congregations, with the exception of Kensington Temple. However, labelling remains controversial; see MacRobert (1989); Trotman (1992); Edwards (1993); Kalilombe (1997).

5 The term 'immigrant' is used here – interchangeably with the word 'migrant' – only as a means of distinguishing these (newer) post-Second World War groups from previous black settlers; it does not imply in any way the political or ideological leanings commonly associated with its usage (Mason 1995; Gilroy 1991).

6 Participant observation and conversations with participants at MTL were conducted from 1992 to 1996. These were followed up by interviews with key informants. A full report and analysis is given in Schaefer (1999a).

7 Collective liminality signifies

> an intense community spirit, a feeling of great social solidarity, equality, and togetherness. People experiencing liminality together form a community of equals ... Religious groups often use liminal characteristics to set themselves off from others ... Liminal features may also signal the sacredness of persons, settings, and events by setting them off as extraordinary – outside normal social space and regular time.
>
> (Kottak 1994:389)

8 This same view was recorded by W.E.B. Du Bois over fifty years earlier in America, reflected in the rhetorical question of whites to blacks – 'How does it feel to be a problem?' (Du Bois 1996:3–4).

9 Brierley identifies 'blacks' as 'black Caribbeans, Africans and others' (2000:134).

10 Formerly the head of the Afro-Caribbean Alliance, Revd Edwards is the current head of the Evangelical Alliance (EA) in Britain. For details about the EA, see Randall and Hilborn (2001).

11 This is a gospel-style technique of singing three or more notes for each syllable (Curtis 1987:58).

12 Sometimes devotees would attend a mainline church on Sunday morning and an independent black church on Sunday evening (Beckford 1998:43).

13 In this regard, the UK black churches resemble Pentecostal churches more generally; see Martin (1990:258).

14 However, for others – namely women, gays and those with physical handicaps – these churches may be a source of oppression, a subject beyond the remit of this study (see Beckford 1998:27–30).

15 Simon Coleman, in his study of *Livets Ord* (Word of Life) in Sweden, makes a similar point; see Coleman (1991:7; 1993:353–73).

16 Ministry estimates tended to be highly inflated (Schaefer 1999b:118).

17 On the basis of admittedly impressionistic data, it appears that Cerullo also draws proportionately higher numbers of African-Americans to his events in the US. This conclusion is based mainly on viewing his TV show *Victory* (UK telecasts) from 1992 to 1993 – which included material derived from revivals held in the US – as well as my own attendance at MCWE's 1996 Easter telethon show (hosted by Cerullo and broadcast live from a San Diego hotel).

18 Remarks made by Greg Smith at the Sociology of Religion Study Group 'Religion and Identity' conference, Durham, UK, 9 April 1999. There is no reason to suggest that Smith's example is atypical, although the precise number of attenders from non-sponsoring churches would be difficult to determine with any certainty.

19 Informants have requested anonymity, almost without exception, due mainly to the controversy surrounding Cerullo's ministry in the UK.

20 Interview, 4 March 1998.

21 However, when the invitation to come forward is given at the end of the service, the music is played softly and at a slower tempo.

22 Indeed, Stephen Hunt notes that a somewhat modified form of faith teaching shows up at Kensington Temple, a major Cerullo supporter. Hunt credits the teaching partly for KT's growth, but points out that it has also damaged KT's relationship with its denominational parent, Elim (see Hunt 2000:337, end note 4).

23 Interview, 4 March 1998.

24 Interviews, 7 March 1996; 17 March 1996; 15 January 1998; 4 March 1998.

25 Interview, 15 January 1998.

26 Interviews, 22 July 1995; 4 March 1998.

27 Interview, 4 March 1998.

28 Interviews, 17 March 1996; 15 January 1998.

29 Interviews, 17 March 1996; 4 March 1998.

30 Contrary to public pronouncements about the intention to reach the 'unsaved', numerous studies have indicated that most participants at these types of events are already believers, and that measurable long-term effects are negligible. However, that is not to say that these ritual events cannot be highly meaningful for attenders. Moreover, clear-cut distinctions between formal rituals and everyday practice may not always hold, as Simon Coleman and Peter Collins persuasively argue in their discussion of British Quakers and Swedish charismatic Christians (2000:317–29).

Bibliography

Aldred, J. (1999), 'Response', in A. Anderson and W. Hollenweger (eds) *Pentecostals after a Century: Global Perspectives on a Movement in Transition*, Sheffield: Sheffield Academic Press, pp. 87–8.

Austin-Broos, D. (2001), 'Jamaican Pentecostalism: Transnational Relations and the Nation-State', in A. Corten and R. Marshall-Frantani (eds) *Between Babel and Pentecost*, Bloomington and Indianapolis: University of Indiana Press, pp. 142–62.

Beckford, R. (1998), *Jesus is Dread: Black Theology and Black Culture in Britain*, London: Darton, Longman & Todd.

Benyon, J. and Solomos, J. (1991), 'Race, Injustice and Disorder', in S. MacGregor and B. Pimlott (eds) *Tackling the Inner Cities: The 1980s Reviewed, Prospects for the 1990s*, Oxford: Clarendon Press, pp. 22–43.

Branigan, T. (2001), 'Nation of Islam Granted Appeal on Leader's Ban', *Guardian*, 31 March.

Brierley, P. (ed.) (1998/9), *UK Christian Handbook, Religious Trends*, London: Paternoster Publishing.

Brierley, P. (2000), *The Tide Is Running Out: What the English Church Attendance Survey Reveals*, London: Christian Research.

Bruce, S. (1996), *Religion in the Modern World: From Cathedrals to Cults*, Oxford and New York: Oxford University Press.

Bruce, S. (2001), 'Christianity in Britain, R.I.P.', *Sociology of Religion*, **62**(2), 191–203.

Calley, M. (1965), *God's People: West Indian Pentecostal Sects in England*, London and New York: Oxford University Press.

The Church of England Newspaper (1993), 20 August.

Cohen, A. (1993), *A Masquerade Politics: Explorations in the Structure of Urban Cultural Movements*, Oxford: Berg.

Coleman, S. (1991), '"Faith which Conquers the World": Swedish Fundamentalism and the Globalisation of Culture', *Ethnos*, **56**(1–2), 6–18.

Coleman, S. (1993), 'Conservative Protestantism and the World Order: The Faith Movement in the United States and Sweden', *Sociology of Religion*, **54**, 353–73.

Coleman, S. (2000), *The Globalisation of Charismatic Christianity: Spreading the Gospel of Prosperity*, Cambridge: Cambridge University Press.

Coleman, S. and Collins, P. (2000), 'The "Plain" and the "Positive": Ritual, Experience and Aesthetics in Quakerism and Charismatic Christianity', *Journal of Contemporary Religion*, **15**(3), 317–29.

Curtis, J. (1987), *Rock Eras: Interpretations of Music and Society, 1954–1984*, Bowling Green, OH: Bowling Green State University Press.

Davie, G. (1994), *Religion in Britain since 1945: Believing Without Belonging*, Oxford: Blackwell.

Du Bois, W. (1996 [1903]), *The Souls of Black Folk*, New York: The Modern Library.

Edwards, J. (1993), 'The British Afro-Caribbean Community', in M. Eden (ed.) *Britain on the Brink: Major Trends in Society Today*, Nottingham: Crossway Books, pp. 100–18.

Edwards, J. (1997), 'Afro-Caribbean Pentecostalism in Britain', *The Journal of European Pentecostal Theological Association*, **17**, 37–48.

Fryer, P. (1984), *Staying Power: The History of Black People in Britain*, London and Sydney: Pluto Press.

Gifford, P. (1998), *African Christianity: Its Public Role*, Bloomington and Indianapolis: Indiana University Press.

Gilroy, P. (1991), *'There Ain't No Black in the Union Jack': The Cultural Politics of Race and Nation*, Chicago: University of Chicago Press.

Hackett, R. (1995), 'The Gospel of Prosperity in West Africa', in R. Roberts (ed.) *Religion and the Transformation of Capitalism*, London and New York: Routledge, pp. 199–214.

Hall, S. (1992), 'What Is this "Black" in Black Popular Culture?', in Gina Dent (ed.) *Black Popular Culture*, Seattle, Wash.: Bay Press, pp. 21–32.

Hall, S. (1995), 'Negotiating Caribbean Identities', *New Left Review*, 209.

Hiro, D. (1991), *Black British, White British*, London: Paladin.

Holmes, C. (1997), 'Cosmopolitan London', in A. Kershen (ed.) *London the Promised Land?*, Aldershot: Avebury, pp. 10–37.

Howard, V. (1987), *A Report on Afro-Caribbean Christianity in Britain*, Community Religions Project Research Papers, University of Leeds (4).

Hunt, S. (2000), '"Winning Ways": Globalisation and the Impact of the Health and Wealth Gospel', *Journal of Contemporary Religion*, **15**(3), 331–47.

Hunt, S. and Lightly, N. (2001), 'The British Black Pentecostal "revival": Identity and Belief in the "New" Nigerian Churches', *Ethnic and Racial Studies*, **24**(1), 104–24.

Hunt, S., Walter, T. and Hamilton, M. (eds) (1997), *Charismatic Christianity: Sociological Perspectives*, London and New York: Macmillan Press.

Ismond, P. (2000), 'Cricket – "Passing the Test"? – Analysis of an Interview with David "Syd" Lawrence', *Journal of Popular Culture*, **34**(2), 127–45.

Jacobson, J. (1997), 'Religion and Ethnicity: Dual and Alternative Sources of Identity among Young British Pakistanis', *Ethnic and Racial Studies*, **20**(2), 238–56.

James, W. (1989), 'The Making of Black Identities', in R. Samuel (ed.) *Patriotism: The Making and Unmaking of British National Identity*, Vol. II *Minorities and Outsiders*, London and New York: Routledge, pp. 230–55.

Kalilombe, P. (1997), 'Black Christianity in Britain', *Ethnic and Racial Studies*, **20**(2), 306–324.

Kershen, A. (ed.) (1997), *London: The Promised Land?*, Aldershot: Avebury.

Kottak, C. (1994), *Anthropology: The Exploration of Human Diversity*, New York: McGraw-Hill.

Lincoln, C. and Mamiya, L. (1990), *The Black Church in the African-American Experience*, Durham, NC, and London: Duke University Press.

McGuigan, J. (1996), *Culture and the Public Sphere*, London and New York: Routledge.

MacRobert, I. (1989), 'The New Black-led Pentecostal Churches in Britain', in P. Badham (ed.), *Religion, State, and Society in Modern Britain*, Lewiston: Edwin Mellon Press, pp. 119–43.

Martin, D. (1990), *Tongues of Fire: The Explosion of Protestantism in Latin America*, Oxford: Blackwell.

Martin, D. (2002), *Pentecostalism: The World Their Parish*, Oxford and Malden, MA: Blackwell.

Marwick, A. (1987), *British Society Since 1945*, Harmondsworth, Penguin.

Mason, D. (1995), *Race and Ethnicity in Modern Britain*, Oxford: Oxford University Press.

MCWE (1994) *There Is a Power*, issues 1–80.

Mission To London Official Programme (MCWE), 1992–6.

Nanton, P. (1997), 'The Caribbean Diaspora in the Promised Land', in A. Kershen (ed.) *London: The Promised Land?*, Aldershot: Avebury, pp. 110–27.

Newman, D. (2000), *Sociology: Exploring the Architecture of Everyday Life*, 3rd edn, Thousand Oaks, Calif.: Pine Forge Press.

Pain, T. and Manning, C. (1993), *Miracles Are Impossible: You Decide*, Robertsbridge, East Sussex: Battle Books.

Percy, M. (1996), *Words, Wonders and Power: Understanding Contemporary Fundamentalism and Revivalism*, London: SPCK.

Pratt, R. (1990), *Rhythm and Resistance: Explorations in the Political Uses of Popular Music*, New York: Praeger.

Randall, I. and Hilborn, D. (2001), *'One Body in Christ': The History and Significance of the Evangelical Alliance*, Carlisle: Paternoster Press.

Rosenberg, B. (1970), *The Art of the American Folk Preacher*, New York: Oxford University Press.

Schaefer, N. (1999a), *'Making the Rulers Tremble!': A Sociological Study of Morris Cerullo World Evangelism in Britain'*, unpublished Ph.D. thesis, University of Aberdeen.

Schaefer, N. (1999b), ' "Some Will See Miracles": The Reception of Morris Cerullo World Evangelism in Britain', *Journal of Contemporary Religion*, **14**(1), 111–26.

Schaefer, N. (2000), 'An American "Faith Healer" in Britain: Another Moral Panic?', *Journal of American & Comparative Cultures*, **23**(3), 1–15.

Schaefer, N. (2002), 'The BBC and an American "Faith Healer": The Making of a Folk Devil?', *Journal of Contemporary Religion*, **17**(1), 39–59.

Scotland, N. (1995), *Charismatics and the Next Millennium*, London: Hodder & Stoughton.

Toulis, N. (1997), *Believing Identity: Pentecostalism and the Mediation of Jamaican Ethnicity and Gender in England*, Oxford and New York: Berg.

Trotman, A. (1992), 'Black, Black-led or What?', in J. Edwards (ed.) *Let's Praise Him Again!*, Eastbourne: Kingsway Publications, pp. 12–35.

Victory [no date, circa 1993], special edition, MCWE.

Victory Miracle Living [VLM] (1996), MCWE, February.

The Voice of Healing (TVH) (1955), March.

Walker, A. (1997), 'Thoroughly Modern: Sociological Reflections on the Charismatic Movement at the End of the Twentieth Century', in S. Hunt, T. Walter and M. Hamilton (eds) *Charismatic Christianity: Sociological Perspectives*, London and New York: Macmillan Press, pp. 17–43.

Wedenoja, W. (1980), 'Modernization and the Pentecostal Movement in Jamaica', in S. Glazier (ed.) *Perspectives on Pentecostalism*, Washington, DC: University Press of America, pp. 27–48.

Wintour, P. (2001), 'Racial Inequality "Set to Widen"', *Guardian*, 7 August.

CHAPTER 9

Protestant Women – Protesting Faith

Tangling Secular and Religious Identity in Northern Ireland

Katy Radford

Shankill Radio 108.5 FM Request – Friday June 1999: 'This one goes out to the Orangemen on the Hill from all the Ladies of the Shankill Women Support Drumcree Group. They say they'll be up again this weekend to offer their support, and in the meantime here's a "True Blue" Medley to keep your spirits high 'til youse get down that road.'

It has been claimed that in Northern Ireland, Catholicism versus Protestantism is the most highly rated ethno-political category, with denominational social identity frequently considered a more important division than either gender or social class (Cairns and Mercer 1984). In this chapter the intention is to describe events at a controversial Orange parade,[1] at Drumcree, as the experience directly relates to a group of Protestant women from the Shankill Road in Belfast.[2] For the women referred to in this chapter, their Protestant identity is most cogently expressed not through religious worship but rather through secular loyalist practices, and their participation in the event will be considered in the light of other protests and demonstrations they are involved with. My prime interest is to position this piece as a demonstration of interdependence between secular and devout practices within political and religious rituals in Northern Ireland. To that end I will introduce the piece by briefly considering the role of the church parade as an example of Orange and other loyal orders' parades, and in addition will look at the background to their controversial stance at Drumcree.

My second concern embraces the subaltern roles accorded to loyalist women at these protests and parades and their seeming acquiescence to playing these character parts. Despite participating as loyalist activists at a number of events which are central to assertions of Protestant identity in Northern Ireland, women who do so undergo a process of peripheralisation (Radford 2001). They are thus rendered subordinate as actors within the political and religious rituals they are engaged in, with plaudits paid to the domesticity of their involvement over their attempts at agitation. It will be demonstrated that an objectification takes place across a number of contexts within both the domestic and the public arenas by gendered expectations imposed by family and fellow activists and, in addition, publicly, through media representation. This in turn presents the women as voiceless images, embodied through media representation as 'product', illustrative of Protestant political intransigence.

Within academic literature, the activities of loyalist women are less covered than those of either republican women or loyalist men (Morgan and Fraser 1994).

However, a few noteworthy exceptions are worth mentioning in light of the ethnographic content of this chapter. Nelson (1984) incorporates oral testimonies of women associated with paramilitary organisations and Sales (1997:148) notes the Women's Ulster Defence Association (UDA) was disbanded in 1974, and suggests that 'women's activities have centred largely on support for male prisoners and welfare work'. These authors' work supports and echoes Edgerton's (1986:70), which claims that women have been 'motivated to political action in most cases by their perceived family responsibilities. Yet the collective power and social identity that women acquired through their public activity has not been reflected in an altered position within the home.'

Church Parades

From Easter Tuesday onwards parades are a significant feature of the Orange calendar. There are regular church parades from local Orange Halls to services to commemorate (among others) Remembrance Sunday, the Sunday before 12 July and Reformation Sunday. Unlike the secular parades where 'blood and thunder' flute bands prevail, accordion bands (whose membership is often dominated by women), when available, provide the accompaniment at church parades. Less popular in urban areas than in previous years, accordions are perceived to be more 'genteel' than flute bands as they are less raucous and therefore deemed 'more appropriate' for Sunday parades. As only sacred hymns or religious music are played on these parades, the atmosphere created by those who turn out to support them is very different from that of other parades. Secular parades tend to command much larger crowds made up of revellers intent on following the bands, and jostling and 'partying' in the streets even when the parade passes out of the local area. Conversely, Sunday parades are often restricted to a short walk from the local Orange Hall to a nearby church. They may only attract the attention of a discreet number of fellow worshippers or individuals and families in the locale who often keep a respectful distance (creating a liminal space between spectators and participants) by not venturing past an open front door to watch the church-goers. Sunday parades are a regular feature along the 2 kilometres that make up the Shankill Road where there are in the region of 25 places of worship, all of denominations within Protestantism. During the marching season, seven parades leave the West Belfast Orange Hall on the Shankill Road, four of which are church parades and one of which is a women's parade. However, the line between the raucous secular and the more mannered church parades has been significantly blurred by the annual church parade in Drumcree which, despite being accompanied by a small accordion band comprising women and children, developed into one of the most controversial parades of the 1990s.

Drumcree One[3]

The year 1995 was one of relative peace in Northern Ireland. In 1994 the Combined Loyalist Military Command (CLMC) and the Irish Republican Army (IRA) had both called ceasefires, though paramilitaries were still conducting 'punishment' attacks. A seeming calm in the wider community was shattered by the events subsequent to senior police officers calling on legislation specific to Northern Ireland (Public Order (Northern Ireland) Order 1987) to determine that a change to a parade route be made by members of Portadown No. 1 District Loyal Orange Lodge (hereafter referred to as Dist. 1). This unfolded into what has become known to loyalists as 'The Drumcree Stand-Off', with badges, songs and other regalia produced annually to commemorate it.

The episode that developed involved approximately 300 Orangemen attending a Church of Ireland service in the Drumcree Parish Church. They wished to parade the 5 kilometres 'home' to their Orange Hall in Carlton Street, Portadown, accompanied by an accordion band from the town, following a route they are recorded to have taken since 1807.[4] The route lasts for approximately 2 kilometres and within a few hundred metres of leaving the church, it crosses a small bridge spanning a tributary of the Bann. There it enters the Garvaghy Road that bisects a predominantly Catholic housing estate.

Activists who campaign together under the banner of the Garvaghy Road Residents' Association represent many of the inhabitants of the estate and they have been lobbying for several years to have the Orangemen's return from the service rerouted. They object to the intrusion and claim triumphalism is displayed on such parades by an organisation whose overt political objectives are the maintenance of the current union of the United Kingdom and Northern Ireland and the defence of this Protestant geography from the spread of Catholicism. The marches are seen by both communities to act as both an affirmation of Protestant identity and an allegiance to a Protestant monarch. Ceremonial swords, pikes, banners and royal memorabilia are prominently displayed and ironically bring to mind Kertzer's suggestion (1988:181) that 'an insurgent force that lacks its own distinctive symbolism and rites is not likely to get far'. Dist. 1's response to the decree was rejection and they mustered support from the parent organisation, the Grand Orange Lodge of Ireland. As residents from the Garvaghy Road demonstrated their concerns over the parade, Orangemen and other loyalists began to arrive to display the unacceptability of the decision. Between the two groups, and vilified in different measures by each, were the police, the Royal Ulster Constabulary (RUC).

The Orangemen refused to talk directly to the Residents' Association, who in their view were being manipulated by nationalist sympathisers led by Sinn Fein, and a series of negotiations was brokered by professional mediators. This resulted in the RUC reversing their decision and permitting the Orangemen (now closer to 600) to walk down the road without the band. Residents silently lined the road in protest and the Orangemen were seen to march solemnly by. However, on arriving in Portadown to tumultuous applause, two highly prominent politicians, Orangeman David Trimble, once First Minister of the Northern Ireland Assembly,[5] and Ian Paisley, a seasoned campaigner and political agitator, were filmed joining hands in a congratulatory jig. This response was in direct contrast to the dignified quasi-religious atmosphere that they had been attempting to create outside the church confines. It was widely reported as a display of triumphalism and produced anger and hurt, in particular in Catholic communities.

Drumcree Two

The following year, 1996, a second stand-off occurred when the police again attempted to reroute the parade on 7 July. Reinforcements were called on by each of the key players: the police were fortified by the British Army who erected barbed-wire fences at the bridge, the residents mustered support from other Residents' Associations, and a large Orange corpus at Drumcree was supplemented by the presence of paramilitaries and other loyalists. Furthermore, rather than the Orangemen attempting to mobilise their fellow 'bretheren' in Portadown, Lodges arranged marches close to Catholic areas throughout Northern Ireland, which put pressure on policing. Over the following four days, the supporters of the Drumcree Orangemen created havoc as they began rioting throughout Northern Ireland: road blocks were set up, bonfires lit, cars hijacked and businesses closed early, 1000 extra British troops were deployed and a Catholic taxi driver was shot dead by paramilitaries. When the decision to reverse the rerouting was taken, Garvaghy residents were forcibly removed from the road and rioting began in nationalist areas. A protester was killed in (London)Derry by an armoured car.

Drumcree Three

By the time of the third Drumcree in 1997, with the decision taken to push the march through once again, the RUC were accused of capitulating to the threat of Protestant mob rule. The small church and the subsequent violence that did ensue once again became the focus of the world's media, with journalists and camera operators juggling for space, stories and the sensational. Similarly, it attracted the attention of many national and international researchers. It was a clear demonstration of how political ritual can both play a role in the construction of an illusion around a community's socially cohesive qualities and simultaneously act as a catalyst for insurrection.

In 1998, the Parades Commission, the body to determine disputes over parades, much to the frustration of the loyalist community, drew on the new 1998 Public Processions (NI) Act to rule then (and each subsequent year) that the Drumcree parade be rerouted. As a defence to the Garvaghy Road residents, trenches were dug around the field by the army and protected by thousands of metres of barbed wire, while a huge metal barrier blocked the Orangemen's route across the bridge. Violence again erupted. Catholic churches and Protestant Orange Halls were burnt out, and the brutality culminated in the death of three Catholic children, brothers killed in a petrol bomb attack on their home in a predominantly Protestant estate in Ballymoney.

As a result, Drumcree has become a political hot potato with huge economic reverberations for the state and commercial sector. Some of the more moderate unionist politicians are now less eager to be drawn publicly on the dispute and have joined some church leaders, including the Church of Ireland Primate, in calling for the protest to end. City-centre traders in Belfast close early or remain shut during the Drumcree period, concerned about potential rioting and loss of business due to many citizens who have no direct involvement in Drumcree (and who can afford to) now leaving Northern Ireland during this tense period. The Orange Order is divided between those members who see its role as the respectable[6] face of loyalism undermined by their association with Drumcree, and those who are supporters of the manner in which Dist. 1 continue their stand. The latter have been engaged in a continued protest over the issue, some maintaining a presence at the hill, and, to the chagrin of the former group, have aligned themselves with widespread civil disturbances in support of what they describe as the pursuance of their civil and religious liberties.

The Shankill Women Support Drumcree Group

As an extension of the protests, boycotts and campaigns some have been conducting in the name of loyalism for the past 30 years, a core group of around 20 women from the Shankill Road, many of pensionable age, come together on an *ad hoc* basis. Their banner reads 'The Shankill Women Support Drumcree Group'.

Their aim is to offer solidarity to the Orangemen through their visits throughout the year to Drumcree where they perform loyalist songs (some of which they have penned themselves), through social evenings and through the weekly attempt to parade down the Garvaghy Road after each Sunday service. The greatest tribute the women pay each other is to verify or acknowledge 'loyalty'. ('See my granny's flag? Her Union Jack is bigger than the one on the Orange Hall!' 'Oh aye, she was always very loyal your granny, very loyal.')

The women's presence at Drumcree is acknowledged by the protest leaders. They in turn demonstrate a paternalistic tolerance of them, projecting them into a role of crowd warmers and address them in terms that stress the domesticity of their activism rather than considering them to be serious political agitators. At an Orange cultural evening organised by Dist. 1, Harold Gracey, the Lodge Grandmaster, introduced them by saying:

> I'd like especially to welcome tonight, (and put your hands together too for) the ladies of the Shankill Road in Belfast. I'd like to thank the ladies on behalf of Portadown District, not only for the money that they've raised, but for their company at the hill. We're delighted every time you come up and we hope you'll come up pretty often – that's if I'm not down the road! [Laughs.] If I have to take my Christmas dinner down there I'll do that – but that's in the Lord's hands. I don't know how to thank these ladies – it is almost impossible. The ladies who come to the soup kitchen, or the café on the hill as they call it – they come out every night and do they really have to do it? They come out whatever the weather to provide the soup, the tea, the stew – my best thanks to them – without you, this would not be possible.

The women standing informally around the edge of the seated crowd were then introduced as 'The Hen Roost Choir'. It was clear that they were no choir in the conventional sense when, encouraged to take the cymbals from the Mourne Young Defenders (a 'blood and thunder' flute band who had previously entertained the crowd) and with an audience clapping in time, the women danced around the hall accompanying the band to the popular loyalist song 'Derry's Walls'. Though a secular song, in the line 'They knew the Lord was on their side, to help them in the fight' it asks for God' s blessing for saving the Williamite Protestant Apprentice Boys in Derry in their seventeenth-century fight against James's invasion. This religious emphasis within secular songs can be seen within a tradition of Protestant witness-bearing, and is a characteristic of several 'Orange' songs.

The women are loosely affiliated through membership of a group that exists with no rules or constitution. As such, they may be considered a quasi group (according to Ginsberg's (1934) and Mayer's (1966) definition of entities), with no recognisable structure but united through certain common interests and modes of behaviour, though some are introduced to the group through kinship ties, with two mother/daughter/granddaughter connections. Their ability to attend individual protests is primarily determined by family responsibilities on that day as these are the relationships privileged above all other commitments. Others come to the group through neighbourly relationships that have developed over a number of years. Their Protestantism is most convincingly demonstrated through their loyalist protests, though two are also Orange women.[7] The organisation of the group is unstructured: membership fluctuates with women who wish to show solidarity only at particular events welcomed into the group for the duration of that protest alone. No single person takes on the role of central co-ordinator; face-to-face encounters and telephone ring-rounds between the women confirm the time and dates of events. They hear about potential protests through a number of sources, primarily through community-based organisations and workers who also provide the means with which to photocopy leaflets for distribution at events or who equip the women with placards when necessary. Occasionally transport is provided to protests, but more often than not the women expect to fend for themselves.

Many of the older women have been involved in political agitation in the Shankill since the 1970s. While this activity was often directly linked to inter-community violence at the time, it was also often initiated to highlight social deprivation including the closing of schools and facilities in the area. Their actions followed a tradition within Protestantism in the North of Ireland for women to mobilise as political agitators (Edgerton 1986; Holmes and Urquhart 1994). Yet once co-opted, women have invariably subordinated issues of particular interest to them to the pursuance of sectarian ideology. Nonetheless, the women see their practices as a necessary and legitimate weapon within the loyalist armoury that they as women have at their disposal. They are encouraged in their activities by male activists and male family members alike, on the proviso that other domestic commitments are not neglected.

It is noteworthy that even when conducted outside the Shankill, their actions rarely bring them into direct confrontation with Catholic communities.[8] Their attentions are primarily aimed at fellow Protestants and are concerned with highlighting political concessions by moderate unionists which they believe may undermine a Protestant hegemony and challenge mass allegiance to the crown. Recent activities include protesting about proposed symbolic changes to the police service which they do through a number of tactics including closing roads and leafleting drivers. They frequently picket the Assembly over the removal of the Union Jack from government buildings and heckle pro-Belfast Good Friday Agreement delegates at Ulster Unionist party meetings whom they see as 'selling out' the 'unionist family'. As protesters, they are photographed by journalists to support articles. However, as there is often no reference to the women within the text, they are presented as two-dimensional illustrative images. Their role in Drumcree as peripheral actors within the context of a religious ritual can similarly be seen to exemplify their subordination as women by both the media and the men, the principal players.

By considering the viewpoint of the women at Drumcree whose role in the male-dominated performance is one of support, it is possible to look inside a contemporary, changing political and religious ritual by the introduction of 'other' human and individual responses. The 'other', in this instance, is based not on a religious differentiation, as is often the case in analysis around Northern Ireland material, but on gender and secular loyalism. By exploring the Drumcree ritual from a gendered perspective, it becomes clear that despite the very prominent face the women are accorded publicly by the press, their attempts at political agitation are measured by conservative expectations of women within their community. The position in relation to male power structures within the community and their media-projected public face is one which they have little opportunity to construct and which reinforces their subaltern status and lack of agency. Such an exploration may help to reveal the very frailty and temporal nature of the ritual, dependent on both the sacred and the 'other' for its validity and existence.

July 2000: Waiting in the Morning

We had met at nine o'clock that Sunday morning at the Woodvale end of the Shankill and had waited beside the park for the rickety old bus to arrive. The park was still full of the debris and detritus left by the Shankill Festival 'culture' day the previous Friday as the festival organisers and the City Council were in dispute as to who should be responsible for clearing it. As the minutes ticked by those women who hadn't been at the event tutted about the state of the park while those who had relayed what a great day it had been and accorded that the entertainment had been 'powerful'.

> 'There was literally hundreds there, from all over. Some even from down the road, down your way too. There was a fair and rides for the children, and that what do you call him was on. The impressions man. He does Gerry Adams and Paisley, you know him. John McBlain.'
> 'Who done the music?'
> 'Oh it was them 'uns. Not Platoon. The other ones, the Young Guns. The ones from Alternatives done the security.'

The short exchange between the women provided a set of markers indicating from where primary support for the event was drawn, namely from one of the main Protestant paramilitary factions, the Ulster Volunteer Force (UVF), but not from the other principal one, the UDA. The signifiers used are in keeping with Burton's (1978) 'telling' which has further been described by Howe (1990:13) and cited in Sales (1997:142) as the 'syndrome of signs by which Catholics and Protestants arrive at religious ascription in their everyday interaction'. But whereas these authors consider 'telling' to denote religious divisions, they are equally used as intra-community markers within Protestantism. In this instance they indicate allegiance to different paramilitary factions. Such allegiances play a salient role in how members of a community regulate their behaviour when dealing with the 'other' (in this case the 'other' is from within the community).

Alternatives is a Restorative Justice programme with close connections to the UVF. Similarly Platoon and Young Guns are guitar- and vocal-led groups that regularly perform throughout Northern Ireland and Scotland at clubs and at events run by the UVF, the Progressive Unionist Party (PUP) and their supporters. Their repertoire comprises no original compositions, but reworkings of club tunes, chart hits, Irish traditional music and rebel songs. The added lyrics both laud UVF paramilitary activists, their battalions and battles ('Brian Robinson', 'Some Gave All', 'Here Lies a Soldier'). They attempt to legitimate the current UVF by drawing on alleged historical connections with the British Army Regiment of the First World War, the 36th Ulster Division ('Daddy's Uniform', 'Gun Runners', 'Private Billy McFadzean'). Performances in sympathetic clubs like the Shankill Road Rangers Supporters Club are sold out well in advance. And on 'fund raiser' nights, in the relative privacy of the clubs, the stage is usually draped with UVF, Ulster and Scotland flags and flags with Red Hand iconography.[9]

The bus arrives. 'Where were you? You're late. Where you drunk last night?' The driver is harangued good-naturedly. Some of the women were going up in cars later in the day and the remaining eight of us, some of whom don't know each other, are travelling by a bus hired through a contact in a local community centre. The driver who had several other jobs on that day had to be cajoled into taking us with the promise of a sizeable tip. The heater on the bus didn't work, and the radio hissed. 'They've given us an auld charabanc. Typical.' 'Sure it's never an easy road to be a loyal Protestant.'

Once in Portadown, no one knows the way to the church. After several wrong turns the driver eventually finds Corcrain Orange Hall. As Ena Mannion gets out to ask the assembling Orangemen the way to Drumcree a quavering old voice from the back of the bus shouts, 'You should get a man here today, Ena.'

Since being left with a young daughter by her husband, an English soldier, 20 years ago, Ena has lived and been primary carer to her invalid mother, now in her nineties. An attractive, well-groomed women just turned 50, Ena ignores the comment. Even with new directions, the bus driver manages to get lost again and ends up at the town end of the Garvaghy Road. Though the streets are empty of citizens, the women are nervous. Ena gets down off the bus again and takes off the bandanna tied round her neck with a picture of King William crossing the Boyne.

'Oh my God but my orange feet shall walk on the Garvaghy Road today', she jokes to one of the RUC men who laughs and redirects the minibus up Obins Street. Ena turns on her heel and shouts back at him: 'To think we're out there fighting for your name badge and you're stopping us getting up that road.'

But the policeman doesn't rise and carries on smiling. The bus eventually deposits us half a kilometre from the church and before speeding off to his next job arranges to return there at five o'clock to pick us up. The rest of the journey is made slowly on foot, picking past stationary cars that line the narrow country road and stopping at various intervals to greet middle-aged and elderly Orangemen in suits and their wives in their sober Sunday best.

The potential congregation for the annual Orange Lodge church service at Drumcree Parish Church promenade like figures from a local contemporary Canaletto. After the service is over, some of the women (identifiable as the church attenders by their skirts and dresses) will return to their cars. There they will serve up hot boxes of roast Sunday dinners prepared earlier to fortify the men before their short walk down to the bridge and back. They are all keen to hear the speeches made by representatives of the Lodge, which will call on the Orangemen to ignore appeals from within the Unionist Party for calm, but to continue tactics of support and civil disturbance throughout the Province. 'We are not on our knees, brothers, but on our bellies.'

The Shankill women identify with the position and lament: 'The whole unionist family's destroyed – it's ruined – why are they givin' in to so much – what are we supposed to do? Sit at the fire twiddlin' were [our] Protestant thumbs?'

At this stage the air is one of a genteel family day out – the participants aim to epitomise the 'respectable' side of Orangeism. Respectability in this instance translates as the advancement of values and mores deemed 'decent' by promotion of observance of the tenets of the Scriptures. It is also coupled with the tradition of an unchallenged patriarchal status quo, both domestically and through the subaltern role that the women's lodges take within the organisation and on parades. In addition to such internal gender stereotyping and subordination, the notion of respectability is further problematised by the explicit exclusivity of the Order, which as a religious organisation prescribes against members marrying Roman Catholics or attending Catholic ceremonies including funerals.[10] Adherence to the *Constitution, Laws and Ordinances of the Loyal Institution of Ireland* (Grand Orange Lodge of Ireland 1967) entails that every Orangeman (and woman) 'should strenuously oppose the fatal errors and doctrines of the Church of Rome, and scrupulously avoid countenancing (by his presence or otherwise) any act of ceremony of Popish worship'.

Caravans are parked along the lanes with their shutters down. During the morning and early afternoon these caravans are redundant props. They won't be opened until the evening when they will do a roaring trade as burger bars with those loyalists who do not come down until later in the day to carry on the protest throughout the evening. Those who come in the evening to offer support and solidarity with the Orangemen bring dramatic, violent tensions and changes to the current pastoral quiet. Their interest is not with the doctrinal messages being transmitted, but with a more explicit loyalist ideology.

It is now eleven o'clock and the church service is about to begin. The Shankill women are there primarily to agitate throughout the day, and in this role, they don't usually attend the church service. Today they do so as there is no more wall space left to sit on outside, and they didn't fancy going into the field just yet because Ena's chest was bad. 'I'd better stay off the grass for as long as I can with this auld asthma of mine! We may as well go inside.' We make our way into the church. Sitting in the warmth of the back pew, the women nudge each other and pass comments on the faces they recognise filing in. 'Hush, stop that, you're not in the Rangers now you know – stick that in your gub.' Renee passes her mother Myna an extra strong mint as the congregation rise. The pretty nineteenth-century church is packed and bathed in a hue of orange sashes.

Though all profess to be loyal Protestants, few of the Shankill women attend church services on a regular basis. When I point this out, it is seen as a criticism with which none are comfortable and an attempt is made to demonstrate their belief.[11] Margaret McArtney, who in her seventies describes herself as 'a true and loyal believer of 40 years', stopped supporting the church when the moderator took a stand on cross-community issues that she could not condone.

> People might call me a bigot, but I do love my faith and my religion, I can't help it now. But I'll have to tell you a story about church. I am a Presbyterian and I did go to church. And then one Sunday I took bad. I'm being honest with you, I kept paying in and my husband still did go – but see the new moderator? An Orangeman and an ex-Shankill Road man too – he went on the TV about keeping the Orangemen out of church. Well from that day on I have paid nothing more. And I now pay into the mission hall. I have a box for the mission hall and that's just what I do now.

Scotch Irene (46) straightens her Orange collarette[12] to the opening bars of the processional hymn sung to the tune of Horsley that the minister refers to as 'Golgotha'. The clarity of the few voices that tentatively warble 'There is a Green Hill Far Away' is drowned out by the mass crescendo of mumbles to the second line. Hymn book pages are frantically turned and glasses adjusted by those disguising their unfamiliarity with the Victorian hymn by Mrs Cecil Alexander, the wife of the Bishop of Derry. The worshippers as Orangemen and women draw heavily on biblical iconography on their banners and insignia and are encouraged by the minister to ponder the geographical similarities between the green hill far away in a promised land and District 1's predicament on a small drumlin outside Portadown. The women's sense of self-righteousness and suffering for their faith is further fuelled by the fact that none of them believe the Lodge will be allowed to return to the Portadown via the Garvaghy Road this year, but will at some stage in the future. 'Let me tell you something, Kate, God's slow but sure.'

The service now over, Drumcree 6 is in full swing. The Shankill women have brought sandwiches and flasks of tea which they're sharing in the field before the speeches start. It is a densely crowded arena of little activity but unmitigated surveillance. Ena looks through binoculars. She sees past the ebbing and flowing sea of loyalist heads to the field across the tributary that leads off the River Bann. On that side of the bridge, cordoned off by a 5-metre-high barricade bedecked in loyalist flags caught up on the razor wire, she views soldiers standing stock still, individuals hidden behind riot helmets, shields and armoured Saracens. They are the Garvaghy residents' first row of defence and in turn they are scrutinising the loyalists through their rifle sights as astutely as the broadcasters and journalists are peering through their lenses.

Given that arguments about the objectification and power(lessness) of women in photographic images often assume a male subject, they have frequently been conducted by assessing the conventions of pornography and the exoticisation of women. However, the fetishisation of post-menopausal women, outdoors, swaddled in trousers, baggy sweaters and waterproof macs and engaged in spitting out a chorus of vitriolic invective or linking arms in a communal sing-a-long, hardly makes the stuff of erotica. Therefore discussions about 'looking relationships' or the 'gaze' in this instance are removed from the confines of the body alone. Rather, focus on the Shankill women throws into relief the objectification of bodies, but falls instead on a unique aspect of their social reality, their loyalism, privileging this constituent element above all others, often without their consent and (depending on the positioning of the camera) sometimes without their prior knowledge. Even when the women are aware that they are being filmed or recorded, they express a sense of powerlessness over how their opinions are decontextualised and presented. As campaigners on a number of issues, their opinions in one situation may be sought with regard to parallel crusades they are conducting. They acknowledge their lack of skills in dealing with the media who they feel misrepresent, deflect or ignore their concerns unless they represent the particular perspective which the press are attempting to elicit from them. Equally, they recognise that to refuse contact with the media removes their opinions from the equation. Ena laments that they can never solicit engagement, rather they are called on when it suits the more powerful party (see Parkinson 1998).

> This American reporter from the BBC asks us 'Sure it's a Protestant force for a Protestant people.' Well I had to chime in there so I says, 'Excuse me dear' – I says – 'don't stand there and tell me it's a Protestant force for a Protestant people, for there's Roman Catholic people in this RUC. There's Roman Catholic people that want to join the RUC but it's the IRA Sinn Fein that won't let them in.' But she didn't put that in. I says to you, Kate, you see all these reporters? No matter what we say, they're just putting in wee comments at the end.

The Shankill women pack away their remaining food and flasks into carrier bags that double up as ground sheets, and a vanguard party of five of the older ones pick their way slowly down the muddy field, spoiling for a sing-song. At the bridge, bored onlookers are temporarily distracted by a BBC crew who are trying to fish a tripod out of the river that loyalist men (not wanting to be filmed) had thrown in. Flag-waving jeerers good-naturedly egg them on. Commenting on a noticeable lack of gallantry on the part of the men, the women teeteringly try to get out of the field by clambering up a small bank and stepping over a low hedge. Once on the bridge they unravel and stand underneath their makeshift sheet banner with red, white and blue writing that reads 'Shankill Women Support Drumcree'.

Sandra's mobile phone rings. 'That was my daughter, we're on UTV, come on we'll give them a song.' They begin to sing 'The Drumcree Stand-Off'. Margaret has the words to the songs printed out and she holds them for the other women to see, but most of them know them by heart. She proudly explains: '"The Drumcree Stand-Off" was written by my daughter Katherine for Drumcree 1998. Katherine as youse know girls just sat down and wrote the words. And when the music goes, well it just really riles up my blood. Oh I *wisht* I had my tambourine with me.' The song is sung to the tune of a UVF song 'Will You Stand' which calls for loyalty to the crown during the First World War.[13]

The Drumcree Stand-Off
Oh will you stand, oh will you stand,
Oh will you stand for God and Ulster as a loyal Orangeman
Will you walk Garvaghy Road with a brave a loyal goal
If you stand then you're a loyal Orangeman.

Chorus
And when the stand-off at Drumcree is over
It's shoulder to shoulder we stand
As we walk down the Road they call Garvaghy
And remember that it still is British land.

Oh will you stand [× 3] against McKenna he's Sinn Fein's right hand man
He plans to take away our rights
But we'll sure put up a fight
If you stand then you're a loyal Orangeman.

Chorus

Oh will you stand [× 3] with Harold Gracey he's a loyal Ulster man
With Bible and with crown
Will you walk in Portydown
If you stand then you're a loyal Orangeman.

Chorus [× 2]

The troops remain impassive. 'Perhaps they're too busy to hear us', says Margaret to no one in particular and no one in particular nods and smiles benignly back.

In Ceribašić's (2000) discussions on how gender is defined through Croatian national discourses during war, she notes that the main body of popular music, though performed by women, is composed, lyricised, arranged and produced by men. The text of the song 'My Loved One Is in the National Guard' (performed by Sanja Trumbic), Ceribašić notes, links concepts of homeland, home and homemaker through fundamental New Testament-inspired Christian values of faith, trust, love and truth. The librettist leads us to believe that with God's intercession, brave, self-sacrificing, devoted male protectors will defend these Croatian ideals. This analysis is an extension of Bradby's (1993:168) suggestions that 'gendering of voices appears as a powerful restatement of traditional gender divisions'.

An initial reading of the situation suggests that the model does not fit the Shankill women's songs where texts are underpinned with the notion that the women can effect political change and challenge the enemy through their solidarity with their male counterparts. Adapting new lyrics to the tune of 'Dad's Army', the women sing: 'We are the girls who will stop your little game, we are the girls who will make you think again.' They call for a loyalist totality which stands together in the face of threats from within and without the Protestant community. Though it would appear that the songs offer an ideal platform for the empowerment of the women, this is not in fact a true reflection of their situation. Though the women's songs (often their own compositions) are welcomed at events and despite a thriving pirate recording industry which disseminates loyalist tapes, their songs are never recorded or distributed through informal or formal channels.

The crowd indicates that the Orangemen are about to walk down to the bridge and before the women move away to listen to the speeches, they are cheered by the crowd as they belt out (to the tune of 'Roaming in the Gloaming'):

Roaming up the Shankill, with a lil accordion band,
Roaming up the Shankill with a lil accordion band,
When the bands begin to play, kick the Pope and Dollie's Brae
Oh it's lovely roaming up the Shankill.

Shankill will be Shankill when the Falls is buggered up
Shankill will be Shankill and we'll keep our colours up
We're as good as any Fenian, as ever went to Mass
And if you don't believe it you can lick my Orange ass.

Hospital and Home

The Orangemen haven't made it past the cordon on the bridge. By the time the bus is due to arrive, the atmosphere has begun to change. Many of the families present earlier have returned home, their places beginning to be taken by other loyalists, the overwhelming majority of them men, some of whom are wearing T-shirts in support of different paramilitary factions and battalions. Margaret, too, left shortly after the speeches which called equally for trust in God and for militant support for the Orangemen. She shared a taxi back the 50 miles to the Shankill in time to make her husband his dinner. Her intention is to return later on that night after her husband has eaten; this, with her daughter's help, she does.

The remaining women reassemble outside the church. Some are having their photographs taken with prominent Orangemen, some with the church in the background. It has been a long day, full of emotion. Ena starts to sway. 'I'm going dizzy, girls,' she says before collapsing to the ground in a faint. Semi-conscious, she is awkwardly lifted to her feet by the women and watched by men sitting on the wall who offer no attempt to help. 'Help us take her over to the church will you?' one of the women asks a man who had been standing beside her when she sang. The man slowly gets down off the wall on which he has been sitting and wanders off. David Jones, the spokesman for District 1, walks by and recognising the women greets them. He agrees to summon a paramedic from further down the hill, but as he walks off, he is waylaid and delayed by a journalist; his priority is no longer the sick woman. Ena, frightened by her faint, begins to have an asthma attack, she is visibly distressed and panicky. 'What about my mommy?' she asks. 'I'll have to get back to look after my mommy.' Georgie calls an ambulance from a mobile phone and suggests that she stay with Ena while the rest go back to the bus. The little country lanes are blocked with cars leaving and arriving. Twenty-five minutes later the ambulance driver edges his vehicle towards the church. She is taken to Craigavon Hospital where she is kept in for observation.

The Shankill women are accorded elder status due to their familiar presence at loyalist protests. But their lack of power when confronted by the media and the casualness with which they are treated by the men they support reflect their limited effect as political agitators. Their activities are looked upon with benign good humour by those ring-siders jostled out of key locations by the women who merely provide a form of light comic relief as the warm-up act before the principal characters take to the stage, be they the Orangemen after the service, or the male loyalists who arrive in the evening. Yet there is no tangible reciprocity of concern when Ena is taken ill.

Power Play in a Political Ritual

Though considering Drumcree primarily as a political ritual, it may be of assistance to bear in mind claims that political ritual 'lies at the interface between "religion" and "politics"' (Boholm 1996). Religious tenets frequently work alongside and bolster the political state through the incorporation of the cosmological into civil life. This is widely demonstrable through Israeli state law, which is derived from the concept of Halacha (Rabbinical law) (Sered 1992). Similarly, Koranic law, Moors (1995) suggests, is used to assert male hegemony in property ownership over women in certain Islamic states.

The role the Orange system has played in the running of Northern Ireland is indisputable. Between the 1920s and 1970s, when Northern Ireland ran as a one-party state, it is arguable that the Orange Order effectively controlled organisation locally along social and political lines. On a decentralised basis, partnerships between the Orange lodges, the Unionist Party, businesses and churches connived in the subordination of Catholic to Protestant interests, in particular in housing and employment. As one contributor to a Belfast newspaper, *Newsletter*, commented in 1861:

> Popery is something more than a religious system: it is a political system also. It is a religio-political system for the enslavement of the body and soul of man and it cannot be met by any mere religious system or by any mere political system. It must be opposed by such a combination as the Orange Society, based upon religion and carrying over religion into the politics of the day.
>
> (Wright 1973)

In light of this prevalent attitude, it may be easier to understand, if not accept, how the Drumcree affair is a legitimate tradition in the eyes of its advocates. It is an event dependent on the continuity and repetition of ritual within a political and religious domain to give unification to many different factions within Protestantism. Supporters further justify the political ritual through an alignment with an unseen, higher moral sacred order by claiming the moral high ground in the name of religious freedom.

However, the marriage of religious and political ritual does not just bolster the state; it can also be used to subvert the status quo. Lan (1995) demonstrates how the mastery of the divine through the imposition of a cosmological order over the secular was used in the liberation of Zimbabwe from a colonial regime. In this instance, guerrillas were successful primarily as they were perceived to be legitimate liberators due to their alliance with the spirit mediums who provided a political and ritual advisory function to Shona chiefs. The chiefs (perceived by the people to have been emasculated by colonialism) were seen to embody the ancestors (an integral part of Shona cosmology and beliefs), yet were powerless against the vagaries of the 'protectorate'. Conversely, when the guerrillas were initiated into chiefdom, their adherence to prescribed ritual practices, food and sexual taboos and the guidance of the spirit mediums facilitated a successful battle against the colonial power.

Some would argue that the paradox of Drumcree lies in the fact that while the Orangemen are attempting to show allegiance and support for a state, that state is

progressively distancing itself from Northern Ireland. Furthermore, the Orangemen's supporters are systematically undermining their own intentions: through a
process of quasi-religious and militaristic rituals whose mimesis of the military
harks back to a Protestant hegemony in Northern Ireland, Drumcree for many
symbolises the obsolete nature of Orangeism. The ritual's appropriation and support
by predominantly secular loyalists who identify with Protestant ideology as an
ethno-political rather than a religious marker weakens the Orangemen's claims of
pursuing a 'religious and civil liberty'. Away from Drumcree, widespread support
for the parade within Protestantism as an example of the incorporation of religious
into civil life has been problematised. Primarily this is due to the dramatic decrease
in the power of and support for the Orange Order over the past 30 years, alongside
the demise of unionist hegemony (McGovern and Shirlow 1997:177). The business
and landowning classes have drastically reduced their connection with the Orange
Order as a state develops where political power is more evenly distributed and less
securely in the hands of an elite few whose allegiances and affiliations were often
conducted through membership of the loyal orders. Another salient reason for the
lack of support is more clearly aligned to the event itself, namely the violence and
paramilitary associations connected to it, however directly or tenuously. While the
Orange Order as a whole dissociates itself from such activity, District 1's rallying
call to all loyalists has coloured the complexion of the public face of Drumcree and
resonates with Tambiah's (1996) work on the 1915 Sinhalese Buddhist–Muslim
riots. It was there that devotees at mosques, offended by the *makruh* (abominable
quality) of music making, challenged the routes traditionally taken by Buddhist
monks whose presence in the area predated the Muslims'. Through processes which
Tambiah terms focalisation (where local incidents and disputes are denuded of their
contextualisation) and transvaluation (where incidents are abstracted into larger
issues of collective national or ethnic interest), the local incident resulted in
extensive rioting throughout Ceylon.

It is worth considering that a necessary component for any ritual to last is its
ability to adapt to change. With reference to Orange parades in Northern Ireland,
this has been looked at diachronically to demonstrate that it is the very subversion
and appropriation of the ritual which ensure its longevity despite challenges to its
'ownership'. This has constantly been interpreted (Jarman 1997; Bryan 2000;
Fraser 2000) within a framework that encompasses Anderson's (1983) model of an
imagined community, Halbwachs's (1980) 'master commemorative narrative' and
Fentress and Wickham's (1992) notion of social commemoration, and which, in
addition, highlights the long-standing associations between the loyal orders and
paramilitarism. The heart of these arguments considers how representations of the
past are controlled by a social/political elite to create and reproduce a particular
ideology. This brings to mind notions of how cyclical time within the ritual context
permits us to determine how ritual allows for the linking of the past to the present
and the present to the future, legitimating past struggles and behaviour with
contemporary life. Having recognised the benefit of a diachronic picture of a rite,
and acknowledging the political arena as one in a state of constant negotiation and
renegotiation, a synchronic look can throw into relief the role of the players and
capture the moment when changes actually occur. This is demonstrable in this
instance by the texts of partisan songs used by the loyalist women that conflate past

battles with contemporary insurgencies both within and without the religious context. Boholm (1996:4) neatly summarises how this relates to those who draw on the sacred to validate the secular. She makes the claim that the power of particular political statements is created through ritually aligning the present political struggle to 'events lying outside time that speak of alternative imaginary worlds that cannot be contested'.

However the role of ritual in the Orange theatre is understood, those parts played by women in the drama are simultaneously integral and peripheral. This subordination is further emphasised by whatever coverage the Shankill women are given by the press during their protests. Their position is always reactive in the face of powerful structures which both rely on and yet doctor their involvement and responses for their own illustrative purposes. This utilisation of the women by the press is not a unique exploitation, but mirrors how they are called on and yet badly supported by interested sections of the community to whom they offer their help. Despite their highly publicised and public presence as community agitators, the reality of their backgrounds is that of domestic patriarchy which they strive to service.

Notes

1 The Orange Order was formed in Armagh in 1795, a Protestant society whose structure and organisation reflected the Masonic background of many members. The Order is now a focal political institution in Northern Ireland. Its underpinning claim for 'Religious and Civil Liberties For All' is seen by some to be undermined by its solely Protestant membership and its constitution (1967) which requires members to 'love, uphold, and defend the Protestant religion, and sincerely desire and endeavour to propagate its doctrines and precepts'.

2 The Greater Shankill is an exclusively loyalist Protestant enclave in mainly nationalist Catholic west Belfast. It has the highest concentration of loyalist politically motivated ex-prisoners (Crothers 1998:39). Some of the worst violence in the past 30 years in Northern Ireland has been perpetrated against and by some of its residents. This may in part account for the history of protest and militancy in the women who appear in this chapter.

3 For full and recent discussions of Drumcree and other Orange parades see Bryan (2000) and Fraser (2000).

4 Despite documentation to support their parading this route since 1807, the parades have not happened on consecutive years. Breaks in the tradition have occurred due to wars and so on. In this chapter I shall be focusing on those parades held since 1995 and will refer to them as Drumcree One, Two, Three, etc., as they are referred to in popular parlance. At the time of writing Drumcree Eight has taken place.

5 At the time of writing, the Northern Ireland Assembly has been suspended and ministerial posts are no longer applied to those members of the devolved government.

6 For further discussions on respectability in Orangeism, see Buckley and Kenney (1995); Smyth (1995:52); Jarman (1997:67); Bryan (2000:44). For a publication that uncritically supports Orangeism as a misrepresented non-sectarian organisation, see Dudley-Edwards (1999).

7 As a religious pressure group, the Association of Loyal Orange Women until the 1990s played a predominantly supporting role to the male lodges. However, they are increasingly organising themselves independently of the men – most noticeably on 'Sunday' parades to services held at the different denominations of churches where the Lodge members are congregants.

8 The exception to this would be when protesting at *interface* areas at parades where bandsmen and women would cross the peace line. Some were also connected (as individuals rather than as part of the

group) to disputes in north Belfast including the prominent protest in 2001–2 in the Glenbryn/Ardoyne area over the access of children attending the Holy Cross Primary School.

9 The Red Hand of Ulster is a prevalent icon in mainstream unionism. It is also one adopted by loyalist paramilitaries (Red Hand Commando is a paramilitary group whose name is used by both principal loyalist paramilitaries). It derives from the mythical story of a warrior in a race with another. The first to reach the province of Ulster will claim the territory. The warrior losing the race ultimately wins by severing his hand and throwing it so that it lands before the challenger. The image is used within unionism and loyalism to denote the depth of allegiance to the territory.

10 David Trimble as First Minister (designate) of Northern Ireland came under criticism when attending the funeral of a Catholic victim of the Omagh bomb in 1998 (Bryan 2000:106).

11 For further discussions on the depth of the role of the church in Northern Ireland, see Morrow *et al.* (1994:19): 'Churches are integrated into the fabric of community lives and provide much of the framework within which apparently secular, social, personal and community life is lived.'

12 Orangewomen do not wear sashes but collarettes.

13 *Oh! Will You Stand?*

Oh! Will you stand. Oh! Will you stand,

With the Ulster Volunteer Force as a patriotic band

Would you fight until the death would you join the UVF

If you can you're a man then you'll stand.

And when the sound of the battle is over, it's shoulder to shoulder we'll stand

And remember the brave young Ulster soldiers who fought for the flag of the red hand.

Bibliography

Anderson, B. (1983), *Imagined Communities: Reflections on the Origin and Spread of Nationalism*, London: Verso.

Boholm, A. (ed.) (1996), *Political Ritual*, Gothenburg: Advanced Studies in Social Anthropology.

Bradby, B. (1993), 'Sampling Sexuality: Gender, Technology, and the Body in Dance Music', *Popular Music*, **12**(2), 155–76.

Bryan, D. (2000), *Orange Parades: The Politics of Ritual, Tradition and Control*, London: Pluto Press.

Buckley, A.D. and Kenney, M.C. (1995), *Negotiating Identity: Rhetoric, Metaphor, and Social Drama in Northern Ireland*, London: Smithsonian Institution Press.

Burton, F. (1978), *The Politics of Legitimacy: Struggles in a Belfast Community*, London: Routledge & Kegan Paul.

Cairns, E. and Mercer, G.W. (1984), 'Social Identity in Northern Ireland', *Human Relations*, **37**(12), 1095–102.

Ceribašić, N. (2000), 'Defining Women and Men in the Context of War: Images in Croatian Popular Music in the 1990s', in P. Moisala and B. Diamond (eds) *Music and Gender*, Chicago: University of Illinois Press, pp. 218–38.

Crothers, J. (1998), *Reintegration – The Problems and the Issues*, Belfast: Epic Research Document No. 2.

Dudley-Edwards, R. (1999), *The Faithful Tribe: An Intimate Portrait of the Loyal Institutions*, London: HarperCollins.

Edgerton, L. (1986), 'Public Protest, Domestic Acquiescence: Women in Northern Ireland', in R. Ridd and H. Callaway (eds) *Caught Up in Conflict: Women's Responses to Political Strife*, London: Macmillan, pp. 61–79.

Fentress, J. and Wickham, C. (1992), *Social Memory: New Perspectives on the Past*, Oxford: Blackwell.

Fraser, T.G. (ed.) (2000), *The Irish Parading Tradition: Following the Drum*, London: Macmillan.

Ginsberg, M. (1934), *Sociology*, London: Butterworth.

Grand Orange Lodge of Ireland (1967), *Constitution, Laws and Ordinances of the Loyal Institution of Ireland*

Halbwachs, S.M. (1980), *The Collective Memory*, New York: Harper & Row.

Holmes, J. and Urquhart, D. (1994), *Coming into the Light: The Work, Politics and Religion of Women in Ulster 1840–1940*, Belfast: Institute of Irish Studies.

Howe, L. (1990), *Being Unemployed in Northern Ireland*, London: Routledge.

Jarman, N. (1997), *Material Conflicts: Parades and Visual Displays in Northern Ireland*, Oxford: Berg.

Kaplan, E.A. (1997), *Looking for the Other: Feminism, Film and the Imperial Gaze*, London: Routledge.

Kertzer, D.I. (1988), *Ritual, Politics and Power*, London: Yale University Press.

Lan, D. (1995), *Guns and Rain: Guerillas and Spirit Mediums in Zimbabwe*, London: Currey.

McGovern, M. and Shirlow, P. (1997), 'Counter-Insurgency, Deindustrialisation and the Political Economy of Ulster Loyalism', in P. Shirlow and M. McGovern (eds) *Who Are 'The People'?*, London: Pluto, pp. 176–98.

Mayer, A.C. (1966), 'The Significance of Quasi-Groups in the Study of Complex Societies', in M. Banton (ed.), *The Social Anthropology of Complex Societies* (ASA Monographs 4), London: Tavistock.

Moors, A. (1995), *Women, Property and Islam: Palestinian Experiences 1920–1990*, Cambridge: Cambridge University Press.

Morgan, G. and Fraser, G. (1994), 'Women and the Northern Ireland Conflict: Experiences and Responses', in Seamus Dunn (ed.) *Facets of the Conflict in Northern Ireland*, Dublin: St Martin's Press.

Morrow, D., Birrell, D., Gree, J. and O'Keefe, T. (1994), *The Churches and Inter Community Relationships*, Coleraine: Centre for the Study of Conflict, University of Ulster.

Nelson, S. (1984), *Ulster's Uncertain Defenders: Protestants, Politics and Paramilitaries*, Belfast: Appletree Press.

Parkinson, A.F. (1998), *Ulster Loyalism and the British Media*, Dublin: Four Courts Press.

Radford, K. (2001), 'Drum Rolls and Gender Roles', *British Journal of Ethnomusicology*, (**10**(II), 37–59.

Radford, K. (2004), 'Red, White, Blue and Orange: An Exploration of Historically Bound Allegiances Through Loyalist Song', *World of Music*. (In Press),

Sales, R. (1997), 'Gender and Protestantism in Northern Ireland', in P. Shirlow and M. McGovern (eds) *Who Are 'The People'?*, London: Pluto, 140–57.

Sered, S.S. (1992), *Women as Ritual Experts: The Religious Lives of Elderly Jewish Women in Jerusalem*, Oxford: Oxford University Press.

Smyth, J. (1995), 'The Men of No Popery: The Origins of the Orange Order', *History Ireland*, **3**(3), 48–53.

Tambiah, S.J. (1996), *Levelling Crowds: Ethnonationalist Conflicts and Collective Violence in S. Asia*, California: University of California Press.

Wright, F. (1973), 'Protestant Ideology and Politics in Ulster', *European Journal of Sociology*, **14**, 213–80, cites W.M. Johnston, Belfast *Newsletter*, 15 May 1861.

CHAPTER 10

Islam, Identity and Globalisation

Reflections in the Wake of 11 September 2001

David Herbert

The primary question for any cultural institution anywhere, now that nobody is leaving anyone else alone and isn't ever again going to, is not whether everything is going to come seamlessly together, or whether, contrariwise, we are all going to persist in our separate prejudices. It is whether human beings are going to be able ... through law, anthropology, or anything else, to imagine principled lives they can practically lead [together].

(Geertz 1983:234)

We recognise there are historic divisions between communities that have separated Asian from white and Afro-Caribbean from Asian and that it will take many years to overcome.

We also recognise that racial prejudice is deep-seated and we need to face it head on and we need to set an example in the public services. But we also accept that we need sensitivity rather than political correctness.

We need, therefore, to lay down challenges on the back of these reports [into the riots in Oldham, Burnley and Bradford in the summer of 2001] in terms of where we are going – to build diversity not separation.

It is a two-way street. If we are going to have social cohesion we have got to develop a sense of identity and a sense of belonging.

(David Blunkett, Home Secretary, in Brown 2001)

If the adherents of religion enter the public sphere, can their entry leave the pre-existing discursive structure intact? The public sphere is not an empty space for carrying out debates. It is constituted by the sensibilities – memories and aspirations, fears and hopes – of speakers and listeners, and also by the way they exist (and are made to exist) for each other. Thus the introduction of new discourses may result in the disruption of established assumptions structuring debates in the public sphere. More strongly, they may *have* to disrupt existing assumptions in order to be heard.

(Asad 1999:181)

Context: The Challenge of Social Integration after 11 September 2001

Sociology has always been concerned with how societies hold together. Its founders all thought this had something to do with religion – as societal self-representation, whether functional (Durkheim) or dysfunctional (Marx), or as an influence on social formations in a variety of ways (such as the Protestant ethic for Weber). However, they also all thought the influence of traditional religions on social integration was declining, and this idea has been further developed and apparently confirmed by secularisation and systems theories. Yet in 2001 in a British society that in terms of religious observance at least is one of the most secularised in the world, we again find ourselves in a debate about social integration that has religion at its centre (Gill *et al.* 1998). In particular Islam and Christianity are in the spotlight of public debate, through the former's supposedly self-chosen ghettoisation and the latter's church schools. Has the mainstream sociological tradition missed something?

The first quotation above, from the cultural anthropologist Clifford Geertz, sets out a basic challenge facing all contemporary societies posed by the combination of increasing global inter-penetration (economic, political, demographic, cultural) and continuing cultural difference. The juxtaposition of law and anthropology as possible means to the imagination of 'principled lives' serves to delineate the boundaries within which a sociological conception of the processes of social integration must lie. On the one hand there is law, which must maintain a sense of impartiality and universality to perform its social role, on the other anthropology with its imperative to recognise and represent in its full complexity the range of human cultural possibility. Somewhere between the two, between the necessity of action, decision and definitive judgement and the endless multiplication of possibilities, lies a model of social integration that recognises both the necessity of the former and the will to autonomous development of the latter.

Not least of the sources of cultural difference mobilised in contemporary struggles over the terms of social integration is religious diversity. Yet in the West from the time of the European wars of religion, disagreements arising from religious diversity are supposed to have been resolved – at least as a cause of public strife – by the privatisation of religion. This process involves the separation of religious devotion and practice from state and communal authority, so that religion becomes a private, personal choice (Stout 1988; Midgely 1989). This solution was first proposed by the founders of modern political philosophy (Locke, Montaigne, Hobbes), and appeared to be confirmed through historical processes of secularisation (Wilson 1994). But religion has proved surprisingly difficult to fully privatise. Not only do its teachings cut across private–public boundaries at the normative level, but it has social and communal dimensions that challenge such boundaries in social practice. For a variety of reasons, this would appear to be particularly obviously so in the case of Islam, not least in Britain.

Recent events, including the disturbances across the north-west of England in the summer of 2001, and of course events following the terrorist attacks on New York and Washington on 11 September, have highlighted this sense of Muslim difference. These most recent events stand in a somewhat longer history of controversy over the terms of integration of Muslim minorities running back to the 1980s, and most recently raised by the Home Secretary David Blunkett in his interview in *The Independent on Sunday* on 9 December 2001 (Brown 2001) from which the second quotation above is taken. These include arguments over halal meat, comments by the Bradford headmaster Ray Honeyford, the 1988 Education Act, Salman Rushdie's novel *The Satanic Verses*, the Gulf War, and long-running arguments over the rights and wrongs of faith schools, currently resurfacing in the light of government proposals to expand such provision. Among these, *The Satanic Verses* controversy is a key turning point for two main reasons. First, because it challenged the hegemony of the concepts of race and class that had previously dominated the discursive field of community relations, by introducing religion as a significant element. Second, because it led to the gradual development of a Muslim 'public sphere', a series of intersecting social spaces for the representation and contestation of Muslim identity in Britain.

The third quotation above highlights the historical character of the British public sphere into which this Muslim public sphere has emerged, and in doing so sheds light on the question of the terms of integration of Muslim minorities. For, contrary to the neutral self-image of liberal political philosophy, especially since the Second World War (Kymlicka 1989), the public spheres of Western democratic polities are formed not only by procedures but by cultural and historical memories. Using Habermas's distinction between system and lifeworld, we may say that Muslim minorities face the challenge of integration not only into British social systems (employment, local government, health, education and so on) but also into British national and regional cultures, or 'life worlds' (Habermas 1987).

Current government thinking would seem to be that discourses of 'multi-culturalism' proclaiming 'unity in diversity' but constricting open debate by 'political correctness' have proved inadequate to address issues of social integration. They point to the civil disturbances of the summer of 2001 and apparent Muslim alienation in the wake of 11 September as evidence. Such alienation is indeed apparent in opinion poll data. An ICM poll conducted for the BBC Radio 4 *Today* programme in early November 2001 showed that while 81 per cent of Muslims thought the terrorist attacks unjustified in any way, 80 per cent were opposed to British and American military action – compared to about the same proportion in favour in the general population. Furthermore, some 30 per cent reported experiencing hostility towards themselves or their family as a result of the 11 September attacks, and 57 per cent were unconvinced by Bush's and Blair's reassurances that the military campaign was not a 'war against Islam' (Aitken 2001).

As well as attempting to rush through emergency 'anti-terrorist' legislation, including measures on incitement to religious hatred, the government also seems keen to open up a broad and 'robust' debate on the question of the social integration of Britain's minority communities, especially British Muslims. By the time this chapter appears such legislation may (or may not) have been enacted, and the campaign in Afghanistan seems likely to have moved towards a post-Taliban stabilisation. But the broader issue of social integration in Britain, and hence to some extent of Muslim minorities in other Western societies, will remain, as will the question of appropriate forms of Western international intervention in conflict and post-conflict situations, not least in the Muslim world. How might the scholar of religious studies, especially the sociology of religion, contribute to debate on these issues, especially the former?

This chapter attempts to contribute to such debate in several stages. First, following Sayyid (1997), it examines the cultural field within which the issue of Muslim social integration arises. Second, it introduces the discourse of 'Islamism', and considers its relevance for British Muslims, drawing on a study of the formation of British Muslims' social identities (Jacobson 1998). Third, it examines Sayyid's argument as to why Islam rather than rival discourses has become the discourse of political protest across large swathes of the popular sector in the Muslim majority world. Fourth, it considers the reassertion of the Muslim identity in the context of theories of globalisation. Fifth, this leads to a discussion of the development of what we have termed a British Muslim public sphere, which finally returns us to the issues of faith schools, Muslim social identity and social integration.

Asserting Muslim Identities and the Fear of Ghosts

In the following passage cultural theorist Bobby Sayyid illustrates some of the ways in which Muslim social identities have proved problematic in Western societies. His evocation of this awkward articulation reminds us that we are not dealing with a bland or mechanical process as the language of 'social systems' perhaps suggests. Rather, we must reckon with a complex cultural exchange in which minorities and majorities both cling to cultural memories and historically developed practices and institutions:

> Ghosts are the remains of the dead. They are echoes of former times and former lives ... Muslims too, it seems, are often thought to be out of time: throwbacks to medieval civilizations ...
>
> It is argued that ghosts do not really exist; they are but fictions, perhaps like Muslims ... There are people from the Magreb, from South Asia, from West Africa – but there are no Muslims. The possibility of Muslim subjectivity is undermined by notions of class and ethnicity, kinship and caste or tribe and clan. These cleavages are said to demonstrate the hollow nature of Muslim identity ...
>
> Even though ghosts do not really exist, they have their uses. When something goes bump in the night we can blame it on a poltergeist. Similarly, you may remember that when some good ol' boys blew up the Federal Building in Oklahoma City, how useful it was to have Muslims around to explain bombs in the night. Ghosts, despite not existing, are also terrifying. Muslims also generate such fear; even though they are often the lowest of the low, Muslims are still capable of making sturdy liberal institutions anxious; and, like ghosts, they can appear everywhere and anywhere.
>
> ... Muslims transgress state boundaries ... [t]heir presence marks a space which seems irreconcilably different and which seems to resist easy absorption into the Western enterprise.
>
> (Sayyid 1997:1–2)

In this extended comparison between Muslims and ghosts, Sayyid draws four parallels between the two. First, association with the past, especially the common use of 'medieval' to describe Islamic customs and practices: here, Islam appears as the 'other' in a Western meta-narrative that tells of emancipation from a medieval past in which social life was dominated by religion. In this story of progress, Islam is narrated as the past. Second, questionable existence: the insubstantiality of ghosts is matched in dominant social scientific discourses by the insubstantiality of Muslim identity, which as we noted has tended to be collapsed into the supposedly more real categories of race, class, ethnicity and so on. Third, transgression of familiar boundaries – in the case of Muslims, of states, of 'Europeanness' and, one might add, of public and private, religious and secular: in particular, the Muslim sense of *umma* – of being one transnational community unbounded by nation-states – has been greatly strengthened by a perception of global injustice against Muslims, whether in the Gulf War, Bosnia, Chechnya or Palestine. Fourth, use as a scapegoat for unexplained phenomena: minorities have always functioned as scapegoats for social ills of unknown origin, and Muslims clearly performed this role in the wake of the Oklahoma City bombing. But in the case of the 11 September terrorist attacks there is good evidence that a group claiming Islamic identity, Osama bin Laden's al-Qaida network, was indeed responsible for the atrocities. In the wake of 11 September the threat of Muslim militancy has taken on more corporeal form. Yet in the face of this development and the militancy of some Muslim youth demonstrated in the riots in Oldham, Burnley and Bradford, it is salutary to recall the history of scapegoating of culturally distinct minorities, and that for all the culture shock of British Muslims' most militant protest to date – against *The Satanic Verses* – this was a non-violent, if culturally transgressive, act.

Sayyid's work is thus valuable in highlighting features of the cultural field within which the issue of the social integration of Muslim minorities in the West is conceived. But the main purpose of his book is to examine the genesis of Muslim militancy more generally, and in particular to explain why the response to the crisis of the 1970s of Arab nationalism and other postcolonial discourses in the Muslim world (that he refers to collectively as 'Kemalism') took a specifically Islamic form, rather than, for example, a liberal or socialist form:

> My concern is to try and account for the emergence of political projects which assert a Muslim subjectivity ... Islamism is a discourse that attempts to centre Islam within the political order. Islamism can range from the assertion of a Muslim subjectivity to a full-blooded attempt to reconstruct society on Islamic principles.
>
> (1997:16)

More generally, we may define as 'Islamist' approaches that seek to understand all aspects of life from an Islamic perspective and in a rationalist mode – that is traditional methods of interpretation are likely to be discarded and a sharp distinction made between culture and religion, especially in diaspora communities. This all-embracing view of Islam often results in efforts to increase the influence of Islam on all areas of life including public life. But such a definition has the advantage of recognising that the overtly political component may vary with circumstances, and hence can be applied both in Muslim minority and majority situations.

The rhetorical repertoire of Islamists is likely to include appeal to the concepts of 'an Islamic state', 'implementation of *sharia*', '*umma*' (Islamic 'nation' or international community) and *shura* ('consultation' – a legitimisation of democracy in Islamic idiom). Given the fact that Muslims constitute a small minority in British society, perhaps 3 per cent, and are unlikely to rise above 5 per cent in the foreseeable future, such concepts have had little influence as practical propositions among British Muslims, except for some small radical groups. But in terms of legitimising an Islamic identity, especially in the context of a sense of Western hostility to Islam, the rise of Islamist discourse is significant for British Muslims, especially for younger people.

Evidence for this comes from Jacobson's (1998) study of young Muslims in Waltham Forest, north-east London. As a focused ethnographic study of 33 respondents (18 female, 15 male), this does not tell us how representative her findings are. But it does have the advantage of showing in some detail how Muslim social identity functions and reproduces itself. Jacobson argues that religion functions as a source of practical guidance, existential reassurance (resolution of a personal quest for meaning) and boundary construction for these young people, the clear definition of the latter serving to reinforce rather than weaken their commitment to it. Several points are of particular relevance here. Religious observance was high – 14 of the 33 prayed at least once a day, 11 of the 15 attended mosque at least once a week, 27 claimed to observe the full fast at Ramadan, 9 regularly and 10 sometimes attended what might be described as voluntary religious activities: talks and meetings organised by various Islamic associations. Twenty of the respondents answered questions about the meaning of Islam in terms of its impact on their behaviour, both at a specific and general level. For example:

> I think everything the Qur'an says has something to do with what I'm doing in life ... It gears me to a different kind of lifestyle. I mean, I don't drink, I don't eat non-*halal* meat, I don't reveal my whole body ...
>
> (Sara; ibid.:105)

> It's not religion – it's a way of life [a repeated refrain] – the way you should be ... Religion's not just praying and wearing a certain dress – it's the way you act towards people. ...
>
> (Nazia; ibid.)

Although the young people were critical of parental authority, including their parents' cultural (Pakistani) background, and also of various aspects of British society, they were generally unwilling 'to look on their religion with any kind of scepticism' (ibid.:111). Furthermore, several of the respondents stressed the compatibility of Islam with rationalism and science (ibid.:113–14). Thus with respect to evidence of Islamist tendencies, although Jacobson argues that only a few respondents showed radical tendencies – for example only a few believed that the West was not just un-Islamic but actively opposed to Islam, and only a few supported proselytising activities – many Islamist tendencies, as we have defined them, are present. These include a tendency towards a rationalist view of Islam, addressing scepticism towards tradition and culture rather than the 'core' of the religion, and a tendency to view Islam as prescribing a whole way of life, albeit one chosen by personal conviction.

Four of the male respondents illustrated a form of 'assertive Muslim identity' without full Islamic practice. This involved commitment to some public aspects of Muslim identity – fasting at Ramadan, not drinking alcohol and eating halal ('permitted') meat. But they also 'made it clear that they were not inclined to lead a lifestyle consistent with the stringent demands of Islamic teachings; for example they told me that they regularly go to night-clubs and date girls' (ibid.:123).

This phenomenon is also noted by Lewis (1994) in Bradford. This turn to Muslim identity as a form of 'cultural defence' (Bruce and Wallis 1992) helps to explain the appeal of Islamism as one way of 'standing up for Islam' in the face of perceived Western hostility. But more broadly it seems that Jacobson's findings broadly fit with evidence that Islamism's universalist and rationalist discourses have proved attractive to educated urban Muslims in other Muslim minority and majority contexts (France (Leveau 1991); Egypt (Starrett 1998)). Sayyid's main argument therefore also seems to be of relevance to the British situation, so we shall now examine it.

Why Islamism? Religion, Semantics and Politics

Sayyid challenges the assumption that the emergence of Islamism as a central form of political protest in the Muslim majority world (and, following the Iranian revolution, as a form of governance too) can be explained in terms of the causes of the crisis of 'Kemalism'. The causes of this crisis include: the failure of national security elites, especially signalled by defeat by Israel in the 1967 war; lack of political participation; a 'nativist' response to globalisation's erosion of cultural identities; and uneven economic development resulting in part from the influx of 'petro-dollars' into the Gulf after the formation of OPEC in 1973 (Ayubi 1991). Within this context, the development of Islamist ideology has also been associated with specific class interests, such as a *petite bourgeoisie* alienated from Pahlavi reforms in the Iranian case, or a frustrated middle class unable to achieve income and status commensurate with their education in Egypt's struggling economy and stultifying bureaucracy (Moaddel 1996; Ayubi 1991). These factors are important, but none of them explains why *Islamism in particular* has become the means of political aspiration and social mobilisation; after all, as recently as the mid-1960s Islam was written off by many social scientists as no longer a significant political factor in Muslim majority societies (Starrett 1998). Sayyid argues that the explanation lies in the semantic function of Islam as a 'nodal point' within several discourses (jurisprudence, ethics and, controversially, politics), a function transformed by Islamist rhetoric into that of a 'master signifier' that links different discourses together.

Following Žižek (1989), Sayyid compares the social construction of meaning to a web, the threads of which consist of 'floating signifiers' tied together into a unified discursive field by a 'nodal point' that – at least temporarily – fixes their relationship to one another. In Muslim societies, Islam has historically served as such a nodal point within several discourses, as indicated. One of the effects of Islamism has been to extend the number of discourses within which Islam functions as a nodal point, to include most notably politics, but also education and even welfare and economics (Starrett 1998). These discursive fields are themselves configured in relation to one another through a 'master signifier', and a further effect of Islamism is to contend that Islam is the master signifier. While linguistic domination may be more or less a conscious aim of some Islamists (though probably not articulated in these terms!), such a process may also be accidental. For example, in Egypt it would seem that the inculcation of a rationalised form of Islamic discourse through the extension of the state education system – a process intended to pacify the population – has backfired on the government. This is because this same discourse is being used to challenge government hegemony across a range of discursive fields (Starrett 1998).

In such a context 'Islam' becomes 'the most abstract signifier', and functions in 'a most generalized way', such that claims made using it are very difficult to refute (Sayyid 1997:48). Criticism of Islamism that 'complains about the emptiness of Islamist programmes and the malleability of Islamic symbols [thus] ... misses the point' (ibid.:44):

> Ultimately, for Muslims, Islam is another word for 'Goodness incarnate'. Thus, when Islamists claim that the best government is an Islamic government, here Islamic refers to the incarnation of goodness, so that the claim becomes: the best government is good government. This is a claim that is difficult to refute, except by attacking the relationship between Islam and the incarnation of goodness. But it is precisely at this point where Islam is strongest, because, for the majority of Muslims, Islam must be the definition of good. It is for this reason that Muslim governments have often responded by arguing that Islamists do not represent true Islam, rather than by claiming that Islam does not represent true goodness.
>
> (ibid.:48)

However, every time a government does this, it reinforces the claim of Islamists that Islam is the master signifier.

By shifting the explanation for the success of Islamist discourse to a semantic ground, Sayyid avoids the dangers of three other modes of explanation. First, he avoids the essentialism of an Orientalist position that ties Islam to a particular historical essence. Second, he avoids the relegation of Islam to a peripheral role by 'explaining' its success in terms of underlying structural – economic and political – factors, although these explanations potentially complement the semantic one (ibid.:48). Third, compared with a functionalist position – Islamism prospers because Islamist-inspired movements 'work', an example being the success of Islamic private voluntary organisations in Egypt (Sullivan 1994) – the semantic explanation can help us see how Islamism can retain its appeal even when Islamist projects fail. It can also help us to understand why Islamist discourse is appealing even when Muslims are a small minority with no chance of creating an Islamic government. It is thus relevant to understanding the appeal of Islamist discourse in Britain.

However, while Sayyid provides an explanation of the semantic function of Islam and its extension in Islamism, he does not appear to answer the question he has set himself, that is why *Islam in particular* has ended up performing this role. Indeed, it seems to be part of his argument that the substantive character of the signifier that comes to function as a nodal point or master signifier is arbitrary and irrelevant. Thus he argues that 'any element may become a nodal point ... the master signifier does not have a substantive identity' (1997:45). All that Sayyid, quoting Žižek, will say about the character of a master signifier is:

> [I]t has something 'that makes people feel that there's something in it' ... It is not a set of features or practices, [but rather] 'something that is present in these features that appears through them'. It occupies the place of master signifier because it holds that community together for as long as the members of the community believe in it.
>
> (ibid.:45–6)

Yet while accepting that the power of Sayyid's account lies in its location of the meaning of 'Islam' in Islamist discourse at an abstract level, one may also argue that it is possible to go beyond such rather elusive statements. In particular, we shall suggest here that there is something in the nature of a religious signifier that enables it to perform such a role. This will enable us to link Sayyid's semantic explanation of Islam's role as signifier with accounts of the relationship between identity and globalisation.

Religion, Identity and Globalisation

In spite of the global dissemination of some cultural forms it is arguably at the level of culture, and not least religion, that pressures towards global integration are most fiercely resisted (Tibi 1998). The assertion of identity plays a key role in these resistance processes (Castells 1997a). Some analysts of new social movements (NSMs) have argued that NSMs are distinctive because, in contrast to traditional opposition movements (such as labour movements), they challenge 'the meaning and value of the social system as whole' rather than the distribution of goods within it (Beckford 1989:144). Examples of NSMs include environmentalist and feminist groups. These groups challenge the social system by 'shifting more and more from the "political" form [of collective action] ... to a cultural ground' (Melucci 1985:789). The shift towards the contestation of meaning rather than the distribution of goods has been linked to affluence: a state of material security in which the costs of 'getting more' begin to outweigh the benefits – a condition known as 'postmaterialism' (Inglehart 1997). However, the contestation of meaning – as well as the distribution of political power – also seems to be central to Islamist movements. Yet the material basis of 'postmaterialism' hardly seems to apply as Muslim groups are often, as Sayyid puts it, 'the lowest of the low' – economically among the most deprived within Western societies and in global terms when Muslim-majority societies are compared with the Western world (Modood 1997). Even if it is not the poorest who are attracted to Islamist movements – rather, it is more likely to be those with a good, especially technical, education, whether in Egypt (Starrett 1998) or France (Leveau 1988) – relative affluence cannot explain their turn to Islam as 'master signifier', because there are better-off groups who have not reacted in this way.

However, before considering the role of religion in culture-based resistance any further, we need to ask, 'resistance to what?' As Beyer points out, different social and political theorists have highlighted different aspects of the globalisation process (1994:14–44). Thus Wallerstein (1979) emphasises the incorporation of ever more local and regional economies into the capitalist world system. Meyer (1980) stresses the role of nation-states in conditioning the functioning of that economy, Robertson (1990) the social and cultural consequences of and resistance to globalising forces, particularly in terms of the *Gemeinschaft/Gesellschaft* (local community/modern society) dichotomy of classic sociological theory. Luhmann (1982) focuses on the tendency towards differentiation that leads to a paradox at the heart of the globalisation process: as functional systems (economic, political, medical and so on) increase their global penetration, their increased specialisation means that they operate increasingly autonomously from one another. Globally, the tendency is towards the dominance of increasingly similar functional systems that are increasingly disarticulated from one another. This creates, among other effects, a democratic deficit, because nationally based political systems are increasingly unable to influence the global economic system.

Written after Beyer's, Castells's work adds a further dimension to the globalisation debate through the concept of the 'network society'. For Castells, the integration of new information technologies into modern societies is leading to radical transformations of their economic, social and political organisation and cultural forms, creating new social cleavages, and enabling the emergence of new identities (1996, 1997a, 1997b). According to Castells, new information technologies have created a new international division of labour: high-value informational labour, high-volume lower-cost labour, producers of raw materials and the devalued 'redundant producers' (1996:147, n. 13). The location of labour no longer coincides with countries. Rather, it is shaped by 'networks and flows, using the technological infrastructure of the informational economy' (ibid.), with the result that even marginalised national economies have connections with high-value networks, while powerful economies have redundant producers in their population – a 'Fourth World' (Castells 1997b). Globally, Muslims are among those most likely to be excluded from these high-value networks, although this does not of course apply to all Muslim individuals or groups.

Castells identifies three kinds of social identity that play a key role in relation to global systems: legitimising identities, resistance identities and project identities. The first is associated with the historically dominant institutions and groups within a society. The second, resistance identities, set out to challenge these dominant institutions in terms that seek to reverse or invert the existing order, but do not challenge its basic structure. Hence Castells sees such identity-based groups as expressions of 'the exclusion of the excluders by the excluded. That is, the building of defensive identity in terms of dominant institutions/ideologies, reversing the value of judgement while reinforcing the boundary' (1997a:9). Certain forms of nationalism, religious fundamentalism (oriented to protecting a cultural enclave) and queer culture are examples of this form of resistance.

In contrast, 'project identities' attempt to challenge the structure of dominant institutions and ideologies, including globalisation:

> [T]he building of identity is a project of a different life, perhaps on the basis of an oppressed identity, but expanding toward the transformation of society as the prolongation of this project of identity, as in the … example of a post-patriarchal society, liberating men, women and children, through the realisation of women's identity. Or, in a very different perspective, the final reconciliation of all human beings as believers, brothers and sisters, under the guidance of God's law, be it Allah or Jesus, as a result of the religious conversion of the godless, anti-family, materialist societies, otherwise unable to fulfil human needs and God's design.
>
> (ibid.:10)

Thus Castells assigns a significant role to religion as a source of communal identity in contemporary societies, alongside nationalism, ethnicity, feminism and environmentalism, and to these 'project' identities (in the sense of projected towards the transformation of society) as sources of resistance to the dominant global systems. The holistic orientation of religious systems makes them well suited to articulate this kind of challenge. This complements the argument of Beyer (1992) that religions' holistic perspectives enhance their ability to respond to the 'residual problems' of the global system, including increasing inequalities of wealth, power and opportunity, greater cultural conflict resulting from increased migration under these conditions, and environmental damage (ibid.:4).

Beyer characterises religion as a 'diffuse ... mode of communication ... broadly rooted in particular cultures' and 'centring around the dichotomy of immanent/ transcendent' (ibid.:7). As such, it is not well suited to specialised functional roles – although the Islamisation of law, politics, education and some aspects of social and economic organisation in a society like Egypt challenges this view to some extent (Sullivan 1994; Starrett 1998; Abdo 2000). But as 'the one mode of communication that is in principle both totalizing and encompassing, [religion] can and does serve as a kind of system specializing in ... residual matters' (Beyer 1992:8). It does so primarily through the 'thematization of the social whole', typified in Islamist concepts such as *umma* (Muslim community, transcending national boundaries), *dunya* ('complete way of life') and *din wa dawla* ('unity of religion and state'). Thus, even in Egypt it is perspectives on the social whole articulated in the name of Islam – in particular, responsibility of the community for the poor and of collective solidarity – that has had most instrumental impact on 'Islamic' hospitals, professional associations and businesses, rather than any specifically Islamic technical knowledge. It is important to note that it is not just Islamic concepts that can be interpreted in this kind of holistic way. Christian concepts such as 'the communion of saints' and 'the kingdom of God', or a concept such as *dharma*, whether in its Hindu ('sacred order') or Buddhist ('right teaching', implying a right understanding of the world) sense, equally imply a transcendent judgement on the immanent order. Hence they are potentially available as a social and political critique of the way things are.

Thus we can move beyond Sayyid in specifying what it is about religious signifiers that makes them particularly suited to function as 'nodal points' within discourses, and potentially as 'master signifiers'. However, this capacity for 'thematization of the social whole' does not necessarily translate into 'integralism', that is the domination of all public spheres of society by religion. The alternative is not simply between integralism and the privatisation of religion. Rather, as Casanova (1994) has shown in the case of Catholicism (and American Protestantism), religion can thrive in democratic modernity by renouncing its claims to the public sphere of the state and political society and becoming a lively participant in the public sphere of civil society. In the British case, there is some evidence that this process is occurring with Islam.

The 1990s and the Broadening of the British Muslim Public Sphere

The decade since *The Satanic Verses* controversy has seen British Muslims achieve important goals. This can be seen by glancing through the pages of *British Muslims Monthly Survey* (*BMMS*), a digest of references to British Muslims in the Muslim ethnic minority, national and local press.[1] For example, in March 1997 an article entitled 'Mosques for Millennium' (*BMMS*, 20 March 1997, p. 1) reported estimates that 100 new mosques were scheduled to be completed by 2000, bringing the national total to over 1000. Alongside this ran comment from national and regional newspapers comparing the rise in mosque attendance with the decline in Christian worship, especially among traditional denominations.

The period has also seen the introduction of state funding for Muslim schools through the granting of voluntary-aided status (though there are only three at present), and the formation of a national umbrella body for Muslim organisations. The latter project had been often attempted but never previously achieved. However, the Muslim Council, although it remains to be seen how successful it will prove in representing Britain's diverse Muslim population, represents a considerable advance (*BMMS*, 20 December 1997, p. 1). This period also witnesses the serious possibility of legal recognition in anti-discrimination legislation, a possibility made more likely in the wake of 11 September but at the time of writing thwarted by the House of Lords (*BMMS*, 20 June 1997, p. 1; *Newsnight*, 13 December 2001). Such developments suggest the increasing maturity, establishment and public recognition of Muslim communities, and their contribution to British society, as indeed did Muslim involvement in the millennium celebrations (*BMMS*, 20 February 1997, p. 5; 20 August 1998, p. 3). They are developments which are underpinned by the growth of forums for debate and negotiation both within the Muslim community (and which indeed constitute it as a community) and with other publics.

Signs of these latter processes include increased voter participation, membership of professional associations such as the Association of Muslim lawyers, membership of mainstream political parties, growth in the number of Muslim local councillors (about 150 nationally in 1995), and the national organisation of these councillors into a National Forum for Muslim Councillors (Purdam 1996). They also include the development of English-language newspapers (*Q-News*, *Muslim Times*), satellite television, creating a South Asian public sphere (*Asianet*) and increased publishing (Alkalifah Press; ibid.).

Anthropologist Pnina Werbner describes three phases in the development of 'the Islamic politics of identity' in Britain in the 1990s (1996:68). First is the increasing visibility of Muslim political activism after *The Satanic Verses* controversy. This, we might add, also involved a diversification of Muslim voices and the growth in public forums for debate. Second is a new development of transnational consciousness resulting from ties not with sending societies but with areas of the world not strongly represented among British Muslims, especially Bosnia. To this we might add Palestine and, controversially, in the wake of 11 September, Afghanistan. Third is the development of a 'gendered diasporic public sphere in which women's independent collective voice has to be taken seriously by men' (ibid.). In contrast to the male-dominated community activism found hitherto, Werbner argues that this gendered and familial space 'is also a space of "fun", that is marked by gaiety, transgressive humour and dance' (ibid.:58).

Werbner illustrates the growth of transnationalism and the gendering of public space with the example of the Al Masoom Foundation Trust in Manchester, a women's organisation formed in the early 1990s and involved in charitable and campaigning work for Muslims groups in Bosnia, Kashmir and Pakistan. Its members comprised mostly devout Muslim middle-class Pakistani women, motivated by the Islamic notions of *khidmas* and *sadaqa* ('selfless communal work' and 'charitable giving' (ibid.:59)). Their activities included taking supplies to the Bosnian border for Bosnian refugees, supporting the construction of a children's cancer hospital in Rawalpindi, organising concerts in Manchester to raise funds for these activities, and lobbying MPs to raise the issue of Kashmir in Parliament. Yet at the same time as attracting the attention and approval of members of the political establishment, and in spite of their impeccable Islamic credentials, the group angered sections of the Pakistani male leadership in Manchester: Mrs Khan, the organisation's founder, has received death threats. The organisation has bypassed the business community, with its traditional male-dominated patronage networks, appealing directly to the local community: one school raised £7700 through a day of sports activities and fairs. But more than that, it has challenged the dominance of men in the public representation of the Pakistani community.

Werbner sees groups like Al Masoom as drawing on the global development of political Islam (Islamism) which has encouraged the growth of women's organisations and legitimised women's struggles against traditional social norms. It has also legitimised the struggle of youth against elders in terms of a distinction between 'true Islam', reconstructed from early textual sources, and later cultural accretions (*bida*, illicit innovations; ibid.:64). In the context of feminist Islamist interpretation (Mernissi 1988; Stowasser 1998), a figure such as 'Aisha, a wife of the Prophet, comes to serve as a role model for contemporary Islamist women. Muhammad died while 'Aisha was still young, and since she never remarried, she conducted the rest of her long life as an independent woman, including leading armies into battle. One should also add that economic factors, bringing more women into work, as well as education, have been important in transforming gender relations among British Muslims (Shaw 1988; Werbner 1990).

As this account of Islamist hermeneutics implies, skills of critical analysis and autonomy in the interpretation of texts and traditions are developed through it. Islamists' attempts to free textual interpretation from traditional straitjackets means that such movements and methods have the potential to (communicatively) rationalise traditional life worlds, and develop skills that can enable public debate and democratic participation. At the same time, however, their modernist insistence on the univocality of meaning of a text ('true Islam') can foster authoritarianism, as has their nurturing in predominantly authoritarian political contexts (Egypt, Iran, Tunisia, Nigeria and so on). Furthermore, traditional elements of respect for authority are also blended with this, for example the reverence for the Maududi (1903–79), founder of Jamaati Islami, an Islamist organisation that became increasingly influential among British Muslims through youth outreach work in the 1990s. The authoritarian inclination of this organisation has been underlined by its support for General Zia's military regime in the 1980s.

The appropriation of Islamist discourse by Al Masoom poses an interesting challenge to the construction of fundamentalism developed by the feminist and non-confessional organisation Women Against Fundamentalism (WAF), formed in the wake of *The Satanic Verses* controversy. WAF comments on the common traits of fundamentalism: 'they claim their version of religion to be the only true one. They use political means to impose it on all members of their religion and feel threatened by pluralist systems of thought' (Saghal and Yuval-Davis 1992:3). WAF emphasises the internal diversity of minority communities and the rights of individuals to shape their own identities. This latter point is especially crucial for women who, according to WAF, are seen by 'fundamentalist' groups as the main agents in the transmission of tradition, and therefore 'at the heart of all fundamentalist agendas is the control of women's minds and bodies' (ibid.:1).

Islamists do, on the whole, insist that their version of religion is the only true one. However, the process by which they validate their readings is one that is in principle open to contestation, even if this may be circumscribed in practice. In a British context, the appropriation of Islamist discourse has, alongside other factors, enabled women to challenge 'the control of women's minds and bodies' which WAF sees as 'at the heart of all fundamentalist agendas'. In the British context at least, it would seem that it is less Islamists than traditional religio-cultural configurations that seek to control women's minds and bodies.

Al Masoom also witnesses to the diversification of the British Muslim public sphere in the 1990s. Such a diversification process is also evident in Bradford, for example in responses to the Gulf War of 1991. The strong line taken by the Bradford Council of Mosques in criticising British government action (and that of other allies and the Saudis), while barely criticising Saddam Hussein, led local politicians to challenge the representative status of the Council. They did so implicitly by presenting alternative perspectives, for example denying Saddam Hussein's interpretation of the conflict as a 'holy war', given the range of Muslim forces on both sides. They also did so explicitly: for example, Tory candidate Muhammad Riaz argued that no person or group has ever been given 'a mandate by ... the Muslims of Bradford to act as their representative or spokesman' (in Lewis 1994:168). Further diversification followed. The business community in Bradford took greater responsibility for organising Eid celebrations through the formation of an Eid Committee in 1991, which also sought to foster non-Muslim participation in the celebrations. Fast FM, a radio station set up in 1992 to support those engaged in the annual fast, broadcast a debate among *ulama* on the disputed dates for starting and finishing the fast: three different dates were given by different sectarian authorities, causing disruption, confusion and embarrassment (ibid.:171).

The 'riot' of 1995, and possibly those of 2001, also witness in their own way to the pluralisation of the British Muslim public sphere, though through an extension of agitational rather than discursive politics. In the disturbance of 1995, a crowd that had gathered at a police station in a Muslim-majority area to protest at the arrest of three youths attacked non-Muslim-owned property and business premises, leading to many more arrests (Burlet and Reid 1996). When Council of Mosques leaders addressed the crowd to appeal for calm, they were shouted down as 'police puppets' (ibid.:151). Interviews with youths from the area showed that they perceived local community relations mechanisms including the Council of Mosques as irrelevant to their needs: 'elders are increasingly out of touch with our reality of unemployment and racism', one young man commented (ibid.:148). The youths also blamed local policing tactics: the arrests that triggered the incident were seen as the latest a pattern of heavy-handed practices, including use of stop and search powers and the construction of a police station described as 'Fortress

Lawcroft'. Gender differentiation is also evident in the interviews conducted by Burlet and Reid: one middle-aged woman commented: 'women wouldn't smash up shops, we direct our energy towards peaceful action' (ibid.:151). Nor did such opinion remain in the private sphere: in response to the riot, a group of Muslim women began a petition aimed at presenting their perspective and facilitating dialogue (ibid.).

Taken together, these developments suggest the pluralisation of British Muslim public spheres within different cities as well as nationally. In many cases they also suggest the rationalisation of the Islamic life world of British Muslims, as traditions become open to question and argument, and identities become more reflexive as well as more complex. While Muslim youths in Bradford may have limited life choices, exposure to a combination of state education, the British media, mosque school and links with Pakistan does inevitably confront British Muslims with choices about values and lifestyle, and engenders multicultural competencies – knowing how to act in different settings, which discourses to deploy (Baumann 1999). Such a process has not necessarily or even usually led to the rejection of Islam, indeed often the reverse, as Leveau found in France: 'The rigorous interpretation of Islam among intellectual believers appears to be a strategy for coping with French society' (1988:112).

Thus we return to the central issue of social integration raised at the beginning of this chapter. We have demonstrated that at least some aspects of Muslim civil society in Britain are procedurally democratic – in the sense of allowing broad participation, encouraging autonomous reflection, and sustaining public debate. We turn to consider whether the specific proposals that have arisen from the Muslim public sphere (especially increased recognition of collective identity, such as separate schools and extension of the law against incitement to racial hatred to cover religion) are favourable to the twin concerns of individual freedom and social integration that underlie liberal concepts of civil society.

Faith Schools, Equal Opportunities and Social Integration

> The refusal to grant Muslim schools, such as Islamia Primary School in Brent, London, voluntary-aided status is perceived by the vast majority of Muslims as clear evidence of the hostility and prejudice prevalent in society at large against them.
>
> (Al-Nisa society in UKACIA 1993:44)

Clearly, some Muslim parents would prefer that their children should be educated in Muslim schools, and more would prefer that Muslim parents should be able to choose faith schools if they want to. Furthermore, parental choice is currently a major factor in the discourse of all the main political parties on the issue of schooling. But there are other considerations, especially the role of education in the reproduction of society. Do Muslim schools give Muslim pupils confidence and a strong sense of identity that equip them to contribute to society, or do they deny the development of autonomous thinking and action (especially to girls)? Do they equip students for confident participation in the wider society, or do they encourage the creation of a ghetto? Let us consider each of these questions in turn. First, we compare these issues, using the arguments of the WAF in contrast to those of the An-Nisa society above. WAF's opposition to religious schools is based on the view that: 'All religious schools have a deeply conformist idea of the role of women. They will deny girls opportunities which they are just beginning to seize' (Saghal and Yuval-Davis 1992:2). But must this be so? Is it either necessarily true, or true in practice, that religious schools deny women opportunities? To take one example, the headmistress of Feversham College, Bradford, has justified her school precisely on the grounds that the provision of a supportive Muslim environment provides parents with the confidence to allow their daughters to continue in education, and thus to benefit from greater educational opportunities.[2] The small number of girls beginning to progress from Bradford Muslim Girls' School to Bradford and Ilkley Community College to train as teachers in the early 1990s testifies to the fruits of this policy. Thus taking account of religious sensitivities may enable wider participation and individual fulfilment. Separate schools catering for religious needs may be supported along these lines.

However, the opportunities which WAF has in mind may be of a broader nature; it may be objected that slightly broadening opportunities from a narrow religiously determined base is an unsatisfactory implementation of equal opportunities. Or that education should involve an initiation into pluralism – an empowerment to make individual choices – which is incompatible with the ethos of a religious school. One important question here is whether a religious school can present students with a sufficiently broad and critical perspective to enable them to make their own life choices.

Drawing on the work of the philosopher Alasdair MacIntyre (1985, 1988), Fitzmaurice (1993) proposes that any cultural practice can be characterised in terms of two dimensions of reflectiveness and embeddedness. She argues that all activities can be located on a continuum between the two, but we suggest that keeping the dimensions separate is better, because the two are not necessarily antagonistic on MacIntyre's understanding. For example, educational practices can be characterised in terms of the extent to which they encourage on the one hand critical reflection on and hence autonomy in relation to existing cultural norms and practices, and on the other hand unreflective reproduction of them.

Differences between the WAF and UKACIA positions may be represented in these terms. For WAF, religious schools will not enable women to develop the autonomy needed to seize the opportunities available. However, for UKACIA without sufficient rootedness in their cultural community, and in particular its religious identity, individuals will lose meaning, purpose and even effectiveness, since they will not know who they are, or where they are going. Fitzmaurice (1993) sees autonomy–tradition/cultural rootedness as representing poles on a continuum, neither of which represents a possible or desirable state in its extreme form of loss of identity or petrified tradition.

This perspective enables us to think around the autonomy–tradition dichotomy posed both by secularist modes of discourse (WAF, most pre-1990 political philosophy and race and ethnic studies, some feminist discourse) and, only with reversed polarity, by some forms of conservative Islam (and other religions) which demonise secularism in a similar way. But seeing the two as independent can take us further, towards a self-critical traditionality that does not insist, as Fitzmaurice continues to, that every step towards autonomous thinking is a step away from tradition. One starting point for the development of such a self-critical traditionality is the recognition that in cases such as *The Satanic Verses* controversy, both secularists and Muslims have sacred memories to protect and reasoned arguments to advance.

But what of the dangers to social integration posed by faith schools? Differentiated societies may be integrated through systems rather than life worlds, but without life world integration they will not be very nice places to live in, as the Bradford riots of 2001 demonstrate. Factors involved here appear to include youth alienation associated with unemployment and racism, the breakdown of respect for parental and other authority, and hostility to non-Muslims fostered by the mosques (Lewis 2001; Roy 2001). Social separation could be implicated in the genesis of all of these factors, and Lord Ouseley's report also points to the dangers of a separate social system created initially by housing and solidified on that basis through education, and to some extent reinforced by the reification of community identities in the competition for public funding. The Ouseley report, based on findings from before the riots, has subsequently been confirmed by the reports on the riots in Bradford, Burnley and Oldham (Brown 2001).

On the other hand, attempts at social engineering (such as bussing) have proved ineffective, and have been decisively rejected by local people (Halstead 1988). Furthermore, 'separate' institutions such as schools do not necessarily foster prejudice, depending on the ability of schools and other community institutions to foster civic pride and achieve participation in local communities in other ways. Thus schools founded on a religious basis – especially where they follow a curriculum that conforms to national standards designed to provide a broad-based education in the skills and knowledge needed to live in today's society, including a measure of personal autonomy and individual thinking – are not necessarily obstacles to wider social integration. Rather, they can conversely aid social integration by developing links with other community groups, hosting adult education classes, having active parent–teacher associations, encouraging students to engage in voluntary work and so on. On the other hand, schools on the whole reflect rather than create the communities they draw on, and in divided and impoverished communities they will tend to reflect that background, although in some cases they may be able to transcend it.

In any case, voluntary-aided and private Muslim schools will only educate a small proportion of Bradford's children for the foreseeable future. The issue is more one of separation within the secular (or 'Christian' voluntary-aided) sector caused by separation of housing. Here, the increasing participation of Muslim organisations in the public life of the city can only help matters, as can the active maintenance of a Christian 'presence' in predominantly Muslim areas (Lewis 2001). Yet clearly there are parts of the population, especially male youths, who are not being effectively drawn into these public spheres, except sporadically in violent protest or through the confrontational politics of extremist groups like Hizb-ut-Tahrir, who were to be found recruiting in the wake of the 1995 disturbances (Burlet and Reid 1996:152). Jacobson's work suggests how an active Muslim identity without Islamic commitment can feed into such situations. Both state and supplementary school systems have responsibilities here.

Conclusion

These problems should not obscure the progress that has been made in terms of the development of public forums for Muslims to debate in (a good thing in the view of both WAF and UKACIA). Furthermore, the evidence presented here also suggests that Muslim tradition is capable of nurturing organisations which embed respect for basic rights in the Islamic life world, and which support a plural public sphere. True, the development of such organisations in the British context and especially in Bradford has been a struggle, but their growth in the 1990s – ranging from UKACIA (formed to campaign to ban Rushdie's book, but committed to arguing the case within British civil and political society and on the basis of human rights), to Bradford City Radio and Fast FM to Al Masoom in Manchester – suggest that struggle is bearing fruit. Empirical Muslim civil society is contributing to normative British civil society.

Finally, we return to the question of whether mainstream sociology has missed something crucial in its neglect of religion as a factor in social cohesion. Certainly, it does seem to have neglected religion as a socially significant factor. In response, we have suggested ways in which this can be redressed, including Beyer's view of religion as a diffuse communication system well suited to addressing (if not correcting) the residual problems of globalisation, Castells's view of religion as a source of project identity, and Sayyid's account of the semantic properties of religious signifiers. Such accounts of the properties of religious systems can help us to understand how, why and when religion becomes publicly active, and to build a public policy that encourages its active participation in civil society. Above all, it can help us to avoid the false and unproductive dichotomy between religion as dominating and repressive and religion as purely privatised that underlies so much current discussion.

Notes

1 Produced by Selly Oak College's Birmingham Centre for the Study of Islam and Muslim-Christian Relations, edited by S. Imtiaz and M. Draper.

2 This information was gathered during an interview in 1992.

Bibliography

Abdo, G. (2000), *Egypt and the Triumph of Islam*, Oxford: Oxford University Press.
Aitken, R. (2001), 'British Muslims Oppose Military Action', *BBC/Today website*, accessed 7 December.
Asad, T. (1999), 'Religion, Nation-State and Secularism', in P. van der Veer and H. Lehmann (eds) *Nation and Religion: Perspectives on Europe and Asia*, Princeton, NJ: Princeton University Press, pp. 178–96.
Ayubi, N. (1991), *Political Islam*, London: Routledge.
Baumann, G. (1999), *The Multicultural Riddle: Rethinking National, Ethnic and Religious Identities*, London: Routledge.
Beckford, J. (1989), *Religion in Advanced Industrial Society*, London: Unwin Hyman.
Beyer, P. (1992), 'The Global Environment as a Religious Issue: A Sociological Analysis', *Religion*, **22**, 1–19.
Beyer, P. (1994), *Religion and Globalization*, London: Sage.

Brown, C. (2001), 'If We Want Social Cohesion We Need A Sense of Identity', *The Independent on Sunday*, 9 December.

Bruce, S. and Wallis, R. (1992), 'Secularization: The Orthodox Model', in S. Bruce and R. Wallis (eds), *Religion and Modernization: Sociologists and Historians Debate the Secularization Thesis*, Oxford: Clarendon, pp. 8–30.

Burlet, S. and Reid, H. (1996), 'Riots, Representation and Responsibilities: The Role of Young Men in Pakistani-Heritage Muslim Communities', in W. Shadid and P. van Koningsveld (eds) *Political Participation and Identities of Muslims in Non-Muslim States*, Kampen: Kok Pharos, pp. 144–59.

Casanova, J. (1994), *Public Religions in the Modern World*, Chicago: Chicago University Press.

Castells, M. (1996), *The Information Age: Economy, Society and Culture*, Vol. 1 *The Rise of the Network Society*, Oxford: Blackwell.

Castells, M. (1997a), *The Information Age: Economy, Society, and Culture*, Vol. 2 *The Power of Identity, III: End of Millennium*, Oxford: Blackwell.

Castells, M. (1997b), *The Information Age: Economy, Society, Culture*, Vol. 3 *End of Millennium*, Oxford: Blackwell.

Fitzmaurice, D. (1993), 'Liberal Neutrality, Traditional Minorities and Education', in J. Horton (ed.) *Liberalism, Multiculturalism and Toleration*, London: Macmillan, pp. 50–69.

Geertz, C. (1983), *Local Knowledge*, New York: Basic Books.

Gill, R., Hadaway, C. and Marler, P. (1998), 'Is Religious Belief Declining in Britain?', *Journal for the Scientific Study of Religion*, **37**(3), 507–16.

Habermas, J. (1987), *Theory of Communicative Action*, Vol. 2 *Lifeworld and System: A Critique of Functionalist Reason*, Cambridge: Polity/Blackwell.

Halstead, J. (1988), *Education and Cultural Diversity*, London: Falmer.

Inglehart, R. (1997), *Modernization and Postmodernization: Cultural, Economic and Political Change in 43 Societies*, Princeton, NJ: Princeton University Press.

Jacobson, J. (1998), *Islam in Transition: Religion and Identity Among British Pakistani Youth*, London: Routledge.

Kymlicka, W. (1989), *Liberalism, Community and Culture*, Oxford: Oxford University Press.

Leveau, R. (1988), 'The Islamic Presence in France', in T. Gerholm and Y. Lithman (eds) *The New Islamic Presence in Western Europe*, London: Mansell, pp. 107–22.

Leveau, R. (1991), 'Islam in France: New Perspectives', in W. Shadid and P. van Konigsveld (eds) *The Integration of Islam and Hinduism in Western Europe*, Kampen: Kok Pharos, pp. 122–33.

Lewis, P. (1994), *Islamic Britain*, London: I.B. Tauris.

Lewis, P. (2001), 'Bradford – More than a Race War', *The Tablet*, 21 July, pp. 1040–2.

Luhmann, N. (1982), *The Differentiation of Societies*, New York: Columbia University Press.

MacIntyre, A. (1985), *After Virtue*, 2nd edn, London: Duckworth.

MacIntyre, A. (1988), *Whose Justice? Which Rationality?*, London: Duckworth.

Melucci, A. (1985), 'The Symbolic Challenge of Contemporary Movements', *Social Research*, **52**(4), 789–816.

Mernissi, F. (1988), *Women and Islam*, Oxford: Blackwell.

Meyer, J. (1980), 'The World Polity and the Authority of the Nation-state', in A. Bergeson (ed.) *Studies of the World System*, New York: Academic Press, pp. 109–37.

Midgely, M. (1989), *Wisdom, Information and Wonder*, London: Routledge.

Moaddel, M. (1996), 'The Social Bases and Discursive Context of the Rise of Islamic Fundamentalism: the Cases of Iran and Syria', *Sociological Inquiry*, **66**(3), 330–55.

Modood, T. (1997), *Ethnic Minorities in Britain: Diversity and Disadvantage*, London: Policy Studies Institute.

Purdam, K. (1996), 'Settler Political Participation: Local Councillors', in W. Shadid and P. van Koningsveld (eds) *Political Participation and Identities of Muslims in Non-Muslim States*, Kampen: Kok Pharos, pp. 129–43.

Robertson, R. (1990), 'Mapping the Global Condition: Globalization as the Central Concept', *Theory, Culture and Society*, **7**(2–3), 15–30.

Roy, A. (2001), 'Muslim Parents and Mosques Are to Blame, Says Hindu Leader', *Daily Telegraph*, 9 July.

Saghal, G. and Yuval-Davis, N. (1992), *Refusing Holy Orders: Women and Fundamentalism in Britain*, London: Virago.

Sayyid, B. (1997), *A Fundamental Fear: Eurocentrism and the Emergence of Islamism*, London: Zed.

Shaw, A. (1988), *A Pakistani Community in Britain*, Oxford: Blackwell.

Starrett, G. (1998), *Putting Islam to Work: Education, Politics and Religious Transformation in Egypt*, Berkeley, Los Angeles and London: University of California Press.

Stout, J. (1988), *Ethics After Babel*, Cambridge, Mass.: James Clarke.

Stowasser, B. (1998), 'Gender Issues and Contemporary Quran Interpretation', in Y. Huddad and J. Esposito (eds) *Islam, Gender and Social Change*, New York: Oxford University Press, pp. 30–3.

Sullivan, D. (1994), *Private Voluntary Organizations in Egypt*, Gainesville: University of Florida Press.

Tibi, B. (1998), *The Challenge of Fundamentalism: Political Islam and the New World Disorder*, Berkeley: University of California Press.

United Kingdom Action Committee on Islamic Affairs (UKACIA) (1993), *Need for Reform: Muslims and the Law in Multi-Faith Britain*, London: UKACIA.

Wallerstein, I. (1979), *The Capitalist World Economy*, Cambridge: Cambridge University Press.

Werbner, P. (1990), *The Migration Process: Capital, Gifts and Offerings among British Muslims*, New York: Berg.

Werbner, P. (1996), 'Public Spaces, Political Voices: Gender, Feminism and Aspects of British Muslim Participation in the Public Sphere', in W. Shadid and P. van Koningsveld (eds) *Political Participation and Identities of Muslims in Non-Muslim States*, Kampen: Kok Pharos, pp. 53–70.

Wilson, B. (1994), *The Changing Functions of Religion: Toleration and Cohesion in a Secularized Society*, Maidenhead, Berks: The Institute of Oriental Philosophy European Centre.

Žižek, S. (1989), *The Sublime Object of Ideology*, London: Verso.

CHAPTER 11

'I'm a Gujarati Lohana and a Vaishnav as Well'

Religious Identity Formation among Young Coventrian Punjabis and Gujaratis

Eleanor Nesbitt

In this chapter I aim to demonstrate the contribution of ethnographic research to uncovering and understanding processes of religious identity formation among young British people from south Asian families. Through an examination of their self-identification, especially as 'Hindu' or 'Sikh' (or with reference to these terms), this chapter will suggest that their self-narration in interviews discloses the processes of comparison between themselves and significant others. The mismatch between the categories of 'Hindu' and 'Sikh' with the self-identification and experience of some young people will problematise the essentialising of religious identities and in particular the role of the education system in conferring and confirming religious identities.

As the research was designed within the context of religious education (RE), the implications of RE for the research, as well as the implications of the research for RE (and indeed for its higher education cousin, religious studies), will be mentioned. RE is a statutory curriculum subject for schools in England and Wales, and is predicated on six 'world religions': Christianity and the 'other principal religions represented in Great Britain' (ERA 1988:8.3) including Hinduism and Sikhism. These must together feature in religious education's locally agreed syllabuses. In each case 'representatives' of the faiths concerned have suggested or at least approved what is presented as their 'faith'.[1]

The data reviewed below result from four periods of ethnographic research between 1985 and 1996 which I conducted in Coventry, UK, while based in what is now the Warwick Religions and Education Research Unit at the Institute of Education, University of Warwick, Coventry, UK.[2]

Coventry, with a population of 300 000, is a formerly industrial city in the west Midlands. Like Britain's other industrial cities its population results from successive periods of migration and settlement, both from within the British Isles (notably from Ireland) and from south Asia and the Caribbean. Coventry's largest minority of non-European background is Punjabi, and of its Punjabi residents the majority (at least 5 per cent of the city's population) are Sikhs, with smaller numbers of Hindus.[3] In many families senior males came to Coventry from the Jullundur Doab area of Punjabi India in the 1950s and 1960s. The Punjabi Hindus are roughly equalled in numbers by Hindus whose family roots are in the Indian state of Gujarat. Most of Coventry's Gujarati Hindu families include grandparents and younger family members who lived in Kenya, Uganda or another African country prior to the 1970s. The fact that residents of Indian background far exceed those of Pakistani, Bangladeshi or African-Caribbean background, together with the predominance of Punjabis among the Indians and the presence of Valmiki and Ravidasi communities (see below), contribute to the distinctive population balance in Coventry.

The four Warwick studies focused on young Gujaratis and Punjabis – three involving 8 to 13-year-olds, and the fourth involving some of the same young people when they were aged 16 to 23.[4] In all 34 girls and 25 boys participated. The Gujaratis all identified themselves when interviewed as Hindu: the Punjabis' self-identification as either Hindu or Sikh was not in every case so straightforward. The first three studies entailed participant observation in places of worship and in young people's homes, as well as semi-structured interviews with both the young people and adult organisers of religio-cultural activities such as Sikh religious music (*kirtan*) classes. The fourth study relied upon three in-depth interviews with 22 of the young Hindus.

Each field study was defined, and the 'subjects' were selected, according to religious rather than, say, linguistic or socio-economic categories, although these received attention as variables. In other words, consistently with my concerns as a religious educationist, the research projects focused on the religious nurture (socialisation) of Hindus and Sikhs rather than on, say, cultural transmission and adaptation in Gujarati and Punjabi communities. This meant that for the first and third studies (of Hindus and Sikhs respectively) the 8 to 13-year-olds were selected from participants in temple-based activity plus supplementary classes (for example, Hindi, Gujarati or Punjabi language classes and *kirtan* classes) that had been set up by Hindu and Sikh organisations. At the same time, in a bid to include the 'less committed' (to use inappropriate Christian terminology), the sample included pupils who were identified in school records as Hindu and Sikh respectively, and whom I had not identified via religious community networks or organisations.

The second study arose from my increasing realisation that members of the Valmiki and Ravidasi communities did not neatly fit the RE syllabuses' and school records' categories of 'Hindu' or 'Sikh'. The young people selected for this study were identified via two places of congregational worship, the Valmik Sabha and the Ravidass Sabha. All participants here belonged respectively to two castes (*zats*) whose names – *chuhra* and *chamar* – are often used insultingly by others. In conversation with me, neither the young people nor their elders used these terms which link them with centuries of oppression by higher-caste Punjabis as landless labourers, toiling in previous generations as, respectively, 'sweepers' and skinners/ tanners.

I extracted my Punjabi and Gujarati interviewees' concepts of their individual and group identity not simply from their replies to questions focused on identity, but also from an analysis of their responses throughout their interviews. These included their responses to visual stimuli (popular iconography – such as trade calendars and framed pictures in their living rooms – and photographs taken in the field). Focused questions included 'If somebody said to you, "What's your religion?", what would you say?' and the young Sikhs were asked whether they identified themselves with any of a list of ethnic, national and religious descriptors which included 'Asian',

'Indian', 'Hindu' and 'Sikh'. The longitudinal dimension of the fourth study allowed for changes and continuity *vis-à-vis* identity over nearly a decade to surface.

The ensuing reflection on articulations of their identity offered by young people in all the studies can be situated by reference to discussions of identity construction and, more specifically, British south Asians' identity formation. The creative tension between the 'between two cultures' literature (such as Anwar 1976; Ghuman 1994) and analyses that recognise a more complex reality (such as Brah 1996; Jacobson 1996, 1997; Raj 1997) plays a key part in my reading of these young people's observations about their personal identity. Midway between these understandings is the 'bi-cultural' position (for example, Drury 1989). According to Drury, '"bi-culturalism" relates to the extent to which members of the second generation internalize and identify with more than one set of socio-cultural norms and values' (1989:557). This approach usefully acknowledges the situational character of individual identity – but, with a tendency to reify 'sets of socio-cultural norms', it can also oversimplify and understate the ever shifting multiplicity of 'sources of identity', since 'identities are in transition, involved in a multiplicity of cross-overs and mixes' (Gillespie 1995:19). As Hall notes, 'identities are never unified ... never singular but multiply constructed across different, often intersecting and antagonistic, discourses, practices and positions' (1996:4).

Non-Religious Self-Identification: British, Asian and Indian

An examination of the young people's non-religious self-identifications exemplifies some of these cross-overs. The young people used many terms, other than explicitly religious ones, to convey their identity. Like Jacobson's interviewees (1996), they described themselves as both British and Asian. Jacobson suggested 'civic', 'racial' and 'cultural' as 'three shifting boundaries of Britishness' (1996), and my interviewees strongly identified themselves as British in the civic and (on occasion) in the cultural sense. Their feeling of being British could surface – as a civic sense of Britishness – in a racist confrontation, or it could strike them – as a cultural identity – when they were visiting their families in India (Nesbitt 1998:193). To quote one male Punjabi university student: 'In India I probably felt more British there than I've ever felt before. I was missing it so much ... I do take England as being my home.'

Other aspects of their cultural identity (in distinction from, for example, white English-style Britishness) were also subsumed in the term 'Asian', a term which they used to refer to themselves as well as when quoting others. 'Asian' implied commonalities of experience such as caste structure, 'arranged marriage' and styles of music (Baumann 1996:149–60), plus (at least for special occasions) dress and cuisine. My interviewees used 'Asian' when commenting on their peers' behaviour, whether as obedient and conformist sons and daughters or manifesting itself in strident, if temporary, reaction against this parental expectation (Nesbitt 1998). One male Punjabi student encapsulated this reaction in his 'rubber band theory', whereby the more pressure their parents apply to Asian girls at home, the more powerfully they rebel at university.

The young people also identified themselves as Indian, and did so (as with 'Asian'), in distinction from being English. For example, to the question 'What are your friends like?' a Punjabi woman replied, 'My closest friends are same as me – Indian.' One identified herself as Indian in emphasising the inappropriateness of the verbal abuse she suffered as a 'Paki'. They spoke of themselves as 'Indian', regardless of where they had been born. Illustrative of this is a statement by a (Punjabi) girl who had never visited India (her father's birthplace) and whose mother had grown up in Singapore. She insisted that she was Indian 'because I came from India, I came from Delhi – our family came from Delhi, ancestors from Punjab, all over India, I think'.

India was, however, also mentioned as the context in which (on visits from the UK) young British Punjabis and Gujaratis felt most keenly aware of their Britishness as compared with their relatives domiciled there. At the same time, for the 16 to 23-year-olds in the most recent study, India was a resource for their individual interests (whether fashion, wedding make-up, music fusion or visiting significant temples), although none envisaged ever living there.

Yet some specific events in India could intensify a young person's sense of identity as Sikh or Hindu. For example a Gujarati law student spoke heatedly about the Babri masjid affair: 'What gave me great satisfaction ... is when we, when Hindus, destroyed the temple at ... Ayodhya.'[5]

In 1991 my 8 to 13-year-old Sikh interviewees were too young to recall the traumatic events of 1984, but in some cases older members of their families linked the violence against the Golden Temple (in June) and the massacre of Sikhs in Delhi later that year to their assertion of their own identity as Sikh (Nesbitt 1999a:326–7). 'Indian', an apparently non-religious identity, in fact carried strongly religious connotations: the young people frequently attributed their identity as Sikh or Hindu to their parents, who, they explained, were 'Punjabi' or 'Indian', and some went on to base this identity as Sikh or Hindu on the fact that their parents (unlike them) had been born and brought up in India. In other words, it was the place, India, that conferred or validated the family's religious identity: '[My dad] was born in India and he's got Indian passport ... That makes him a real Sikh' (nine-year-old boy). Consistently with this one ten-year-old boy said of another boy, 'He's not a Sikh, he says his mum was born in Africa.'[6]

In addition to 'Indian', other identities too connected strongly with my interviewees' self-identification as Hindu or Sikh, and these identities are the subject of the next section.

Ethnicity and *Jati*

Despite a tendency increasingly to use 'ethnic' for groups in fact differentiated by religion (Searle-Chatterjee 2000:499), 'ethnicity' in this chapter means individuals' identification in terms of an Indian region of family origin and the associated mother tongue – which south Asian language was most used in the home even where English had replaced it as the dominant language – plus distinctive cuisine, marriage customs and so on. It is on this basis that I describe my young British interviewees as Punjabi or Gujarati. The very small numbers of Gujaratis in

Coventry of any faith community other than Hindu meant that for both Punjabis and Gujaratis, Gujarati meant Hindu. At the same time, the young Sikhs' association of being Sikh with being Punjabi and speaking the Punjabi language was made more explicit than the Hindus' sense of connection with either Punjab or Gujarat. Indeed, the Sikhs equated speaking Punjabi with being Sikh, even though there are many Punjabi-speaking Muslims, Hindus and Christians in Coventry, and despite the fact that most of the young Sikhs were reluctant to use Punjabi in situations where English could be spoken instead (Nesbitt and Jackson 1993).

Several of those who identified themselves as Hindu in the study of 8 to 13-year-old Hindus used the terms 'Hindi' and 'Hindu' interchangeably. Hindi, which together with English is one of the national languages of India, was not the first language of any of the young people and was spoken as a first language by only one of the parents. However, the tendency to equate (or at least associate) Hindu with Hindi is important for several reasons. There is the tendency for Punjabi-speaking Hindus to regard Hindi as their community's language, in distinction from Punjabi, so that those children who attend language classes go to Hindi classes, not Punjabi classes. This tendency has its origins in a political cleavage between Sikhs and Hindus along language lines in Punjab during the twentieth century. Furthermore, the interchangeable use of 'Hindi' and 'Hindu' echoes the confusion and resultant inaccurate usage of the two similar-sounding words by teachers and other non-Indian adults whom the children hear. The children's language and so their concepts and categories had not evolved in some Indic isolation from their English schooling and environment. By drawing attention to this factor I am in this one respect querying Searle-Chatterjee's confidence in shifting the 'confusion' from the children's apparent mixing of categories to Jackson's and my supposed assumption 'that the informant ought to share the same categories as the researcher' (Searle-Chatterjee 2000:504, commenting on Jackson and Nesbitt 1993:29ff.). Thus their use of 'Hindi' for 'Hindu' and vice versa is not necessarily evidence of their having a concept of culture in which language and identity and religious community are undifferentiated.

The Hindi word *jati* – like the Gujarati *nat-jat* and the Punjabi *zat* – denotes the hereditary, traditionally endogamous groups to which the young people's families belonged – but such Indic terms were not used by my interviewees. In their conversation the young people used neither these Indic terms nor European ones such as 'caste' for this phenomenon, but they referred instead to their 'community' and – in the case of some Gujaratis – to their *samaj*. *Samaj*, literally 'society', denoted the organised networks, such as the Lohana *mahajan* or Prajapati *samaj*, which produced address lists and arranged social events – notably celebrations of the autumn nine-night festival of Navaratri. Conversely, on the few occasions when my interviewees used 'caste', it was to refer to an ethnic group or community such as 'English people', 'Gujarati people' or 'Muslims' rather than to a *jati*.

As with their geographical region of sub-continental origin and associated ethnicity, these young British Asians clearly linked those two aspects of their experience for which I am deploying the analytic terms *jati* and religion, and in some instances they treated these, no less than ethnicity and religion, as interchangeable. This was especially true of the Punjabis. Thus, for Ramgarhia Sikhs (from families historically occupied as carpenters, smiths, bricklayers and masons) being Ramgarhia meant being more thoroughly Sikh (see also Kalsi 1994). So a member of the local Ramgarhia *gurdwara* management committee assured me that 'if kids are in the Ramgarhia school [the *gurdwara*'s Punjabi class] they are as good as *amritdhari* kids [initiated into the Khalsa, the nucleus of committed Sikhs, and observing the associated discipline]'.[7] Similarly, young people from the Jat, or traditionally farming, *zat*, that is both numerically and economically the most powerful in Punjab, used 'Sikh' and 'Jat' interchangeably, and British children in Jat families unhesitatingly emphasised this equation. For example, particularly striking was a Jat girl's assertion that 'of course' the *panj piare* (five orange- and blue-attired, bearded Sikhs) in a local procession marking a Sikh festival must be Jats.[8] I had anticipated that when she saw the picture of the five men in ostensibly traditional Sikh clothing she would tell me that they were very religious or that they had been initiated (were *amritchhakia* – the verb that some interviewees used adjectivally for *amritdhari*), not that she would leap to conclusions about their *zat/jati*.

Ravidasi children – all from families which were *chamar* by *zat* – also equated Jats with Sikhs, describing them as 'true Sikhs' (to quote an 11-year-old Ravidasi boy) as compared with their less Sikh selves. Easton's *chamar* interviewees in Wolverhampton articulated the same perception (1999:5).

Sampradaya

Jati intersected in a variety of ways with the devotional groups and networks in which families were involved. For example, like the Ravidasis and Valmikis, some devotional congregations, and the larger organisations to which they belong, are *jati*-specific or at least certain *jatis* preponderate – Lohanas among Pushtimargis, for example. In others (for example in the International Society for Krishna Consciousness, ISKCON, with its mix of Gujarati, Punjabi, other south Asian and non-south Asian worshippers) *jati* is less significant. For these groups and networks *sampradaya* (guru-led movement) serves as an appropriate analytic term, even though – like *jati* – it was not used by my interviewees. Their family's ritual activity and religious idiom was in many cases, however, distinctive of a *sampradaya*. In practice the term *sampradaya* is used quite flexibly. Flood (1995:11) provides a useful – if tighter – definition: 'a tradition focused on a deity, often regional in character, into which a disciple is initiated by a guru. Furthermore, each guru is seen to be within a line of gurus, a santana or parampara, originating with the founding father.' *Sampradaya*-specific congregations gathered in *gurdwaras*, *mandirs*, houses and hired halls. Some of these groups owed particular allegiance to a living master, such as the Babajis of two *gurdwaras* (see Nesbitt 1985; 2000) and Sathya Sai Baba (Jackson and Nesbitt 1993:122–6).

Williams has suggested that '[a]llegiance to religious leaders ... seems easier for immigrant parents to transmit to their American children than language or ethnic identity' (1988:283). Certainly some of the young Coventrians' under-standing of being Sikh or Hindu was strongly influenced by a specific *swami*, *sant* or guru.[9] Indeed, the influence of Morari Bapu is proof that such an individual need not belong to a succession of masters, so representing in himself a *sampradaya*, but may instead be a charismatic performer and exponent of the tradition – in his case of the Ramayana epic (Nesbitt 1999b). In many cases, however, the spiritual master or woman guru is venerated as the latest in a line of succession, and he or she is in some cases the living focus of a *sampradaya*. For example, two young Gujaratis' families worshipped as Pushtimargis in the homes of other Pushtimargis and venerated charismatic hereditary leaders including the occasionally visiting, Gujarat-based woman guru known as Betiji (Jackson and Nesbitt 1993:116).[10]

*Sampradaya*s do not necessarily fit neatly into a Hindu or Sikh slot, but the reasons for this differ from one group to another. Some devotional groupings (such as Sathya Sai Baba's devotees – see Exon 1997) present themselves as universal, transcending narrow faith confines. So, for a female Gujarati psychology student, her devotion, and her family's, to Sathya Sai Baba stood in an ambiguous relationship with being Hindu. Her musings include the issue of whether ritual observance is a prerequisite for being Hindu: 'But then the question is "what is a Hindu?" Are you born with Hindu blood? ... I would say I'm born a Hindu. I'll die a Hindu. But then, maybe, I shouldn't call myself a Hindu in the first place, because I don't actually practise Hinduism.'

For the Valmikis and Ravidasis, however, neither their level of observance nor the extent of their spiritual encompassment was the issue, so much as their community's *zat*-based solidarity forged by centuries of discrimination. The fact that some were more ready to identify themselves as Hindu, others as Sikh, others as both or neither, illustrated the inadequacy of taxonomies, such as that perpetuated in religious education, based on the 'world religion' model (Nesbitt 1990).

Significant Others

As is evident in some statements quoted above, implicit – and indeed often explicit – in interviewees' affirmations of their identity, and in their musings upon it, were comparisons and contrasts. For example, when I asked 8 to 13-year-olds 'What makes you a Hindu/Sikh?' one key distinction that they drew was between themselves on the one hand as 'brown' (that is darker-skinned) and white people on the other hand, to whom they referred as '*gore*' (pronounced 'goray' and meaning light-skinned). Using religious labels, rather than pigmentation, many also distinguished themselves during their interviews from others whom they referred to as Hindu or Muslim or Sikh. So the one young man in the most recent study who mentioned 'gangs' spoke of Hindus and Sikhs joining different gangs from Muslims.[11]

The young Coventrian Valmikis and Ravidasis located their identity in relation to Sikhs and Hindus, and without asserting difference in strong terms: 'I know what I am, what culture I am, Hindu. But it's not as if we're constricted to Hindu, because we believe in Sikhism as well' (12-year-old Valmiki girl).

This tendency to understand their family's tradition in terms of both Hinduism and Sikhism was not unusual. Certainly, none of my Coventry interviewees distinguished themselves as emphatically from either Sikhs or Hindus, as Easton's older Wolverhampton *chamar* respondents (members of the Ravidasis' *zat*) distinguished themselves from 'Sikhs':

> Chamars in this Wolverhampton study spoke most often of their identity in relation to 'the Sikhs'. For example, despite outlining many congruencies between Sikh and

Ravidasi religious practice informants emphatically refused to be labelled as Sikh and blamed the Sikhs for excluding them from their religious community. One had taken the images of Sikh Gurus from the shrine at home and put them in the bin.

(Easton 1999:4)

Here, 'Sikh' actually refers to Jat, that is the traditional landowning agriculturalists as contrasted with the historically landless *chamar*/Ravidasi. In other words, even when employing the terminology of religion-defined communities, the young people are actually building their identities with reference to other *jati*s. The Jat/*chamar* interface was unusual in the degree of animosity that could surface – continuous with the oppression and resentment of this in the Punjab. Easton's respondents in Wolverhampton 'expressed conflict' and she comments, rightly in my view, that: 'In England not only do Punjabis of all castes live alongside each other but they are also under pressure to assert their differences and mutually position themselves in the face of an indigenous discourse which views all Asians as the same' (1999:5).

Young people from higher *jati*s also articulated their identity with reference to other *jati*s, but never with so much feeling as the *chuhra*s and *chamar*s did in relation to Jats. However, both brahmins and non-brahmins occasionally indicated awareness of the religious significance of being brahmin. So a 10-year-old Anavil brahmin (a Gujarati), while talking about diet, explained that brahmins pray more and do not eat meat:[12] 'It's not very special, but it's something to be proud of. If you're one you got to be proud of it.'

A male student, a Kathiawari Soni (goldsmith *jati* from Kathiawad/Saurashtra region of Gujarat), whose mother outdid most of her brahmin contemporaries for religious – including dietary – observance, informed me that: 'I know that brahmins are classed as very high class people ... A lot of brahmins go further into more depth in their religion.'

Like the nineteenth-century developments in Caribbean Hindu communities (Vertovec 1988), the *jati*-based comparisons that young people voice are more apparent at the extremes of the hierarchy. However, the hierarchy is not only the classic purity/pollution-ranked *varna* model with brahmins at the top and *shudra*s and *dalit*s[13] at the bottom, but also the economic ranking of rural Punjab, dominated by Jats proud of their history as landowners.

The comparisons through which the young people constructed their identity were ones not only of pigmentation, a world religions-defined faith community, *jati* and *sampradaya* but also (as already noted) of their degree of association with India and Britain. The young Coventrians' sense of themselves as British was heightened by comparison with relatives in India. Some distinguished their shallower 'knowledge' of their religion from their parents' deeper knowledge which they attributed to their closer ties with India. Similarly encounters with peers at school who had recently arrived from the sub-continent, and were less fluent in English, could contribute to feeling 'English'. A young Punjabi woman recalled: 'There was [*sic*] some kids that came from different countries where they couldn't speak English ... They were more Indian and I was more English.'

In addition to the polarities of brown/white, Indian/British, Brahmin or Jat/lower caste that surfaced in the young people's self-identifications there was also a scale of religious observance. For those who identified themselves as Sikh, comparison between themselves, members of their families and others resulted in a scale of what I have elsewhere termed 'Sikhness' (Nesbitt 1999a:319). Young Punjabis connected being Sikh with several factors: appearance (including turban and the five Ks, the external signs of commitment – especially uncut head and facial hair), belief, being born into a Sikh family, and being *amritchhakia* (initiated). They recurrently articulated a distinction between two orders of Sikh: Sikhs on the one hand and 'proper Sikhs', 'pure Sikhs', 'real Sikhs', 'true Sikhs' on the other. This two-tier model was evident when conversation in the course of interviews turned to personal appearance – especially hair – or to the *amrit* ceremony, to the subject of functionaries in the *gurdwara* or, as suggested above, to the topics of India and *jati*. While Punjabis of the lowest two *jati*s did not all identify exclusively with Sikh or Hindu, the Jats and Ramgarhias all came across as secure in their identity as Sikh, but equally sure that they themselves were not 'proper' Sikhs as they did not maintain the discipline of a Khalsa Sikh. However, they did not use the term Khalsa or for that matter *keshdhari* or *amritdhari*, terms familiar in Sikh studies as designating respectively Sikhs whose hair was uncut, giving them 'the Sikh look' (Gell 1994), or *keshdhari* Sikhs who had additionally committed themselves to keeping the Khalsa code of discipline by receiving *amrit*. Instead, in addition to 'proper Sikhs' two girls spoke of '*pagwala* Sikhs' (turbaned male Sikhs) and of being '*amritchhakia*'.

Some Sikh writers and speakers, in the diaspora at least, are beginning to reserve the name 'Sikh' for Khalsa Sikhs, paralleling some Christians' restriction of 'Christian' to those who have 'asked Jesus into their lives' in contrast to 'nominal' Christians. Thus Amarjit Singh insisted that most of the people who think they are Sikh are 'non Sikhs' as 'the most important thing that defines Sikhs is the practice of Sikhism', that is Khalsa discipline (1992:27–8). However, only one of the young Coventrian Sikhs followed this line, distinguishing (a strict Khalsa minority's) 'Sikh weddings' from the 'not Sikh weddings', that is those of the majority of (nominal) Sikhs, characterised as they are by bridal splendour and conspicuous hospitality involving alcohol and non-vegetarian food.

This contestation, and the fluctuating restriction and encompassment in the application of religious labels, exemplifies the continuous processes of comparison between the self and others, and between different others, whereby individuals construct and give meaning to their own identities. In Hall's words 'identification ... requires what is left outside, its constitutive outside, to consolidate the process' (1996:3). The Coventry data illustrate the ways in which individuals categorise groups in Britain's complex society, and exemplify the related comparison between one's own group and others' groups which 'contribute in turn to some important aspects of [people's] definition of themselves, of their social identity' (Tajfel 1981:165).

Life Stages

As already indicated, in articulating their own religious identity the young people often made reference to their parents, and indeed to their grandparents, contrasting their own relative ignorance of their tradition with their elders' more extensive knowledge or more disciplined practice. For example, I was told of two Gujarati Hindu (Vaishnav, that is Pushtimargi) grandmothers who maintained their kitchen's purity through strict vegetarianism (Nesbitt 1999c), and of visibly Sikh grand-fathers – turbaned and maintaining the five Ks.

What is less clear is whether young people were simply contrasting themselves and their parents or grandparents (whose upbringing in India could never be theirs) or whether they were also acknowledging a traditionally expected difference between an individual's religiousness at different stages of life. Deep in Hindu tradition is the model (at least for high-caste males) of *asramadharma* – an assumption that one's appropriate path through life will entail varying balances of spiritual and material concern at different ages. One male Gujarati sixth-former's observations accord with this model:

> Once you ... become like teenagers, 14, 15 ... it's up to you whether you're interested in tradition or not. But for some reason ... married kids ... tend to go back to tradition ... Like my brother ... when I was 10 he was listening to pop music at that time. Now I'm 17 and he's 30 something he's listening to more *bhajans* [devotional songs], he's watching more Indian films ... When I become an adult people are going to expect me to start watching Indian films, staying at home, being grumpy.

Similarly, a female Gujarati science student anticipated learning to conduct *puja* and *arati* in the way her mother-in-law does, 'so one day, when she's not around any more, I can still pass on to my children and it will go on in that way'.[14]

Although the Sikh gurus replaced *varnasramadharma* (the appropriateness of different duties to different social classes and stages of life) with an emphasis for all, regardless of *jati*, on the *grihasthi* (family duties) of the *sant-sipahi* (saint-soldier) who combines family responsibility with spirituality throughout life, in practice not only the young Hindus but also their Sikh counterparts envisaged different degrees of religious commitment at different life stages. Two sisters anticipated that they would go through the act of commitment (*amrit chhakana*) and observe the consequent discipline in the future. Other children reported the marked increase in an older relative's observance after taking *amrit*.

As 8 to 13-year-olds my Hindu interviewees looked forward, whereas from their vantage point nine years on as young adults interviewed in the fourth study, they could also look back. Accordingly, they described changes in their religious understanding and practice during the past decade: 'When you progress you realise that all the different gods are in fact the same, and that's when you start to talk about the world being an illusion ... The real reality is that of being one with God ... You can look back and think "then I thought this"' (male Gujarati mathematics student).

The longitudinal study also provided evidence of a decline in some young people's actual observance during the period. The female Gujarati Sai devotee quoted earlier explained: 'Nine years ago I would be practising my religion much more because my father would tell me to, but now by choice I don't actually practise any religion: I just believe in Sai Baba or whatever he teaches.'

Several interviewees linked the decline in their ritual activity with the demands on their time as students and the difficulty of remaining so observant away from home. None, apart from the Gujarati psychologist quoted above, even began to question their own identity on the basis of distance from observance.

Such reflections on temporal shifts in individual interviewees' religiosity did not in other cases suggest any changes of felt identity. However, since it is processual, identification as Hindu or Sikh can be periodised in a few cases, and the years spent in primary education merit attention. The field studies showed, in the case of some pupils, the role of schools in this identity formation. Not only did primary school teachers (like the nineteenth-century census-takers in British India) ask pupils or their families for their 'religion', but they also helped to answer the question, in some cases providing the label: 'First I used to say [my religion] was Indian, but then my teacher told me that it's not really Indian, it's Sikh. So I start sort of saying, "It's Sikh"' (Nesbitt 1991:31, quoting a Ravidasi girl).

> I just found out that I'm Hindu; well my mum told me because this teacher said, 'Are you a Hindu?' and I said, 'I don't know', so she said, 'Go and ask your mum and tell me'. And when I told her the other day she said, 'OK' and she wanted to know about Divali.
> (Jackson and Nesbitt 1993:162–3)

Teachers in secondary schools might also precipitate pupils' linkage of knowledge with their identity. In particular, RE, with its syllabuses framed by the world religions model, provided some content of 'belief' for a pupil's religious label. This can be illustrated by my interviews with, respectively, a 16-year-old female Gujarati brahmin and a 13-year-old female Punjabi Ravidasi. The first interviewee, asked if she had heard the word 'karma', answered: 'Yes, I can't remember. I did it in my exam ... Is that the cycle? ... Is it the reborn?' The second said: 'When I heard it [reincarnation] at school ... it had a great effect on me because it [Hinduism] was my own religion and I thought it was true' (Nesbitt 1991:31).

This is of particular interest, given that the second interviewee identified herself as 'Punjabi Hindu' on her parents' strategic advice in order to counter other pupils' inquiries about her 'caste', even though, as she and her brother explained to me, by going to a *gurdwara* their family seemed to resemble what the curriculum presented as Sikh practice rather than Hindu practice.

RE teachers' formalisation of 'beliefs' and 'practices', based on RE syllabus requirements, is a far cry from the informal nurture, such as 'just sitting around and with my mum cooking' through which young Hindus for the most part learn what it means to be Hindu (Raj 1997:124). So, too, is the academic reinforcement and problematising of identity in undergraduate courses followed by the young Gujarati woman quoted in the title of this chapter and by the Gujarati psychology student and the 13-year-old just quoted.

Conclusion

In a more nuanced way than quantitative research on identity (for example, Short and Carrington 1995) the Warwick studies provide data that support theories of identity as 'not ... an artefact or an outcome, but as a construction, a process never completed' (Anand 2000:273).

The young people situated their identity horizontally by reference to other communities and vertically both by reference to their parents and grandparents and by looking forward and backward to different stages of their own lives. In these two vertical explorations 'Hindu' and 'Sikh' frequently emerged – like Punjabi and Gujarati – as core identities, continuous through their own lifespan and across the generations, whereas 'African' and 'British', and to a lesser degree 'Indian', could be used to differentiate the generations according to place of birth and upbringing in successive generations.

As I have argued in more detail elsewhere (Nesbitt 1998) it is encounters that precipitate their identity construction, and one encounter – the ethnographic interview itself – not only discloses but also generates, or at least facilitates, individuals' narration of their identity. In this narration of religious identity, outsiders including teachers – especially religious education teachers – and researchers are implicated and they may influence the labels that individuals select. At school identities are aligned with 'world faiths', even when the culture of home challenges such allocation and spans supposed boundaries. As these studies suggest, young Gujaratis and Punjabis have learned that 'Hindu' and 'Sikh' are 'acceptable categor[ies]' (Searle-Chatterjee 2000:499) so that the distinction which she draws between using these and 'actual thinking and practice' (necessitating questions such as 'who is your guru?' or 'to whom do you do *puja*?', not 'what is your religion?') is itself increasingly anachronistic.

The individual's narration illustrates Tajfel's processes of identity construction through categorisation and comparison (1981). For the Warwick interviewees the categories included ethnicity, *jati*, *sampradaya* and 'faith community' (although these were not the terms that any of them employed). These aspects of their identity came to the fore more strongly in some situations than others, and the intensity with which each is felt depends upon context and is responsive to events (Nesbitt 1998). The variations in feeling, so vital to identity, are less likely to be evident from censuses, and quantitative research's use of scales can at best only supplement the fluctuations that qualitative data can capture.

Ethnographic research serves also to alert us to differences between the terminology that I used (in conceptualising and reporting the research) and the terminology of my interviewees. It is not simply that I and other anthropological writers used 'Pushtimargi' where my informants used 'Vaishnav' or that they used '*samaj*' where I used 'caste' and anthropologists used '*jati*'. These terms refer to overlapping and shifting conceptual terrain, and both my interviewees and I use different terms for the same category or concept in different contexts. This was particularly evident when a young 'Hindu' woman admitted in her final interview that she was Jain, but explained that she only identified herself in this way when talking with (other) Hindus, as other people would not understand the word 'Jain'. Had I not introduced my investigation as a study of young Hindus, had I questioned her differently, had I declared more insider knowledge, and if she in turn had felt more confident to explain what 'Jain' meant, she would perhaps have identified herself differently, both to me and in her school.[15]

As we have noted, some of the 8 to 13-year-old interviewees used 'Hindu' and 'Hindi', 'Sikh' and 'Punjabi', 'religion' and 'language' or 'religion' and 'caste' interchangeably. This fluid usage apparently challenges categories. It does not invalidate the appropriateness of 'religious identity' as an analytic term. It does, however, serve as a reminder that variations in usage indicate the dangers of defining too narrowly, or without questioning the inbuilt Western assumptions in many current definitions of religion, culture and community, and it may also indicate the contribution of teachers who have no understanding of the diversity of south Asian language, region, identity and practice.

Baumann's 'cross-cutting cleavages' (1996) and the language of plurality and diversity in postmodern analyses such as Anand's and Gillespie's best fit the Warwick data, with Østberg's (2001) emphasis on the integration of identity according with their narratives more closely than the rifts and tensions enunciated in the 'between two cultures' literature or, for that matter, in Hall's description of their identity construction as 'never unified' (1996). These young people can certainly draw upon a repertoire of cultural skills, knowing which are appropriate to which situation. But in terms of identity it would be erroneous to overuse the metaphor of navigation (Ballard 1994), entailing as it does alertness to avoid fatal collisions. Rather, identity is a form of self-knowledge that emerges through encounters, in some of which individuals are called upon to articulate their identity. In so doing (to substitute a metaphor of weaving) they single out strands in an unfinished fabric which they are continually weaving out of both certainties and tentativeness.

In this process gender does not emerge as a significant factor – and the sample is too small for statistically based conclusions. It is interesting, however, that the only two young people who mentioned any involvement in an organisation which in India is associated with the 'Hindu right' (Searle-Chatterjee 2000), namely the Hindu Swayam Sevak Sangh, were both male, and that it was a male who articulated communal feeling on the Babri masjid conflict. On the subject of the likelihood of personal change, both male and female interviewees suggested that levels of religiosity change according to different stages of one's life.

By uncovering the dynamics of identity construction and ascription the Warwick field studies problematise the world religions approach to religious studies as well as to its school-based relative, RE. First, as Geaves has argued (1998), ethnographic data challenge the reification of discrete, bounded 'faiths' and 'faith traditions'. On the Sikh–Hindu interface Coventry's Valmikis and Ravidasis, while not numerically significant, illustrate the arbitrariness of supposed boundaries between faith communities as well as the complex relationship between *jati* and 'faith'. Second, fieldwork challenges the essentialising of internally homogenised 'faiths', which so often devalues, marginalises and even excludes the experience of many who self-identify with the faith label in question.

This marginalisation results from the ignorance or disapproval of 'leaders' and spokespeople, all of whom have their own perspectives and agendas. These may include a recognition that for strategic purposes *vis-à-vis* British authorities, such as city councils, a religious identity will serve them better than an overtly caste-based one (Searle-Chatterjee 2000:500). Thus fieldwork poses questions for the design of the research itself and for the selection of research populations. This is especially true in view of the implications of the content of both scholarly writing and religious education in relation to some political agendas – in particular that of the Hindu 'right' (as discussed by Searle-Chatterjee 2000) and that of Khalsa

Sikhs. The latter deny the name 'Sikh' to non-Khalsa Sikhs, so prompting Lall to write her report as a concerned non-Khalsa Sikh parent and religious educationist (1999).

Identity lies, as Hall has pointed out, where psychology and politics intersect (1996). '[T]he "unities" which identities proclaim are, in fact, constructed within the play of power and exclusion' (ibid.:5). Field studies such as those reported in this chapter can sensitise educationists and others to both the psychological processes of categorisation and comparison and also the political implications of religious identity construction, in which – to invoke a contested dichotomy – outsiders, such as interviewers and teachers in schools and universities, are involved alongside insiders.

The particular Coventry context (as being, for example, one of the six or so areas in the UK with a Ravidasi and a Valmiki community) must not be overlooked. But the issues raised by the research are more generally applicable to teasing out the relationship between religion, culture and identity and between continuity and change. As such the University of Warwick studies offer insights into the dynamics of experience and self-understanding in south Asian diasporas.

Notes

1 See Rose (1998) for a discussion of the inconsistencies in this consultation process.

2 For discussion of theoretical and curriculum development associated with the ethnographic research see Jackson (1997).

3 At the time of writing Coventry City Council's most recent figures for Hindu, Sikh and Muslim population were those published by the Lord Mayor's Committee for Racial Harmony (1989) based upon the 1981 census, which – like the 1991 census – did not contain a religious question. Given the greater rate of population increase among south Asians than in the UK as a whole, the approximate figures of 15 000 Sikhs, 5–6000 Hindus and 4–8000 Muslims, and their percentage of the total Coventry population, will have increased substantially.

4 Of the studies of 8 to 13-year-olds (A) 'Hindu Nurture in Coventry' 1985–1987 (see Jackson and Nesbitt 1993) and (B) 'Punjabi Hindu Nurture' 1988–1989 (see Nesbitt 1991) were funded by the Leverhulme Trust and (C) Sikh nurture (see Nesbitt 2000) was supported by the Economic and Social Research Council (project no R000 232489). The fourth study (D), 'A Longitudinal Study of Young British Hindus' Perceptions of their Religious Tradition' (see Nesbitt 1998), was funded by the Leverhulme Trust. In studies B and C all the young people were Punjabi, while in A and D Gujaratis outnumbered Punjabis, although not sufficiently to reflect estimated local and national percentages of roughly 70 per cent of UK Hindus being Gujarati and 15 per cent (the second largest group) being Punjabi (Knott 1991; Vertovec 2000:88). Nesbitt (2001) provides an overview of all the Warwick studies.

5 Interestingly the only interviewee to mention the destruction of the Babri mosque, sited on the birthplace of the divine king Rama at Ayodhya (in Uttar Pradesh), was the only one with a European father.

6 Unlike the Jats who migrated direct from India, most Ramgarhia families' history includes a period between 1900 and 1970 in East Africa (Kalsi 1992:61–2; Bhachu 1985).

7 *Amrit* means the sweetened water that is used to initiate or confirm candidates as members of the Khalsa. The term *amritdhari* for initiates appears in literature about Sikhism, but my interviewees did not use the term.

8 *Panj piare* means 'five beloved ones' in an incorporative allusion to Guru Gobind Singh's first five volunteers in 1699 for initiation into his dedicated Khalsa community.

9 *Swami* ('lord') is a title for some Hindu spiritual masters. Sikhs designate charismatic teachers *sant* or *baba*. Whereas Hindus call religious teachers 'guru', for Sikhs the title is reserved for Guru Nanak and his nine successors as well as for the scriptures and for God.

10 In the present chapter, following other observers (such as Dwyer 1994), the designation 'Pushtimargi', meaning 'devotee of Pushtimarg', the way of grace, promulgated by Vallabhacharya, is mine: the two young people concerned used the more generic term 'Vaishnav' (Sanskrit Vaisnava), worshipper of Vishnu, to denote their particular worshipping community.

11 See Alexander (2000) for analysis of perceptions of Asian gangs.

12 Anavil is a category of Gujarati brahmins, identifiable by their family names.

13 *Dalit* (Sanskrit for 'oppressed') is the term which members of formerly 'untouchable' castes in India apply to their communities. Searle-Chatterjee and Sharma (1994) discuss hierarchical models of caste.

14 *Puja* denotes worship involving offerings, for example of light and sweetmeats. *Arati* is the act of circling a light in front of the focus of worship, while singing an *arati* song.

15 Jains' acceptance of being both Hindu and non-Hindu can be understood as illustrating Jain emphasis on *anekantavada*, the many-sidedness of reality.

Bibliography

Alexander, C. (2000), '(Dis)Entangling the "Asian Gang": Ethnicity, Identity, Masculinity', in B. Hesse (ed.) *Un/settled Multiculturalisms: Diasporas, Entanglements, Disruptions*, London: Zed, pp. 123–47.

Anand, D. (2000), '(Re)imagining Nationalism: Identity and Representation in the Tibetan Diaspora of South Asia', *Contemporary South Asia*, **9**(3), 271–88.

Anwar, M. (1976), 'Young Asians between Two Cultures', *New Society*, **38**(December), 563–5.

Ballard, R. (ed.) (1994), *Desh Pardesh: The South Asian Presence in Britain*, London: Hurst.

Baumann, G. (1996), *Contesting Culture: Discourses of Identity in Multi-Ethnic London*, Cambridge: Cambridge University Press.

Bhachu, P. (1985), *Twice Migrants: East African Sikh Settlers in Britain*, London: Tavistock.

Brah, A. (1996), *Cartographies of Diaspora: Contesting Identities*, London: Routledge.

Drury, B.D. (1989), *Ethnicity amongst Second Generation Sikh Girls: A Case Study in Nottingham*, unpublished Ph.D. thesis, University of Nottingham.

Dwyer, R. (1994), 'Caste, Religion and Sect in Gujarat: Followers of Vallabhacharya and Swaminarayan', in R. Ballard (ed.) *Desh Pardesh: The South Asian Presence in Britain*, London: Hurst, pp. 165–90.

Easton, B. (1999), *Aspects of the Experience of Young Ravidasis in Wolverhampton: A Field Study*, unpublished study for MA in Religious Education, University of Warwick.

The Education Reform Act (ERA) (1988), London: HMSO.

Exon, R. (1997), 'Autonomous Agents and Divine Stage Managers: Models of (Self-)Determination amongst Western Devotees of Two Modern Hindu Religious Movements', *Scottish Journal of Religious Studies*, **18**(2), 163–79.

Flood, G. (1995), 'Hinduism, Vaisnavism, and ISKCON': Authentic Traditions or Scholarly Constructions', *ISKCON Communications Journal*, **3**(2), 5–15.

Geaves, R. (1998), 'The Borders between Religions: A Challenge to the World Religions Approach to Religious Education', *British Journal of Religious Education*, **21**(1), 20–31.

Gell, S. (1994), 'Duleep Singh and the Origins of the Sikh "Look"', unpublished paper, South Asian Anthropologists' Group, London School of Economics, University of London, September.

Ghuman, P.A.S. (1994), *Coping with Two Cultures: A Study of British Asians and Indo-Canadian Adolescents*, Clevedon: Multicultural Matters.

Gillespie, M. (1995), *Television, Ethnicity and Cultural Change*, London: Routledge.

Hall, S. (1996), 'Introduction: Who Needs "Identity"?', in S. Hall and P. du Gay (eds) *Questions of Cultural Identity*, London: Sage, pp. 1–17.

Jackson, R. (1997), *Religious Education: An Interpretive Approach*, London: Hodder.

Jackson, R. and Nesbitt, E. (1993), *Hindu Children in Britain*, Stoke on Trent: Trentham.

Jacobson, J. (1996), 'Perceptions of Britishness', unpublished paper, Conference on Multicultural Competence: A Resource for Tomorrow, August, Hogskolen i Bergen.

Jacobson, J. (1997), 'Religion and Ethnicity: Dual and Alternative Sources of Identity among Young British Pakistanis', *Ethnic and Racial Studies*, **20**, 238–56.

Kalsi, S.S. (1992), *The Evolution of a Sikh Community in Britain*, Leeds: Community Religions Project, University of Leeds.

Kalsi, S.S. (1994), 'Sacred Symbols in Sikhism', unpublished paper, British Association for the Study of Religions, University of Bristol, September and Punjab Research Group, October.

Knott, K. (1991), 'Bound to Change? The Religions of South Asians in Britain', in S. Vertovec (ed.) *Aspects of the South Asian Diaspora*, New Delhi: Oxford University Press, pp. 86–111.

Lall, S. (1999), '"I Know Who God Is": A Study of Sikh Children's Spirituality within Various Expressions of Sikhism', unpublished report, Farmington Institute, Oxford.

The Lord Mayor's Committee for Racial Harmony (1989), *Coventry Multi-Cultural City*, Coventry: The Lord Mayor's Committee for Racial Harmony.

Nesbitt, E. (1985), 'The Nanaksar Movement', *Religion*, **15**, 67–79.

Nesbitt, E. (1990), 'Pitfalls in Religious Taxonomy: Hindus and Sikhs, Valmikis and Ravidasis', *Religion Today*, **6**(1), 9–12.

Nesbitt, E. (1991), *'My Dad's Hindu, My Mum's Side are Sikhs': Issues in Religious Identity*, Charlbury: National Foundation for Arts Education.

Nesbitt, E. (1997), '"We Are All Equal": Young British Punjabis' and Gujaratis' Perceptions of Caste', *International Journal of Punjab Studies*, **4**(2), 201–18.

Nesbitt, E. (1998), 'British, Asian and Hindu: Identity, Self-Narration and the Ethnographic Interview', *Journal of Beliefs and Values*, **19**(2), 189–200.

Nesbitt, E. (1999a), 'Sikhs and Proper Sikhs: Young British Sikhs' Perceptions of their Identity', in P. Singh and N.G. Barrier (eds) *Sikh Identity: Continuity and Change*, Delhi: Manohar, pp. 315–33.

Nesbitt, E. (1999b), 'The Impact of Morari Bapu's *Kathas* on Young British Hindus', *Scottish Journal of Religious Studies*, **20**(2), 177–92.

Nesbitt, E. (1999c), '"Being Religious Shows in Your Food": Young British Hindus and Vegetarianism', in T.S. Rukmani (ed.) *Hindu Diaspora: Global Perspectives*, Montreal: Chair in Hindu Studies, Concordia University, pp. 397–425.

Nesbitt, E. (2000), *The Religious Lives of Sikh Children: A Coventry-Based Study*, Leeds: Community Religions Project, University of Leeds.

Nesbitt, E. (2001), 'Ethnographic Research at Warwick: Some Methodological Issues', *British Journal of Religious Education*, **23**(3), 144–55.

Nesbitt, E. and Jackson, R. (1993), 'Aspects of Cultural Transmission in a Diaspora Sikh Community', *Journal of Sikh Studies*, **18**(1), 52–66.

Østberg, S. (2001), *Pakistani Children in Oslo: Islamic Nurture in a Secular Context*, Leeds: Community Religions Project, University of Leeds.

Raj, D.S. (1997), *Shifting Culture in the Global Terrain: Cultural Identity Construction among Hindu Punjabis in London*, unpublished Ph.D. thesis, University of Cambridge.

Rose, D. (1998), 'A Study of Representative Groups on SACRE', *Journal of Contemporary Religion*, **13**(3), 383–93.

Searle-Chatterjee, M. (2000), '"World Religions" and "Ethnic Groups": Do These Paradigms Lend Themselves to the Cause of Hindu Nationalism?', *Ethnic and Racial Studies*, **23**(3), 497–515.

Searle-Chatterjee, M. and Sharma, U. (1994), *Contextualising Caste: Post-Dumontian Approaches*, Oxford: Blackwell.

Short, G. and Carrington, B. (1995), 'What Makes a Person British? Children's Conceptions of Their National Culture and Identity', *Educational Studies*, **21**, 217–38.

Singh, A. (1992), 'So You Think You Are a Sikh?', *The Sikh Reformer: Quarterly Review of the Sikh Cultural Society, Coventry (UK)*, January to April, 27–8.

Tajfel, H. (1981), *Human Groups and Social Categories*, Cambridge: Cambridge University Press.

Vertovec, S. (1988), 'Hinduism in Diaspora: The Transformation of Tradition in Trinidad', in G.D. Sontheimer and H. Kulke (eds) *Hinduism Reconsidered*, New Delhi: Manohar, pp. 152–79.

Vertovec, S. (2000), *The Hindu Diaspora: Comparative Patterns*, London: Routledge.

Williams, R.B. (1988), *Religions of Immigrants from India and Pakistan*, Cambridge: Cambridge University Press.

CHAPTER 12

Kinship Identity and Nonformative Spiritual Seekership

Matthew Wood

Introduction

Michelle's mother had been dead only a matter of weeks before Michelle attempted to contact her. The medium Michelle consulted to do this told her that not enough time had passed, that her mother would not yet be ready to re-establish a link with this world. But Michelle's urge to encounter her mother was so strong that she decided to take on the task herself, employing the meditation techniques she had learnt at various groups. Very soon, after practising sitting quietly and picturing her mother's image night after night, Michelle heard her mother's voice telling her, 'I'm only in the next room'. A few nights later, Michelle's mother appeared and took her to the place where she now lived – they walked over fields with mountains in the distance, reminding Michelle of Scotland, of which her mother had been very fond. They met up like this time after time, until one night Michelle's mother took her to a place with buildings and people, and pointed to a hospital where she worked. She was wearing a uniform and looked very happy. Michelle realised that her mother's dearest, but unfulfilled, wish in this world had come true in the next – she had become a nurse.

When parents, other relatives and lovers are encountered during the course of spiritual techniques like meditation, they clearly have significance beyond simply being actors in games centred on the lone practitioner. Michelle's mother, for example, had figured prominently in her spiritual development, as will be seen further on. Since spiritual experiences cannot be understood in isolation from people's wider lives, it is important to recognise and take account of kinship. In particular, this chapter argues that it is the ways in which people identify with their kin that is important and that such kinship identity forms an essential part of spirituality[1] because of the family's location in the class structure of society.

To explore these themes, this chapter draws upon ethnographic research carried out within a network of groups in Nottinghamshire from 1992 to 1996 (Wood forthcoming). Five groups were studied through participant observation and interviews: an Essene meditation, the Anthroposophical Society, an occult study group, a spiritualist healing group and a spiritual fair; also various channelling and holistic healing events and workshops. It was found that the sort of spiritualities within this network focused on spirit possession principally in the forms of channelling, mediumship and shamanism, but also in the forms of meditation, holistic healing and divination. The network did not exist as a publicly identifiable and bounded entity, but was chosen for research because there was much movement of people between the groups. Its description as 'the Nottinghamshire network' is therefore not meant to suggest an emic identity, but is merely a convenient way of referring to groups with many links that were geographically proximate to each other. Although each group had its own characteristics in terms of leaders and attenders, on the whole there was an equitable spread across ages and genders, although nearly all were white British. But as will be argued further on, the majority of people were working class or lower middle class rather than middle class.

Before the ethnography is discussed, however, it must be stated that the sorts of spiritualities practised in the Nottinghamshire network are usually considered part of a New Age Movement. There are grave difficulties with such a formulation, for apart from the fact that, as Steven Sutcliffe (1997:100–2) has suggested, the term 'New Age' is largely meaningless as applied to such phenomena, it is also crucial to point out that their social structure did not constitute a movement. Although there were many links, both social and in terms of religious practices and beliefs, between the groups, they cannot be said to have produced a movement. This was because there was neither a movement in the sense of a stable organisation with goals or projects, as seems to be the case in British paganism, as Simes's ethnography suggests (1995:365–9, 490–500), nor a movement in the sense of a development of ideas, as for example in the Green movement, in Kvaloy's analysis (1990). The Nottinghamshire network can be understood as a network of family resemblances, as Barker suggests for the New Age Movement (1989:189), but only if both the significance of the network links (see Mitchell 1973:28) and the structure of resemblances is made clear. This chapter aims to classify these spiritualities by introducing the concept of nonformativeness and to show why kinship identity, which has been largely overlooked in New Age studies, is important for understanding them.

Nonformative Spirituality

The lack of a common belief system, common meanings attributed to concepts and practices, and common aims in the groups of the Nottinghamshire network meant that a new conceptualisation of their structures of social power was required to further academic understanding. The term 'nonformative' was developed to refer to the relative absence of formal social structures compared to those established in churches, sects and other organisations which exist in a consistent form for their members (Wood forthcoming). This should not imply that social authority does not exist in nonformative spiritualities, for in each group there were leaders who organised meetings and events. Rather, 'nonformative' refers to the inability of such authorities to establish and maintain an organisation that is structured in terms of common goals and meanings, in other words in terms of consistently maintained collective actions and understandings of experiences. Instead, in these groups, participation was idiosyncratic.

This may be illustrated by a fortnightly meditation group, attended by around 15 people, which had been established along the lines of teachings attributed to the ancient Jewish sect of the Essenes. It had arisen out of the Essene Network, created and led since the mid-1980s by one couple, Janet and Chris Lovell,[2] but their attempts to mould attenders' experiences at the meditation into an Essene way of life largely failed. When the group began, the Lovells employed the Essene method of carrying out an inventory, in which everyone reflected on the situations in which they had found themselves since the last meeting and sought guidance from members who could help them. They regretted that this had since been abandoned, leading the group to become more oriented to individual interpretations. Now their authority in Essene matters could be displayed only in the occasional retreats which they organised for members of the Network – most of whose members lived outside Nottinghamshire and none of whom attended the meditation – which, they said, 'has a more sharing and caring group atmosphere'. This failure to make the meditation conform to an Essene spirituality may be attributed to two causes, which were explored during the 18 months of fieldwork with the group.

First, another couple, Julie and Andrew Spencer, in whose home the meditation was held, promoted a quite different approach to spirituality. The Lovells' may be described as displaying a static performance, in which new experiences were located within the pattern of healing and guidance of their Essene lifestyle. But the Spencers' spirituality was dynamic, with a continuing openness to new activities that would upset their previous ones. For example, at one stage they became fascinated by ufology, seeking to understand the powers encountered during meditation in terms of alien life forms and introducing the attenders to books and tapes which dealt with this issue.

Alongside this first check to the Lovells' authority was a second, more important, one. Despite the regular attendance of a core group of half a dozen people at the meditation, many others were casual attenders who came with their own purposes in mind. To take one example, during a period of three months, Sally, a woman in her late 20s, came to meetings, with her brother Noel and a friend, Beth, having heard of the meditation through someone with whom they had practised Reikei, a healing technique in which Earth energy is directed by someone initiated to draw on it (for a sociological interpretation of the practice of holistic health therapies in the network see Wood 2000). These three were explicitly seeking new experiences of energies alongside their involvement in holistic therapies, and admitted in interview that they were not interested in the interpretations given to the meditation energy by the Lovells in terms of their Essene notions of angels and 'the father-mother god'.

The significance of the meditation group therefore needs to be understood in terms of individuals' wider spiritual contexts, rather than simply either its leadership or beliefs. Attenders can be interpreted as holding an attitude towards their experiences, comprising eclecticism, non-dogmatism and holism. That is, they sought experiences from a variety of sources, which they did not treat as definitive authorities, but sought to integrate with their previous experiences in a provisional, temporary manner. This triad of nonformative attitudes contrasts with the greater tendency towards exclusivism, dogmatism and particularism of formative spiritualities, although it appears that these are less prevalent on the ground level in churches and sects than is generally assumed. As Grace Davie shows (1994:39–41), seekership is an increasingly common feature of contemporary British religion and this has been empirically explored with regard to the sorts of spiritualities as found in the Nottinghamshire network by Sutcliffe's Scottish study

(1997:105–11; cf. 2000). Indeed, some in the network moved between formative and nonformative groups. This showed, on the one hand, that nonformative attitudes did not function as a framework of belief to which people strictly adhered and, on the other hand, that formative groups could be attended in a nonformative manner, although this was likely to be short-lived due to the pressures to conform in formative groups. Further, the constraining elements of formativeness that could exist in nonformative groups, such as the exercise of social leadership and promotion of textual authorities, could be temporarily focused upon by attenders if they were thought to be particularly useful.

These theoretical issues may be rehearsed by considering fieldwork in another part of the network, a monthly spiritual fair. Many people from the Essene meditation and from the other groups studied either attended the fair or held stalls or lectures there. Michelle was a regular, having been good friends with the fair's organiser when they were both studying with a shaman of the Native American tradition, and Sally and Noel both presented talks on their respective practices of reflexology and Bach flower essences. Another regular was Alvin, a spiritualist healer who held a stall where he used his spirit guide to practise clairvoyance. On several occasions he gave talks on spiritualism, focusing on how the powers he uses can be drawn upon by anyone, rather than talking about the spiritualist churches to which he belonged and which had introduced him to them, as shall be seen further on. The fair was a welcoming ground for a bewildering variety of practices: participant observation and interviews, including with the organiser Michael, showed that it acted in the same manner as did the meditation for its attenders. There was little overall formal authority but much idiosyncrasy towards beliefs and interpretations of experiences. Michael, describing his role as a facilitator, said how he had lessened his control of the fair, letting others take a part in choosing who could set up there; this had led to a greater mix of talks, less concentrated on the 'psychic phenomena' which particularly interested him. Indeed, originally called a Psychic Fair, its name had been changed to the more general Mind-Body-Spirit Festival, and at the time of research had grown to accommodate about 150 people, with over 20 stalls, 10 40-minute speakers and 4 half-day workshops.

This nonformative aspect of the Nottinghamshire network, whereby there was a distinct limit to the endurance and influence of power structures, means that a sociological understanding cannot rest on analysis of spiritual practices alone. Life histories, whose importance for sociology was recognised by Howard Becker (1974), must be considered, since participants' present experiences gained significance for them as part of their development, or what might be called their spiritual careers. This shift of focus also means other aspects of their lives can be seen as relevant to their development of spiritualities, in particular relations with kin. That is to say, nonformative spirituality did not provide a haven by which to escape from their lives and focus on themselves. Rather, it was a means by which people could attempt to interpret and deal with their wider lives. The importance of kinship for understanding nonformative spiritual seekers may be considered through the three different ways in which identity with family was illustrated. First, there is the relationship of participants with sexual partners, second, relationships with parents and third, kinship motifs in beliefs and practices.

Kinship Identity

The importance of the significant other in someone's involvement with nonformative spiritualities was not just a matter of domestic convenience. In the groups studied, roughly a quarter of all participants attended as couples and once their life histories were investigated, there was found to be a recurring pattern of development of partnership alongside development of spirituality. Also, two of the groups – the Essene meditation and an occult studies group – were led by couples. The Spencers, the couple in whose house the meditation was held, had divorced their previous partners after they had met through an interest in biorhythms, a holistic healing which assesses people's health through bodily energy flows. This was at the start of their respective careers of seekership, after each had become disillusioned with the formative groups to which they belonged: a spiritualist church in the case of Julie and the Church of England for Andrew. In fact, increased seekership went hand in hand with Julie's growing intimacy with Andrew: for example, she learnt how to read runestones in order to find out whether they should move in with each other.

In the case of Michelle, introduced at the start of this chapter, is found the belief that spiritual gifts are passed down between generations. Michelle said that in her teens she began to see ghosts and receive premonitions from dead family members on her mother's side. Her mother informed her that all the female line in their family had the gift of sensitivity to the spirit world, and while she had decided not to develop it, Michelle could if she so chose. Until her death Michelle's mother remained an important figure in her experiences – at one time forbidding her to see Anglican church friends who had reacted badly to Michelle's reports to them of psychic experiences. Michelle described her mother as a 'sister, friend, mother and comforter; everything all rolled into one'. In recent years, it has been Michelle's turn to explain their family's gift to her own daughter, after she too began to see ghosts. Likewise, her daughter has accompanied her to different churches and groups, as their spiritual development grows together.

Alvin also illustrates this identity with parents. After being brought up an Anglican, Alvin did not interest himself in religion until his twenties, when both his first wife and father died within six months of each other. This led him to ask what he called 'the two fundamental questions' of whether there is a God and whether there is an afterlife, the answers to which he sought in the spiritualist churches which at that time, in the 1960s, had a strong base in Nottingham. From people there, he found out that both his father and paternal grandmother had been practising mediums. Comments by a medium at one service convinced him that his dead father's spirit was alive, and led him to train in a spiritualist circle and then to set up a small home circle at his mother's house.

Although these examples show the presence of family – usually parents, grandparents, children and lovers/partners – in people's spiritual development, the importance of kinship identity is further attested by the many kin motifs that feature in beliefs and rituals. In *The Development of the Family and Marriage in Europe*, Jack Goody drew attention to the prevalence of kin terms in Christianity, 'not only for addressing the gods and the priesthood, but also for addressing all the fellow-members of the sect, and later those specially chosen as spiritual kin or godkin'

(1990:194). This points to the importance of considering the wider society of nonformative spirituality, existing as it does in the predominantly Christian societies of Britain, North America and continental Europe. Christine, a regular attender at the Essene meditation, had her two young children 'christened' on an Easter Sunday, at a special ceremony led by the Lovells, who took on the role of their 'spiritual guardians'. Christine chose this day because it had been named by the Ascended Masters as the day on which new energies would be directed to Earth. She had heard this information from Shah, who had been invited by the Spencers to lead a one-day workshop on channelling, which she and many others from the meditation, though not the Lovells, had attended. At this event, Shah channelled the Masters, a clique of highly evolved beings that oversee the spiritual evolutionary development of humans. Thus, Christian elements – the christening of children, the appointment of parental figures to watch over them, and the importance of Easter Sunday – had been appropriated but altered in a nonformative manner. This matched the spiritual development of many of those in the network: they had often had quite extensive contact with Christian churches earlier in their lives, but had left them to pursue practices not countenanced by them, yet without rejecting many elements of Christian spirituality.

As mentioned above, the Lovells employed the notion of 'the father-mother god' at the Essene meditation and there, as at other groups' practices, the imagined resolution of family and relationship troubles was a prominent theme. At one meditation, participants were taken in a visualisation to 'the eternal and infinite garden' where they were to see the conflicts of their personal lives float away as clouds and evaporate under the heat of the sun. The meditation ended with the closing of each of seven chakras – visualised as either 'an equi-sided cross surrounded by white light' or 'a flower closing to a tight bud' – in order to protect the meditators on returning to physical, earthly reality, but also to keep intact those changes which were effected during visualisation. Julie came away from the meditation saying, 'Well, that was a surprise! I certainly had a lot of stuff to deal with, with my dad – at least I've made a start on it.'

Kinship motifs also extend to other areas of spirituality, such as Green spirituality and conceptions of communities of believers. One of the meditations focused on the environmental destruction of 'the earth mother, we have neglected'. The International Association of Reiki is described as a 'family organisation' and represented by a symbol called 'The Heart of the Family', in which people hold hands round a baby (Hall 1997:3, 136). These motifs may be seen as reflecting the concerns of nonformative spiritualists with their wider lives and it is in this regard that the importance to them of psychotherapeutic techniques and discourse may be understood. Paul Heelas has looked at the link between psychotherapy and modern forms of religion, indicating their cross-fertilisation especially through the human potential movement (1996:46–54; Heelas and Kohn 1986). However, by focusing on theories of the self and its liberation that these share, Heelas tends to obscure the concern with kin relations that lay at the heart of Sigmund Freud's project as indicated by his views on psychoanalysis throughout his career (1976:77–9, 120–6). Nor were such concerns dropped by those of his pupils from whose ideas humanistic psychology grew: Wilhelm Reich concentrated on sexual energy and its control in the individual's social relationships, while Carl Jung's theory of archetypes included many familial representations. However, it is crucial to recognise that the importance of kinship to nonformative spirituality lies not only in beliefs and symbols but also in spiritual practices. In this regard, spirit possession demands close attention.

Spirit Possession and Kinship

Spiritualism is commonly overlooked in New Age studies, yet the Nottinghamshire network was strongly shaped by it. It was influential in the form of people's involvement with groups such as the spiritualist churches for Michelle, Alvin and Michael, and Christian Science for the Lovells' development. It was also influential through traditions such as the Theosophical Society and its offshoots like Anthroposophy. Equally important was the influence of channelling and channelled discourses (see Wood 2001). These remained prime sources of practices and teachings for nonformative spiritual seekers, as well as being the starting point for many spiritual careers.

Consideration of possession helps elucidate the place of nonformative spirituality in people's lives. For those in the network, spirit possession could be seen as the key performance that tied together their other practices, which were threefold: meditation, holistic healing and divination. Experience of direct possession by spirits – such as by vocal or written channelling, spiritualist mediumship or shamanic practices – formed the bedrock of their wider nonformative spiritual seekership, a pattern which recurred again and again for those in all locales within the network. This direct, or primary, possession may be seen as the vicarious basis for three forms of indirect, or secondary, possessions: meditation, healing and divination. In these three forms of secondary possession, there usually was no direct contact with spirits, but contact with extraordinary spiritual energies or forces, where these were understood to come from a part of the person not normally accessible, often described as the higher self, or from a wider plane, such as the Earth energy drawn upon in Reikei. These secondary possessions were understood by their practitioners to gain power from primary possessions: experiences of channelling or channelled messages or experiences of the deceased in spiritualism legitimated other practices and a person's spiritual development as a whole.

This view of possession in relation to people's other spiritual activities draws on Maurice Bloch's comparative anthropological theory of rebounding violence, whereby the ritual process of movement away from the everyday world to a transcendental world, and the bringing back of the latter to conquer the former, is understood to effect a transformation of those involved (1992:4f.). Applied to spirit possession, the first violence, or movement, can be seen in the disruption of spirits and their actions in this world, especially in the mediums' bodies (ibid.:35). The second violence, although not considered by Bloch who is more concerned with ritual sacrifice, may be viewed as the controlling of spirits by the mediums and the consequent directing of the spirits' energies. These energies may be powerful explanations of the state of the evolutionary development of the Earth and those on it, as in channelled discourses, or they may be healing powers, as in spiritualist healing. In both cases, possession acts to legitimate and reinforce people's spiritual seekership and, importantly, to establish their own social authority. Experience of possession therefore commonly enables seekers to feel secure in maintaining their nonformative attitude in the face of other authorities in the groups to which they belong.

In connection to this debate, it is important to point out that direct possession in the Nottinghamshire network was generally a communal affair. Groups would go along to hear channellers, just as spiritualists performed for congregations or circles. Even if a person's first experiences of direct possession took place during solitary times, these were quickly transferred to situations in which others were present. In this sense, the development of experience of possession may be likened to Ioan Lewis's 'mystical career' of shamans, whose initial, spontaneous and involuntary experiences become controlled and voluntary through involvement with a cult (1989:88–91). Although spiritualist groups often have cultic organisation as Geoffrey Nelson has shown (1987:53–8), and may therefore be described as a formative spirituality, for many spiritualists they become part of a wider pattern of seekership and are therefore used in a nonformative manner. However, the value of experience of direct possession remains and it is this, with its vicarious relationship to the three forms of secondary possession – meditation, healing and divination – which acted as the structure of family resemblance of the various groups in the network.

Recognition of the centrality of spirit possession in nonformative spiritualities reinforces the link with kinship identity, for the two are commonly found together. From its inception, spiritualism was family oriented, dealing with problems between kin, often through exploration of gender relations, as Alex Owen shows (1989). This continued to be true throughout the twentieth century, as Vieda Skultans's study of Welsh spiritualism makes clear (1974). As well as running the Essene Network and meditation, the Lovells were registered healers with White Eagle Lodge, established in 1936 by Grace Cooke, who channelled a Native American spirit teacher and healer known as White Eagle (White Eagle 1992). Cooke's husband, Ivan, took on the task of communicating White Eagle's teachings after her death in 1979, and since his death in 1981 this has passed to her two daughters. This pattern is similar to that of the Theosophical Society, whose lodges were commonly run by a succession of female channellers (Godwin 1994:333; Washington 1993:70–4), and of the Church Universal and Triumphant whose leader, Elizabeth Clare Prophet, channels the Ascended Masters and is known as 'Mother' (York 1995:48). This link between possession and kin is found cross-culturally: spirits who possess are often seen as ancestors or as related to a particular clan, and possession is frequently associated with other forms of religious practice such as divination and healing (Lewis 1971:133–48).

Once the magnitude of spiritualism for nonformative spiritualities is taken into account, it is easier to see how kinship identity locates participants in wider society. For kinship is not present in isolation in the social world of nonformative spiritual seekers, rather it is intimately related to their social class. In particular, spiritualism may be seen as a working-class religious tradition, as in Bryan Wilson's thaumaturgical type of response to social distress (1975:102–20). The majority of people in the network had predominantly working-class backgrounds and could not be said to have achieved middle-class status in their careers. Rather, they may perhaps best be described as lower middle class, occupying positions of lower management or professionalised working-class jobs such as social carer. As such, they may be seen as embodying a key dilemma of contemporary capitalism, being caught between middle-class aspirations of professionalism and working-class conditions of insecurity and disempowerment (Kumar 1978:192–219, 258–71).

Michelle, for example, worked in a string of low-paid care jobs before finding temporary stability as a cook in a home for the elderly; Chris Lovell had been a manager before setting up as a herbal healer with Janet; Andrew Spencer was a time and motion assessor; and Alvin was a hospital porter. That this dilemma has repercussions for family life was made clear both in people's spiritual experiences and in their pursuit of nonformativeness. As stated above, spirit possession was found to be the key to their various spiritualities, and these typically enacted damaged relations with kin. This function of spirit possession to deal with personal dilemmas is highlighted by Laurel Kendall's analysis of South Korean contemporary shamanism, which those 'at the margins of the Korean economic miracle' turn towards as 'a means of apprehending, of attempting to exert some control over the seemingly arbitrary notions of the political economy' (1996:516–22). Further, the networking aspect that was vital to nonformative spirituality can be understood to reflect networks of kin and, as already seen, often took place through the family.

However, the working-class position of those in networks such as the one studied in Nottinghamshire may pose a problem for recent analysis, both sociological and anthropological, and its ability to contextualise people in society. To investigate these issues, attention is now turned to theoretical considerations of them in the work of Anthony Giddens, Paul Heelas and Marilyn Strathern.

Kinship and Class

The argument in this section is that people's active identification with kin is an unduly neglected area in Giddens's sociology of high modernity, Heelas's analysis of the New Age Movement and Strathern's consideration of English life in a postplural age. It is insightful to consider the reasons for these views.

Giddens's work in the 1990s focused on risk and lifestyle choice in an increasingly technological environment. For him, identity is concerned with the self as it creates its own form within the ambiguities of this environment. As such, traditional sources of identity, which include kinship and, to a lesser extent, class, have largely become obsolete. In *Modernity and Self-Identity*, Giddens writes that, 'Even if they are now quite weak, there are obligations which relatives have towards one another, specified by the tie of kinship. Moreover, while these obligations may be general and vague, kin ties, where they are blood relations at any rate, cannot be broken off (1994b:90).

However, in practice, his sociology does not take account of the strength of kin ties, whether of blood relations or marriage, and turns instead to friendships within lifestyle choices. So, in distinguishing between 'pre-modern culture' and modernity, Giddens states in *The Consequences of Modernity* that the kinship system has been replaced by personal relationships (1993:101–2).

By his phenomenology of what he calls the 'pure relationship' in which, as in Alfred Schutz's method of analysis of the 'we-relationship' (Schutz 1972:164), Giddens treats modern friendships in abstract terms, he serves to lift them out of context in order to build up an ideal of self-identity (Giddens 1994b:96–8). As he writes, 'in conditions of modernity, the more a child moves towards adulthood and autonomy, the more elements of the pure relationship tend to come into play' (ibid.:98). But, like the sociological phenomenology of Schutz, this tears people away from the structures of social power which alone allow meaningful consideration of their lives, although this was recognised by Giddens in his earlier appraisal of Schutz (Giddens 1977:53). Such an approach, according to James Beckford, 'subsumes "power" under [the] concept of "order" which, in turn, is subsumed under the concept of "meaning"' (1983:13). This encourages a view 'of religion as primarily a matter of knowledge susceptible to understanding in the same way as other cognitive products – in particular, language' (ibid.:12). The people of Giddens's world become so denuded of kinship that it becomes a residue which, like the body's appendix, may uncomfortably remind them of its existence only when things have gone wrong and which is otherwise forgotten.

The reason Giddens does not do anything with kinship identity seems to be because he considers it a factor in traditional working-class culture and therefore not wholly relevant to today's increasingly classless society. To be sure, Giddens is aware of the inequalities that modernity engenders in society, but this is viewed in terms of suppression of self that yet does not obviate lifestyle choices. According to Giddens, 'Holding out the possibility of emancipations, modern institutions at the same time create mechanisms of suppression, rather than actualisation, of self'; but in the same paragraph he claims that, '"Lifestyle" refers also to decisions taken and courses of action followed under conditions of severe material constraint' (1994b:6). However, it would surely be more accurate to say that suppression entails a decrease in possibilities, not a revolution from one arena of possibilities to another. The emphasis that both Giddens and Ulrich Beck (1995:67–9) have placed on choice within situations of risk becomes less relevant in situations where suppression exists, particularly given the dominance of tradition in cultures within society where the family still plays a crucial role. Since choice in risk-taking is essential for Giddens's idea of the reflexive self (1994b:39–40), it follows that reflexivity is limited for most people by a far greater degree than he allows. To take one of his examples of a risk environment, the stock market may be what he calls 'a theorised domain of sophisticated reflexivity' (ibid.:118) for those wealthy enough to invest and pay for financial consultancy. But for the majority of people what the stock market embodies is not a risk with which they can play in their careers of self-actualisation, but an external force determining whole areas of their lives – which foods and goods they can afford and whether they are to continue working, if indeed they have a job in the first place.

Anthony Giddens's sociology of the reflexive self bears strong resemblances to Paul Heelas's seminal work on the New Age Movement.[3] Heelas has influenced the way in which those phenomena which this chapter calls nonformative spiritualities are treated in British sociology of religion, for example in Steve Bruce's recent book, *Religion in the Modern World* (1996:196–229). According to Heelas, New Age religion is a project of the self, created through reactions to modernity, much as

Giddens views the individualism which resulted from the breakdown of old communal orders as a concern for 'self-fulfilment' akin to 'spiritual quest' (Giddens 1993:122–4). Heelas charts contemporary self-exploration as arising with the expressivism of the 1970s, when the psychological wing became radicalised as 'self religions' which, he writes, lie at the 'heart of the New Age' (1992:139–43). Just as Giddens (1994b:70–80) builds his analysis through the concerns of Janette Rainwater's book *Self-Therapy* (1989), so Heelas (1996) makes repeated use of Louise Hay's writings, such as *You Can Heal Your Life* (1987). But this extended use of texts causes problems for their sociological analyses, leading to a decontextualisation of those they claim to study and therefore a shift in focus from power to meaning and language, as noted before. It is no surprise that Heelas's conclusions match those of Wouter Hanegraaff's (1996a) explicitly text-based study of New Age religion, as Hanegraaff himself has pointed out (1996b), for they focus on the same authors, such as Marilyn Ferguson, Louise Hay and Shirley MacLaine.

In his book, *The New Age Movement*, Heelas concludes that, 'The New Age shows what "religion" looks like when it is organized in terms of what is taken to be the authority of the Self' (1996:221). New Agers' self-actualisations, he writes, are pursued through reaction to 'capitalistic modernity' (ibid.:30–2), such as in management training where key elements of capitalist enterprise are employed as means to such change (1991; 1996:62–6, 90–2). However, in Heelas's analysis, the presence of social authorities takes second place to New Agers' perceptions of their selves, which, as Rachel Kohn has pointed out (1991), is confusing given Heelas's emphasis on authoritarian groups – which would be classed as formative in the terms of this chapter – such as Werner Erhard's est, Robert D'Aubigny's Exegesis and the Rajneesh Movement (Heelas 1987; 1991; Thompson and Heelas 1986). It is not surprising, then, that New Agers are commonly identified as middle-class lifestylers, who create their own selves rather than being social persons created by conditions such as kinship. Again it appears that too much concern with perception, meaning and language has obscured an investigation of social power and therefore a proper appraisal of what this form of spirituality is and its place in wider society.

These issues of self-reflexivity, capitalism and kinship come to a head in Marilyn Strathern's analysis, *After Nature: English Kinship in the Late Twentieth Century* (1992). Strathern's aim is to trace the development of anthropological kinship studies through the changing conceptions of kinship of the English middle class, from the point of view of a postplural world where what she calls the 'modern dimension of grounding or context' has been lost (ibid.:7). Strathern views such contextualisation as merographic, whereby, 'nothing is in fact ever simply part of a whole because another view, another perspective or domain, may redescribe it as "part of something else"' (ibid.:73). The reason she dismisses this plural perspective for a postplural one is because she traces its origins to an English way of looking at the world, which was taken up by anthropology. Yet Strathern's postplural perspective is as much constructed by the society in which she lives as was the plural perspective: she takes up the changes effected by Thatcherism to view the middle class as a 'plasti-class'[4] constituted by affordable choices (ibid.:142). As such, and like Giddens (1994a), she believes the difference between left- and right-wing politics has collapsed (Strathern 1992:143). This revolution has led to the cancellation of 'a certain relational facility' between society, individual and family;

for example, social relationships, she writes, are now very hard for the English to visualise, such that, 'They insist on making families visible by their lifestyle, and then all they see is the lifestyle' (ibid.:145).

This analysis leads Strathern to claim that the former British Prime Minister Margaret Thatcher's infamous statement, 'There is no such thing as society. There are individual men and women and there are families' (quoted in ibid.:144), could just as well have dispensed with individuals or families as it did with society (ibid.:145). But this is to misunderstand the class conflict which Thatcher engaged in to weaken strong trade unions and apply laissez-faire or neo-liberal economics across the country (as shown for the coal mining industry by Milne 1995). The very ideology in which Thatcher cast this conflict was one that articulated a reaction against society and towards individual entrepreneurship based upon family self-sufficiency. By interpreting social relations as choices rather than as the conditions in which people are collectively bound together, Strathern fails to recognise the essential role that family inevitably plays in people's lives. The recognition of this, as for example by Brigitte Berger, is important for understanding the choices that individuals do make, although Berger's adopted view of a stable and benign bourgeois family which is conducive to 'producing self-reliant, morally accountable, and entrepreneurial individuals who become the carriers of political responsibility and economic prosperity' (1993:24) does not necessarily follow, as feminist and socialist sociologists have pointed out (Barrett and McIntosh 1982).

Ironically, it is the very quality of Strathern's fine analysis of kinship studies that damns the method of anthropology that she presents. For she explicates anthropology by socially contextualising it, a method that she claims is no longer valid. Thus she inadvertently vindicates that which she presents as outmoded. The shame is that in doing so, Strathern does not provide a real account of contemporary English kinship, one which could have built upon her study of kinship in an English village, Elmdon, in the 1960s (1981). Here, she pointed towards the negotiation and choice in bilateral kinship identities that enabled individuals to locate themselves within social groupings (ibid.:14–17). By documenting how class and kinship identities are conceived by the villagers in her study in static and fluid terms (ibid.:148), Strathern laid the ground for extending analysis of multilateral kinship links that could usefully be employed in today's society, where geographical and social disruptions to family life and networks of kin have increased. That this situation is not qualitatively different from that in Elmdon is shown by her recognition that mobility and immobility have always been central to the image of the English village as constituting a residential core and mobile periphery, with movement facilitated through the different domains in which identity is located (1992:140).

The continued presence of kinship patterns in social life is pointed out in Goody's most recent contribution to analysis of the European family (2000:137). He shows that while industrialisation reduced the significance of larger kin groups such as clans, wider ties of kinship remained despite geographical separation and isolation caused by the demands of labour (ibid.:149). Thus, the complexities of the past need to be appreciated so that the changes that have taken place are not misconstrued as cataclysmic but instead are seen to relate to changing variables over time: 'To talk of the end of the family, of marriage or of kinship, is to . . . offer rhetoric rather than analysis' (ibid.:155). In particular, Goody challenges Giddens's concepts of modernisation and confluent love,[5] claiming that marital and parent–child relations in the past were affective and companionate and thus that the concept of modernisation is too vague, slippery and all-embracing (ibid.:133, 148, 150–5, 170).

The reason for Strathern's apparent refusal to examine kinship today is what unites her with Giddens and Heelas: each focuses on texts to the detriment of contextual analysis of either the lives of the writers they utilise or, more importantly, the lives of those who do not produce texts. For example, Giddens's formulation of confluent love – as an active, contingent love based upon the pure relationship which contrasts with romantic love – relies on the charting of reflexivity provided by therapeutic works and self-help manuals which he views as emancipatory (1992:61–4). Thus, attention is skewed away from people's experiences within society, onto the concerns of the minority who have the time and means to publish.

This diversion of attention detracts from the many salient points that Giddens, Heelas and Strathern develop. To be sure, kinship has changed in recent times, but it has been extended rather than foreclosed. The reason why kinship remains important is because it is a fundamental source of social power through which people enter and build networks, as Young and Willmott's study (1976) of the London working class in the 1950s and Firth *et al.*'s study (1969) of the London middle class in the 1960s most clearly showed. It is possible to view the extension of kinship as coming about through an apparent disestablishment of the family, due to increased social mobility in employment caused by the flexibility that is increasingly demanded in today's capitalist economy (Kumar 1995:59). For while expanding numbers of families may be broken up, links between them remain as potential sources of power which are regularly fed and occasionally utilised. In particular, the matrifocality that emerged in nineteenth-century England has endured (Goody 2000:134–6). Thus, Heelas is right to focus on the importance of contradictions of capitalism for what he calls the New Age Movement, but his analysis serves to displace the significance of this from individuals in their social contexts to individuals as reflexive selves.

Conclusion

This chapter has sought a new conceptualisation of spiritualities normally classed as New Age not only in terms of their social organisation but also in terms of the social identities of those involved. The notion of nonformative spirituality has been explored alongside kinship identities of the lower middle class in order to show how kinship, contrary to New Age studies and recent sociological and anthropological theorising, remains central to an understanding of religion and society in contemporary Britain.

Fieldwork for the study on which this chapter is based suggests that the very significance of the continuing place of kinship identity under capitalism assists an understanding of nonformative spirituality. Like kinship, such spirituality is built out of flexible networks to which individuals turn again and again during the course of their spiritual careers. In an important way, then, the tensions between nonformativeness and formativeness in seekers' networks and spiritual careers map out the conditions of social life of the lower middle class, caught as they are between middle-class and working-class conditions. In particular, it is through experiences of spirit possession and matrifocality that identity is often centred. As the case studies and biographies presented in this chapter have shown, nonformative spiritual seekership was the means by which people attempted to interpret and deal with the disruptions to kin relations in their wider lives, allowing kinship identities to be affirmed and renewed. These extensive webs of strongly meaningful human interactions, in which identities are founded and persons thereby formed, are what need to be investigated if this form of spirituality is to be properly located by the sociology of religion.

Notes

1 'Spirituality' has recently become a contested term in religious studies, as its increased usage by popular writers has led to a certain vacuousness and variability in its meaning (King 1996). In this chapter, it is used in place of 'religiosity' to draw attention not only to the individual practices and explorations of many people in the network but also to the multiplicity of authorities that are thus encountered and engaged.

2 All field subjects' names in this chapter are pseudonymous.

3 A related area of theorising between Heelas and Giddens is their concern with traditional society, although there is not room to explore their thoughts on this matter (see Beck *et al.* 1994:56–109 and Heelas *et al.* 1996:1–20).

4 Compare with Giddens's description of sexuality in the late twentieth century as 'plastic sexuality', marked by severance from its integration with reproduction, kinship and generations (1992:27).

5 Unfortunately, Goody mistakes Giddens's term as 'congruent love' (2000:154).

Bibliography

Barker, E. (1989), *New Religious Movements: A Practical Introduction*, London: HMSO.

Barrett, M. and McIntosh, M. (1982), *The Anti-Social Family*, London: Verso.

Beck, U. (1995), *Ecological Politics in an Age of Risk*, Cambridge: Polity Press.

Beck, U., Giddens, A. and Lash, S. (1994), *Reflexive Modernization Politics, Tradition and Aesthetics in the Modern Social Order*, Cambridge: Polity Press.

Becker, H.S. (1974), 'The Life History', in P. Worsley *et al.* (eds) *Modern Sociology: Introductory Readings*, Harmondsworth: Penguin Education, pp. 115–19.

Beckford, J.A. (1983), 'The Restoration of "Power" to the Sociology of Religion', *Sociological Analysis*, **44**(1), 11–32.

Berger, B. (1993), 'The Bourgeois Family and Modern Society', in J. Davies (ed.) *The Family: Is It Just Another Lifestyle Choice?*, London: Institute of Economic Affairs, Health and Welfare Unit, pp. 8–27.

Bloch, M. (1992), *Prey into Hunter: The Politics of Religious Experience*, Cambridge: Cambridge University Press.

Bruce, S. (1996), *Religion in the Modern World: From Cathedrals to Cults*, Oxford: Oxford University Press.

Davie, G. (1994), *Religion in Britain since 1945: Believing without Belonging*, Oxford: Blackwell.

Firth, R., Hubert, J. and Forge, A. (1969), *Families and Their Relatives: Kinship in a Middle-Class Sector of London*, London: Routledge & Kegan Paul.

Freud, S. (1976), *Two Short Accounts of Psycho-Analysis: Five Lectures on Psycho-Analysis and the Question of Lay Analysis*, Harmondsworth: Penguin Books.

Giddens, A. (1977), *New Rules of Sociological Method: A Positive Critique of Interpretive Sociologies*, London: Hutchinson.

Giddens, A. (1992), *The Transformation of Intimacy: Sexuality, Love and Eroticism in Modern Societies*, Oxford: Polity Press.

Giddens, A. (1993), *The Consequences of Modernity*, Oxford: Polity Press.

Giddens, A. (1994a), *Beyond Left and Right: The Future of Radical Politics*, Cambridge: Cambridge University Press.

Giddens, A. (1994b), *Modernity and Self-Identity: Self and Society in the Late Modern Age*, Oxford: Polity Press.

Godwin, J. (1994), *The Theosophical Enlightenment*, Albany: State University of New York Press.

Goody, J. (1990), *The Development of the Family and Marriage in Europe*, Cambridge: Cambridge University Press.

Goody, J. (2000), *The European Family: An Historico-Anthropological Essay*, Oxford: Blackwell.

Hall, M. (1997), *Practical Reikei: A Practical Step by Step Guide to this Ancient Healing Art*, London: Thorsons.

Hanegraaff, W. (1996a), *New Age Religion and Western Culture: Esotericism in the Mirror of Secular Thought*, Leiden: E.J. Brill.

Hanegraaff, W. (1996b), 'The Role of Nature in New Age Literature', paper presented to 'Nature Religion Today: Western Paganism, Shamanism and Esotericism in the 1990s', conference organised by the Department of Religious Studies, Lancaster University.

Hay, L.L. (1987), *You Can Heal Your Life*, Cape, South Africa: Aliveness Unlimited Movement.

Heelas, P. (1987), 'Exegesis: Methods and Aims', in P. Clarke (ed.) *The New Evangelists: Recruitment Methods and Aims of New Religious Movements*, London: Ethnographica, pp. 17–41.

Heelas, P. (1991), 'Cults for Capitalism? Self Religions, Magic, and the Empowerment of Business', in P. Gee and J. Fulton (eds) *Religion and Power, Decline and Growth: Sociological Analyses of Religion in Britain, Poland and the Americas*, British Sociological Association Sociology of Religion Study Group publication, pp. 72–7.

Heelas, P. (1992), 'The Sacralization of the Self and New Age Capitalism', in N. Abercrombie and A. Warde (eds) *Social Change in Contemporary Britain*, Cambridge: Polity Press, pp. 139–66.

Heelas, P. (1996), *The New Age Movement: The Celebration of the Self and the Sacralization of Modernity*, Oxford: Blackwell.

Heelas, P. and Kohn, R. (1986), 'Psychotherapy and Techniques of Transformation', in G. Claxton (ed.) *Beyond Therapy: The Impact of Eastern Religions on Psychological Theory and Practice*, London: Wisdom Publications, pp. 291–309.

Heelas, P., Lash, S. and Morris, P. (eds) (1996), *Detraditionalization: Critical Reflections on Authority and Identity*, Oxford: Blackwell.

Kendall, L. (1996), 'Korean Shamans and the Spirits of Capitalism', *American Anthropologist*, **98**, 512–27.

King, A.S. (1996), 'Spirituality: Transformation and Metamorphosis', *Religion*, **26**, 343–51.

Kohn, R. (1991), 'Radical Subjectivity in "Self Religions" and the Problem of Authority', in A.W. Black (ed.) *Religion in Australia: Sociological Perspectives*, North Sydney, Australia: Allen & Unwin, pp. 133–50.

Kumar, K. (1978), *Prophecy and Progress: The Sociology of Industrial and Post-Industrial Society*, Harmondsworth: Penguin.

Kumar, K. (1995), *From Post-Industrial to Post-Modern Society: New Theories of the Contemporary World*, Oxford: Blackwell.

Kvaloy, S. (1990), 'Green Philosophy', in J. Button (ed.) *The Green Fuse: The Schumacher Lectures 1983–8*, London: Quartet Books, pp. 1–25.

Lewis, I.M. (1971), *Ecstatic Religion: An Anthropological Study of Spirit Possession and Shamanism*, Harmondsworth: Penguin.

Lewis, I.M. (1989), *Religion in Context: Cults and Charisma*, Cambridge: Cambridge University Press.

Milne, S. (1995), *The Enemy Within: The Secret War Against the Miners*, London: Pan.

Mitchell, J.C. (1973), 'Networks, Norms and Institutions', in J. Boissevain and J.C. Mitchell (eds) *Network Analysis: Studies in Human Interaction*, The Hague: Mouton, pp. 15–35.

Nelson, G.K. (1987), *Cults, New Religions and Religious Creativity*, London: Routledge & Kegan Paul.

Owen, A. (1989), *The Darkened Room: Women, Power, and Spiritualism in Late Nineteenth Century England*, London: Virago Press.

Rainwater, J. (1989), *Self-Therapy: A Guide to Becoming Your Own Therapist*, London: Crucible.

Schutz, A. (1972), *The Phenomenology of the Social World*, London: Heinemann Educational Books.

Simes, A.C. (1995), *Contemporary Paganism in the East Midlands*, unpublished Ph.D. thesis, University of Nottingham.

Skultans, V. (1974), *Intimacy and Ritual: A Study of Spiritualism, Mediums and Groups*, London: Routledge & Kegan Paul.

Strathern, M. (1981), *Kinship at the Core: An Anthropology of Elmdon, a Village in North-West Essex in the Nineteen-Sixties*, Cambridge: Cambridge University Press.

Strathern, M. (1992), *After Nature: English Kinship in the Late Twentieth Century*, Cambridge: Cambridge University Press.

Sutcliffe, S. (1997), 'Seekers, Networks and "New Age"', *Scottish Journal of Religious Studies*, **18**(2), 97–114.

Sutcliffe, S. (2000), '"Wandering Stars": Seekers and Gurus in the Modern World', in S. Sutcliffe and M. Bowman (eds) *Beyond New Age: Exploring Alternative Spirituality*, Edinburgh: Edinburgh University Press, pp. 17–36.

Thompson, J. and Heelas, P. (1986), *The Way of the Heart: The Rajneesh Movement*, Wellingborough, Northamptonshire: The Aquarian Press.

Washington, P. (1993), *Madame Blavatsky's Baboon: Theosophy and the Emergence of the Western Guru*, London: Secker and Warburg.

White Eagle (1992), *The White Eagle Lodge – Purpose and Work*, High Wycombe: The White Eagle Publishing Trust.

Wilson, B.R. (1975), *Magic and the Millennium*, St. Albans: Paladin.

Wood, M. (2000), 'Holistic Health Therapies in Comparative Analysis', in M. Bowman (ed.) *Healing and Religion*, Middlesex: Hisarlik Press, pp. 81–94.

Wood, M. (2001), 'Playing with Spirits: Channeling and Nonformative Spirituality in Contemporary Britain', *Focaal: European Journal of Anthropology*, **37**, 49–60.

Wood, M. (forthcoming), *Possession, Power and the New Age: Ambiguities of Authority in the Contemporary World*, Aldershot: Ashgate.

York, M.O. (1995), *The Emerging Network: A Sociology of the New Age and Neo-pagan Movements*, Lanham, Md.: Rowman & Littlefield.

Young, M. and Willmott, P. (1976), *Family and Kinship in East London*, Harmondsworth: Penguin Books.

Index